PENGUIN BOOKS

GHOST MILK

Iain Sinclair is the author of *Downriver* (winner of the James Tait Black Memorial Prize and the Encore Award); *Landor's Tower*; *White Chappell, Scarlet Tracings*; *Lights Out for the Territory*; *Lud Heat*; *Rodinsky's Room* (with Rachel Lichtenstein); *Radon Daughters*; *London Orbital*; *Dining on Stones*; and *Hackney, That Rose-Red Empire*. He is also the editor of *London: City of Disappearances*.

Ghost Milk

Calling Time on the Grand Project

IAIN SINCLAIR

PENGUIN BOOKS

PENGUIN BOOKS

Published by the Penguin Group
Penguin Books Ltd, 80 Strand, London WC2R ORL, England
Penguin Group (USA) Inc., 375 Hudson Street, New York, New York 10014, USA
Penguin Group (Canada), 90 Eglinton Avenue East, Suite 700, Toronto, Ontario, Canada M4P 2Y3
(a division of Pearson Penguin Canada Inc.)
Penguin Ireland, 25 St Stephen's Green, Dublin 2, Ireland (a division of Penguin Books Ltd)
Penguin Group (Australia), 250 Camberwell Road, Camberwell, Victoria 3124, Australia
(a division of Pearson Australia Group Pty Ltd)
Penguin Books India Pvt Ltd, 11 Community Centre, Panchsheel Park, New Delhi – 110 017, India
Penguin Group (NZ), 67 Apollo Drive, Rosedale, Auckland 0632, New Zealand
(a division of Pearson New Zealand Ltd)
Penguin Books (South Africa) (Pty) Ltd, Block D, Rosebank Office Park, 181 Jan Smuts Avenue,
Parktown North, Gauteng 2193, South Africa

Penguin Books Ltd, Registered Offices: 80 Strand, London WC2R ORL, England

www.penguin.com

First published by Hamish Hamilton 2011
Published in Penguin Books 2012
001

Typeset by Palimpsest Book Production Limited, Falkirk, Stirlingshire
Printed in Great Britain by Clays Ltd, St Ives plc

ISBN: 978-0-141-03964-0

www.greenpenguin.co.uk

MIX
Paper from
responsible sources
FSC
www.fsc.org   FSC® C018179

Penguin Books is committed to a sustainable
future for our business, our readers and our planet.
This book is made from Forest Stewardship
Council™ certified paper.

ALWAYS LEARNING   **PEARSON**

In memory of the huts of the
Manor Garden Allotments

'Alas! poor ghost'
 – William Shakespeare

Contents

NORTHLAND

FARLAND

Lostland

Abraham Ojo

It was my initiation into East London crime. If Stratford can be called East London. A bulging varicose vein on the flank of the A11, which fed somehow, through an enigma of unregistered places, low streets, tower blocks, into the A12. The highway out: Chelmsford, Colchester. A Roman road, so the accounts pinned up in town halls would have it, across brackish Thames tributary marshes. A slow accumulation against the persistence of fouled and disregarded rivers.

Stratford East. The other Stratford. Old town, new station. Imposing civic buildings arguing for their continued existence. A railway hub that, in its more frivolous moments, carried Sunday-supplement readers to Joan Littlewood's Theatre Royal, for provocations by Brendan Behan, Shelagh Delaney, Frank Norman. For pantomime Brecht. *Carry On* actors moonlighting in high culture. That was about as much as I knew, when the person at the desk in Manpower's Holborn offices told me I would be going to Chobham Farm.

'Chobham Farm, Angel Lane, Stratford. Right now. This morning. If you fancy it.'

This is how it worked: when I was down to my last ten pounds, I would take whatever Manpower had to offer. Employment on the day, for the day. Bring back the docket on Thursday and receive, deductions made, cash in hand. An office of Australians living out of their backpacks, woozy counterculturalists and squatters from condemned terraces in Mile End, Kilburn, Brixton. It was a dating agency, benevolent prostitution, introducing opt-out casuals to endangered industries desperate enough to hire unskilled, dope-smoking day labourers who would vanish before the first frost, the first wrong word from the foreman. There were always characters at the Holborn desk, justifying themselves, whining about the hours they spent trying to locate the factory in Ponders End where they would be invited to scrape congealed chocolate from the drum of a sugar-sticky vat with a bent teaspoon.

Everybody knew, on both sides of this deal, that it was 1971 and it was all over. The places we were dispatched by the employment agency were, by definition, doomed. From my side, beyond the survivalist pittance earned, there was the excitement of being parachuted into squares of the map I had never visited; access was granted to dank riverside sheds, rock venues in Finsbury Park, cigar-packing operations in Clerkenwell.

'The social contract is defunct,' I muttered. I had been dabbling in Jean-Jacques Rousseau, not listening to politicians. Rubbish strikes and rat mountains enlivened our 8mm diary films. If the post didn't arrive, bills wouldn't have to be paid. We collaborated with civic entropy.

On Upper Thames Street, in a cellar under threat of inundation, I sorted and packed screws and bolts alongside a man in a tight, moss-green, three-piece suit. A Nigerian called Abraham Ojo. I remember that name because I inscribed it across the portrait I painted: *Abraham Ojo floats a company*. Steps dropping vertiginously to a sediment-heavy river. A schematic Blackfriars Bridge. Wharfs. Hoists. Black-windowed warehouses on the south bank. And a stern Abraham with his arm raised to expose the heavy gold wristwatch. Those long wagging fingers with the thick wedding band. Like many West Africans in this floating world, and the ones met, eight years earlier, in my Brixton film school, Abraham Ojo never dressed down. Smart-casual meant leaving his waistcoat on the hanger he carried inside his black attaché case (with the pink *Financial Times* and the printed CV in glassine sleeve). He might, with mimed reluctance, shrug a nicotine-coloured storeman's coat over his interviewee's jacket, but he would never appear without narrow silk tie, or fiercely bulled shoes. He favoured hornrim spectacles and a light dressing of Malcolm X goatee to emphasize a tapering chisel-blade chin. Like the Russians I've been coming across, in recent times, running bars in old coaching inns in Thames Valley towns, ambitious Nigerians made it crystal clear: *I'm not doing this.* Not now, not really. I am only here, on a temporary basis, because I have a scheme in which you might be permitted to invest: if you forget the fact that you saw me foul my hands with oily tools in a dripping vault.

It was a privilege of the period to encounter men like Abraham. I was fascinated to witness how he patronized his patrons, sneering at them as a caste without ambition or paper qualifications. He refused to register where he was, the specifics of place meant nothing. The chasms of the City, the close alleys and wind-tossed precincts, were knee-deep in banknotes, he assured me. Loose change waiting for a sympathetic address. My mediocre literary degree qualified me, barely, to be a low-level investor in Abraham's latest scam: the importation of cut-and-shut trucks into Nigeria. Documentation would be juggled. Sources of supply, in Essex and the Thames Estuary, were obscure. When we had enough in the fighting fund to tempt the right officials, cousins of cousins, we would be in clover.

As we talked, in our lunch break, down by the river, he kept his back to my wreck of a street-market bicycle. When I invited him to Hackney for a meal, he came with folders of papers, financial projections, lists of contacts. He enthralled the others at the table, potless painters, students without tenure, the manager of a tyre-replacement operation in Leytonstone, with a vision of hot-ripe places, deals with Russian diplomats and shaven-headed entrepreneurs from Bethnal Green who were looking to reinvest surplus loot from the black economy. He spoke of new cities on the edges of old jungles, a vibrant economy hungry for reliable or prestigious European motor vehicles. The voodoo of capital. The madness. Pooling our resources, the whole Hackney mob might have raised the funds to rent a beach hut in Margate. Seeing or not seeing the hopelessness of his pitch, Abraham continued. Mopping his brow with a linen napkin, pushing away the wine glass. Maybe it worked, maybe he's out there now, gold-plated Merc and bodyguards, in the oil fields of the Niger Delta. He never returned to the warehouse.

His replacement, a man from Sydney, was a few inches shorter than me, but otherwise a Stevensonian double. The pure Aussie doppelgänger. Another Sinclair. I never found out the full story of my great-grandfather's experiences in Tasmania, after his investments evaporated. He retired, came back from luxuriant Ceylon to bleak Banff on the North Sea, at the age of forty.

'Now for the next ten years,' he wrote, 'I extracted as much enjoyment out of life as perhaps ever falls to the lot of ordinary unambitious mortals; but at the end of this time I fell among thieves, and as misfortunes rarely come single, the *Hermileia* must needs play havoc with securities in Ceylon at the same time, so that I began to look abroad again for investments and occupation, resulting in a trip to *Tasmania*, an adventure often talked of with friends now gone.'

Looking back, the astonishing aspect of life in my late twenties was that I had time to paint Abraham Ojo's portrait. The balance was still there, I suspect, between weeks lost to casual labour, that infiltration into the mystery of how a city works, involvement with a communal film diary, and the writing and publishing of invisible books. Fifty pounds of my wages saved from random employment in 1970 produced my first small collection of poems and prose fragments. The first shift towards separating myself from the substance that contained me, a living, working London. Its horrors and epiphanies.

A Pretty Average Mess

The first days were warm and, in spirit, close enough to the now remote and legendary Beat ethos to be comfortable. I mean that the short journey across Hackney Marshes to Stratford appeased, or held in check, our various demons: Tom's projected expeditions to Nepal, Afghanistan, silk routes and hippie trails he would never take; Renchi's testing of extreme psychic states in search of a sustaining vision and a way of life; paintings worked and reworked, or coming, direct and plain, as remembrances of episodes from a diary of walks and labours designed to capture the vanishing essence of place. Victoria Park. Pole Hill. Dancing Ledge in Dorset. As we drove in our communal blue van, we continued the debate. Was the movie of history, as I contended, lodged in the memory-bank, every cell and squeak of it, to be sifted and sounded? Or did past experience, as Renchi asserted, pulse in reflex spasms, unexpected flares brought forth as panels of shimmering light?

Collective dreaming. A nagging monochrome film plays in the head as we load and unload slithering brown sacks of talcum powder in the autumn yard, alongside the promiscuous spread of Stratford's railway lines. Dirty, weary, underpaid, we were inspired by this new location to flights of fancy, talking excitedly as we wrestled with those perverse sacks. Where we had come from, where we were going? What we could scavenge, this day, for supper?

A self-published gathering, my first book, was the proof of Renchi's thesis: prose Polaroids with no past and very little future. A spray of borrowed blood on my exposed feet, which were shuffling along in flip-flops, one green and one blue. While I wrote up a slashed-wrist suicide attempt, an Irishman sprawled in the street, gazing at the newly completed and unoccupied tower blocks of the Holly Street Estate.

The road across Hackney Marshes was shadow-dressed, tree-screened. A warm breath, windows down, of a green morning. The 8mm film of those days, a confirmation that they actually happened, adopts the rhythms of a slide show by interspersing flashes of live action with black frames (lens covered by hand): domestic intimacies, breakfast-in-the-dark, bath and bed, cut with the mud yards of Stratford, stubby lorry-cabs backing into forced clinches with topless trailers. ACL. HAPAG-LLOYD. SEA CONTAINERS LTD. It took me a few weeks to find out what HAZCHEM meant. Chobham Farm was no inner-city pastoral interlude.

Homerton Road and Temple Mills Lane were solid with traffic, white vans on the burn, the usual agitated stream. The road carried the weight of a working city; printers, breakers' yards, food distribution. Temple Mills, once the corn-grinding mills of the Knights Templar, is a name that has retired from history. It has been trampled into the marshes like that sea of bottle caps into contemporary London Fields, where early walkers confront the hard evidence of spontaneous barbecues and picnics. A dun confetti of cigarette stubs around scorched rectangles of black earth. A summer-long garden party requiring no invitation, the overspill of Broadway Market. The lesson of London Fields is that you can't legislate for how humans will decide to make use of territory. Council planners provide tables and benches and they are occupied, within hours, by a loose association of convivial drinkers who appreciate the solidity of the furniture. Anchored platforms in a tilting world. Foxes watch from bushes. Crows strut among the detritus of inadequate bins.

I pick my way through half-naked bodies, fascinated by the books they are reading. Geoff Dyer in Venice. Retro-gothic of Sarah Waters. Robert Macfarlane's *Wild Places*. One morning I found a bunch of keys among the blue cans and took them to the ranger's office, by the revamped lido. A glimpse at the pool was enough: exercise purgatory, goggled swimmers ploughing their roped lengths, tight-capped like a regiment of the bald, wrinkled by too much chlorine. 'There is some provision, free access for senior citizens,' the attendant said. 'But not here, we're too popular.'

Driving to Chobham Farm in 1971, employment cards at the ready, we were disconnected from local politics and objects of confusion to hardworking, established parents who had put us through the long and expensive haul of private education. We had failed, not only to follow in their footsteps, but to make visible progress in our alternative careers as independent film-makers. Tom Baker had received some critical visibility through his collaboration with Michael Reeves on *The Sorcerers* and *Witchfinder General*. But Reeves died in 1969, the year we bought a terraced house in Hackney. An accidental overdose in face of the pressures of success, having to do the thing he had pushed so hard to achieve, step out on the studio floor for a new feature film. Another fraught encounter with Vincent Price. A first shot at Christopher Lee. Reeves was Tom's age, they had been to the same public school, Radley. Renchi, through similar contacts and connections, directed a neatly calculated programmer about his mother's Cambridge ballet school, young girls and bicycles in the dappled sunlight of a perfect English summer, camera operated by future Oscar-winner Chris Menges. Unfortunately, the producers failed to secure music rights from Duke Ellington's estate and the film was never seen. My own documentary career began and ended in 1967. Coming down the gentle slope of Homerton Road, beneath the hospital, past the Lesney Factory, over the Lea, we identified the right landscape in which to lose ourselves. To start again. With a wiped slate.

Everything begins with the fact of the river, the Lea and its tributaries. Like a wig of snakes. A dark stream sidling, fag in mouth, towards the Thames at Bow Creek; foam-flecked, coot-occupied, enduring its drench of industrial pollution, cars with the ambition of becoming submarines, skinned bears, overexcited urban planners. Men like Lou Sherman, the Mayor of Hackney in 1961, whose messianic schemes clashed with the modest expectations of twitchers, allotment holders, dowsers and edgeland wanderers. The Lea Valley was our Poland, fought over by eco-romantics, entrenched Stalinists and political visionaries with a compulsion to erect plasterboard barriers, electrical fences.

Laurie Elks, in an investigation published in *Hackney History* (2008), tracks the makeover neurosis of the Lee Valley Regional Park back to source. They mean well, the invaders from the Town Hall, and they fight tooth and nail to secure their legacy. When I met Elks, the smiling, hovering custodian of St Augustine's Tower, that remnant of Templar Hackney, he offered me, as we stood on the roof, facing east towards the emerging Olympic Park, a copy of his essay. I respected Laurie's engagement with the bell tower, which was open to visitors on the last Sunday of every month. He challenged interlopers, with a polite cough, to explain themselves, the backstory of their lives, in the shadow of the church. Were we faking it, exploiting locality? Or did we have something to offer, in cash or influence? It wouldn't be hard to picture the gaunt ecclesiastical relic and its keeper as twin entities, the building existing to hide a man who had become the spirit of place. The tight bore of the tower, a blind lighthouse plugging the passage from Mare Street to Clapton, reverberates with the loud mechanism of a clock. Having been squeezed in the spiral ascent, elbows drawn close, before an awkward tumble through a low door to the leaded roof, the totality of the cityscape, the panoramic spread of Hackney, is overwhelming. Any two persons, clutching the rail, will struggle to articulate scraps of knowledge against the impulse never to return to ground, except by the shortest possible route, a wild leap. Laurie's area of special interest, the Regional Park, nudges our gaze, past watercress beds that became the car park of the Tesco superstore, to the cranes, mud mountains and skeletal hoop of the Olympic Stadium.

They couldn't leave the eastern margin of the borough alone. Patrick Abercrombie, the conceptualist of London's post-war city of orbital motorways, bright new schools, lidos, the one that never happened, eyed up the Lea Valley. His Greater London Plan of 1945 was a blueprint, benevolently patronizing, for future crimes and myopic blunders. They will not accept, the politicians, that the beautifully executed proposal, with its fold-out maps and paragraphs of utopian copywriting, is all that is required: a charm against the night, an object for contemplation. You do not have to summon the bulldozers after reading Blake's *Jerusalem*. There is no requirement to set a budget, to fiddle a penny on the rates. Much better to inspect maquettes of impossible marinas, miniature Persian gardens, Babel towers that balance on the palm of your hand. The trajectory from Abercrombie's reasoned proposal to the insidious CGI promos of the 2012 Olympic dream is inevitable. The long march towards a theme park without a theme.

August 1961: Mayor Sherman hires a boat and rounds up the town clerks of West Ham, Leyton, Walthamstow and Tottenham, for a Lea voyage, stuttering between locks, nosing through weed beds and electric-green duckweed blankets. An Hieronymus Bosch outing, stiff dignitaries rattling their metaphorical chains of office, nibbling and swilling, convivial and concerned, through territory so assured in its indifference to progress that it cries out for revision. Sherman is attended by his sidekick, Hackney's town clerk Len Huddy. They are the Laurel and Hardy of this stupendous wheeze: rescuing a lost landscape by making an urban park; a necklace of leisure facilities running from Broxbourne, through reservoirs and reed marshes, to the Thames. Sherman's riparian picnic, a sightseeing drift to the gentle chug of the motor, anticipates backriver circuits laid on to promote the 2012 Olympics.

Novelists of the Abercrombie period, returning from war, recalled the golden hours of childhood, camping trips to Epping Forest or rides out along the Lea Valley. It's an important mythology, having an escape, fields and woods, so easily accessible by cheap public transport, or by mounting a boneshaker bicycle. Even Harold Pinter, who lived in Clapton, and who took care to bleed specifics of place out of his glinting psychodramas, paid his dues to the Lea, to Victoria Park and Hackney Marshes. Wide skies under which to nurse grievances, to argue with himself, to exorcize pressure. By walking and rehearsing interior monologues. Walking and betraying. Walking where there were no eyes, no witnesses.

Sherman's legacy was confirmed by the Lee Valley Regional Park Act in 1967. The Duke of Edinburgh was tapped up to act as cheerleader, a man who could be relied upon to chivvy doubters, while pitching the brochure for a nation of leisure warriors. Professional hobbyists (they can afford it), our royals have always enjoyed a special relationship with the Olympics, taking part, sitting on committees, making speeches. Now the Lea Valley would be an engine for regeneration. Proposals were floated for a 'sea-front' promenade, tree-lined, with pubs, cafés and restaurants, from which to delight in the passage of regular 'water-buses with gay awnings'. There would be pleasure gardens, cinemas, dance halls, boating lakes, bike tracks. And slapped down in Mill Meads, to rise out of dereliction like an anticipation of Anish Kapoor's 2012 helter-skelter monument, was that symbol of the 1960s, Joan Littlewood's Fun Palace. Kapoor's £19-million proposal had the curious title of the *ArcelorMittal Orbit*, making it sound like the X-ray of some hideous shunt on the M25, underwritten by Europe's richest man, the steel magnate Lakshmi Mittal. The pitch was size, nothing beyond that. Bigger than Gormley's *Angel of the North*, the Meccano stack was the Angel's twisted calliper.

Joan Littlewood's never-built pleasure dome failed for the opposite reason: too much was asked of it, it contained the world. Littlewood was an inspirational theatre director, an irritant, a goad, the best kind of cross-river cultural migrant. Her power base was in the wrong Stratford, the Essex one, while her home was a substantial property on the edge of Blackheath. After working with the guerrilla Theatre of Action in Manchester, she collaborated with Gerry Raffles on the Theatre Workshop in East London. Banned from broadcasting on the BBC, because of her alleged association with the Communist Party, she asserted the integrity of her double life, between bohemian suburbia and agitprop drama, by pointing out that she remained under surveillance by the secret services from 1939 to the late 1950s, when her Stratford shows began to transfer to the West End. The idea of the Fun

Palace, conceived and developed with the architect Cedric Price, was a blueprint for all future Lea Valley schemes: ambitious, exciting as a proposal, and impossible to achieve.

In architects' drawings, this 150-foot tall, open-frame playpen resembled an Ikea warehouse, the distinguishing structure of future edgelands: the blank-walled storage shed. An all-purpose unit modelled on a Kleenex dispenser. The Fun Palace would, like the asbestos-saturated Palace of the Republic, in Marx-Engels Platz, East Berlin, be all things to all men: debating chamber, bowling alley, boozer. A non-space given interest by ramps, travelators, walkways and 'variable escalators'. As in the Turbine Hall of Tate Modern, it would take you several visits to work out a way of navigating from one floor, one viewing platform, to the next. The Fun Palace, unlike the Millennium Dome, had the good sense to remain a series of drawings, PR puffs and rhetoric from culture hustlers. An heroic failure charming us with its non-existence. The thing that doesn't happen displaces its own weight in our imaginations.

Wick Woodland, where tinkers and travellers parked their caravans under the motorway bridge, was nominated for a Japanese garden, an English eighteenth-century garden and a landing stage. The planners of the Civic Trust, unconvinced by the need for separate cycle tracks, lobbied for a series of recreational centres linked by a four-lane, dual-carriageway park road. An eco-friendly green highway of the kind originally proposed by Abercrombie. 'A pleasant drive is hard to find,' said the commissioned engineers, Sir William Halcrow and Partners. And where better than an urban parkland motorway, up on stilts in the spirit of J. G. Ballard, a tarmac causeway across the marshes?

Financial constrictions, the difficulty of sustaining the alliance between the boroughs, between local and central government, dished most of the options. The 1979 Broxbourne rowing centre came with so much baggage from the council that it was left, permanently, in the pending file. Most of the grand schemes crumbled and failed, before settling into their comfort zones: as ruins, squatted husks, discontinued adventure parks, graffiti auditions. In

September 2008, as budgets were trimmed to fund the biggest extravaganza of them all, the Broxbourne Leisure Centre was closed. Leisure was being privatized. Elite athletes would swallow whatever loose change could be found, to offer them a reasonable chance of bringing home the medals that would promote Britain as a viable world power.

The excitement of winning the bid for the World Athletics Championships of 2005 was premature. The development package for the stretch of the Lee Valley that touches on the satellite estates and retail parks of Waltham Abbey and the M25 corridor couldn't be made to work in time. Westfield didn't fancy a superstore in Picketts Lock. One hundred million pounds was promised by the Sports Council (now rebranded as Sport England). It wasn't enough. Somebody took one of those corporate helicopter rides over the territory and noticed the awkward proximity of the London Waste facility at Edmonton. The smokestack belching its toxic filth over the proposed 43,000-seater stadium. The project was abandoned. A disaster was not allowed, not then, to become a catastrophe. Total financial meltdown. Debts that would never be cleared.

The Duke of Edinburgh, making the opening address to the Civic Trust, in Hackney Town Hall, back in 1964, revealed that he frequently overflew the Lea Valley in his crested helicopter. 'The place on the whole,' he said, 'is a pretty average mess.'

Chobham Farm

We come off the road, through the gate, across the mud, into the farm: Chobham Farm. A progression of clapped-out warehouses, divided into high-stacked alleys, set hard against a mesh fence and the spread of the Stratford rail yards, sidings, national and international freight terminals. A hub. A junction. A defunct investment portfolio. A clanking, hissing, weed-and-wild-flower theme park of labour history and social stagnation, in close proximity to all the other cemeteries and memorial gardens in that convenient fold of the map, between the new tower-block estates of Hackney and the collided villages, swollen hamlets and dispersal zones of late-industrial Essex.

If you have seen Robert Hamer's 1947 film, *It Always Rains on Sunday*, you'll appreciate the romance of East London rail yards; the night-and-fog drama of a fugitive dodging through shunting coal trains, leaping over glistening tracks, to demonstrate, in his doomed flight, the scale and majesty of these forbidden places. A mundane, workaday reality overwhelmed by metaphor: ramps, cattle cars, misty haloes around light poles, agitated guard dogs. The poetry of the rail zone works everywhere. The French with their yellow cigarettes and zinc-bar passions, train drivers seething with lust and rage: Jean Gabin and Simone Simon. American Beats making poetry of the ironhorse highways of the Far West: Allen Ginsberg sitting beside Jack Kerouac, 'under the huge shade of a Southern Pacific locomotive', to eulogize a soul-shuddering sunset. Kerouac and Neal Cassady, those brakemen of language, struggling to keep alive the ride-the-rails hobo myths, in a time of war-world innocence. Short-term labourers addicted to dry-mouthed Benzedrine riffs and the holy legends of trailer parks and wood fires under bridges. Young men reconnecting with old landscapes.

The reality of Chobham Farm was very soon apparent; we were a disposable element at the bottom of the food chain in a speculative operation that might collapse at any moment, and whose legacy would be strikes, picket lines, low wages, aggravation. At first we were general labourers, beasts of burden, unloading containers and loading lorries. Slippery, brown-paper sacks of talcum powder that bent awkwardly in our arms, like small drunk children, slithering away from the grip: one sack at a time was too easy, three sacks impossible to control. Bags burst. We slid and skidded. The ghosts of defunct railway lines came under the perimeter fence and into the sheds. We tripped on raised metal, stubbed our toes on sharp-edged concrete pillars. We wrestled dripping barrels of putrid animal stuff, suspended in vinegar. We cut our fingers on the wire bands holding together rancid sheep casings. We were confused but willing, over-whelmed by the richness and strangeness of this location, charmed by the exoticism of our workmates. They asked few questions, made no judgements; all of them prepared, as we were, to wait and watch.

Faces. Chobham faces. Lived-in, puzzled and generous faces of men confronting a camera. The little, lithe, 'Cape Coloured' South African with the beanie cap pulled down to his eyebrows in autumn warmth; the dazzling smile of supersize false teeth like the fenders of a Detroit motor on a Dagenham forecourt. They joshed him, the others. And he took it in good part, until young Freddie snatched off his cap. Baz had been a sailor, Merchant Marine, he dressed in expectation of foul weather, a clear unblinking gaze scanning the Stratford horizon for signs of trouble. In breaks, between jobs, I leant against his forklift, while he advised me, in a whisper, to make the best of the situation, but to be ready, as soon as opportunity presented itself, to move on. Never trust the bosses beyond the next pay packet. As casuals, we had to report back to the Holborn office, after work on a Thursday, to pick up our wages: £15 for a week of early starts, dirt, hard graft and no facilities.

'Join the firm, full-time,' Baz said. 'Don't give those bastards a slice of your money for nothing.'

He was saving. He was plotting. Kitbag packed beneath the bed. He kept his own counsel. He never read a newspaper.

Liam, the smiling, pink-faced Irish checker with the red hair, shoulders too solid for his donkey jacket, had no problem with type-casting: conviviality, physical strength, a temper. He would give you the chat, a loud 'How you doing now?', to signal the end of conversation, not the beginning; there was another agenda beyond the bonhomie of the yards and I would never be a party to it. Another lorry to stack: boxes, tea chests, slim packages, bundles of rods, washing machines, drums of honey. The first driver in the queue would present a docket, and the checker, on his forklift, would set off to locate the specified cargo in its numbered slot. We were doing dockwork, four miles inland from the Thames. Once a week, no choice about it, we paid our dues to the Transport and General Workers' Union. A mark on the pink card. The only way out of the drudgery was politics. If I had to do this for life, I would exploit my gift for bullshit, never letting facts get in the way of a good story, and become a spokesman, a fixer. As a labourer, I was willing but handless.

After a month or so, Renchi dropped out. Tom, calmed by the regular slap of the brown envelope, the simple tasks that defined a soothingly proscribed world, decided to stay on. Chobham was an inland voyage, an interlude of physical labour, a palliative to mental torment. The Hackney phone might ring while he was out here, behind the wire, inside the gloomy warehouse, a private space where nobody could find him. It would ring in an empty room. He wouldn't have to agonize over taking the job, hacking out another script. They might pick up on one of his Hammer Films outlines: revenging plants maddened by the greed of humankind, vampires who read Thoreau and made their own coffins out of recycled packing cases. But he would never hear that terrible bell. He would not be at home to answer the call. Chobham Farm, Angel Lane, E15, was an oasis, a Zen monastery. With the mystique of rail tracks, the yarns of itinerant workers, the flood and flux of cargoes, Tom was journeying without going anywhere. The ponytailed hippie-pirate drivers, gold rings in the ear, joints burning yellow fingers, spoke of the open road: India, Nepal. It was enough. We sat in the sunshine, in our rags, books in pockets, mesh fence supporting our aching backs, and admired the persistence of giant sunflowers growing out of oily gravel. We would sign on, we would stay for the winter. Perhaps for ever.

Looking back now, watching the 8mm films, the story breaks down into two elements: faces and terrain. Our films are mercifully silent. But I miss the voices of those Chobham men, the monologues and sharp banter that I struggle to recover.

The Cob, I remember him. I gave him that name and it stuck. After the Welsh cob ponies, short-legged, strong in the back. Uncomplaining. The Cob was a welcome addition to any work gang; shirt off, jeans with cowboy turn-ups, scars and tattoos, constant motion. The times when there was nothing to do, contemplative, roll-up intervals between lorries, hurt him. He jumped on and off tailgates. He hurdled barrels. He rolled drums and then kicked them back where they came from. He did robotic press-ups in the mud, calling out numbers. He shadow-boxed. He punched holes in rotten wood. Then the shout – YES! – and another tottering stack of tea chests to manhandle, another rattle of pipes and random packages. The jagged tin edges of the chests slashed the Cob's palms. He licked his wounds and grinned like Dracula.

Mick watched him. He was as strong, physically, but he wouldn't venture one drop of sweat more than was strictly necessary. There was something held back and threatening in Mick's silence; the way he stood, arms folded, at the edge of alien conversations – cinema, books, newspaper babble – and studied our faces. Mercury-grey eyes. The twitch of his lips, at the pretension, the absurdity. In tea breaks, Mick became the dominant presence, as others like the Cob and Liam, through a furious response to the challenge of moving obstacles from one place to another, did when we serviced the queue of lorries from far-flung places.

A packing case stamped ROCKLEA QUEENSLAND becomes an

improvised card table. Cribbage. Pegs in a board. Mick's stubby hands: an indelible compass rose blue-inked over a river system of veins. A bird with spread wings. Four needle-sketched diamonds echoed by the playing cards spread, face up, by his thick fingers. A stained white mug with broken handle. Mick knows how to occupy dead time. He has come straight from prison to Chobham. He's waiting to get away and talks about Canada. The card games are a useful interlude in which, without specifics, dates and methods, to plot future crimes. They say he killed a man in a pub brawl. He doesn't drink. He doesn't talk about women.

They owe us. This much is agreed. The owners, the operators. A modicum of low-level pilferage, self-awarded bonus payment, is tolerated: tins of fruit, sardines, paperback books, broken wax from which to make candles against the threat of power cuts. Traditions of the docks are honoured, within unspecified limits. It's a cowboy operation in an unresolved wasteland. One of the lads, from a Canning Town family, is putting in a few months before he gets his dockers' card. He is treated with respect, an aristocrat of labour. He will take up the position vacated by a relative who is retiring to the sun. Seasoned Chobhamites, caps, dungarees, donkey jackets, their dark-rimmed eyes, pinched faces mapped with worry-lines like ridges in wet sand, harbour no grudges against those who are more fortunate than themselves. There is an established hierarchy of caste: workers with union connections, foremen out of the army, ex-paras with a limp and the habit of command, unknowable bosses, white shirts and braces, figures of fate. Workers are trapped within the minutiae of whatever is proscriptively local: niggles, feuds, blocked toilets, cold tea, a permitted Christmas drinking session and the hope of overtime. The bosses, when we see them, are embarrassed to be caught on the site from which they make their money. The details of the operation are shameful: all these men standing around, talking, scratching their bollocks, slapping cold hands together, breaking up good pallet boards for oil-drum fires. And the sheds themselves, with their inverted W roofs, broken-glass panels, dead chimneys and twisted smokestacks, are a rebuke; a daily reminder that it takes serious investment to translate a set for the last act of *The Sweeney* (screaming rubber, *you're nicked, you slag*) into an automated, multifunction coldstore.

Tom and I are the only ones who leave the yard during the course of the working day, because we want to explore and evaluate the ground that envelops us. I volunteer for sandwich duty, a walk out of the gate, down Leyton Road into Alma Street, to the small precinct of shops intended to service the surrounding estates, the dejected scatter of railside industries. Cigarettes, cans of fizz, crisps, chocolate bars. 'Take your time.'

My pocket is heavy with change. The Chobham boys know the precise cost of their mid-morning sugar hits, the quantity of tobacco required to pace the day. They wait by the fence: big Horse and his pie-munching mate, Streak. Horse is no cob, a shaggy, heavy-boned shire. Monobrow. Dense sideburns like wings on a helmet. Dandy's floral neckerchief, knotted at the throat, to dress the brown smock. A giant and a fop, despite the flat-footed, stately waddle towards the incoming lorry. The thump of greeting. Streak is a Dodger figure, quick, funny, neat as a knife. Quilted waistcoat over denim jacket, muffler at the throat in the old Silvertown fashion. A type. An archetype. But they are men of this place, both of them; the lumbering Horse and his goading, protective mate. Who snaps through bacon rolls, pies, cheese sarnies, mugs of tea, without putting on a pound of weight. Married with kids, responsible at twenty-two, and advising Horse how to go about it, how to get a good woman into his bed.

Why Horse, I wondered? From the TV show *Bonanza*, the dim brother of the Ponderosa ranch? Wasn't he Hoss? It was a family thing, the big man told me, while we waited on a case of spanners that couldn't be found. A desultory chat between accidental colleagues. They were fishermen, his folk, from the mouth of the Thames Estuary, the mudflats. They pushed a sledge-like device called a horse out in front of them. And it took some pushing. To the line of nets in all weathers. That was the legend. Horse belonged in *Great Expectations*, where Streak with his natty outfits, his chat, was a man of the city, comfortable with coded language and arcane practices. A survivor with the eyes of a ferret.

One of the strange aspects, thinking back, is that we didn't talk football. Tom and I, middle-class dropouts, we talked football. We made expeditions at the weekends to White Hart Lane, Highbury, Upton Park, even Stamford Bridge, without any convinced tribal allegiance; a nod towards Tottenham, an antipathy for Arsenal, but essentially it was the journey to the ground, the theatre of it, in through the turnstile on a whim. Upton Park: the monkey chants for Clyde Best. The fabled wit of that academy of footballing science: 'Where's your handbag, Moore?' As Bobby, comb in hand, strolls through another routine encounter, not yet sainted and marooned on a triumphalist plinth in Barking Road. The Chobham mob, drawn from everywhere, grafting to get by, would take overtime before Saturday spectatorship without a moment's hesitation. Football was no longer the opiate of the workers and not yet the corporate monster devouring the world's financial systems, smokescreen respectability for oligarchs, arms dealers and corrupt statesmen.

There was another reason for leaving the site during working hours. And it shocked me. One of the young married men passed, at a clip, as I emerged from the newsagent. 'Can't stop, mate. Only got twenty minutes.' He was seeing a woman on the estate, a quickie, before her husband came off shift. This was accepted behaviour, a casual genetic exchange, a break in the day for both of them, reflecting the chirpy atmosphere of Joan Littlewood's 1962 film, *Sparrers Can't Sing*. Every man a James Booth. Every housewife in the new tower block a Barbara Windsor. Details of the encounter, positions achieved and attempted, kitchen table, shower cabinet, enlivened our early-afternoon torpor. 'She said, so I said. Wash your fucking hands, before you put your fingers up my arse. I told her. Dirty mare.' Then home to the wife and kiddies for tea. Life happened in separate compartments. One law for the terrace, one for the high-rise. The Chobham Lothario didn't look much like James Booth or

George Sewell. Still less Michael Caine in *Alfie*. He could, at a pinch, have been number three or four from the left in the Dave Clark Five.

Freddie Tanner, our checker, was a youth of about eighteen, very sure of himself, unfazed by coping with two members of a different species. We did the job, he took the piss. Skinny. Long-fingered. Cupped cigarette. One-handed virtuoso of the forklift. He lived at home with his mum and dad in a tower block overlooking what is now the Olympic site. He loved the way you could move from room to room to enjoy sunrise or sunset. The complexity of all that life: railways, Stratford Broadway, Lea Valley. Hoists, scrub woods, marshes, roads where the traffic never stops flowing.

The view that Freddie describes is a novelty, no working Londoner has ever seen it before. He buys into the utopianism of the planners' vision, the vertical streets with their smart Swedish kitchens and bathrooms: the setting for Joan Littlewood's film. New buildings provoke new energies. You drudge down there in the mud, hassled by foremen and time-keepers, underpaid, underappreciated, and you are still in the great hive, the buzz of argument, jokes, rucks, snatched sex, thieving, comradeship. Then you retreat, at the end of the day, to the pristine flat. The floating pod that demands an upgrade in furniture, bed linen, electrical goods. A social space inspiring adulterous encounters, no strings, by evading the constant vigilance of the terraced streets, the twitching curtains. Gossip at the front step. Accountable neighbours.

After a few months as a Chobham labourer, the system was changed. No longer did we receive pay, cashmoney, in little envelopes (deductions itemized). It was a pinched season of power strikes, rubbish strikes, ineptitude and obfuscation: with not a cigarette paper between the political strategies on offer. Wage snatches were a natural extension of industrial work practice. Professional villains, local firms in Canning Town and Forest Gate, operated on the model of dying Lea Valley enterprises. The checker (or wheelman) and his group of tried-and-trusted associates. Put in the graft and spend the profit before the week is out. The only difference between hardened thieves and disaffected workers is the rush, the adrenalin boost of high-stakes risk. The wages you collect, as an over-the-pavement merchant, belong to someone else. You cut out the middlemen, the accountants shaving their percentage. You drop the tedious business of card-punching, the long hours. Crime was a logical response to illogical conditions.

Management at Chobham Farm responded by instructing their workers to open bank accounts: thereby initiating them into the slippery world of credit, the festering itch of material ambition and future catastrophe. The old cash exchange worked pretty well, you could see what you had. Money was divided to pay the week's bills. What was left over went on pleasure. You started each week with empty pockets and a clean slate. Or so I rationalized the process. As we ambled down Angel Lane, saluting that lovely creeper-covered Victorian cottage, towards Stratford. The paperback in my pocket was a beat-up, grime-fingered Dante. When I stole a few minutes, lolling on an Australian sack, in a furtive alcove, I leafed back and forth through the sticky pages, to find the stanzas I would reread before I nodded off. The stuff about lost wretches who prostitute themselves for gold and silver. The torments waiting for usurers in red braces.

Bankers with heavy bellies, advocates of fiscal alchemy, let them dance on hot coals and wade, up to the chin, in tides of their own excrement. Delightful reveries for a walk to the Midland Bank. Most of the boys handed over their cheques and took their weekly wages in cash. Others were seduced by the potency of slim new cheque-books. They were in the system now. Tom, his film money not quite depleted, banked his tithe and built up his reserves. Freddie, he considered, was a natural for the new City. A whippet on the trading floor. Lively. Quick-witted. Amoral. Uninhibited by education. Why wrestle a forklift truck over buried rails when you could be cruising tarmac in a silver Porsche?

The panorama from Freddie's Stratford tower was echoed by the establishing shots in *Bronco Bullfrog*, the 1970 film by Barney

Platts-Mills. I took this as a timely conjunction of two worlds: the independent, low-budget cinema we had left behind and the dramas of territory in which we now worked. Freddie, if he hadn't been otherwise engaged, could have played a part. Non-actors, inspired by Joan Littlewood, and given just enough of a framing structure by Platts-Mills, enacted a fable of place, shot in the wake of Italian neo-realism and the mood of British Free Cinema. The way Oxbridge directors, living vicariously, explored aspects of proletarian life, boys' clubs, funfairs, bikers' cafés, the seaside. Platts-Mills was the son of the barrister who defended Ronnie Kray at the 1969 trial in which he received a guilty verdict and a life sentence, with the recommendation that he serve 'not less than thirty years'.

Viewing *Bronco Bullfrog* while working alongside the rail yards where a fictitious robbery occurs was a disorientating experience. The film was produced by Andrew St John, a friend of Renchi Bicknell, and the man who set up *Mari's Girls*, Renchi's abortive ballet short. The editor was Jonathan Gili, an associate of John Betjeman. And in later years a customer for my used-book catalogues. Beyond his involvement with Betjeman's topographic excursions, Gili designed the illustrated bear story *Archie and the Strict Baptists*. Philida Gili, whose drawings accompany the Betjeman text, was Jonathan's wife and the daughter of the celebrated engraver Reynolds Stone. It struck me that the credits for *Bronco Bullfrog*, this modest Stratford story, shot at the optimum moment of social transformation, with disenchanted kids breaking away from the limited expectations and timid conventions of their parents, represented an honourable form of cultural tourism. The modest budget of £18,000 was enough, even then, to buy two or three terraced houses in the area, or a large property, with established garden, on a Victorian square in Hackney. The crew were West Londoners, while the cast, or most of them, came from the streets in which the film was set. The entire episode, like much that followed, was an invasion, a raid on exoticism. East London was a tribal, sexualized wilderness. The docks were dying, but you could smell the river.

Cinema, like rock music, was a way for connected public-school boys to slipstream the energies of a romanticized underclass. The process of colonization went back to the post-war landscape of ruins, when London thrillers exploited bombed docks, rubbled terraces, street markets and rail yards. Among the jobbing repertory company of English gargoyles, you might find Dirk Bogarde as a quiveringly neurotic cosh boy, slumming spivs with strangulated RADA elocution, and teenage psychopaths impersonated by Dickie Attenborough. The movies paralleled, or anticipated, regeneration packages. If an area was striking enough in its dereliction to work as a film set, it was ripe for development. The Barney Platts-Mills expedition to Stratford, for all its virtues, was a signifier of coming land piracy. The arrival of our small troop of counterculturalists at Chobham Farm represented the same process in a different form. I was not there because I wanted to lose myself in a George Gissing abdication of status and identity. The landscape seduced me, it was an unwritten nowhere in which to launch a lifelong journal. My workmates were not heroic presences, trapped by economic pressure in degraded wage slavery, they were characters who might or might not turn up in a future fiction. Fortunately, the typed blue sheets, bound with twine, on which I kept a record of that winter's work, have been lost. I can recover the diary film of the yards, bruised light, burning railway carriages, autumn sunrises, but the emotional formulae of the time, stark language seizures, have vanished into the attic jumble where everything has an equal value and nothing can be located on demand.

The double-barrelled film-makers of the Platts-Mills era (*Bronco Bullfrog* was photographed by Adam Barker-Mill) were the pre-forgotten. Respectable British Film Institute footnotes. The valiantly unnoticed waiting to be discovered by media-studies theorists. Platts-Mills came east to collaborate with local kids doing classes at the Theatre Royal. In workshop exercises, initiated by Joan Littlewood, youths from the estates pantomime the toffs: class satire taking the crap out of judges and bent briefs, a milieu with which Barney Platts-Mills had some familiarity. He documented these sessions, preparation for *Bronco Bullfrog*, in a short film called *Everybody's an Actor, Shakespeare Said*. As with all period footage, it is the random details of time and place that catch our eye. A torn centrefold from a vanished publication, *Parade*: Jayne Mansfield, her augmented bosom in a wispy white wrap, recalling her visit to Hackney for a budgerigar show. A poster for Edward Judd in *Invasion*. 'Aliens crashland near a hospital and mount a night attack on an English village.' Scratchy young men in considered outfits that don't cohere, tight trousers showing white socks, work boots with cardigans and trilbies, negotiate with the camera: actual and simulated boredom, snorts of derisive smoke.

'Hang about the streets, it's all I've ever done . . . Stratford, Plaistow, Forest Gate, East Ham, Leyton, Chingford, everywhere.'

'It's not acting,' one of the lads says, 'it's remembering.'

Washed-out colours of Hackney Marshes. Blue-grey prairie divided by scraggy rivulets and clogged canals. The Stratford boys, time out from work, kick a ball around, encumbered by one-size-fits-everybody overalls. They decide that the theme of their drama will be redevelopment. They have done the research. They know that civic structures have been torn down to provide a car park. They pretend that the marshes are a private golf course, on which developers schmooze corrupt politicians. 'From St John's Church to Maryland Point, that's what I want to bung you for – to get the buildings off it, to build a car park.' The fantasy is recurrent and persuasive. A reflection of the late 1960s and an anticipation of the coming millennium. 'I'll make a bomb off it, off every car that comes in there . . . Take everything down, no clubs on Stratford Broadway.'

The script of *Bronco Bullfrog*, unconstricted by a bullshit narrative arc or conventional three-act structure, derives from the earlier Theatre Royal exercises. Characters, remembering not acting, move around just enough to quantify a portrait of place. Allotments. Prefabs. Tower blocks. Steamed-up, all-day-breakfast caffs. Launderettes. And the rail yards that provide the setting for the fateful robbery: the Borstal runaway Bronco Bullfrog, in his premature braces, wedged in a room of useless white goods. Territory is familiar, life-long, and endured with affectionate exasperation: circumscribed lives made awkward by hormonal surges and the transitory beauty of youth. You can't help wondering about the afterlife of Anne Gooding, who was discovered by Platts-Mills while 'working in a dairy shop'. Her presence on the screen, docile but dissatisfied, not yet resigned and defeated, is easy and authentic. Tumble of hair and panda eyes. That sense of always looking out of the frame in any conversation, expecting the worst. Del Walker uses a flair for troublemaking as a badge of integrity. 'He challenged Joan's or anyone's authority,' Platts-Mills said. Del is the one slumped at the back of the class, cranking up the volume on his alternative soundtrack. The actors were given a share in the phantom profits of the film's brief notoriety.

The problem in *Bronco Bullfrog* is Stratford's dust overcoat, the sucking gravity of place, how the young are held to what they already know, the fact that lives are fated, the story is written: they will wither into their despised parents. The liberating run on the motorbike to 'the other end', up west, is a failed attempt to see the *Oliver!* of Carol Reed and Lionel Bart. Too expensive. 'Winner of 6 Oscars.' Too popular. The young lovers give themselves up to the hopeless melancholy of Hackney Marshes, a bench near the dog track. The Anne Gooding character is unconvinced by the promise of high-rise living. 'It's nice up 'ere, innit?' The spoilt panorama and the distant prospect of Epping Forest. An empty Mateus Rosé bottle is in evidence. And Dad is 'away'. Armed robbery. A detective tells her mother that Del is 'the sort of kid who would take drugs – and introduce her to them'.

The youths of *Bronco Bullfrog* can aspire to an apprenticeship, working as welders or labouring in warehouses and rail sheds. Or they can freelance in crime, graduate in yobbery and vandalism, aspire to Parkhurst, men of reputation. Barney Platts-Mills got his start in the film business when his father met the director Lewis Gilbert at a cricket match. There were early days at the edges of Kubrick's *Spartacus* and games of poker with Steve McQueen on the set of *The War Lover*. Then Barney took a summer off, aiming at Turkey and reaching Corfu. He drops in on Norman Douglas on the Isle of Ischia and stays with Freya Stark, who takes him along to a production of *Aida* in 'the magical candlelit setting of the arena in Verona'. With his brother, Barney buys a Victorian racing yacht: before he decides to return to London and a career in film. Out of the discovery of Free Cinema, low-budget improvisations, Paddington youth clubs, he arrives at Joan Littlewood's Theatre Royal in Stratford.

Talking about this period, Platts-Mills said: 'Probably, on reflection, Joan's ideas were never of much interest to the powers-that-be, but what a difference they might have made in removing the dead hand of building contractors, architects, landowners and surveyors which has lain so expensively on Britain's Cultural Industry and which the Dome so clearly represents.' The failure of the Fun Palace along with the construction of that millennial tent on the East Greenwich peninsula were the moments of fracture. Stratford abdicated its fixed identity and willingly prostituted itself as a backdrop for experimental malls, rail hubs and computer-generated Olympic parks. The O2 Arena was New Labour's Xerox of the Littlewood Fun Palace, a circus that was all sideshow, freak show, bringing the dead back as holograms. Making the whole idea of fun terminally depressing.

When they offered us a full-time contract at Chobham Farm, we took the paperwork to an overgrown cemetery, where we signed away our freelance identities. Like Platts-Mills we had traded on connections, public school or film school, but that was all over. It looked very much as if we were in this for the duration. Every day we explored another thicket on the marshes, another backriver. When we climbed the mounds, to roam or kick a ball, we looked out over a classic edgeland of inconvenient, dirty, fly-by-night enterprises and abortive pastoral relics. Industrial hoists. Football pitches. A cycle track. A river shared by oarsmen, narrowboat dwellers, dog-walkers, wanderers who were not filmed, not challenged by security, trusted to make their own mistakes.

Tom Baker

The view from the converted squash court, into the green lozenge of a hidden garden, carried me back to another, older England; one that had been there all along, out of reach, conforming to unwritten rules and prohibitions that were more real than those who serviced them. I remember Tom's home in Berkshire, from student days, and how, after the evening meal, there was a special cloth for the glasses, another for the cutlery; colonial habits respected long after the age of servants was over. Tom's father, a senior civil servant, produced a guide to Spanish architecture and asked us what we intended to visit and why, which churches, museums, sites of cultural significance. When, in truth, there was nothing ahead of us but the open road; accidental discoveries and encounters, Velázquez, Goya, El Greco, in parallel with a dubbed version of Nicholas Ray's *Rebel Without a Cause* at an open-air cinema in Barcelona, and the crowd at a bloody, small-town bullfight hooting and chanting when a black American tourist won a television set in the between-bouts bingo session. You could see the glint of the Mediterranean over the low white wall, new apartments rising from the dirt shore. Coming back through France, after two months sleeping under the stars, we tried the tent for the first time: only to discover that it had been stolen.

Every journey out of London in 2009, if it's not made on foot or by water, is a negotiation with rage, frustration, stalled traffic, confusing signs, cone avenues without a hint of work in progress. The run to Thedden Grange was no exception. I won't rehearse the tedious details, but that motorway shudder, the weariness, is with us as we sit in the gallery above the former squash court, taking solace from a visible square of mastered garden. Palpable evidence of a job well done gave Tom permission to perch in an easy chair, rest a book in his lap, sift the *Financial Times*. He left London in the mid 1970s, part of a group who were buying a large country house, with stables, cottages, land. After Chobham Farm and work as an occasional builder, he never went back to film. He contributed to the Hackney 8mm diary, and then began to shoot, on Super-8, his own lyrical 'songs', multiple superimpositions in forests and fields as a final renunciation of the burden of narrative. The fiddle of editing. What passed through the camera, that was the story.

Treating memoir as an element within a larger social argument, I had to pay some attention to structure. Could I trust my unsupported account of our days at Chobham Farm? Now that my blue-paper journals had vanished. Laying out the photographs on Tom's table, I saw at once how he responded to details I had chosen to ignore or play down. He was struck by the romance of youth, the floor-length cloak and shoulder-length hair of his first wife. And our curious notion that a walk over the mud dunes and railside paddocks of Stratford constituted a suitable Sunday-afternoon outing for the family. Bridget Baker, smiling gamely, carries the Bolex in her gloved hand. In the background are hoists, pylons, tower blocks. In junkshop coats and wellington boots, we are a time-travelling Pre-Raphaelite coven rambling through a Tarkovsky wilderness. Climbing the track towards the site where the Clays Lane community estate would be built – and destroyed – we were harbingers of the coming plague of surveyors, hard-hat engineers, fence erectors. Toxic blight was all around, the ghost milk of dying industries. Accompanied by an ecology of resistance and unsponsored fecundity. The women wrap themselves in their military coats and woollen cloaks. The men grin. Anna is photographed in front of a board announcing: MAJOR ROAD WORKS AHEAD.

I decided to record Tom's version of our period at Chobham Farm. He was happy to take part in this exercise, offering an improvised meal, salad and wine, on his return from a stint as a gardener. He did two half-days a week, helping to manage private estates in the area, and spent the rest of the time looking after the vegetable beds at Thedden Grange. This, as might be expected, was a complicated arrangement. The philosophical basis of the original community had been factored by practical considerations. There were systems within systems. Four people agreed to sign up to Tom's scheme: that he would dig, plant and service the vegetable garden. For a fee. Pick as much as you like. Three stakeholders would pay. One wanted to take a part in the labour, independently, but supervised by Tom, for credit in terms of the crop. There were further difficulties. What, for example, if you spurned Brussels sprouts and craved a bumper dividend of mangetout peas? As might be imagined, such theological niceties led to hours of discussion and debate, of the kind that make communal life so challenging. For Tom, there were contemplative silences to be relished as he bent over the trenches. He prepared the soil, he sowed the seed: he did not harvest, weigh out, make division. If he frustrated greenfly and other pests, he had to do it without chemicals. The pitch was organic, its laborious methodology would have been approved by the Prince of Wales. In its tedium was a necessary virtue.

When Judith, another former Hackney resident and our fellow guest at Tom's table, spoke of 'the community', I thought of Iris Murdoch and *The Bell*. This was not the enforced, all-for-one against the greater evil, of the Chobham workers. This was a voluntary alliance of urban escapees, solicitous, in their differing ways, of the good life. A community of interest which, having survived thirty-five years of separations, schisms, marriages, children and grandchildren, was itself interesting. And settled, established, viable. Hidden at the end of a wooded drive. Screened behind walls of dark strawberry-coloured brick. Clock towers, dovecots, dairies. Lines of large cars parked on gravel.

Tom's squash court was a permanently ongoing project. His computer, wedged into a corner, balanced over a sheer drop to the floor below. There was no supporting rail alongside the improvised stairs. But the room was pleasantly occupied, wood burnished in early-evening light: a long table, plenty of books. *Falling Man* by Don DeLillo had been taken out of the library for the second time, when Tom failed to crack it at the first attempt. He wouldn't be contriving the screenplay for David Cronenberg, who seemed to be involved with a one-man campaign to turn a collection of modern first editions – Burroughs, Ballard, Martin Amis and now DeLillo's *Cosmopolis* – into over-respectful movie interpretations. A heritage of sanitized nonconformity.

I had been talking about swimming in the Usk, a cold brown river in the rain. Tom mentioned his birthday. He had set out with his girlfriend for a drive through the New Forest, before a celebratory supper at Ikea in Southampton. Never before had he experienced a hot dog. 'One of those long sausage things, rather good.' And you could drink as much fizz as you wanted from the dispenser. For 30p. 8 July: a day to remember.

'I've read about the place where you stayed in a John le Carré novel,' Tom said. 'My son gave it to me for Christmas.' He meant the country-house fishing hotel, nestling above the Usk, a mile or so outside Crickhowell on the Welsh borders. 'Something odd happens there, a meeting, Philby and Graham Greene.'

I knew that he had the wrong author, a very reasonable mistake. The thriller in question flags a comparison with Le Carré on the cover. It's by Chris Petit and it's called *The Passenger*. Petit knew that hotel and used it as the setting for an assignation between English spooks, as recalled by a dead American: James Jesus Angleton, the certifiably paranoid poet of the CIA. Angleton, like Jeremy Paxman, had been to school a few miles down the road at Malvern. If the world was an ungodly conspiracy, he was the one weaving it: out of his own sweaty entrails. History, Petit reckoned, was a series of mislaid files edited by a posthumous dreamer. Pretty much everything going on in contemporary geopolitics fits between two of the most dramatic grand projects: the Berlin Olympics of 1936 and the Beijing Games of 2008. When Chris made a film in Berlin, prophesying the collapse of the Wall and exploiting metaphors of cultural leakage, he called it *Chinese Boxes*.

'Interesting book, but I couldn't get my head round it,' Tom confessed. 'I let it sit too long between sessions. I could never figure out what was happening, who was alive and who was dead.'

The Thedden Grange episode, as darkness enveloped the garden and familiar shapes dressed themselves in an attractive ambiguity, was another debriefing. Another attempt to fix the past. Judith told us that she was keeping a journal. Her work took her out on the road, long hours at the wheel, up and down the country; before she checked in at another strange hotel, to appear in court, next morning, as an expert witness. She relished the cut and thrust of the trial, the forensic precision of language in her meticulously prepared evidence. Every night, without fail, she recorded her observations. This meal, she assured us, would be documented. We were playing a part.

I had been on the move now for six months, promoting an old book and researching a new one: riding buses on a Freedom Pass, scribbling notes, walking too fast through unfamiliar cities. I was beginning to believe that I would never return to Hackney. Where Tom was fixed in an incomplete ark, which he was condemned to revise and improve on a daily basis, I was stuck on the Bunyan treadmill of elsewhere. I was becoming addicted to my status as a Travelodge tramp: check in, not too far from the airport, scrape breakfast from pre-filled containers, before another hike through industrial dereliction, generic malls, hapless public art dumped in windy, privately owned squares. A catalogue of unfunny punchlines without the necessary preamble. Everything, from my exhaustion to the spread of Chobham photographs, to the consciousness that individual witnesses were forming their own versions of a lingering meal, pushed this event closer to Petit's interpretation of middle-class English society as a spy story. In the spirit of Michelangelo Antonioni, he demonstrates that the set always overwhelms its incidental human puppets: dry fucks in empty swimming pools carpeted in the curled leaves of dumped newsreels. A Petit out-take from *The Passenger* imagined Angleton visiting Philby's house at Crowborough in Sussex. Finding the hard-drinking spook away from home, and having to deal with a bitter wife, Angleton is trapped in the febrile stasis of an English summer: unraked gravel drive, burnt lawn, an embarrassment of rhododendrons. Boredom, as his shirt sticks to his back, and he sniffs the foxy reek of the captive woman, becomes transcendent. This is the place, here is the story. Petit takes cricket as a metaphor for espionage, double-dealing, civilized treachery. The off-break delivered with a leg-break action: the Chinaman.

Crowborough has a marginal distinction that Petit does not mention. It is the town where Edwin and Willa Muir translated *The Castle* by Franz Kafka. Windlesham Manor, once the home of Conan Doyle, is the most famous literary shrine in the area. After the death of the creator of Sherlock Holmes in 1930, the house was ritually exorcized.

These were some of my fictions as I invited Tom to dredge up his account of our Chobham Farm days. I was hoping for details I'd missed. The kind I stumbled on when digital technology allowed me to freeze-frame the VHS tape of the old diary films. I saw myself in the bath reading a letter I'd forgotten from an American woman, the mother of a friend who had gone missing, so it appeared, in Afghanistan. Before this man set off on his great adventure, the mother, English-born but long resident in New York, treated us to a meal at Rule's in Covent Garden. She recalled, a highlight of her youth as a publisher's secretary, being propositioned, over lunch, by a rather flushed Graham Greene.

I took Tom right back to the start. We relocated to a corner near the kitchen. He had crafted the work surfaces, fittings and cupboards, but left out the sink. He fetched water from the floor below in a plastic bowl, saying that he relished the inconvenience. It taught him patience. A proper kitchen was at least thirty years in the making. He flicked through the photographs for a few moments and then spoke, without hesitation, laughing over forgotten follies, the innocence of those times. Stratford East: 1971.

I don't know that I gave up on film, but film had given up on me. Chobham only started a few months before we went there. It was clearly set up to circumvent the docks. Once the container system was in place, containers could be unloaded anywhere. We were dealing with mixed containers.

They had to be emptied. A container might have goods in it from ten different companies.

They came off a ship in the docks, on to a lorry. And instead of having to pay the dockers to unpack it, they sussed that they could recruit the riff-raff of the world. Which was us. On the lowest possible wages.

That was my interest in Chobham. The people who had drifted in from everywhere. They had no careers, they went from job to job. I didn't get to know many of my fellow workers very well. I was struck by one man, an old man, he'd been a waiter on a train. A steward. Serving meals on night trains to Scotland.

My strongest memory of that winter was of February 1972, the earliest flower to come out in England. I can't remember its name. It pokes its nose out of the rubble. In the darkest days of the year, a yellow daisy.

So much of the stuff in the containers got broken. One of the saddest sights was the goods coming back from Australia, domestic stuff, tea chests of emigrants who had decided to come home. If you fill a tea chest up completely, it's bloody heavy. Pots and pans and books. We found it very difficult to unload tea chests without damaging the goods. Everyday domestic things were tipped out on the floor.

There was a lot of root ginger at one time. Chickpeas too. I was eating chickpeas for months and they're not very tasty. Sacks of chickpeas.

The worst thing was plastic glazing material. Whole containers full of the stuff. We didn't have the equipment to unload them. We had to do it by hand. That was ghastly.

The most fun was driving the forklift truck. You press the left-hand side of the accelerator and you go forward. You press the right-hand side and you go back. It's very quick. Two levers to lift or lower the forks. And another to tip them back and forth. You have three movements going on at the same time. It was lots of fun.

I wasn't frustrated by working in such a cold, dirty environment for so little money. There were no facilities, but I didn't want facilities. In the tea breaks, everyone else would go into the tearoom and play cards. You and I would sit outside on the forklifts and read the newspapers. Mostly we had to read the Sun, *because that's what people left lying around. I don't think I ever bought a paper. I do remember reading a book. I read* The Wisdom of Insecurity *by Alan Watts. Wonderful. I must have read Thoreau's* Walden *at that time.*

I do remember being horrified, quite late on, when I discovered that staff, the office staff, had a separate lavatory. Which had its own key, to stop the riff-raff getting in. I thought, 'Shit! This isn't right.' I can see now, thinking about how filthy we were, that the social distinction might not have been such a bad thing.

We were a little different. John the foreman knew that we would understand things. We could do forms. We had to fill in these forms when they took us on. And, foolishly, we put down all our degrees. They did tease us about that. Mostly they said, 'Wow, what are you doing here?'

There was a certain sense of liberation in this. You didn't have to feel guilty about not having a career. I had no idea really what the hell I was doing. Not at all. I'd stopped making money out of film, but I hadn't started making anything out of building, painting and decorating.

I left Chobham because my son, Ned, was about to be born. Most people who are having a child try and earn more money. I became unemployed. Family was more important, I thought. With hindsight, my attitude was totally irresponsible.

I can't remember what else I did. Motorbike messenger? That was in the winter. I skidded in the snow on Old Street. A year or two later, I got a job in a tomato greenhouse. Then Renchi's brother-in-law asked us to work on his house in Essex – so I gave up the greenhouse. And learnt a bit more about being a builder. I've done that for ever.

Film had completely petered out. Partly because I wasn't at ease in the film world. I was never any good at ringing people up. It went on for a time after Mike Reeves died. My first wife had met a man called Max in Hollywood, an Englishman. She'd been working as a nanny for Raquel Welch and Pat Curtis. This man Max came back to London and took me on, with the William Morris Agency. A tremendous start. He got me various jobs in television, rewriting television, story-editing. I was commissioned to write a number of outlines. None of them were ever taken up. This went on for quite a while, a couple of years. Perhaps my ideas weren't good enough. Hammer Films didn't pick up on any of my outlines.

Things drifted. Then I met Barney Platts-Mills. He knew of me through Renchi. He contacted me and said the word was that Ringo Starr wanted to be in a pirate movie. Barney and his partner, David Astor, were looking for a pirate script. Would I write a pirate movie? I said, 'OK.' I wrote rather a good pirate script, I think. The deal was they would pay me a cut: if it was taken up . . . I think that was the last film job I ever did.

I had meetings with Andrew St John, a friend of Renchi. He'd been at school with him, Winchester. He produced Bronco Bullfrog *and also Renchi's ballet film. There was an office in Hereford Road. In Notting Hill. They were operating a bit. But nothing came of it. Ringo didn't bite.*

A similar thing happened, you remember, in Mike's days. When we did a story for the Shadows. Mike was living in Yeoman's Row. Paul Ferris, who wrote the music for Mike's films, also did quite a few Cliff Richard songs. So we were drawn into writing that outline, about the Shadows and their alien doubles running about Ireland. They knocked it back. Cliff decided he didn't want to copy the Beatles. Ha! He'd keep clear of the Dick Lester stuff. Pity. I like musicals. No violence. You went off and did that Conan sword-and-sorcery script.

I liked the marshes. We went there as soon as we moved to Hackney, to the house in De Beauvoir Road. I remember picking a stalk of dock. Or was it teasel? To give to someone. A waste plant from a wasteland: as a birthday present!

We walked down Angel Lane into Stratford, the town centre, to get paid. Down past that old cottage and the Railway Tavern. Over the humpback bridge. The Theatre Royal was out in the open. They pulled down a number of streets and terraces around it. It stood alone. The theatre was the only reason I'd ever heard of Stratford.

When Ned and I walked around the Olympic zone, a few months ago, at the nearest point you could get to Chobham Farm, just past the old entrance, I noticed that the famous Japanese knotweed was coming up. They thought they'd got rid of it: at considerable cost, thousands and thousands. But on *this little side road that goes into an industrial estate, the knotweed is back. They have bright new fences. And surveillance cameras. But it doesn't matter. On the wrong side of the fence, Japanese knotweed is pumping up through the tarmac. Quite astounding! It has no respect for fences. It will be back inside the Olympic Park in no time.*

I remember the one-day strike, after Barbara Castle's 1969 White Paper, 'In Place of Strife'. She was suggesting methods to control the unions. To fix the fact that there were always strikes.

I went into work, absolutely. I thought, 'Why should I lose a day's pay? This strike isn't going to make a hoot of difference. I'm in this for the money.' So I climbed in my car and went to work.

All was well until I turned off the road and drove up to the gates. And there to my horror were a bunch of my mates as serious pickets. I thought, 'Shit, this isn't a good idea.' People were waving at me. I either had to stop and turn round or keep on going. As it happens, I kept going. Luckily, they weren't that serious. The foreman didn't send me home. I worked a full day. There were a number of other people in the warehouse. I wasn't the only scab.

I was a bit concerned the next day, but there was no bad feeling. I was embarrassed. I was a bit scared.

Then, later, after I'd left Chobham, the dockers decided to take it over. They started picketing in earnest. They told management that they had to give employment to dockers. To be a docker you had to get a ticket.

I did feel for the guys who worked there. So many had dodged about all their lives. By the time I left, three-quarters of the place had been demolished. There were bulldozers and giant claws ripping the site apart.

I was amazed by that huge area on the edge of our yard. It wasn't totally derelict, but all those buildings we worked in had railway lines into them. Trains did go past every now and again. They were marshalling yards.

I don't like horses very much, but I like western movies. It struck me that being a forklift driver was the nearest thing to being a cowboy. You could move these things around like a cowboy flicks the reins and the horse changes direction. We would tweak one of the levers.

We weren't skiving. I never bloody skived at all. I liked physical work. It doesn't do you any good, but it's very enjoyable at the time.

I had a near bust-up with one of the bosses, after you left. A fat man. The boss of bosses. One day, we didn't have any trucks coming in. I must have been a checker at the time. I decided to park my forklift at the head of the queue, just where the trucks would arrive, and to read a book until the first truck appeared.

The fat man clocked me. He wasn't rude to me, directly, but he was bloody rude to John, the foreman. He said: 'I'm not having people out there, looking as if they've got nothing to do.'

I don't know what he was scared of, his investors perhaps. He didn't own the place. He was dead scared that a man seeming to do nothing but read a book, on a 6-litre forklift truck, might be perceived as a serious risk. A bad impression for anybody passing on the road.

I think, on the particular occasion when I got into trouble, I was reading Alan Watts. What does he say? Something about how in each present experience you are only aware of that experience. You can never separate the thinker from the thought or the knower from the known. All you are ever going to find is a new thought, a new experience.

Manson is Innocent

We found our own ways to excuse the pilfering. For some of the men it was part of the long-established traditions of the river – and we were honorary dockers, were we not? – to take a tithe, little extras for the table. It had been difficult, dangerous work, in years gone by; memories were part of their inheritance, the Irish boys and the others had scores to settle. The odd can or bottle. An ornament or a holy picture to dress a bare room. The routines of Chobham, on the flank of Stratford, beside the railway, were as dirty as ever, as badly paid, if not as life-shortening.

They came in from Forest Gate, Upton Park, Leytonstone, men willing to put in a full day, somewhere near the bottom of the heap, for a minimal wage. It was their right, and their duty, to balance the books, to reassert their manhood, their duty as husbands and fathers, by showing the bosses that they couldn't be exploited. Underneath the banter, acquiescence in the face of hierarchies of unreasoning authority, was a constant nod and whisper of petty conspiracy. A few, not many, bunked off to see convenient women, to proclaim their masculinity that way, by talking it through afterwards. Others argued the case for union action, fraternal relations with revolutionary comrades to the east. The only constant, as I saw it, was the landscape, the place in which we found ourselves, this miracle of sunlight burning through mist across the marshes. An endless parade of lorries heading out on to the roads of England.

Like Tom I recoiled at the idea of taking anything from the tea chests of the failed emigrants, household goods shipped back from Australia. The pocketing of dry beans, wax, sardines, or the gulping on the spot from a punctured wine keg, could be justified as legitimate, live-off-the-land strategies. Mao's red plastic-covered book, about the size of a snout tin, nestled in my pocket: unread, unopened.

What is work? Work is struggle. There are difficulties and problems in those places for us to overcome and solve. A good comrade is one who is more eager to go where the difficulties are greater. Our chief method is to learn warfare through warfare.

Tom's warrior credentials went as far as his army surplus jacket with the deep pockets. We were of an age to have escaped National Service, narrowly, while catching what purported to be an education between European and colonial wars. There was a residue of guilt, emphasized by memorials to the 1914–18 generation, parades and sermons. Bad Wednesday afternoons, bulled boots and blanco'd gaiters, drilling with the Combined Cadet Force. When Tom crossed the open yard at Chobham, back to his car, a few rescued strips of magnetic tape about his person, he recognized our ex-para foreman as a figure very much like the school sergeants of old. A professional brought in to get his revenge on the inadequacies of the future officer class. A man of honour who knew when to look the other way. 'Pick those bleeding feet up – sir.'

It was a few months before we were let in on the scam. We had worked our way up to the forklifts, jockeying down long aisles, scraping prongs beneath sheep bales and packing cases. Tom had his own vehicle and a new gang. I stayed with Freddie and Mick. One afternoon, the under-foreman, truly one of life's lance-jacks, stood us aside, before issuing us with pickaxe handles.

'Smash 'em,' he said. 'Smash the fucking lot.'

But with discretion. An old-style CID kicking, if you like: rolled-up directory, no visible bruises. The word had come, on a nod and a wink, that a consignment of gleaming launderette machines was to suffer a malicious and unprovoked assault. An insurance thing. Crushed, splintered, traumatized in the container. Rough seas. Bad roads. Act of god. Property insured far beyond its real value.

At first our blows were apologetic: Freddie cupping a cigarette on the inside of his hand, Mick hunched in donkey jacket. Bright enamel chipped and showed grey. Viewing panels splintered. The multiplied novelty of the innocent machines, stacked in their dim bay like Rachel Whiteread's reserve stock, was a crime. They were asking for it, weren't they? All paint and flashy Italian finish. The tarts. It was hard graft, not as easy as it might seem, to play the sanctioned vandal. We tumbled Arctic-pure cubes out of their packaging, down from the top of the heap, and the madness took over. When Leslie the under-foreman returned, clawing back crow-slick hair, chewing thin lips, the job was done. A field of ruin, disembowelled white goods, powdered crystal. There were official forms, pink and yellow sheets, to be completed. Les licked his indelible pencil: 'Damaged in transit.'

From that episode, the slide into more serious, potentially gaol-time criminality was swift. Chobham Farm was my first intimation of how future grand projects would operate: put up a fence, trade on misinformation, turn a blind eye to misdemeanours. So long as targets are met. One of the defining aspects of current politics is that impossible trick: the manufacture of new clichés. *Direction of travel.* Whatever the mire, whatever revelations of malpractice and incompetence, you trot out this phrase: direction of travel. A committee is sanctioned to draft a report on the latest catastrophe, but all is well in the best of all legacy worlds. We have it sorted: direction of travel. Only the sourest critic would quibble over a sack of lost spanners in Chobham's mud, or the £100 million misplaced by the London Development Agency, on the same ground, in the run-up to the 2012 Olympics.

The *London Evening Standard* (24/6/09) informed its readers that Gareth Blacker, the man who oversaw the purchase of the Olympic site in the Lea Valley near Stratford, was now on indefinite leave, as was his accountant. 'There is no suggestion of wrongdoing by either of them.'

Forensic accountants are attempting, without much success, to trace the vanished loot. Millions, allocated as compensation for businesses forced to relocate from the Lea Valley, have evaporated like sweat on blotting paper. A spokesperson for the LDA admitted that there had been 'unforeseen spending commitments', but any shortfall could be made up from 'savings elsewhere'. Whose savings he did not say. And none of these local difficulties would affect the confirmed direction of travel. To hell in a handcart.

When I hear these words, in close conjunction, 'Olympics' and 'legacy', I remember that legacy is a two-edged sword; it cuts both ways through time. And I repeat this mantra: Berlin '36, Mexico City '68, Munich '72. Count the cost. Heap up the dead. Bury that in the direction of travel.

Freddie and Mick are operating a little number on the side, topping up their miserable wages with an unapproved bonus system. And so is Liam. And Clancy. And Gary. And Patrick. It's never discussed, but there is enough in it to keep a generally depressed and ill-informed workforce happy. They are encouraged to believe, it's good for their self-esteem, that they are putting one over on the bosses, on the cruel fate that landed them in this wind-swept, hole-in-the-roof, hazchem mire. Foremen and under-foremen, the eyes and ears of the operators, the ones with a key to the toilet, know what is happening, but they say nothing. It can be lost in the paperwork. Your cargo never made it from Tilbury. Road pirates. River thieves. You know what those bloody dockers are like.

The lorry drivers and independent van operatives were grudgingly admired. They pulled away from the gates, they were free men. One cheroot smoker with a black leather cap, like Oskar Werner in *The Spy Who Came in from the Cold*, was known as the Oncer, meaning he was rumoured to trouser the legendary sum, a sort of sound barrier or four-minute mile for Stratford peons, of £100 a week. Cashmoney. Then there were the ponytail-and-elastic-band, rings-in-the-ear, slogan-T-shirt working hippies, standing off by the rusty chain-link fence to smoke and admire quotation sunflowers, while we trundled boxes on to the flatbed: soon they would be away to Italy, Greece, Turkey. I was never party to those deals, the unlicensed substitutions and additions of freelance travel agents. And their desperate human cargoes. Some of whom, unpapered, would be working alongside me. Their stories, when they told them, when they had the language, merging into the universal babble, the threnody I sometimes imagined in the song of the pylons, the robot-speak of reversing trucks.

The most basic villainy was the old cargo switch. Driver presents bent checker with docket for five cases of baked beans. Bay and slot numbered. Forklift zooms off. Labourers climb among the stacks of unclaimed goods. Lorry departs, papers initialled, with three cases of beans and two cases of tools. A bung for the checker, a few quid for the others. The whole accountancy system is a preamble to insurance forms, misattributions, amnesia. The cargoes of the world sweep in and out again. It's a lucky dip. You receive the expected number of items, but the contents will be mysterious. Spanners, hairdryers, golf clubs: they vanish. Into pubs and street markets. Sheep casings, slithery talcum powder, outdated Balkan foodstuffs, they are in the Farm for the duration. Kick through bindweed, they're there now.

All of this winked-at naughtiness, as in a British caper movie with Jack Hawkins, was a rehearsal for the big one. The whisper went around that certain characters – Fred, a bad-lad favourite of the foreman, among them – would be given overtime, night overtime, when the rest of the workforce had dispersed. We would be handling a secret shipment, on bonus. Gold, banknotes marked for incineration, nobody knew. The rumour was confirmed when dark-windowed security vehicles arrived, late in the afternoon, and began setting up silver-dazzle light poles. *It was a film set.* A compound within a compound. The lowlife wanted a piece of this, but they didn't know what it was.

Duckboards went down across the mud. The goods would be heavy, *heavy.* Uniforms took up positions around their fence within a fence, arms folded. Some of the Chobham suits, careful about where they stepped, looked in, nodded, and drove away. They never risked contamination by talking to the labourers. Come close, by accident, on a fact-finding tour laid on for investors, and the fat man would not acknowledge your presence. You didn't register. You were not there. If he heard the voice, the RP, the subjects under discussion, he visibly flinched. Then pretended it wasn't happening. I could see one illuminated window, the outline of the fat man, staying late, keeping out of the way, watching us.

The main gates are closed and secured. Armed, helmeted and visored mercenaries surround the brightly lit pathway between the truck that is more like a safe on wheels and the unmarked vans brought in, one after another, to take the drums away. Now we hear, a guard mentions it, what the cargo is: platinum. More valuable, so they say, than gold or silver. Weighty to manhandle, impossible to divert. The drums will be redistributed and gone in a single session. They come off a train in an unregistered siding and they will be departing who knows where. And every canister, every nugget, is accounted for, ticked off on the manifest.

Freddie can't see a way round this, it's out of his league. Mick laughed when the boy smoker suggested piercing the drum with the tines of the forklift. The men from the Mint were too canny for that: no forklifts, no mechanical assistance. Heft, sweat, manhandle, two to a drum. Checked and numbered. But Mick had the tattoos on his knuckles, the mythical past. Mick was away to Canada. He studied the necklace of lights, the halogen lamps, and identified a small pool of darkness. The drums were standard issue. We had others very much like them. After an hour of repeated journeys, truck to van, we were given a tea break.

'Get the forklift,' Mick said.

Freddie, extinguishing his cigarette, was away. He could navigate the aisles at night, using his radar like a bat. If the switch could be made, the heavy drum, the one packed with nuggets of platinum, money purer than money, rolled into the dense undergrowth, out by the fence, they would come at it, before morning, from the other side. Wire-cutters and white van: an uncanny replay of *Bronco Bullfrog*. Neither Mick nor Freddie had a car, or a licence. Nothing to search. They were clean. The presumption, when the switch was discovered, next day or soon after, was that outsiders had broken through, while the operation was in progress. An inside job. Lengthy, sweated interviews for all concerned. Freddie would brazen it out. Mick would be gone. Mick had a record. Mick would be fingered. If they could find him.

Freddie told me, if his story had more validity than any of the other legends of Chobham, that the platinum nuggets were the coldest metal he had ever held in his hand. He lost his nerve, went out fishing with a mate, dropped the half-full canister into the Lea, not far from the Manor Garden Allotments. Mick was never heard from again. The single nugget Freddie retained was a fetish for what might have been. It didn't happen. On my last Thursday, after we'd been down to the bank to collect our wages and gone across the road to a panelled pub, Freddie put the nugget on the table.

'I'm off,' I said. 'I've saved a couple of hundred. We're going back to an island called Gozo.'

'Do what?'

He couldn't get his head around it. No clubs, no action. No work-mates. No women. I wasn't stupid enough to mention the writing, the book I wanted to complete.

'Pick it up.'

The nugget was the size of an after-dinner mint, curved, silvery. It rocked, on and on, when you set it down on the flat surface. As if it had absorbed the rhythm of the world. It was fused from two separate parts; smooth on the surface and like glinting charcoal in the crack. A mysterious and beautiful trophy I had no desire to possess.

Years later, addicted to circumambulations of the Olympic site in the Lower Lea Valley, I found myself drawn back to Angel Lane in Stratford, the site where Chobham Farm had once been. In September 2009, entrance to the Greenway, running from Old Ford to Beckton, was prohibited.

WELCOME TO THE PEOPLE'S PARK.

The latest security guards are Gurkhas, beneficiaries of a campaign by Joanna Lumley. An invading regiment, self-contained, easy in movement, with whom pedestrians are not inclined to argue.

Helmeted, they sit in kiosks or invigilate tiny portions of mesh fence, making time into a grid, witnessing this monumental project of reverse archaeology. To the lazy occidental eye, the Gurkhas suggest a terracotta army nodding visitors through, waiting to be buried in the trenches of a structure in which they have no investment. An artist of the edgelands has pressed a bunch of yellow tennis balls into the fence, strange fruit losing its fur to the weather.
SECURITY DOGS PATROL THIS AREA.

A technician in a yellow hard hat, raised by the arm of a yellower cherry picker, is knitting extra strands of wire into the new perimeter fence. Fences replace fences, at mounting cost, as the grand project evolves. The Greenway landscape is like one of those ever-rolling advertising hoardings you watch while waiting for the lights to change on the A11 into Stratford. The operatives have a name that captures, quite accurately, the keynote of the Olympic development: Teutonic efficiency (engineering, surveillance) and Celtic PR (otherwise know as bullshit). VolkerFitzpatrick (a VolkerWessels Company).

Ah Stratford, my Stratford! If there is a less enticing blot in this country, than the haemorrhaging roadcrash of the area surrounding the transport-hub station, I've been fortunate enough to avoid it. The air around here *isn't*. It's something else, something new, requiring gills and built-in decontamination filters. Particulates, red dust. Carcinogenic dreck painstakingly excavated to facilitate economic adventurism and botched vanity architecture. Labyrinthine pound-stretcher malls. Ramps going nowhere. You can't breathe. You don't want to breathe this stuff, it shreds your lungs. The treacle of incineration: human, plastic, verminous. A crazy street-preacher screaming into a loudhailer. Mobs seething towards escape hatches, viral-torpedo buses. A state-of-the-art station with the same old cattle-car service. Now enhanced by disembodied voices bringing you up to speed on the latest cancellations.

The thing Stratford has going for it, at the point where visitors are collected by safari vehicles or minibuses for their tours of the Olympic site, is a world-class fence.

GATEWAY TO LONDON'S OLYMPIC PARK. OVER 300 DYNAMIC BRANDS. 1.9 MILLION SQ FT OF RETAIL AND LEISURE DESTINATION. WESTFIELD.

Access to the virtual stadium is by way of an Australian supermarket. High screens feature a blurred sprint to athletic supremacy and a lifetime of endorsement. Pedestrian permeability, that's the catchphrase: out of the station, holding your breath, and into the mall.

On Angel Lane, where tethered piebald ponies crop the verge, I try to identify the entrance to the obliterated Chobham Farm. A gigantic hoarding, layers peeling away, features a manic John Lydon (formerly Rotten) doing a number on behalf of Country Life butter. The western horizon is cancelled in a sandstorm of construction dust.

I remember coming out of the gates, on the morning after the platinum heist, and deciding that this would be my final week as a Stratford labourer. I stood on this spot, looking over the rail yards, across the mounds and hoists where rogue capital was busying itself to squeeze a living out of an undervalued strip of territory. There was a new graffito on the wall now hidden behind Lydon's butter advertisement: CHARLES MANSON IS INNOCENT.

Parkland

Fence Wars

China is the myth, the money opera. On 21 February 1972, as I was contemplating my exit from Chobham Farm, Richard Milhous Nixon, bloodied in the proxy wars of Vietnam and Cambodia, stepped from the presidential plane, Air Force One, on to the Chinese mainland for the photo-opportunity of a lifetime. Two posters met. The American political bagman, liar, serial opportunist, and the doped, moon-faced enigma of Mao, long marcher, swimmer among maidens. Kissinger and Chou En-lai hovered in the wings. Pat Nixon was presented with a glass elephant and invited to check out pig farms (as if auditioning viruses for export). She was greeted by marshalled children. And spoke of a time when consumer luxuries must give way to simple Quaker virtues. The 1987 John Adams opera confirmed what we now know: China was fit ground for the greatest show on earth, the Olympic Games of 2008. Rehearsals began at least two thousand years ago.

The neurotic swirl of activity around this grandest of projects – building, destroying, promoting – brought regiments of freelancers to Beijing. Commentators, essayists without tenure, loose poets: they ballasted aircraft in the rush to get ahead of the story. The dollar fountains, the packed forecourts of slick used cars in place of market gardens along epic highways. Neon rain. Face masks for cyclists. Glazed food to be eaten on the run. Jellyfish macerated in China-Cola.

Dazzling proposals were unveiled by peripatetic Dutch architects. Swiss designers in mean spectacles astonished audiences at conferences celebrating 'City of Culture' status in Norwegian fishing towns, prudent with their North Sea oil revenues. Laptop magicians screened CGI visions of impossible towers, interlinked orbital motorways stretching the ancient capital hundreds of miles, so it appeared, into the Mongolian wilderness.

The pulse of the world was out there and I wanted to be a part of it. The siren song of the six orbital motorways was irresistible. What could be more challenging than to set the afterlife of the Beijing Games against our own emerging Olympic Park? Many of the containers now snaking along railway embankments through Hackney Wick towards Stratford, alongside the ghosts of Chobham Farm, are stencilled with the logo CHINA SHIPPING. White lettering on green metal boxes. Loud signage in a landscape of burning-eye graffiti, breakfast cafés, junkyards, closed roads and plasterboarded pubs.

I watched driving footage, shot on a mobile phone, sent back from Beijing as an appetizer: soft enough, generic enough, to be anywhere. Dallas. Milton Keynes. Or a spin on the virgin Chiswick flyover, shortly after it was declared open by Jayne Mansfield in 1959. And a few years before J. G. Ballard blew a tyre, rolled over the central reservation and demolished street furniture (for which he was charged £100). When asked by an interviewer if he knew any Chinese, Ballard replied: 'I wish I could say I did. I was born in China and lived there till the age of sixteen. I didn't learn a word.'

Beijing taught us that the interval between posting a development promo on the screen and walking through it is undetectable. If you can't smell the kitchen, or scrape shit off your shoes, you are not there. This morning, there is a clinging, overripe perfume that people say drifts in from the countryside, a folk memory of what these clipped acres used, so recently, to be. Aromatic mulch of market gardens. Animal droppings in hot mounds. The distant rumble of construction convoys. A heron dance of cloud-scraping cranes. Flocks of cyclists, clustering for safety, dip and swerve like swallows. Hard-hats and yellow tabards monkey over the jungle scaffolding of shrouded towers, the exposed steel ribs of emerging stadia. Grass has the irradiated sheen of an ancient toothbrush. Early risers, in the privilege of first-use recreation, a smudge of sun burning off the fug of pollution that hangs over a pre-Olympic city, fall into quiet conversation.

Ice-cream kiss of almond blossom. A bridal abundance of cherry:

pink-and-white froth. Yellow pompoms of japonica. In a corner, under a high wall that gives away the previous identity of this public park as an energy-generating plant, retired workers sway, stiffly and slowly, in t'ai chi ballets.

I'm fascinated by the elderly Chinese couple who circle, for more than an hour, around the perimeter fence of the newly laid carpet of a sports complex achieved in advance of the Great Event. They are there when I set out and still there, moving at the same brisk unhurried pace, when I return. The pavilion and the new pitches are a compensatory gesture towards those who must endure years of drilling, dust, demolished schools and theatres, banishment from functioning but inappropriate housing developments. The block-building, assembled overnight, has no vernacular element, it could have been designed anywhere for any purpose; blinding whiteness complemented by the deep blue of the interior, an aspirational colour we must learn to associate with the culturally unifying message of the Games.

The Chinese woman walks, right shoulder to the fence, in a clockwise direction, while her husband short-strides the other way. When they meet they do not acknowledge one another, not so much as a nod or a wink. My impression is that he is less enthusiastic about the regime. He wears a hooded monkish top and looks like a sixty-a-day man who has given up his addiction, reluctantly, after receiving bad news. A drag of burnt air, one final smoke-chase, is his reward for completing the hour's penance. The woman, in flat cap, arms pumping, is remorseless, gaining ground with every circuit.

'The opportunity has come for them to lift up their heads,' said Chairman Mao. 'The authority of the husband is getting shakier every day.'

The comrade walker pistons forward on her self-imposed generator: by force of will, she drives the engine of the city. At her side march unseen battalions.

And this is East London, four years short of that seventeen-day corporate extravaganza, the 'primary strategic objective' to which we are so deeply mortgaged. Haggerston Park, E2, a modest enclosure factored out of war-damaged terraces, the vanished Imperial Gas, Light and Coke Company, has long been an oasis. It was launched as a public park in 1958. Its scandals are old scandals and have no bearing on the current frenzy for makeovers, wooden obstacles for training circuits, laminated heritage notices. Spanking new carpets are woven for clapped-out football pitches, changing rooms erected to replace shower blocks opened in the dark ages by Wendy Richard of *EastEnders* fame.

Back in the 1820s, Gas Company funds were misappropriated, illegal payments made to council officials, stock accounts falsified. In more enlightened times, when bureaucratic malpractice is exposed on a daily basis, hidden parks win prizes for visionary planting schemes. Unnoticed, rough sleepers in thin bags utilize the stone terrace of a café that has been shut for years. Late risers, having nothing much to rise for, burrow deep into dismal kapok-stuffed cocoons, while dog-accompanists use ballistic devices to hurl soggy yellow-green tennis balls for their hunt-and-retrieve pets. Designated wilderness zones quote wild nature.

Artificial grass is better than the real thing, tougher. False chlorophyll glistens like perpetual dew, the permafrost of conspicuous investment. The rough sleepers are not victims of property mania or traumatized war veterans, they are construction workers, often Polish, saving their wages and choosing to kip down close to where the action is: the tsunami of speculative capital, wanton destruction, hole-digging. The throwing up of apartment blocks, dormitory hives, warehouse conversions along murky waterways. A much-lauded development calling itself Adelaide Wharf (an aircraft carrier ploughed into a wood yard) replaced a long-standing cold-store operation. 'With its 147 units (prices up to £395,000), this is a tremendous example of aspiration coming to fruition,' said Stephen Oaks, area director for English Partnerships.

Inch by inch, the working canal between Limehouse Basin and the Islington tunnel has become a ladder of glass connecting Docklands with the northern reaches of the City. Footballers, with loose change to spare, are rumoured to be buying up entire buildings as investment portfolios; many of these gaudy shells, low-ceilinged, tight-balconied, are doomed to remain half-empty, occupied by employees of the developer. Ikea storage boxes gimmicked out of swipe cards and toothpicks. The urban landscape of boroughs any-where within the dust cloud of the Olympic Park has been devastated with a beat-the-clock impatience unrivalled in London since the beginnings of the railway age. Every civic decency, every sentimen-tal attachment, is swept aside for that primary strategic objective, the big bang of the starter's pistol.

When did it begin, this intimate liaison between developers and government, to reconstruct the body of London, to their mutual advantage? Dr Frankenstein with a Google Earth programme and a laser scalpel. In the early 1970s, when the deepwater docks were already ruined by containerization, restrictive practices and fearful-angry 'Enoch is right' marches, Maxwell Joseph acquired Truman's Brewery in Brick Lane. The brewery with its stables, cellars, cooper-age, cobbled yards, acted, along with the Spitalfields fruit and veg market and Nicholas Hawksmoor's Christ Church, as buffer-reefs against the encroachment of the City. A paternalistic employer was lost, along with the heady drench of hops from the brewery and the wild gardens of adjacent streets. Joseph flogged the Gainsborough portrait of Sir Benjamin Truman, the brewmaster, asset-stripped the operation, and bought up surrounding acres in canny anticipa-tion of future development packages, the coming world of retro frocks, Moroccan internet cafés and 'plastinated' freak-show corpse art by Gunther von Hagens. The eastward shift, towards off-catalogue territory, was launched. Spitalfields Market, with its parasitical life forms (allotment gardeners, twilight prostitutes, vagrant drinkers around wastelot fires), was expelled to Hackney Marshes. Where it would function quite successfully up to the point where the football pitches, alongside the new site, would be required as parking space for the 2012 green Olympics.

Johnnie Walker, chairman of the Hackney and Leyton Football

League, was enraged. Despite assurances from a multitude of face-less authorities, that work would not begin for four years, the diggers arrived before the start of the 2007 season. Eleven pitches, trampled by hard-swearing enthusiasts, were lost. Anne Woollett of the Hackney Marshes User Group complained that the ODA (Olympic Development Authority) had sequestered portions of East Marsh, a year ahead of their promise, to construct 'a huge 12-lane motorway'. Challenged, a spokesperson for the ODA admitted that two trenches had indeed been dug, for 'archaeological' research. Animal bones and beer cans were photographed and preserved; along with the rubble of blitzed Second World War terraces over which the football pitches had been laid out. 'The heritage must be protected.'

Much of this tricky element, heritage, can be recovered from vintage films as they are reissued on DVD. The tall chimney of the Brick Lane brewery, a significant territorial marker, appears like an accusing finger in stills taken from Carol Reed's *Odd Man Out*, which was released in 1947. War-damaged Bethnal Green masquerades as an expressionist Belfast. James Mason is an IRA gunman on the run. Twenty years later, his Hollywood career in decline, Mason returned once more to an East End of smoky pubs, dark shadows, charity hostels: to narrate a documentary version of Geoffrey Fletcher's *The London Nobody Knows*. Umbrella rolled, vowels clipped, he sleep-walks through a gone-in-the-mouth city, struggling to make conversation with marooned mariners and fire-eyed witnesses. When he performed his dying fall in *Odd Man Out*, clutching at the gate, before staggering across the snow towards the lights of the police cars, he is in Haggerston Park, E2.

Another film, so sharp in its exposure of aspects of the coming land piracy that it seemed prophetic, arrived in 1979. *The Long Good Friday* was efficiently directed by John Mackenzie, but the meat of the thing is in Barrie Keeffe's script, his intimacy with tired ground that is about to be invaded, overwhelmed, rewritten. The advent of Margaret Thatcher was announced, as Mackenzie's crime fable makes clear, by local government corruption ('the new casino's gone through'), kickbacks to Irish Republicans in the burgeoning construction industry, bent coppers and heritaged Kray hoodlums making overtures to the New York Mafia with their 'property law-yers, lawyers specializing in gambling tax'. Much of this had happened and continues to happen. It is the Thatcherite legacy we are now experiencing. London topography is reconfigured accord-ing to the movie finances of the moment, first as proper cinema, then as budget television.

A persistent urban myth has the gang who robbed the Brinks-Mat warehouse at Heathrow on 26 November 1983 quadrupling the estimated £26-million value of the gold bars by investing in river-side regeneration. Swashbuckling capitalism led the way for timid hedge-fund managers and Bishopsgate sharecroppers. The defining image of this era – Bob Hoskins with his sleek pleasure craft moored in St Katharine Docks, Margaret Thatcher schmoozing the Reich-mann brothers in Canary Wharf – is the maquette of the proposed marina, the city of towers. A Lilliputian theme park of unimaginable wealth-creation. An anticipation of computer-generated presen-tations for the Olympic wonderland. 'Water City', a new Venice (without the memory-mud of centuries), will rise from the stink-ing tilth of backrivers and duckweed canals.

Keeffe's 'Corporation', a confederacy of villains, is a direct trans-lation of alliances in contemporary political life. Hoskins, a pumped-up Dalston Mussolini, presenting himself as 'a business-man with a sense of history', spiels a pitch as his oligarch's gin palace makes waves under Tower Bridge. Thirty years on and he could be making his final presentation as a candidate in the London mayoral election, right across the river from the crumpled buttock of City Hall. Which is neither a hall, nor in the City, but a post-architectural doodle with the futile ambition of bringing Manhattan to Bermondsey. 'We have mile upon mile and acre after acre of land for our future prosperity,' drools Bob. 'The right people master-mind the new London.'

This was a period when blowing the whistle on corrupt practices brought retribution in a traditional form. A Dalston solicitor, on the point of presenting evidence about fraudulent building practices, the use of the cheapest materials coupled with invoices for the most expensive, a dossier assembled by an outraged foreman, was warned off with a sniper shot, from a rooftop, as he stepped from the court-house. The quality of the marksmanship was professional: the bullet missed by inches. He got the point. And had a story to tell.

But the scam of scams was always the Olympics: Berlin (1936) to Beijing (2008). Engines of regeneration. Orgies of lachrymose nationalism. War by other means. Warrior-athletes watched, from behind dark glasses, by men in suits and uniforms. The pharmaceutical frontline. Californian chemists running their eye-popping, vein-clustered, vest-stripping androids against degendered state-laboratory freaks. Bearded ladies and teenage girls who never have periods. Medals are returned by disgraced drug cheats: to be passed on to others who weren't caught, that time. The holy grail for blue-sky thinkers was the sport-transcends-politics Olympiad. The five-hooped golden handcuffs. Smoke rings behind which deals could be done for casinos and mosques and malls: with corporate sponsorship, flag-waving and infinitely elastic budgets (only challenged as an act of naysaying treason).

The Long Good Friday has a neat tracking shot through the deserted quays of the future Docklands. The TV comic Dave King, playing a bent detective, reprimands Hoskins. A car has been detonated outside a Hawksmoor church. 'We can't have bombs going off, Harold. We can't have corpses.' But that, unfortunately, is the price on the tin. Well-rehearsed spontaneous celebrations, dancing, hugging, shoulder-punching in the studios, then private grief, explosions on the Underground. Mutilation, carnage. A fluster of BacoFoil suits and on-message medallists bouncing up and down as heavyweight political arm-twisting pays off. PR assaults, camera-kissing by Blair and Beckham: we get the Games on 6 July 2005. And the shock of a traumatized London on the following morning, death toll rising, dazed survivors captured on mobile phones as they stumble through smoke-filled, soft-focus tunnels. Bomb carriers looped on CCTV: malignant tourists at a Metroland station.

Their posthumous journey, long after the event, a surveillance-television spectacular: motorway, car park, train. The Olympic project, from the start, would be about security. And budget. Baghdad conditions imported. Green zones staked out, helicopter-patrolled. Leaflets in the street with boxes to tick. Managed populism. Subverted dissent.

'So this is where we're going to build the 1988 Olympic Stadium,' King muses. 'Can you imagine nignogs doing the long jump along these quays?' We can: vividly. We've watched Leni Riefenstahl's *Olympiad*, her Wagnerian, body-fascism evocation of the 1936 Games, the triumphs of Jesse Owens, the grim-faced Hitler, the stiff-armed salutes of the Austrian, Italian and French contingents. The map montage in which the Olympic torch crosses Europe, Olympia to Berlin, is like an invasion rehearsal.

When Horace Cutler, the Tory leader of the Greater London Council, made the speculative proposal, in 1979, that the 1988 Olympics should be held at the Royal Victoria Dock in Silvertown, right alongside Bow Creek, the point of access to the Lower Lea, he was ridiculed by the man who succeeded him, Ken Livingstone. 'A gimmick.' A megalomaniac right-wing fantasy. The worst sort of land piracy.

By 2008, in a frank admission, during the run-up to the mayoral election, Livingstone boasted that he had feigned enthusiasm for the 2012 Olympics as a way of generating funds for brownfield development in East London and Thames Gateway, seeding his favoured pylon-forest estates alongside landfill mountains and poisoned creeks. The recklessly underestimated costs, based on nothing more than jottings on the back of an envelope, were simply a snare to ensure government approval. The initial tab of a couple of billion, liberated from lottery loot and siphoned from Arts Council vanity projects, escalated very rapidly as the reality of the damaged topography was investigated: up towards ten billion (and climbing). Japanese knotweed, radioactive watch dials, endangered newts: another £100,000. No breaks on this rocket-propelled debt elevator. Direction of travel. Paymasters held to ransom.

'This was exactly the plan,' Livingstone told his audience at St Martin-in-the-Fields. 'It has gone perfectly.'

In boroughs affected by this madness, the 2012 game-show virus, long-established businesses closed down, travellers were expelled from edgeland settlements, and allotment holders turned out of their gardens. As soon as the Olympic Park was enclosed, and therefore defined, loss quantified, the fence around the site became a symbol for opposition and the focus for discussion groups. A seminar convened by PNUK (Planners Network UK) was held at the boxing club in the old Limehouse Town Hall. Attending this public debate, I heard the Hackney solicitor Bill Parry-Davies describe how, after a series of mysterious fires, Dalston Lane lost its Victorian theatre and sections of Georgian terrace, to facilitate a new transport hub that would service the vital axes, south to the City, east to the Olympic Park.

'Most of the development will be buy-to-let investments,' Parry-Davies said. 'Huge amounts of Russian and Saudi money. Tenants will move in and out constantly. There will be no community at all.'

A few yards down Commercial Road, to the west of the Town Hall, was another defunct institution, the former Passmore Edwards Library. In front of the library was parked a black box, like an upended coffin made from offcuts of Olympic-fence plywood. It came with spray-on slogan: ATTLEE WUZ ERE. It contained the memorial statue of the former Mayor of Stepney, post-war socialist prime minister, Clement Attlee. Who was receiving a compulsory makeover and not being prepared for removal, like Lenin or Stalin, to some theme-park knackers' yard. Perhaps Clement was, as a courtesy to the dream of the welfare state, being shielded from the self-regarding towers of Canary Wharf.

Limehouse is a dormitory of unsummoned ghosts. The once-celebrated author of 'yellow peril' fictions, Sax Rohmer (Arthur Henry Sarsfield Ward), had a particular interest in the pyramid in Limehouse Church. It was known to his evil genius, Fu Manchu, a man of fiendish plots achieved through intimacy with London's downriver reaches. A panel in the pyramid gave entry to a network of underground tunnels.

But the fabled Chinese Limehouse of Thomas Burke and Sax Rohmer has long gone. The opium dens of Wilde, Conan Doyle and Dickens have been replaced by dockside bars with awnings and heaters. And now the Good Friends Restaurant in Salmon Lane, to which hungry diners travelled from all over the city, has been converted into a store for building supplies. The spirit of Fu Manchu, with his merciless cadre of martial-arts bodyguards and assassins, lives on, accompanying the Olympic torch on its progress between the two prime examples of bungled and underestimated grand projects: Wembley Stadium and the Millennium Dome (where the feeble flame ignited a burger-roasting shrine).

On the morning the blue fence went up – OLYMPIC PARK: ROAD CLOSED HERE FROM MONDAY 2 JULY, FOOTPATH CLOSED, KEEP CLEAR – I met a man called Keith Foster. Mr Foster, who described himself as a 'fieldwork photographer' for Waltham Forest, had been keeping a meticulous record of the Lower Lea Valley, the shifts in land use, for more than thirty years. Until today. When he was challenged, and threatened with summary arrest by private security guards, for the crime of pointing his camera at the fence. A fence which shadowed the towpath, accompanied the Greenway, stuttered through Stratford, and marked out the half-abandoned estate due for demolition on Clays Lane. Foster's dispiriting experience was a commonplace. Stephen Gill, another compulsive cyclist-photographer, haunter of scrub woods, produced two finely observed elegies to the doomed territories. A celebration of the sprawling, Babel-voiced boot fair held at the former Hackney Wick Stadium. And a documentary record of the Olympic Park in its limbo, before the first conceptual stadium slid from its computer screen.

'I used to wander the Wick, completely on my own, exploring and taking photographs,' he told me. 'Now there are lots of people in yellow coats, boots and hard hats. "Sorry, mate, you can't come in here." Suddenly there are places where you can't walk freely. "Health and safety. You're not insured." It's always the same: health and safety.'

On Waterden Road, that improbable assembly of exotic food warehouses, evangelical African churches, steel-door nightclubs, bus garages, Gill snapped the Queen of England. On a private and unannounced tour. (Brave smile, like her late mother, tripping over rubble, as she visited the East End war zone.)

'I was standing by the roadside. There were a lot of helicopters overhead. I waved. She waved. I took a few shots. The policeman said, "That's enough." The big black car purred through all the barriers, down the length of Waterden Road, past padlocked allotments, the abandoned travellers' camp, sweeping back towards the motorway. She looked quite relieved to be getting out unscathed.'

Gill has another nice capture: Lord Coe and David Cameron. Ties coordinated with the blue of the coming fence, dark suits, hands in pockets. Cardinals of capital strolling through the ruins of a captured city. It was in that moment I realized the game was up for Gordon Brown: he doesn't stroll, he can't do hands in pocket. He doesn't drop in on Hackney Wick, he hits Washington looking for consoling handshakes, shoulders to squeeze. Brown won't look good schmoozing athletes and freeloaders, he'll have to go.

On Sunday 6 April 2008, I set off down the Northern Sewage Outfall, our Greenway, to Stratford. We had been promised an Olympic taster, the procession of the torch through London. The elevated footpath is accessible through Wick Lane, as it passes beneath the A102. Here is the fault line where the virtual collides with the actual: a Second World War concrete pillbox, a stutter of built and half-built apartment blocks, a lock-keeper's cottage converted into the set for a breakfast-time television show. Pylons are being disassembled and cables buried. A patch of wild wood is tamed with screaming chainsaws. Concrete-producing tubes cough and spew.

The blue of the perimeter fence is tactfully echoed by ribbons of fluttering plastic, convenience-store bags caught on razor wire. Beyond the fence is a sanctioned view of never-ceasing convoys, showered and scoured dunes of treated soil. Everything aspires to the grey-blue colour of drowned meat. White boxes have been attached to slender poles, but they are not cameras; further surveillance is unnecessary with the Gurkhas in position. The boxes are 'Air Quality Monitors' produced at the Northwich Bus Centre by Turnkey Instruments Ltd. A contemporary version of the budgerigars taken down coal mines to provide advance warning of noxious gases. When the boxes begin to hum, it's too late.

The new fences, with their pointillist panels, are beautiful as Japanese screens. Mock-ups so convincing that it is churlish to disbelieve them. The real Canary Wharf skyline, fading into spectral blue, is stitched on to a computer-generated Olympic Stadium. Which looks like a frozen smoke ring. A souvenir ashtray from Berlin in 1936. And good for nothing very much, after the event. Lord Coe, in the vanity of his quest for legacy, has insisted on preserving running lanes which promise to go the way of the old Hackney Wick dog track: boot-fair oblivion. Coca-Cola, McDonald's, Visa, edf, Samsung, Lloyds TSB, The National Lottery, The Department for Culture and Media, The Mayor of London: they want their expensive tags sprayed on that shiny fence.

Along with multiples of that skateboarder logo for 2012. In shocking pink. Hundreds of thousands of pounds spent to mimic a street signature: a bubblegum swastika. Some aggrieved local has sprayed a response: A POX ON THE OLYMPICS.

It's a question of following the helicopters. I emerge on the A11 where a frenzy of indifference awaits the Olympic torch. Motorcycle outriders in yellow jackets cover the side roads and form threatening lines, white-helmeted against the blue shutters of emerging tower blocks. A procession of police cyclists puff up the hill, reluctant box-tickers for the eco-lobby. A scarlet open-top Coca-Cola bus – 'Supporting the Olympics Since 1928' – waits for the action, somebody to enthuse. The low-loader, with its line of shivering Samsung cheerleaders in white tights and heavy blue mascara, blasts out a triumphalist chorus. The girls charm-assault motorists held back by cycle cops. They semaphore, dementedly, waving furry pompoms that look like Persian cats dipped in blue-dyed toilet cleaner. But the ultimate blue belongs to the shell suits of the phalanx of stone-faced Fu Manchu guards in baseball caps who protect the sacred flame as it wobbles towards us out of Stratford. Lord Coe, in thrall to the Sax Rohmer stereotype, refers to the torchminders as 'paramilitary thugs'. The Chinese ambassador insists that they are mild-mannered students, volunteers. The expected London mob is elsewhere, down the pub, or at home watching playbacks of the mayhem that attended the flame on its faltering progress across the city, on and off buses, under constant attack from kamikaze cyclists.

Two or three mobile phones are raised in tribute from behind a steel sculpture that resembles a dynamited palm tree. A Chinese gentleman from the takeaway waves a tiny red flag. Poor David Hemery, the 400-metre-hurdles champion from Mexico City, is obliterated by his protectors. The torch is a cone of flaming banknotes, a brand to light a witch's bonfire. Black-clad APS Crowd Safety operatives with shaven heads, and thuggish joggers in aciddrop cycle helmets, shoulder-charge a solitary Free Tibet bannerwaver. Smashing him backwards into the Gala Club bingo hall. Members of the security services, with cameras registering dissidents, outnumber the embedded television crews in their blast-resistant trucks. The whole circus more of a foretaste of the real thing than anybody could have predicted.

When, a few days later, I return to Stratford, a city state with a population 'the size of Leeds', it seems that nobody has given them the news of their status as a post-Olympic jewel. The Rex Cinema is defunct. The main road difficult to cross and vandalized by public art. The Labour Party offices are boarded up. The library is operative: it features a scale model of the coming Stratford City tended by legacy fundamentalists, sharp suits pouncing like Mormons on casual observers.

'Is there anything you'd like explained?'

I back off, instinctively, in the English fashion. 'How did you get away with it?' doesn't need asking. Here, in essence, is the solution to the Olympic mystery, the enigma hidden behind the smoke-screen of upbeat PR, websites, viewing days, junk-mail publications and professional obfuscation. Stratford City will be 'the largest retail led mixed regeneration in the UK'. In other words: a shopping mall. With satellite housing we must call, for convenience, the Athletes' Village. But the heart of it, the land swallower, is a gigantic mall conceived and delivered by the Westfield Group, which is controlled by Frank Low, the second-richest man in Australia. Westfield are the fourth-biggest shopping-centre developers in the world. They have assets of £30 billion. A last-minute deal was struck for them to take control of the 180-acre Stratford site, for which privilege they paid £180 million.

The brothers David and Simon Reuben, who held a 50 per cent stake, were put under some pressure to sell out. Ken Livingstone, with characteristic tact, invited the Indian-born siblings 'to go back to Iran and see if you can do any better under the ayatollahs'. City Hall and the various Olympic quangos prefer to deal with a single monolithic entity. Westfield would also take on the White City shopping mall (a traffic island separating the Westway and Shepherd's Bush). Planning permission has been given to Westfield for 13 million square feet of 'mixed use' development, with the Olympic Village being converted into housing after the Games. The word on the street being that if nobody can be persuaded to take up residence in this reclaimed wilderness, the tower blocks (generic and architecturally undistinguished) will serve as holding pens for asylum seekers and economic migrants, until they can be shunted back through the conveniently sited Channel Tunnel link.

In the gold-rush land grab of flexible futures – hyper-mosques, evangelical cathedral-warehouses (£13.5 million offered to the Kingsway International Christian Centre to move off the nine-acre site they were illegally occupying) – legacy is all-important. It's like reading the will and sharing the spoils before the sick man is actually dead. 'The legacy the Games leave is as important as the sporting memories,' said Tony Blair. And the legacy is: loss, CGI-visions injected straight into the eyeball, lasting shame. We have waved this disaster through, we have colluded: dozens of artists roam the perimeter fence soliciting Arts Council funding to underwrite their protests. It's so awful, such a manifest horror, we can't believe our luck. All those tragic meetings in packed cafés, the little movies. Blizzards of digital imagery recording edgeland signs clinging to mesh fences alongside compulsory-purchase notifications: we buy gold, we sell boxes. Gold from the teeth of dying industries, cardboard boxes to bury murdered aspirations.

In Stratford I met some of the legacy professionals. They have an office in Westminster, close to Green Park. A typical career path to the business of fixing the future might come out of Hackney Council in the bad old days, when they were £72 million in the hole, and on through the selling of Thames Gateway. And now this: the invention of something that will never happen by people who won't be there when it does. In the entrance hall of the library, I notice the head of Keir Hardie in a perspex box. He's not quite forgotten, the first Independent Labour member of parliament, voted in at West Ham on 4 July 1892. Cast in bronze by Benno Schatz, Hardie has his place in the scheme of things: a paperweight, a legacy we prefer to ignore. A tongueless bust in an airless cabinet.

On 26 September 2007, I stood outside Stratford Station – like those unfortunate celebrities on Millennium Eve, waiting two hours for their connection to the Dome – in the hope of spotting John Hopkins with his black Land Rover. And his sidekick Nathan, the name-badged driver. Hopkins has the title of 'Project Sponsor, Parklands and Public Realm'. He is employed by the Olympic Delivery Authority: as an explainer, facilitator, tour guide. He is an affable, well-informed man with an interest in London history. He recently attended, so he tells me, a public conversation between Peter Ackroyd and a journalist 'who looked like Hugh Grant'. Stephen Gill accompanies me; he has photographed the site so often, before the occupation, that he can't pass up this opportunity. The spill-zone in front of the station has a triumphal arch with an electronic timer ticking down the minutes to Olympic glory, a corkscrew clock tower (with broken clock), a steam engine called 'Robert' (home to dozens of incontinent pigeons). Beggars, junk-dealers and god-ranters, expelled from more salubrious districts, are much in evidence. Across the road is a labyrinthine mall-tunnel of resistible bargains, sachets of 'Calf's Pizzle' at £1.99 a hit. There is an under-pass with prints of night-blue skies dedicated to the legacy of Stratford's own poet, Gerard Manley Hopkins.

> Look at the stars! look, look up at the skies!
> O look at all the fire-folk sitting in the air!
> The bright boroughs, the circle-citadels there!

Circle-citadels indeed. The Jesuit poet's smoke-ring conjurings have come to pass. Stratford Circus, as we drive to our entrance gate, has choked Joan Littlewood's Theatre Royal in a rash of Pizza Expresses and Caribbean Scene restaurants, budget multiplexes fronted by an ugly silver-hoop sculpture. 'Ah well,' wrote Hopkins, 'it is all a purchase, all a prize.' David Mackay, author of the original Stratford City plan and lead architect for the Barcelona Olympic Village, is horrified by what is happening: 'The silliest architecture seen for years. The Olympic legacy will be more like a Hollywood set for a ghost town or an abandoned Expo site.'

The first thing that goes, as we emerge beyond the fence, is any sense of place. There is nothing by which to navigate, except the legend: 'Bronze Age, Viking, Roman and Norman inhabitants have enjoyed the temperate climate, fertile land and powerful river . . . A once-in-a-lifetime opportunity to revitalise the valley, leaving in its footprints world-class sports, business and leisure facilities.' Twelve thousand new jobs; 1.2 million visitors. 'Billions of TV viewers.' And statistics beyond number. Statistics are the cash crop of Stratford. Our slow circuit is respectful of tadpole beds, Museum of London ditches, wire fronds and crushed concrete arranged in gallery-quality exhibition piles. Gill wants to record these abstract patterns, but permission is refused.

He emailed me, soon after I got home: 'I had a kind of territorial feeling, everything had been taken away. I almost cried in the back of the car, it is such a political experience. Whenever the guide talked about removing fish, saving the newts, making homes for insects and butterflies, I always checked on the opposite side to the one he suggested, it was much more interesting.'

Nathan, our gap-year chauffeur, told us, while we waited at yet another checkpoint, that they had given him another job, filling in tax-concession forms for the contractors, allowances for asbestos removal, handling pollutants. Manufacturing cake. That's what they call the heaps of rendered mud. Treats for cloned cattle.

One area I do recognize, even in its peeled form, is the mound on which the Clays Lane Estate once stood. Bill Parry-Davies was employed to represent tenants who felt themselves threatened by the documented evidence of radioactive material, used in the manufacture of luminous watch dials, buried in cesspits on the site.

'There was concern,' Parry-Davies told me, 'when the contractors started boring deep holes . . . The nature of radioactive material is that it only becomes dangerous once it's been disturbed. Once you release it into the air, as dust, it becomes a major problem . . . At the end of last year, they undertook tests on the run-off into the River Lea. They found levels of thorium in the water. Atkins, the engineers, considered that it was possible that thorium had dispersed along the water table. Thorium is ductile and malleable, it's used as a source of nuclear energy . . . When they found the run-off in the Lea, it was enough to confirm the engineers' prediction of what could happen. The effect being that the entire Olympic Park is contaminated with thorium at water-table level.'

Even if figures are fudged and scare stories buried, it is going to be tricky to fulfil Ken Livingstone's promise that the money for the construction of the Olympic Park will be earned back, afterwards, by flogging the land. 'They won't be able to do it,' Parry-Davies confirmed, 'unless they clear the whole thing up, which is a huge undertaking.' It's a grim scenario, especially for the travellers expelled from their established camps at the base of the Clays Lane mound and for the tenants who tried to hang on to home and community. 'Those who are still there,' Parry-Davies reported, 'are woken at five in the morning, to find a police and army exercise going on, anti-terrorist war games, bombs and guns and helicopters, clouds of smoke. Nobody told them this was going to happen.'

The Olympic Park is zoned like a city under siege. You listen for the muffled thrum of a big-bellied airlift squadron. Murphy, Morrison, Nuttall: they have strategic checkpoints and private armies. The shadow of old Berlin is unavoidable. But this time the corporate entities have walled themselves, by their own choice, inside their defended stockade. Only by erecting secure fences, surveillance hedges, can they assert their championship of liberty. The threat of terrorism, self-inflicted, underwrites the seriousness of the measures required to repel it. Headline arrests in the Olympic hinterland followed by small-print retractions.

We have to sign our names on clipboard forms at every barrier. We splash through troughs of blue disinfectant. John Hopkins, with his interesting grey moustache, keeps up the patter. 'New jobs are being created,' he says. 'Look at those Polish women from the relocated salmon-packing operation enjoying their alfresco lunches.' The next night, on local-television news, I recognize Hopkins, in a boat, giving the identical word-for-word pitch. Say it often enough and it becomes true. They are very good, the explainers, at delivering an unchallenged monologue, but when the hard questions come, a momentary time-delay kicks in. They struggle like flak-jacket correspondents unsynched by video-phone technology on a desert road.

Gareth Blacker, a deathly pale, black-suited Irishman, was sent by the LDA – before the unfortunate business of the mislaid procurement funds – to patronize the folk at the Manor Garden Allotments. He had the same soft-spoken, infinitely reasonable pitch as John Hopkins. Perhaps they have media professionals to teach it. Blacker stood in the rain, under a golfing umbrella, staring at highly polished shoes, while his PR consigliere, Kinsella, hovered in the background. When Blacker responded he seemed to be answering the wrong question, the one asked a minute ago. The allotments, an island oasis ticking every possible regeneration box, stood in the way of the perimeter fence.

'This is part of the Olympic Park and the Olympic Park legacy. It's a temporary move. We want the allotments back after the Games. Everything will be in place. The only thing that will come out is a lot of concrete.'

'How can something return after it has been obliterated?' I asked.

Blacker checked his laces. A question of national security, simply that. 'The highest levels of security on a building site for a long, long time,' he said. 'More security than this country has ever seen.'

Consultation concluded. Sheds come down, blue fence goes up. Some of the gardeners relocate to a dank swamp and start again, others shrivel like the summer crops they will never see. The afterlife of the allotments, the home-made sheds in which so much time and love had been invested, would be a series of affectionate portraits by Stephen Gill and a clear-eyed elegy on film by Emily Richardson. Direction of travel. Letting a hidden camera run, while she toured the Olympic site on an official bus, allowed Richardson to record a Tourette's syndrome spill of upbeat statistics combined with tracking shots across a panorama of blight and ruin. A superimposition that reduced audiences to hysterics.

The tacky blue of the perimeter fence does not appear on any of the computer-generated versions of the Olympic Park. The prospect from the north is favoured, down towards Canary Wharf, the Thames and the Millennium Dome. The heritage site looks like an airport with one peculiar and defining feature: no barbed wire, no barrier between Expo campus and a network of motorways and rivers. The current experience, in reality, is all fence; the fence is the sum of our knowledge of this privileged mud. Visit here as early as you like and there will be no unsightly tags, no slogans; a viscous slither of blue. Like disinfectant running down the slopes of a urinal trough. Circumambulation by the fence painters is endless, day after day, around the entire circuit; repairing damage, covering up protests. Sticky trails drip into grass verges, painterly signatures. Plywood surfaces never quite dry. Subtle differences of shade and texture darken into free-floating Franz Kline blocks.

But the major artworks, self-sponsored galleries of opposition, occur at the back of the fence, and on the unexposed panels of giant off-highway hoardings. Two artists in particular, white boys emerging from the squatting and warehouse-occupying nexus, have undertaken astonishing projects: mile after mile of two-headed crocodiles, grinning gum-pink skulls, clenched Philip Guston fists. A punk codex using industrial quantities of emulsion to revise railway bridges and condemned factories. We are here, they shout: Sweet Toof and Cyclops. Ghost-ride mouths eating the rubble of development, the melancholy soup of black propaganda.

You have to believe that the muralists of Hackney Wick are responding to Daniel Pinchbeck's apocalyptic text: *2012: The Year of the Mayan Prophecy*. Pinchbeck is convinced that the year of the London Olympics is an 'end date'. Stone calendars warn of the dying of one great cycle of time, of environmental catastrophe. The neurosis of stadium-building is nothing more than an unconscious desire to prepare sites for ritual sacrifice: Westfield ziggurats, Barratt pyramids. That horror mantra whispers once more in its echo chamber.

Berlin '36: The setting in which boy soldiers will be executed for cowardice in the last days of the Third Reich. In the forest that surrounds the Olympiastadion.

Mexico City '68: President Gustavo Díaz Ordaz is instructed by Avery Brundage, president of the International Olympic Committee, to deal with protests inspired by this moment of global attention. 'The Olympic tradition is at stake,' Brundage warns. Ordaz orders 10,000 troops of the Olympic Battalion, accompanied by light tanks and water cannons, to occupy Ciudad Universitaria. The final reckoning, the death toll, according to John Ross in *El Monstruo: Dread and Redemption in Mexico City*, is 325. A figure confirmed by a *Guardian* journalist buried under a heap of corpses on the second floor of the university building. Two thousand protesters are arrested, stripped to their underwear and held in secure pens in a military camp. Black power salutes, the gloved hands of podium athletes. Future newsreels.

Munich '72: The city of putsches is remembered for the massacre of eleven Israelis, athletes and coaches, by members of the Black September group. A secure Olympic village. Admired architecture. Hooded figures on balconies. Bungled response. Hijacked Lufthansa airliner. Revenge assassinations in an operation known as 'Wrath of God'. Documentary feature films. Exorcism by Oscars.

The spray-can artists are not responding to remote legends, their work has a feral intensity. Zany, psychedelic bestiaries informed by pre-Columbian models, more Robert Crumb than Diego Rivera. The social message is: Look at me. Admire me. Give me a show on Brick Lane.

Painted eyes on the walls of the Lord Napier pub melt in an acid attack, but are never extinguished. In every crack and crevice among the crumbling detritus of the Wick, snakes and teeth appear. Priapic buddleia. Vagina dentata.

Coming home one evening, I encountered a group of muralists on the Olympic front line near Whitepost Lane. I was impressed by their quiet efficiency, the speed with which they underpainted, squared up and set to with roller brushes. The boy in charge issued terse instructions. He stood off, letting apprentices fill in the background, before he stepped forward to finesse signature wings and flames. Within a few hours, digital snoops were cataloguing this latest exhibit as a potential CD cover. The process of spontaneous reproduction is the defining characteristic of the area. What begins on the wrong side of a temporary hoarding soon becomes the colourful backdrop of a TV cop show. By which time, the original wall has been obliterated under fresh tags and aerosol doodles.

The pressure of regeneration, force-fed by the Olympics, is such that zones once tolerant of impoverished artists have to turn every wastelot, every previously unnoticed ruin, to profit. To provide more theoretical housing, it is necessary to unhouse those who have already fended for themselves. Walking down the Regent's Canal from Victoria Park, on the morning of 8 May 2008, I witnessed another eviction. Around thirty police, with attendant vans, bailiffs, hired muscle. Council officials in dark suits clutching protective clipboards. Loud bangs, crunched hinges: the door is battered down.

A towpath cyclist is enraged. 'How long was that building empty? Twenty years? The squatters cleaned the whole place up, it was going to be a community centre.'

A barrel-fronted property, dressed in weeds and tendrils, between the Empress coach garage and the gas-holders. I noticed, a few years ago, a sticker on the cobwebbed window: BACK THE BID. Squatters reclaimed this ghostly shell, using Tibetan gods and prayer scrolls for blinds.

Plodding home from Stratford, after discovering that much of the Olympic Park was fated to become a termite shopping centre, I picked my way down what was left of Ruckholt Road and Eastway. They were taking down the blue fence. Panels were hacked out and dumped on a carpet of wood chips, around the stump of an inconvenient ash tree. The blue tourniquet had served its purpose. Plywood was being replaced by more of those virtual-reality panels: archers, swimmers, cheering crowds. High-definition digital photography and ethically challenged fakery.

Signs are unreadable, arrows point towards mesh fences and motorways. I try to cross the Quarter Mile Lane Bridge, but I'm soon engulfed in security checkpoints. They don't understand the concept of walking, wandering without a fixed agenda.

'You want a job?'

I'm about to become an example of positive discrimination, those slots reserved for decrepit locals.

'See that caravan? Go down there and they'll take you on. Start straight away.'

I'm tempted. Why not return to the era when I cycled out here, to paint white lines on 200 football pitches? And, before that, to

Chobham Farm. After all these years, I was being offered regular employment: I could help to dismantle the blue fence of the Olympic Park.

Arriving at Victoria Park, in the golden hour, I am stopped by a troubled and short-sighted Chinese man. 'Excuse me, sir.' He is flanked by five women of various ages and the same height, daughter to grandmother. They have lost something, somebody, and recognize me as a park regular, foot-dragging, respectably distressed.

'A little man. No teeth. Not normal, simple. Very, very small.'

He was spotted, twice, last Thursday, by a dog-walker. Nothing since. This tiny simple man has disappeared. He carried an umbrella.

I don't want to ask if he is Chinese.

'Does he speak English?'

'Not at all.'

A man seduced by crowds, a grand public event, noise: the 'Love Music, Hate Racism' free concert. He meandered into all that fuss and was never seen again.

Disappointed in my response, the bereaved family move east, in the direction of Hackney Wick, where everything vanishes or is revised. And nothing returns, in the same condition, to the territory it left behind.

Raids

The incident I'd witnessed by the canal, the collaboration of police and council bailiffs, was a commonplace of our early-morning walks. Raids happen at first light, youths congregate at dusk. 'Pond life are out,' say the watchers at their surveillance screens, stirring coffee mugs, leaning forward on their elbows. Life on the street is budget television and the police are the major producers. Digital technology at every demonstration. Hours of CCTV footage of suspect corners. Targets (drug actors) audition for remote viewers as the lack of action goes down: the circling bikes, the sprawling on benches, compulsive phone-babble. A virus from boxed sets of *The Wire* infects the canteen boredom of state-sponsored technicians: in shooting crime, you create it. Postcode soldiers yawn and scratch.

There was a powerful outwash from the Olympic Parkland. A cosmetic imperative. To set and reset paving slabs on busy boulevards. To plant bushes in unlikely places. To throw water at a few yards of tarmac. Nobody builds, they improve the image of construction. Loudly, and on camera, raiders break into the flats of low-level dealers. They evict squatters from doomed theatres and cafés. When stylish swings are installed, down by the canal, they become nests and hammocks for rough sleepers. 'Working with the community to make a difference,' says Tesco Express.

In Broadway Market there was an all-day-breakfast operation run by a Sicilian man, Tony Platia. A local facility of mixed reputation, popular with many, and true to this depressed backwater in the lean years of neglect and bureaucratic indifference. When the crunch came and Hackney Council's £72-million black-hole finances were challenged by central government, an initiative was launched, whereby the usual motley of independent traders were sold out to serious but invisible developers. It simplifies the regeneration process. The legal arguments ran on for years. The Italian café, and the Nutritious Food Gallery managed by a Rastafarian, Lowell 'Spirit' Grant, were predictable casualties. Community activists, eco-warriors, journalists and professional malcontents occupied the café formerly known as FRANCESCA'S. White lettering on a green signboard.

It was a bitter winter. My gesture of support amounted to dragging around a heavy gas heater and a spare canister. The scene inside the boarded-up building was nostalgic, taking me straight back to the squatters of Redbridge in the late 1960s and the M11 extension protesters I'd visited during my *Lights Out for the Territory* wanderings in the 1980s. The certainty of defeat was ameliorated by lifeboat humour: hatches battened down, in it together, sharing a brew. Rollups. Caps and gloves indoors. Radio on. And a constant procession of image-makers. That was the difference now. The small group, enduring the elements, paying their respects to a building that would very soon disappear, appreciated that they were performing in a documentary. Crews arrived from Holland, Germany, Italy. Tony Platia, squat, hunched, zipped into black leather, stood beside the bespectacled, stocking-capped Arthur Shutter, spokesman for the occupying guerrillas. Emblems of a suppressed history.

After the first invasion by bailiffs and council-approved heavies, the squatters regrouped, waited, then moved in for a second time on Boxing Day. They repaired much of the damage and kept guard in shifts to repel the demolition crew. They were allowed to shiver through the worst of the weather, cocooned in sleeping bags like economic migrants bivouacking in the shrubs of Victoria Park. There were about forty people sustaining the occupation, more customers than Tony would serve on a good morning. The roof was patched, the wrecked building creaked back to life.

I was coming through the market on my dawn circuit when they smashed the door down, evicted the squatters, ripped through stairs and roof, rendering the space uninhabitable: except by guard dogs. Whatever survived the assault stood as an ugly symbol, among the retro boutiques, estate agents, nice bookshops, wine bars and deli-catessens of Broadway Market: a bunker dressed in razor wire, metal door sticky with flyers. The developer, a Citibank broker called Roger Wratten, has several active properties on this street, but the old café, promoted as a community theatre, stays empty. A scar and a blight behind the fruit and veg stall which was there before all this madness started.

The distance between Broadway Market and Portobello Road lies in the nature of promotional films that trade on a form of topo-graphical branding. Over in the west they get the sanitized absurdity of Richard Curtis's feel-good *Notting Hill*, with its ethnic cleansing and bumbling New Tory toffs. We get David Cronenberg's tattooed Russian hoodlums in *Eastern Promises*, the pantomime version of what is rumoured to be happening. The reinvested loose change of state industries, flogged off in the boot sale, after the collapse of Communism.

I tried the Broadway Market barber whose shop was dressed down for the film, but he didn't have much to report. Some of the set designer's green paint lasted as long as the razor-wire bunker. News-clippings about the movie were taped to the window. Through an interview conducted for a Hackney documentary, I discovered that my informant's uncle owned the barber shop, the restaurant on the corner and a couple of other businesses; which he picked up for a few thousand pounds, back in the 1980s. The uncle preceded the artists into Beck Road. Now he had decamped, so I was told, to a large property, a farm with horses and kennels, on the other side of the river, above Thamesmead. Where he enjoyed a gracious retire-ment, living on his investments.

The final glimpse of Tony Platia, as reported by the journalist Oliver Duff, has him 'huddled over an electric heater in the remains of his shop, avoiding the snowflakes coming through a hole in the ceiling'. Tony muses on the showers of banknotes that are sup-posed to fall from the sky as the 2012 effect brings inevitable benefits to the area.

'It is people like me, local traders who fought very hard to bring

Broadway Market back into a proper community, who should be celebrating the Olympics,' Tony says. 'All the developers want to do is take money coming into Hackney straight out of the area.' To Moscow, the Bahamas, Saudi Arabia. Useful liquidity for picking up distressed Premier League football franchises. That is the other symbol, when you walk down the canal: the gleaming white nest of a stadium processed by corporate debt, in a wilderness of condemned terraces and discontinued industries.

Living with the threshold nuisance of pre-dawn sirens, the warning screech of police cars heading back to the canteen, made me responsive to a request from Robin Maddock, a Hackney-based photographer, that he show me a portfolio drawn from his experiences when accompanying the Stoke Newington Entry Squad on their raids.

Maddock was a photographer who looked like a photographer: young (to me), smart-casual, on the move. His captures, unlike my own snaps, were not part of a logging process, the laying down of an archive from which a more mediated account would be teased. There was nothing proprietary about the way Robin spread out the prints. They might have been taken by a stranger, an earlier version of himself that he barely recognized. Only now, in the act of telling the story, did certain details come to light. He was open about his doubts and difficulties, a talker uninhibited by not having his promotional pitch resolved and polished. A becoming hesitancy, a grasping for the right word, gave way to self-mocking laughter. He was most comfortable near the window. There was no obligation to lock down history. His work was about energy, the life of the streets, balanced by sudden epiphanies: the view from the green carpet of the Lea towards Canary Wharf. A way to position his characters against an ever-shifting backdrop.

I kept the record of the police raids with me for weeks, turning over the prints, placing them against each other, editing a film of my own from Maddock's raw material. He was on to something, without question: a troubled witness coping with the responsibility of shaping a true report. The person you never see, the one with the camera, is omnipresent; in the way that, however alien the set, every portrait becomes a self-portrait.

Nothing is quite what it seems in Maddock's Hackney, a terrain trapped in that mysterious interval, after street lights go out and before the sky begins to acquire colour in the gap between tower blocks. Any attempt to register cultural difference has to be undertaken in direct competition with the evidence-gathering machinery of the state.

While Robin was accompanying the group from Stoke Newington on their raids into what they understood as hostile territory, Hackney councillors decided that the best tactic for combating litter abuse was to establish a snoop squad, undercover agents stalking the borough with camcorders. 'In one incident,' the *Evening Standard* reported, 'two enforcement officers burst into a café in Mare Street, searching for a woman who had dropped a cigarette butt on the ground outside.' The raids, recorded by Maddock, are a more dangerous version of the same strategy. There is no distance now between art projects blessed by Olympic legacy funding and the fetish for current technologies espoused by the state. You can listen, with one ear, to successful applicants babbling about art-for-all digital cameras fixed on bus shelters and, with the other, to post-Orwellian paranoids (like me) whimpering about surveillance systems: the footage is identical. In the age of the spinner, content means nothing; the apparatus of explanation, the word-weaving, tells us what we are looking at and how we should react.

Walking the streets, I frequently witness preparations for the sort of incidents Maddock documents with such an innocent eye. Slow procedural hours, in the aftermath of the smashed door, inspire a catalogue of small revelations. The drugs themselves, at the centre of all this fuss, are 'glamorous in their absence'. There seems to be an agreement between cops and postcode gangs to avoid collision. Screaming sirens work like a courtesy call, allowing offenders to melt into the shadows before they become tedious paperwork.

The underlying theme of Maddock's practice is a tribute to place:

as it is, not how it should be. Featureless blocks, sedated by blue television-light, in an oasis of bare branches and unloved grass. Hooded spectres are nightmare emanations of the buildings themselves. The police, with their padded vests and short-sleeved white shirts, spread out to advance on that dark place, a city within the city. A Welfare State favela. The poetry of estrangement is nicely managed: the photographer's attitude is alert, but never forensic. He brings a measure of humane record to a brutal process. Once inside, surrealism is on the cusp of farce; pornographic magazines and accidental soap operas act like a parallel text, a commentary. Here is the bent head of an old man, as unknowable as Samuel Beckett, sitting on the toilet alongside the life-size transfer of a grinning skeleton. Here is an officer with a disposable yellow camera, which he grips, so fastidiously, with purple rubber gloves. Maddock's archive is a mass of random documentation waiting for a curator.

I asked Maddock if he would record his account of riding with the Entry Squad convoy. How did the world look from inside the van? He made it sound ordinary, a job like any other. Domestic space is violated and the evidence, as the photographer amasses it, is of tedium: smeared colours, ghosts in petrol stations, ripped bingo cards, rumpled sheets, yawning kids, bandaged guns. He calibrates suspended time, using fright-sheet headlines as his chorus.

A&E DEPARTMENT SHUT AFTER PATIENT THREATENED
TO KILL STAFF WITH GUN . . .
PALACE PAVILION CLOSED AFTER KILLING OF TEENAGER
IN A HAIL OF BULLETS . . .
BIKE YOUTH HELD GUN TO PC'S HEAD
ALL FOUR CYCLISTS ARE BLACK . . .
DRUG DEALER SMASHES CAR INTO GARAGES AS RAIDS
SHUT DRUG DENS . . .

Maddock distrusts the sensationalist tone, the rictus of moral outrage. He has the gift of being surprised, working outside a script that is already written. Of finding solace in gazing from the balcony at deserted streets and mute canals.

When I went out in the van with the Stoke Newington police it was sup-posed to be a one-off. I didn't know what I was doing. It felt like just another piece of the Hackney jigsaw. I wanted to move out into a part of Hackney that I hadn't photographed. I was shooting on a large-format film, black and white. The wrong film to capture things you see by being more journal-istic. As soon as I looked at the pictures I'd missed, because of using the wrong camera, I realized I would have to start again, using a more docu-mentary style. But in a way that wasn't about iconic newspaper images.

I had to report, early in the morning, to the Stoke Newington police sta-tion. Too early for me, about half-five or six. Sometimes it's quite nice to be out in the city at that time. Sometimes they'd give the characters they were going to raid a bit of a lie-in, until half-nine. Of course they're still in bed.

The briefings are really interesting, you find out about what people have done. The raid feels like a personal choice on the part of the police, a ven-detta. We need to show them we are going to do something about it. The push comes from information received. Somebody on the estate complains about loads and loads of people visiting a certain flat. Loads and loads of people at night.

I don't know how the police summon up the enthusiasm to go through all that junk. The more you are on the edge of society, the more stuff people hoard and collect. Many mornings it was like raiding a car-boot sale.

I love to be there when the doors are smashed in, catching the rush, the commotion. If I was at the front, right behind the first man in, I probably shouldn't have been. Most of the time the specials would be shouting. There was a whole lot of screaming going on. The normal police would follow in later, to deal with the mess. Usually, the person they are looking for isn't there.

Then we'd go back to the police station and the word would come back that the drugs were in the garden shed, but nobody had actually let them know, until it was too late.

The squad thought I was the grim reaper. Every time I went out was the touch of death. Then they started to get quite a good hit rate. They didn't really mind me coming along. It was amazing. They have a real confidence that what they're doing is the right thing.

You could probably map a policeman's mind in its physical form. They say that people's brains actually change shape according to what jobs they do. The police mind is: 'This is the law, therefore it is right.' They don't have a lot of faith in the legal process. They see a lot of the people they arrest walking, the same night. Straight back to business.

In so many of my pictures, people are sitting there silent, or with a bit of banter, because they know the police are not going to find any drugs. And if they do, the people arrested will be out on bail in a few hours. When you see a kid caught throwing his gear into a hedge, the cops will tell you how rare this is. One boy broke down in tears straight away. He knew, it was the third time he'd been warned, that he'd been caught red-handed. He was going to do time. These kids don't believe they are going to be caught.

Everybody's got a TV. Everybody's got a microwave. Everybody's got a full fridge. It's a strange kind of poverty. You're on that line where it could go into poverty. You might not be able to do anything else, because you haven't got any money. A lot of kids are in that position. What would I do?

There is a massive blurring now, white kids act like black kids. When I went out with the police, there were a lot of mixed-race kids. Single white mothers. The parents live in denial or they are big smokers themselves. They might be part of the same drug scene.

I probably went out on about ten raids. It was difficult to stop. You are always left with a smell in your nostrils and feeling a bit grotty. I was challenged by the people we were invading and by the police.

I'd try to get closer and closer before it kicked off. Before my presence affected the situation, I would back off. There is an awful sneakiness about making those pictures.

One policeman said, 'You're a voyeur, aren't you?'

You find yourself playing a role, getting along with the police. I'm sitting in the van, it's a bit quiet. And they're all in their element, having a good time. If you do the raids, same area, same prostitutes, the action is always interesting. As interesting for them as for me. Even if they have to pick through a lot of dirty laundry.

They work together, they have a laugh together. They have the same sort of mentality about things. They have a very dry sense of humour. Sitting there, little by little, I got to feel how much of an outsider I had become.

The main sergeant who looked after me, and gave me the call most mornings, she was very much on the way up. She's now gone to the Entry Team, the people who smash doors in. The guys in the helmets, the ones who go inside. She made the jump from community policing, head of that, to the Entry Squad. She was so trusting, so nice about it, I nearly went out cycling with her. I'm almost glad I didn't. She was a married woman. But we got along. We're both into running and cycling. And yet we come from different worlds.

I went to her leaving party, to see them all very drunk. That was about as close as I'd want to get. Actually it would have been good to photograph because they were dressed up as nurses and firemen. Can you imagine? It sounds pretty weird. They're all very straight, but when they go out, alcohol is allowed, so it's lively. It was nice to meet people from a different world and to feel their generosity. And to be allowed the space to work.

Most of the police would say, 'Hackney! Where are we going for a drink?' They think they're in the Wild West. They see the worst of it. And, like all the taxi drivers, they have taken flight to Ilford. They are out there in Essex. Maybe there's a racial profile. The head of the Stoke Newington police, when I was there, was a black guy. Great presence. He was really confident about the structure and very helpful. And yet I felt some of the black and Asian officers had taken a traditional white role. They are ambitious. Doors are open to them. They're in a weird position when they're standing with the youths and the banter is going on. 'Why are you hanging around the streets?' And the kids say, 'This is where we live.' They don't want to go and sit with their mothers or their grans in the flat.

I lived out in Hackney Wick for a while, when people were having their flats bought out from under them. I saw a few warehouses being demolished. The allotments went. This wasn't an area where anyone would choose to be. It's a weird island. You'd get police horses trotting through in the daytime, but they are nowhere to be seen in the evening when the stuff is really going on.

The girl I lived with was a bit of a depressive, a designer. She used to rearrange the flat every day. A beautiful, big old fabric factory. She'd move all her stuff across the room, every week. She couldn't get organized. She couldn't work. One of those procrastinators. She had a relationship with the Kurdish guy from the local shop – who turned out to be a raging alcoholic and a nutter. He was breaking our door down in the evening. I got accused of sleeping with her. Always drama, always someone dying.

The blue fence was going up at this time. I saw a documentary on the allotments. It's a terrible shame that they haven't the imagination to say, 'Let's keep the allotments and let's have the flyover going over them.' Those gardens were so visually beautiful.

The problem is that we don't have any style when we do these things. When you look at the stadium going up, you see those big girders. Compare that with the Bird's Nest in Beijing. What an incredible piece of architecture. It's half-baked. We have no sense of tradition about what we're doing.

Funny Money

'It isn't money, exactly,' Sancho suggested, 'more like new debt.'
  – Thomas Pynchon

Suddenly I was rich. At a time when banks were collapsing, bankers topping themselves or selling their apologias before doing some rehab in an open prison, loot was rolling in. The technology made it so easy; every morning, as the screen cleared its sticky-eyed scrot, a good-news assault provided my wake-up call. The Spanish were blush-makingly generous, emphasizing my turn of fortune in block capitals and promiscuous underlinings. The Lotería Primitiva in Madrid was not so primitive after all. They could hardly contain their pleasure in letting me be the first to know that my ticket number 015-11-464-860 had come home. **You have therefore been approved for a lump payment of NINE HUNDRED AND EIGHTY FIVE THOUSAND NINE HUNDRED AND FIFTY EUROS ONLY.**

I loved that **ONLY.** And I loved the pleasure they took in my good luck. **CONGRATULATIONS!!!!!!** And the most astonishing aspect was that I didn't even have to buy a ticket. I had never bought a Spanish lottery ticket or any other kind. Nothing, in my prejudiced view, was more depressing than witnessing the urban poor queuing to shell out for their shares in the Millennium Dome and all the other Nude Labour vanity projects. There are more scratchers addicted to loss in the minimarts of Dalston than the fleapit cinemas of 1960s Dublin, or the dockside brothels of a malarial sump.

All that was asked was that I keep my award from public notice. And I should pay 10 per cent of my winnings to an agent. (No change there.) An attached form made it a simple matter to pass on the relevant banking details.

Before I could trouser this first rattle of Spanish doubloons and plot my retirement to the coast, watching the horizon, doing a little painting, there was another download of Iberian largesse. This time the El Gordo sweepstake had drawn a ticket, which once again I had not been obliged to purchase. Here was a new form of gambling, every one a winner. A way, after the urban renewal of the Barcelona Olympics, to foster a climate of European goodwill, by offering funds to difficult authors, and disguising cultural awards as lottery triumphs. Over in Madrid, a favourite city of mine, last seen at the age of twenty, they recognized quality when they saw it. How discreet of them to avoid vulgar prize-giving ceremonies, for which, in any case, I had permanently disqualified myself by blundering into a form of writing that was neither fiction nor non-fiction.

This time it was **SIX HUNDRED AND FIFTEEN THOU-SAND EIGHT HUNDRED AND TEN EUROS.** It was mounting up nicely. The conditions were the same, keep it buttoned, 10 per cent to the agent. I'd soon have enough to buy a flat in one of the new towers overlooking the site of Chobham Farm. Contracts were on the point of exchange when Lotería Primitiva came back to top up the pot – only three exclamation marks after the **CONGRATULATIONS!!!** – with another tidy lump: **EIGHT HUNDRED AND FIFTEEN THOUSAND EIGHT HUN-DRED AND TEN POUNDS ONLY**. Maybe they'd mistaken my failure to activate my claim for a prejudice against euros.

And this was far from the end of my winning streak. I began to think that I was personally responsible for the credit crunch, by mopping up all the global slush funds, the shiny trinkets hidden in hedges. I was operating at a Bishopsgate-bonus level. I should be out there, propping up the secondary economy of Shoreditch by sniffing, snorting, guzzling, shoving wads of readies into the vestigial underwear of lap dancers. Even the formerly staid *Reader's Digest* – did you know they operated a Finance Department? – got in on the act. Noble of them, I thought, given our differences over style and content.

> You may want to savour this moment, Mr Sinclair, because great news like this doesn't come along every day.
> The reason I am writing to you is because you could soon be confirmed as the Sole winner of our £5,000 Immediate Payout Draw. **Important documents will arrive at your address in an orange envelope marked 'Urgent, Time-Sensitive'.**

I'm still waiting for that orange envelope. But as the cheapskates were only offering five grand, who cares?

The really creepy stuff kicked in when total strangers started paying cheques into my apparently secure account. £4,500. £4,300. £9,500. £4,900. And £9,500 again. By the close of play on 5 January 2009, I was £32,700 to the good. A gesture, perhaps, from an unknown well-wisher in response to the difficulties surrounding the launch of my new book, *Hackney, That Rose-Red Empire*? The bulk of my readership, so I understand, consists of Hackney-born sentimentalists exiled to the north and the far west. A pretty cover qualified this item as a suitable present, given by new London Fielders, so that old folk can write to let me know where I got it wrong.

Who was the mysterious Mr N. Lardja? A man who felt a compulsion, several times a day, to fill in a credit slip. Was he suffering from some form of dementia, memory-wipe? An unfortunate condition causing him to donate substantial amounts to a person he had never met, at regular intervals, as he went about his business. 'Another coffee, sir?' 'Just a minute, while I find my chequebook. Time to give old Sinclair his dibs.'

And what of Mr C. Lai? With his blatantly coded name: *see lie*. Did they know each other? Had I been elected to a society so secret no member would ever learn the identity of any other? Was Mr Lai in the employ of Dr Fu Manchu?

The telephone, interrupting my soap-opera reverie, broke the spell. The HSBC bank security division wanted to query the rush of blood that had me spraying cheques out, as wildly as Messrs Lardja and Lai, to a gentleman whose name rang no bells. My security code meant nothing. My mother's maiden name, my special place? Familiar knowledge to the fellowship of the Lai. I don't use internet banking, but that was no protection. I was haemorrhaging money I didn't have. By a curious coincidence, hinting at psychic powers on the part of the thieves, payment for the sale of my archive to an American university had just come in. And now, before I could access a penny, had gone out again like the tide. The large cheques could be blocked, but they'd started modestly with fifty. And then a few hundred. And a few hundred again. Those sums had gone and would have to be reclaimed. In one day, they'd cleared £37,000. Which was never there and which left me staring at a black hole as fantastic as the promises of the Spanish lottery.

My account was being used as a clearing house for intricate drug-connected deals. When I arrived at the bank and found an actual person to talk to, in one of those comfortable little partitioned areas, she was relaxed about the whole affair. It was, so the lady admitted, a commonplace. Happens all the time. But especially in the early part of the year, after Christmas. There is no such thing as money any more, as we once knew it. The metaphor has collapsed: anachronistic as a DeLorean car. Money has moved away from an Adam Smith or a Maynard Keynes cod-scientific rigour to a dopey, psychedelic soap bubble. We should think of the Wall Street jackals, the Lea Valley visionaries, as poets of a new unreality, where anything is everything. The virtual world has been carved up between accountants and curators, both of whom recognized right away that content is finished and contempt is the tool of the times. Contempt for truth. Contempt for place. Contempt for the human animal. The post-ironic explanation, the slick pitch, the masterly deployment of statistics, the belated apology: that's what it's about. Accountancy, I told myself, is what I've been doing all along; a form that is neither fiction nor fact. An unacknowledged hybrid medium. Collaboration between author and invigilator. Signed off when you pay that meaningless cheque (plus interest). Maintaining an in-credit account was fiscal innocence of the worst kind, an open invitation to online scavengers in rented Leytonstone rooms, the new invisibles who spend their days picking over the landfill dunes of cyberspace.

I interviewed a media-savvy architect in his riverside studio. He doodled as he spoke: towers, floating rings like a manifestation of the hoops of smoke he puffed as he whaled a French cigarette in three drags. I recorded his riff.

The Olympic Park will be a disaster. The press are so mealy-mouthed. Everyone knows when it's all done we'll have a bill of at least twenty billion. The starting figure means nothing at all. But the civil servants are right behind it. They announce budgets that are acceptable to the politicians, budgets that receive full political backing. They have no bearing on the truth at all. They say, 'We can always blame it on the architects and the planners.' Which is what they always do.

It's the same with all grand projects. I was invited into the competition for Tate Modern. At that time the budget was eight million. I did ask the question: 'If you just make the thing watertight, clean up the brickwork, get rid of the crap inside, repair the windows, so you've got bare walls and a big shell, how much would that be?' They said, 'Two to three million.' I thought, 'Christ, it's got to be ten at least.' No one knows the true budget, but I have it on reliable authority that it was in excess of 140 million.

The world of grand-project accountancy is completely unreal, figures are just floated. If you tell the truth you won't get the job. Sadly, the public sector is the worst. Why did we make such a mess of Wembley? The Emirates Stadium is a much more intriguing structure. Much more lively. If we accept that we need a new athletics stadium, and Crystal Palace is difficult to get to and past its sell-by date, let's do it properly.

Behind the Olympic Park, whatever anyone says, are the architects HOK. They were responsible for Sydney. They got the job by saying they would fund it themselves. They are a huge organization. They put in additional seats. They get revenue from the additional seats and they take it away. They make a lot of money. And they reduce the risk.

So what happens here? They are going to remove part of the structure of the Olympic Stadium. We're not going to have a proper stadium as legacy. It's got nothing to do with architectural quality. HOK specialize in stadia. They will do a deal with finance. No other architect would do that.

The closer you get to the Stratford construction site, the more money, as civilians understand it, loses its meaning. I think that what they are actually building, in those tunnels and bunkers, deep inside the dangerous, unexploded-ordnance-infested clay is a gigantic particle accelerator like the facility at CERN in Switzerland. Why else would they need to curtain the landscape in blue plywood? To employ regiments of Gurkhas? My Lea Valley string theory, attempting to reconcile quantum mechanics and relativity, blunders into previously unsuspected dimensions, which include multiverses of insecure investment, global terror websites and a wilderness of counterfactual theology. Cutting-edge physics cohabits with Mayan 2012 endgame prophecies to deliver a new economics. The more you owe the richer you are: we understand that perfectly well. But the more you owe, the more you fuck up, the more you will be given? They call this 'anomaly cancellation'. In other words, if a flaw can be described, wipe it out. Sue the shit out of anybody who complains about radioactive dust drifting over their pristine estates. And, if the worst comes to the worst, establish a committee to elect another committee to draw up a report, to be evaluated by government-appointed experts, before being binned by the incoming administration, because it is nothing to do with them. Improving the image of construction. Public autopsies for Iron Age bogmen dug from the peat.

I was uneasy about a few thousand pounds coming and going from my bank account, the grand-project managers were made of sterner stuff. The HSBC associate who dealt with the fraud I had experienced as casually, more casually, than an overdraft exceeded by a fiver, explained that the Olympics had set off a deluge of cyber-crime. A notion supported in an article by Mark Prigg in the *Standard*. Prigg alluded to a plethora of websites punting premature souvenirs, tickets for seats that would never exist. You could buy, if you were sufficiently deluded, a 'virtual Olympic torch'. Graham Cluley, of the online security firm Sophos, is reported as saying: 'The 2012 Games is going to attract a lot of criminal attention. There is going to be an explosion in junk mail and scams.'

Things are not as bad as they might be. Given the regularity of postal strikes and the mountainous backlog to be cleared, the junk mail won't get through. And the scams will not come close to the sanctioned disappearances and escalating budgets of the Olympic Park developers. The LDA, with a generous allowance to buy up land from those about to be evicted from the Lower Lea Valley, managed to mislay £100 million. The managers responsible for closing down the allotments will now take an extended gardening leave. Forensic accountants expected an overspend of £32 million, but discovered that the figure had crept up by almost five times that amount. 'There has been no evidence of fraud, just mismanagement.' Another cancelled anomaly, they said, to be made good when land is flogged off after the Games.

Meanwhile, the survivalist economics I had practised from those days as a labourer at Chobham Farm in the early 1970s were drawing to a close. The old freelance life of the Lea fringe boroughs was over. Rubbing along on fees from talks or readings, up and down the country, was no longer practicable. When my wife took charge of chasing outstanding invoices, she discovered a stack of seventeen, going back over six months. One government-funded arts institution kept a promise of £100 in play from March to October: emails were ignored, calls vanished into answering machines and were never returned. The finance department has no contact with the creatives who commission work and who move on to another gig as soon as your piece is safely delivered. Eventually, it was admitted that the cheque had gone out: to the wrong person. No payment was possible, naturally, until the fee was returned. We learnt about new accounting systems with teething troubles, mislaid paperwork, files that couldn't be downloaded. We shipped off passport photographs, sworn affidavits, photocopies of petrol receipts. Articles solicited in the most extravagant terms back in February were an embarrassment to all parties when they were submitted, as required, in December.

As the postal service imploded, the old 'cheque's in the post' excuse became a fact of life. Nothing made it on to the mat other than junk mail, free council propaganda (funded from the rates), invitations to long-concluded art shows and gilt-edged stiffies from such as Debrett's: who wanted my company at a wine tasting preceded by a talk on trust and estate planning. 'The aim of this service is quite simple: to provide authoritative advice on matters of wealth protection and innovative ways to mitigate tax.' After which, we would sit down for a performance of Mendelssohn's Violin Concerto and Mussorgsky's *Pictures at an Exhibition*.

I was otherwise engaged. In the Hackney twilight I was taking my payment for council tax, along with the usual blustering red-letter bills and summonses, to the new multimillion-pound offices, around the back of the white-stone edifice on Mare Street. Land deals in Shoreditch, development packages in Dalston Lane: the bloated cash cow was milked straight into the civic bucket. Stylish new premises, like an upmarket betting shop, for the black-suits, the clipboard bureaucrats with the razor-cut hair. The high-heel smokers with badges. But nobody, it seemed, was authorized to deal with something as inconvenient as actual payment.

'We can't accept that,' said the woman at the desk.

'What if I went outside and put my envelope in the box? Would you accept it then?'

'Different department.'

'This is the only address on your demand: 2 Hillman Street, E8. Cashiers' Offices.'

'Have you got a banker's card? We can't take cheques without a banker's card.'

I knew this Hillman before he was a street. From the days when he was a fellow drudge at the North East London Technical College in Walthamstow. Quite an amiable cove. An orthodox eccentric with an interest in sewers and tunnels. Author of *London Under London: A Subterranean Guide*. President of the Lewis Carroll Society. Which struck me as being an excellent qualification for the dedicatee of this open-plan rabbit hole, where all the furniture is on the wrong scale. Ellis Hillman had risen in the educational and political worlds as I had retreated underground.

The rules and regulations in the Council Tax Payment Booklet were pure Lewis Carroll. 'Even if we receive your payments later that same month, we may still send you reminders or final notices.'

The keeper of the desk issued me with a pink ticket, 5002, and told me to wait my turn. I could see her, as she buffed her nails, watching me, ready to summon security if I made one wrong move. Could a person, straight off the street, brazen into new, architect-designed offices, and expect to hand over a naked cheque? The ponytailed, white-shirt cashier knew that I was pulling a scam by paying a bill, directly, straight into the system, but he couldn't work out what it was.

'Can I have a receipt?'

It was almost closing time. Dozens of drones yawned over their all too visible computer screens. He hit the button and my contribution became available for redistribution by our elected representatives, the ones for whom I have never cast a single vote. Votes are volatile in this territory. I remember following a woman into the voting station in the school on the other side of the road from where we live. 'Name?' asked the official. The woman was disconcerted by such a direct challenge. She gestured vaguely towards the printed list of registered voters. 'This one?' 'Thank you. That will do nicely.' A pile of postal voting forms was found in a hedge, but there was no suggestion of malpractice. Hackney is not Afghanistan. My youngest daughter, late home from work, queued for an hour to play her part in the democratic process. She reached the desk and was turned away.

Retreating from the Mare Street zone the council has colonized with sleek block-buildings, it is easy to understand that it's only a matter of time before the Tesco development around Morning

Lane will collide and connect with the offices of the tax gatherers. That refurbished music hall, the Hackney Empire, will be closing its doors for a few months, a relentlessly upbeat and approved diet having failed to attract the punters. You can't legislate for the disreputable humour, the sexism, racism, spit and sawdust, that went into making the original theatre so attractive. As a sanctioned freak show. A knocking shop. Gilt and gingerbread viewed through a haze of alcohol, a curtain of smoke.

Flying north across a darkening sky a squadron of geese squawked in an asymmetrical V formation, the long arm on the left. An uplifting symbol for the way I felt. It might be time to sell up and go. The river. The road. And China too?

They had a new measure for poverty out there. A Plimsoll line for deprivation. Albania, Armenia, Bosnia-Herzegovina. And, most recently, Iceland. It sounded like a reverse-order Eurovision Song Contest. It was actually a list of the only countries denied the pleasures of the McDonald's franchise, the pampas-grazed, offal-sweeping, official burger-bun providers of the 2012 Olympics.

Resurrection

Sitting stiffly, posed on a hard chair for two hours, is not as tough an assignment as it might seem. Time, during that first hour, overlapped me, kindly, quietly. There were few choices to be made and nowhere to go. The buzz of the city faded with the light in the uncurtained window. Nobody spoke. Five amateur painters dabbed and scratched; stood off, staring at the presented obstacle – myself – without excitement or impatience. Stephen Gill, the previous sitter, the one who got me into this thing, took a couple of photographs of the artisans at their easels, then he went away. Nothing else occurred. The young guy at the back did some fancy roll-up smoking, which was almost too dramatic to endure. Smoking was his gift, his special subject.

Motes dance in a cone of dying sunlight. You learn to breathe with your gills. I had no desire to see the evidence of my unavoidable mortality. After twenty minutes, your knees ache and your neck locks. You walk away or you become part of the set. Part of the long room at the back of St Mary of Eton Church in Hackney Wick. I doubt if I could find the place again. It won't be there, not in its present form, with velvet shadows creeping across blackened boards. And the company of spectres from another age. Those who will never be evicted. Until the walls come down and the developers win the day.

Downstairs, the click of ivory balls from the former snooker room confirms the legend of two ancient, near-blind members of the Eton Mission who arrive from nowhere to play out their weekly challenge. Wheezing, they crouch to shoot the odd frame, before subsiding against peeled leather, while waiting to disappear into it. The wild young boys with cropped heads, behind cobwebbed glass up on the wall, are slightly less dead than their portraits. Which have bleached into obscurity. Faces like acid-scorched thumbs. Stern teams of vanished sportsmen. Wilderness lads press-ganged by god's storm troopers, public-school missionaries from the Victorian and Edwardian eras. Benefactors of the territory like Major Arthur Villiers and Gerald Wellesley.

Henry Allingham, the oldest man in the world, survivor of Jutland and Ypres, a living fossil of the last century's tragic absurdities, was an Eton Mission oarsman. Active on the River Lea from 1909 to 1914. And again from 1919 to 1922. Returned, at the last gasp, to the canalside club, just before it vanished into the Olympic Park, Henry said, 'It's wonderful. This has taken ten years off my life.' After 113 years, he was ready to go.

Distracted by the unseen pull of the submerged Hackney Brook, I was about to take ten years off my life too: by walking straight into the diesel-storm of a motorway slip road. With no way out, until I managed to climb a fence and scramble through bushes, thorn thickets, camera poles, back to the edges of civilization. To the Gothic hulk of the padlocked church. Where the artists hung out; meeting at regular intervals to attempt mass portraits of current Wick enthusiasts who have volunteered to fade alongside the images of the long-dead footballers, rowers, athletes.

Which is why that first hour on the chair was so soothing. Part seance, part dumb confession, the sitting was an effortless unburdening. A remission from troubled thoughts about the devastation of the Lower Lea Valley achieved through the concentrated labour of others. I would become an approximate rendering of husbanded flaws and imperfections. Moment by moment, I was opened to a version of the past curated by the space into which I had been admitted. Liberation derived from the practised skills or the technical inadequacies of the artists. As they drew me out of, and away from, my earlier selves.

There were difficulties in my life, many of them stemming from local estrangement. The good thing about Hackney, over the last forty years, was that nobody cared. Nobody noticed the place.

Transport was hopeless, it was better to walk. A reasonable burden of debt hobbles the politicians, tempers their excesses. The trouble started when our crapness began to be celebrated with a post-ironic fervour: we manufactured enamel badges with broken hearts. And then the Olympics arrived to swivel a searchlight on the dark places, to impose a fraudulent narrative. Everything they boasted of delivering, as legacy, after the dirt and dust and inconvenience, was here already. It had always been here, but they didn't need it. They lived elsewhere. They lived inside their illusions. Hackney ceased to be a game reserve and became a career. To prove how much they loved the ugly old borough, town hall politicians agreed to rub along on a pittance (ten of them having to share not much more than a million pounds in the last financial year), before decamping on an expenses-paid, fact-finding mission to Beijing. Travel, they informed whinging critics, heightens the perception of what has been left behind.

'These people are individuals who want to make a difference to their community and they must be rewarded for that,' said Councillor Merrick Cockell: from his totally impartial viewpoint. It's boom time on Mare Street. On bling central. Penny Thompson, chief executive of Hackney Council, receives an annual salary of £164,839. Director of housing, Steven Tucker, is on £126,000. Timothy Shields, director of finance, and Kim Wright, corporate director of community services, earn £120,000 each. And worth every penny. Read about their achievements in the council-funded, eco-friendly *Hackney Today*.

My second hour was less comfortable. The organizer, an American woman called Leigh Niland, discovered that her watch had stopped. A consequence, I suppose, of experiments in relativity being conducted out on the marshes, in the tunnels and bunkers. So I was deputed to monitor the passage of time, to warn the painters of their final countdown. Time was no longer seamless, a reverie interrupted by the clatter of trains on the high embankment.

From a window at the back you could look on a cancelled future of unstrung cricket nets, bits of lawn where feral youths had been encouraged to engage in community sports. Eton Manor, Eton Mission: young gentlemen, in striped blazers and celluloid collars, arrived in this uncolonized edgeland to import the ideals of Empire; buying up farms, preaching amateur-football morality, constructing boathouses. Public-school and university men, fired by the challenge of Satanic gloom, the lurking thieves and prostitutes, were conspicuous, according to Michelle Johansen, 'for striding purposefully straight up the middle of the road'. Hackney Wick was a shanty town, reached without weeks at sea. A suitable landscape for the opium wars of religious doctrine.

Oxford Movement missionaries, often at their own expense, countered gang-related violence issues by establishing a direction of travel that offered a legacy to coming generations of East Londoners: playing fields recovered from industrial squalor, rowing clubs on backrivers, allotments presented to those without gardens. They created everything that has now been torn down to make way for the Olympic Park. The football pitches stolen for VIP parking. The popular cycle track destroyed against the promise of an elite facility. Locals forced to improvise training exercises in the corners of a retail park. Swimming pools shuttered and standing idle. Allotment holders expelled to a flooded patch of yellow clay, alongside a busy road, up against the shell of the doomed Eton Manor clubhouse. The uniform sheds, with which they were provided, in place of previous tumbledown assemblages, were like battery-farm chicken coops.

An Old Etonian, E. M. S. Pilkington, wanted to do great things for the youth of the area, denizens of railway arches and rabbity terraces. But the marshes were never easy to locate. That was part of their charm. 'Having searched diligently through *Mogg's Guide to London and the Suburbs* for the correct geographical position of Hackney Wick, and all the Metropolitan timetables for a suitable train to Victoria Park Station, I duly started off one evening in search of adventures in the Wild East.'

Those adventures included the instigation of drawing classes: in the room where I now posed for Pilkington's elective descendants. Loving water, the muscular Christian solicited funds to establish a swimming club. All the fine young men, rising at 4 a.m., would troop down to the Lea, for a restorative plunge, right opposite an active factory.

'On early summer mornings the men from the dye works used to stand out on the edge of their wall and look on. They were sometimes a rich blue all over, and they were sometimes red, according to the dye which they were working at the time, and their appearance was always picturesque.'

To read about the achievements of the Eton Manor philanthropists (who were not cleaning up the territory to present it to a mall developer), is to discover one crucial difference in their presentation. The spinners of the ODA and LDA speak of what is to come. The sporting pioneers write of what has already been achieved. In 1923, using their own money and money raised from friends, four Old Etonians acquired thirty acres of wasteland, near the River Lea in Leyton, and turned it into 'one of the most conspicuously beautiful recreation grounds in the metropolitan area'. It was known as the Wilderness: 'a vast sporting Eden or nirvana, with nine football pitches, two rugby pitches, a cricket pitch, six tennis courts, a squash court, running track, bowling green and swimming pool for the Eton Manor Boys and Old Boys to share.'

The floodlights alongside the running track were the inspiration of Major Arthur Villiers, the benefactor who presented Manor Garden allotments to the landless folk of East London, to enjoy in perpetuity. Villiers, a man with no great cultural pretensions, endured the classical European tour. He motored around Italy, under a cloud of grim necessity, a chauffeur at the wheel. A friend, coming across him by chance in Pisa, was astonished to see the former officer studying the famous leaning tower and the Campo Santo. It was the floodlighting, not the architecture, he was interested in. Villiers grasped at once how electrical technology could be adapted for the running track at Hackney Wick. He built himself a house on the edge of the Wilderness and stayed there until he died in 1969. Like an old India hand, puffing a cheroot, on his veranda in Bournemouth.

Everything promised, swimming pool, cycle track, rivers enjoyed by working men and women, had already happened. The post-Olympic facilities were here all along, getting on with their business, struggling for funds. The poisons of industrial exploitation were in the ground, undisturbed and inert. If the drama of international competition, man against man on the track, was required, then Hackney Wick found ways to provide it: as a modest private investment. The nation didn't have to go into hock to pull in the punters. It occurred, spontaneously, before the age of multilayered development agencies, the tearing out of gardens, the expulsion of small traders, the removal of travellers.

The 2012 Olympics were a noisy sequel. The original Hackney Games had been witnessed by vast crowds. In 1857, James Baum, an impresario based at the White Lion public house in Wick Lane, created a running track on one acre of his own property. He organized boxing matches and the 'Victoria Park Races', a modest version of the current extravaganza. The White Lion track was made from gravel and followed the natural features of the ground. Spectators massed in the centre of the track or up on the railway embankment. There were long-distance pedestrian races, handicapped runs and wrestling bouts. A number of records were set. William 'The Crowcatcher' Lang came down from Middlesbrough in 1865, to take the world one-mile record with a time of four minutes seventeen and a half seconds. Not bad on an uneven track with an uphill section and a mob pressing tight to the verge. John 'The Gateshead Clipper' White established a six-mile record that stood for sixty years, before it was broken by Paavo Nurmi, the legendary Finn, in 1921.

The fame of the White Lion track was such that Louis Bennett, a Native American known as Deerfoot, crossed the Atlantic to challenge our English champions. Four thousand people, many arriving after the race started, travelled from Fenchurch Street Station. As the series progressed, crowds grew: 10,000 were expected when

Baum put up his own version of the blue fence, around the back of the course, to secure it from freeloaders. The railway embankment was enclosed to form a grandstand. Private boxes were provided for the great and the good (the wealthy). 'Every nook and crevice from which a glimpse of the contest could be obtained was occupied,' reported the *Sporting Life*. 'And no little merriment was caused by the repeated break downs of lottery platforms.'

Baum, as Warren Roe reports in a thoroughly researched piece in *Hackney History*, 'was also a bit of a philanthropist, always keen to promote events that would benefit the poor and under-privileged'. He organized fund-raisers for the distressed cotton workers of Lancashire.

It couldn't last. That moment of balance between the fading pastoral of the marshes and the industrial imperative of dye works and fish-curing sheds. The argument between Arthur Villiers, who wanted to see Eton Manor funds used for practical projects, clubs for urchins, and the Church authorities, who proposed the construction of a great tower, was a rehearsal for much that would follow. The vertical thrust of a single structure, dominating place by overlooking it, would be opposed, repeatedly, by horizontal energies: which are always democratic, free-flowing, uncontained.

Sneaking a glance at my watch, tracking every tick of time, fixed to my stiff chair in the limbo of the Eton Mission, I played over the stories I had read: the races run, the forgotten benefactors recovered through research by local historians in vanishing libraries. It was left to the *Sporting Life* to compose the tragic elegy.

'Hackney Wick – alas! what a falling off! . . . The place has been allowed to fall into such a state of decay that it is enough to give one the horrors to look at it . . . The whole wears such a woebegone aspect as to plainly betoken that the once famed Hackney Wick must soon be numbered among the things that have been.'

Not Here

Under the dust of development, the brutal imperatives of the current regime, I sickened. Books, paintings, and property, were a burden, symptoms of the disease. I wanted to walk away and to keep walking. I had not recovered from my orbital circuit, my tramp around the M25 motorway loop, that perfect icon of endlessness. I dosed myself with German road movies (better without the subtitles). And Chinese poets, driven out of China, seeing London with fresh eyes. Yang Lian, relocated to Stamford Hill, contemplated the margins of the River Lea. 'People he meets all his life are as unavoidable as this place.'

Lying awake at first light I hear the click of the letter box, the sound of a single item hitting bare boards. I do not leap from the bed: another bill. Small businesses are going under, which seems to be part of the great scheme of things. Talk to an established postman, if you can find one, and they'll describe a gradual erosion of confidence, grotesque schemes thought out by computers and enforced by clipboard management: impossible rounds, no overtime, no incentives to deliver a decent service. The landscape, in the shadow of the Olympic Park, is in the process of being brought on-stream as a virtual paradise. The model is German, old East and older West: Honecker's urban planners, the propaganda of Dr Goebbels. A surgical removal of stubborn traces of the local makes way for a mindless verticality. Statements of control. New blocks, lacking Berlin's communal courtyards, are positioned for convenient access to the extended malls that will replace the free-flowing anarchy of the street market. Tessa Jowell, dismissing a critic of the Stratford grand project, remarked: 'He's a man who doesn't like shopping.'

The white envelope, with the latest bill, addressed by hand, had wedged itself neatly into a crack between floorboards. Where I left it, quivering slightly, when I walked out to meet the Chinese-British photographer Ian Teh. A man whose surname my monoglot laptop sniffily corrected to the definite article.

After the incident – we'll return to that later – film crews arrived on my doorstep from all over Europe. America too. A brief item on the *Today* programme, followed by a blog from the presenter, making a bullet-point summary of a long-winded essay I'd written months ago, provoked an Olympic feeding frenzy. Belgians, Germans, Italians, French: civilized and serious-minded communicators solicited a guided stroll through the dust storm. Their reports might run for as long as two minutes, probably less, so they were never going to walk the entire blue-fence circuit. A hired people carrier, stacked with camera boxes and tripods, would park on Wick Lane, near the barrier with the weave of memorial flowers. The presenter, after checking hair and make-up in a hand mirror, would follow me on to the Greenway. They never got further than the site where the skeletal stadium was emerging from the clay like a waking crocodile. Wraparound weirdness overwhelmed the cultural tourists, huge skies the like of which they had not previously encountered. Concrete funnels dispensing liquid slurry into a perpetual stream of trucks. Rinsed earth in mounds. Swaying cranes. New developments with picture windows mesmerized by the virulent green of the duckweed-clogged canals and backrivers.

'I am becoming paranoid for people like yourself who regularly visit or live on land around the Olympic Park,' Bill Parry-Davies told me. 'The Lloyds Shoot tip is where some really nasty stuff was found, a forgotten dump situated on the Olympic arena site. The West Ham tip and the banks of culverts also appear to have been randomly covered with radioactive substances. God only knows what they dredged out of the Lea.'

Much of the work, so it appears from an article by Ted Jeory and David Jarvis in the *Sunday Express*, was to facilitate the construction of a massive bunker, 'the size of half a football pitch'. It was hidden beneath an approach ramp, 'next to a site where new homes will be built before the 2012 Games'. Toxic soil, 7,300 tonnes of it, lined with a plastic membrane, was buried in a 'disposal cell', between the railway station and the river. Residue from luminous watch dials, churned up in the development process, leached into the water table. Thorium, a radioactive isotope, has an estimated half-life of fourteen billion years. But who's counting?

Olivier Pascal-Moussellard, from the Paris magazine *Télérama*, came over to do an interview, as part of a special London issue. Checking his copy, on his return, Olivier rang me: 'Is it really so bad?' The London issue was intended to promote the place, to prove that we are not just beefeater heritage and Oxford Street shopping. (Now you can shop at Westfield in Shepherd's Bush or a quarry in Thames Gateway.) 'Have you perhaps been a little negative in your opinions? Can you strike an optimistic note for the future?'

'I'll do my best,' I said. 'The quality of the complaints has improved. Now we have an active response in the edgelands. More anger, more subversion than I've seen in decades. Thatcher brought about the punk moment. Nude Labour have midwifed the 2012 apocalypse.'

The London offered by *Télérama* was a pop version of that design classic, Harry Beck's Underground map, with Charles Saatchi as the destination hub in the west and 'Peter' Doherty in the east. The significant geographical zones are: Hackney, Brixton, Chelsea, Kilburn, Notting Hill, Ilford, Paddington, Charing Cross Road. Ian Teh wanted me to point him in the direction of images that would do justice to my reinvigorated borough. A problematic assignment.

Teh moved lightly and easily, it was hard to know if he was a stranger in this place or if, holding back, he wanted to see it through my eyes. This was 1 April, the Day of Fools in the City, the G20 shindig: an economic summit confronted by protestors. Climate camps had been attempted in Bishopsgate and squats invaded by police enforcers. I decided not to walk down there, as a witness, on the assumption that the morning would pass off peacefully and that the dramas would come, with the usual kettling, thuggery and violence, later in the day; when boredom, frustration and a warped sense of entitlement let unidentified paramilitaries off the leash.

The photographer concurred. 'Nothing to shoot,' he said, unwilling to compete with the massed cameras of the men in Plexiglas helmets, snoops in blacked-out vans. Image-harvesting is the favoured security technique: watch and wait, gather evidence for retrospective action. But the obsessive practice of recording an event, as it is happening, or before it happens, incubates paranoia. There is always the requirement to justify budget. Demonstrations, as the G20 battle proved, are simply image wars. Robotic surveillance footage in real time. Directed portraiture of potential malefactors, frozen headshots of figures isolated from the seething mob, is a process as deluded and obsolete as the taxonomies of criminals, lunatics and sub-humans by Alphonse Bertillon with his 'Synoptic Table of Facial Expressions for the Purposes of Systematic Identification' in 1895. Footage, as Pudovkin and the early theorists of film editing knew, can be organized to create guilt by association. If you are wired to hopped-up American cop-show TV as you sit around the station house, you go out to find it. Eyes bulging, fists bunched, weapons primed. The key actor is the cameraman. The sequence of events leading to the death of the unfortunate newspaper-seller Ian Tomlinson was revealed, not through the sworn statements of officers, or dubious medical reports, but through an accumulation of scatter-footage from the mobile phones of people in the crowd.

It's almost impossible now to walk, by back ways, from Shoreditch to Dalston, Hoxton to Victoria Park, without encountering some species of film crew. Blood-splash forensics. Fashion shoot. Soap opera. Certain pubs, certain stretches of towpath, abandoned hospitals, are quotations: ghost milk. Invasive caravans of wardrobe and catering. Hurtful bursts of light. The priestly attendants in puffa-jacket black. The episodes of yawning, aggressive, public boredom.

I led Teh to a number of the standard Hackney photo opportunities, locations distressed and diminished by over-recording, but he would have none of it. 'Light's wrong.' Most of the characters who turn up, flustered, between commissions, are only too happy to catch a bit of fence, a shimmer of canal, and away. Not this man, not at all: we weren't even close. He didn't touch his camera. And he asked no questions. Rather, I interrogated him. He told me about his Chinese coal-mine project, the coking plants at night. Dystopian realism at its most extreme. In a collection called *Dark Clouds* he demonstrated how the neon flicker and the hard bright surfaces of the Chinese economic miracle were rooted in coal dirt, sweating grey walls, brutally circumscribed lives.

I offered him, more as a trial shot than anything else, since he was reluctant to reveal any notion of what he was after, the canal bridge where Tony Lambrianou dumped the car keys after the murder of Jack 'The Hat' McVitie. You get water-shadows rippling on the curve of bricks. You get the immaculately painted sign for RON'S EELS AND SHELL FISH. (You don't get Ron himself. His van has probably been declared a health risk; the pubs he serviced are boarded up.) The sign is a commissioned irony, an artwork trading on nostalgia. You get a slab of corrugated fencing: TOWPATH CLOSED. And you get the recent development, Adelaide Wharf, part-occupied and presenting rectangles of furtive electricity, blues, reds, oranges, to contrast with the dying of the afternoon.

Cat and Mutton Bridge? The view towards the gas-holders? Not worth breaking our stride, for even a moment. Development spasms in Broadway Market and along the canal were discreet, sensitively achieved, when compared with what Teh had witnessed in pre-Olympic Beijing, the banishments to remote tower blocks in gaps between orbital motorways. Communities based around court-yards, teeming with noise and life, were dispersed. One example of the old way was left, as heritage for tourists. Teh met an old man who travelled back, every week, to sit in the street, in the space where his former home had once stood. The new stadiums were unused. They had served their propaganda purpose.

Not one shot had been taken. This was becoming interesting. I was pushed to go beyond the story I had been peddling so long, stones stamped flat by repetition. There was a sentence in a piece I'd written for the *London Review of Books* about how the Victorian cobbles near the canal survived because we never developed a revolutionary class angry enough to tear them out, to smash the windows of council offices and police stations. The editors, passing no comment, cut the whole thing.

A cyclist, coming out of the canal-bridge café where they mended punctures and served ethical coffee, was heading south towards the City protests. 'Basically, they've put all their eggs in the carbon-trading basket,' he said. To a slim blonde girl in black bodysuit, trotting off to London Fields, a spotted-Dalmatian accessory at her heels.

The thing Teh noticed, coming to Beijing from London, was that security around the Olympic Stadium was far more lax. The Chinese were less anxious about cameras, passes and papers. He was not searched with the same frequency. In the evening, he found a themed comedy restaurant, where local schoolteachers and tourists mingled, wearing Mao masks and having a good time, unmolested.

By taking the decision to walk down a street I barely knew, I blundered into what Teh needed. Later, examining prints from *Dark Clouds*, I understood why Wharf Place triggered an immediate response. The Malaysian-born photographer liked the trick of diminishing perspective, a domesticated avenue closed off with a monster cooling tower. The eastern horizon of Wharf Place was end-stopped by skeletal gas-holders. I was positioned, mid-street, like one of the 'shadowy figures out of science fiction' critics located in Teh's portfolio. He was a ghost hunter, nudging those on the point of disappearance against backdrops of dying industries, soulless architecture. Manifestations of transition, decay, impermanence, took his fancy. The twenty-storey tower block that emerges, overnight, from a swamped paddy field. The titles of Teh's shows underline a fascination with entropy: 'The Vanishing: Altered Landscapes and Displaced Lives on the Yangtze River', 'Noctambulations', 'Blackpool Weekend'. From Blackpool it's a small step to

Morecambe Bay and the deleted footprints of the drowned cockle pickers. Teh has been described by Christian Caujolle as 'a curious *flâneur* who searches China for elements of his identity and roots'.

Ada Place, a nondescript tributary on the Hackney border was a set which, being unvisited, had much to offer. It is always more revealing to investigate the out-takes of regeneration, cul-de-sacs excised from the story. GLASS CUT TO SIZE was the boast of a bygone era. Roll-up shutters were dressed with five padlocks in a vertical line. Ian Teh didn't need to ask; I stood beside the wavy metal curtain while the portrait that went into the magazine was framed. Bald man in blue shirt, at attention, beside a locked door, so tall that it goes out of the frame.

Comment voyez-vous le futur de Londres?

Je suis pessimiste: Londres s'enfonce dans les dettes et les projects de développement inutiles . . . Je ne suis pas porteur d'espoir, vous voyez, mais à mon âge on ne réinvente pas la résistance, et on ne change pas sa manière de vivre.

This unresolved hinterland, between canal, gas-holders, and half-built flats, was the perfect ground for our casual encounter. The real dramas of the day, blood, bruises, death, were happening elsewhere. Here was an ordinary absence of the kind that is often to be found within earshot of battle. Cardboard box factories closed down, council agencies with bright blue walls newly opened for business. A gaunt Lithuanian church heavy with flowers. A traffic island called 'The Oval' in the middle of nothing. A squatted, emptied, re-squatted hulk, choked in ivy. A coach garage. A wall cartoon, now vanished, not by Banksy, but one of his imitators. A stencilled angel, dying, or slumped over an anvil monument. In the angel's left hand is a startling red rose.

'I imagine my work,' Teh said, 'as a series of short films made out of stills. I want to encourage the viewer to take the narrative beyond the limits of my frame.'

After this excursion – the photographer drifted off, job done, before I noticed he had gone – I looked at familiar things from a different angle. I didn't walk home along the towpath, but on the road beside it. I took time to peep inside the iron foundry and to investigate the little tangled gardens at the back of the solitary row of cottages.

In Broadway Market, I stopped to restick a notice that had drooped from the wall, to press down the sticky hinges: 'Learn Chinese With A Private Tutor'. Rain-warped colour images, crudely printed text. There were little strips you could tear off with the contact details for Grace. I think I might just do that, contact Grace, as my preparation for a journey that will never happen. Beijing emerging out of Hackney Wick. Hackney councillors drinking toasts in the Forbidden City. A DVD from the Film Shop in Broadway Market: a Chinese remake of De Sica's *The Bicycle Thief* offering 'a strong political statement about the corrupting power of capitalism'.

Retribution

As soon as I put the phone down, and still in shock, I knew that my Hackney book would benefit from a deluge of council-inspired publicity. The poor librarian deputed to give me the bad news kept insisting that it was not her fault, there was nothing she could do, orders from above. My first reaction was relief: one less promotional outing to prepare and deliver, more time to write. This gig came under the heading of duty, as any trek to Stoke Newington must. Church Street is so reasonable, so well stocked with righteous organic outlets and historical traces, that it is unendurable. There is an excellent bookshop on Stoke Newington High Street. I'd be performing there, close to the pub, with an audience you could rely on to be engaged and lively to the point of falling-down drunk. You have some great conversations, with German incomers, walking home after Stokie events, as they interrogate you about where the famous Dalston lesbian quarter is to be found. Where are the fashionistas of the moment? Is that Gilbert or George marching towards the kebab house?

The library people were doing their best to inspire readers and writers by initiating a series of events, to prove that the culture of this place grew out of a long and honourable tradition of debate and dissent. Inherited awkwardness. Work produced in the teeth of neglect, incomprehension, yawning indifference. Daniel Defoe endured a session in the stocks. Edgar Allan Poe recovered from the nightmare of a Stoke Newington education by inventing American Gothic and drinking himself to death. I got off lightly. Being barred from Stoke Newington is like landing on the get-out-of-gaol card in Monopoly. I had been there before, in a hall at the back of the building, talking about neglected Hackney authors: Roland Camberton, Alexander Baron and the rest. Now I was one of them, promoted to the status of non-person. I took it as a tribute, after all this time, to be thought worthy of being invited to leave the premises. It's a tough act to get yourself banned these days and I had pulled it off three months before my book was even published.

'So sorry. The launch is off. You've dissed the Olympics.'

My docu-novel closed with the erection of the blue fence around the Olympic Park. It's true that the shadow of the grand project hung over the borough and the backstory, but the impetus was personal: how I came to be here, why I stayed. What qualities were particular to Hackney and why were they worth celebrating? The council censors were gifted with second sight. Anticipating slights before they had been delivered, they got their retaliation in first.

Kim Wright, corporate director of community services, a woman charged with 'improving the quality of life for all', ordered the library to withdraw my invitation. As public relations go this was a disaster. If the launch in the Stoke Newington Library had taken place, there would have been around thirty people present. A plastic beaker of publisher-sponsored plonk, some discussion of local issues. Reference made to the fact that, just down the road in the council offices, a wall of surveillance screens in a secure basement was monitoring the renegade comings and goings of the citizens of Hackney. With some of the funding for this Orwellian system coming straight out of library funds and the rest from council tax. 'At the forefront of directorate thinking,' says Wright's mission statement, 'is the maximizing of the many opportunities presented by the 2012 Olympics.'

The next morning I was on the *Today* programme with John Humphrys. By that evening, I'd done two television interviews and fielded many calls from the broadsheets. I'd chatted with an instantly concerned Vanessa Feltz. The 'banned' book had acquired a momentum that would carry it, even at £20, through six printings.

The one thing, perhaps the only thing, New Labour did well, was spin. Their legacy was built on it. How could they be so crass? The two institutions to animate the English middle classes, the bloggers and letter-writers, are libraries and allotments. Now the cultural panzers of the Olympics had trashed them both. How could they have got it so wrong? The main players were out of town, lapping up Chinese hospitality, on a fact-finding excursion. Terence Blacker, writing in the *Independent*, called the library episode 'censorship Beijing would be proud of'. So the trip to the city of the six orbital motorways wasn't wasted.

The Hackney press office took the phone off the hook. They stuck by the favoured New Labour tactic of putting nobody up, saying nothing, denying nothing. Eventually, a statement was released: it was policy that controversial subjects – they mentioned stem-cell research and Afghanistan – could not be discussed on council property. It was a duty of care to see that Hackney libraries remain controversy-free, purged of topics that might inflame the volatile reading groups of Stoke Newington.

By now the other political parties, sensing a major own goal, were getting in on the act. Munira Mirza, the Director of Arts, Culture and Creative Industries Policy for the Mayor of London, describing the cancelled launch as a 'bizarre attack on free speech', called for the ban to be rescinded. 'We may not agree with Mr Sinclair's view of the 2012 Olympics, but we defend his right to express his opinions without fear of censure. The Olympics are strong enough to withstand scrutiny and criticism without Hackney's heavy-handed tactics.' The Liberals in Islington, visibly gloating, offered alternative venues, emphasizing their generosity with a battery of hand-squeezing officials and accompanying photographers. In a sense, the council prophecy was fulfilled: for months I was condemned to do nothing except talk about the Olympics, the book I had published totally deformed by its presentation as a social critique.

Distrust of the politics of mendacity, the suspicion that ugly truths were being concealed behind the Olympic smokescreen, seemed to be confirmed by the absurdity of the library ban: that highly paid officials could spend so much energy on so trivial an affair. One adviser, it emerged, had warned of the consequences of the prohibition, how the media would fall on it. The advice was spurned in the thirst for retribution, making it clear to malcontents and naysayers that they would be up against the wrath of an all-powerful bureaucracy, happy to be in agreement, for once, with central government.

It took the *Hackney Citizen*, an independent, self-funded freesheet, to get to the truth of this affair. Using the Freedom of Information Act, they uncovered a series of emails exposing the pronouncements of the council as misinformation or blatant lies. The ban was directly to do with the Olympics, nothing else. And the decision to implement it, whatever the cost, came from Jules Pipe, the Mayor of Hackney.

Two journalists, Josh Loeb and Keith Magnum, recovered an email, dated 24 September 2008, from Polly Rance, Head of Media.

It is clear that we cannot allow the event to go ahead. I have discussed this with the Mayor and his direction was clear.

He feels, as I do, that we should not host an event on Council premises promoting a book which has an overtly contaversial [*sic*] and political (albeit non-party) agenda, and actively promotes an opinion which contradicts our aims and values as an organisation – in this case the 2012 games and legacy . . .

If pushed we can explain that we do not want it to appear that the Council is in anyway condoning or endorsing the content of Sinclair's book. I have discussed the PR ramifications of this with Jules Pipe and he is comfortable with this approach . . . It is a position he would feel comfortable defending.

The wise ones of Hackney convened a meeting for 'book launch risk analysis'. The docu-novel, unread, and as yet months away from publication, is found guilty, with no right of reply, of being political but somehow outside politics. Unaligned. And therefore controversial. The council's own decisions, to rip down terraces, vandalize Victorian theatres, construct 52-storey blocks, are not political: they are strategic and never taken without full public consultation, numerous forms on offer, big tents in the park. Before they do precisely what they were always going to do, go with the development package: blitz, banish, build. The dust never settles. Travellers are invited to keep travelling. It is gratifying that, despite the manifold problems facing a sprawling metropolitan borough, with all its cultural diversity, poverty, crime, our councillors can make time for a debate on the tactical implications of cancelling a reading in a Stoke Newington library.

The borough's chief librarian, Ted Rogers, pointed out that blocking the event would run contrary to the ethics of his profession and with Hackney's professed policy on 'Intellectual Freedom and Censorship'. Rogers was overruled by Jules Pipe, a smart operator convinced that the council could ride out any minor problems from 'the high number of media professionals who live in the borough'. Muesli grazers. Ignore them. Bats squeaking in a wind tunnel.

Non-professionals, writing to the local press, connected the library ban with the mayor's jolly to Beijing. Neil Cooke, of Lauriston Road, wonders if Jules Pipe 'has already resigned, paid back the cost of his holiday in China and left office, or is he just hiding behind a big desk in the vain hope that by staying quiet the people of Hackney will forget and carry on as normal?'

A man called Rob Mackinlay contacted me to say that he had recently surveyed Hackney councillors for their 'views on the supernatural'. This struck me as a useful angle of approach. Mackinlay admitted that he had 'forgotten about the witchcraft, exorcism and child abuse scandal storm of 2005'. And the sensitivities activated by returning to those areas.

Professor Chris French, Head of the Anomalistic Psychology Research Unit at Goldsmiths College, invited to comment on the responses, remarked that 'supernatural beliefs do have significance for a number of issues that politicians may be asked to act upon'.

Matthew Coggins, Conservative, recalls a house in Stoke Newington where temperature and smell change dramatically and unexpectedly. 'Just a curiosity,' he said.

Julius Nkafu, Labour, believes in the 'HOLY ghost' and knows of 'many instances of the Lord's divine interventions to our everyday lives'.

Michael Desmond, Labour, turned on a tap. Rickety plumbing gushed with words as well as water: 'Get away from here! Get away from here.' The phenomenon convinced him not to become an accountant.

Ian Sharer, Lib Dem, admitted to being 'open to views on these things'. Jewish books he had studied warned that 'if you could see what was standing next to you, you would die with fright'.

Mischa Borris, Green Party, was convinced that ghosts were 'some kind of blip in the time continuum'.

Michael Levy, Conservative Chief Whip, had enough on his plate without 'having to delve into the unknown'.

Meg Hillier, Labour, on maternity leave, was excused an opinion.

Diane Abbott, Labour, left it to her researcher to discover that, unfortunately, she had no comment to make.

Jules Pipe, Labour, stated: 'I am happy to confirm that I have never felt the need to attribute any event to "supernatural" causes. Whilst I accept that people are entitled to hold whatever beliefs they like – as long as this causes no harm to others – this is not a subject to which I would ascribe any significance, nor which I would wish to see taken any more seriously than it already is.'

Mackinlay, assessing the responses to his questionnaire, concludes that the people of Hackney take the topic far more seriously than the politicians. Council policy, to an outside eye, can only be attributed to occult forces, possession by the demonic spirit of capital, future world visions. Sacrifices conducted in pyramidical block-buildings by a priestly caste. There is an intimate relationship between financial adventurism and ritual blood-letting.

The report concludes with a cameo from a court case in Essex.

A woman who produced human fingers in court in a bid to explain her involvement in a £925,000 tax credit fraud has been jailed for five years.

Remi Fakorede, 46, from Hackney, east London, told Snaresbrook Crown Court she had been forced into crime by a voodoo curse on her and her family.

Stepping outside for a breath of air, I met a neighbour at the garden gate. 'An ambulance has been stoned on Mare Street,' she said. 'Why?' I asked. 'Why not? There are 149 kids out there denied secondary-school places and plenty of others roaming about on the loose. Some people moan about barbecue trays scorching the grass on London Fields, others are dodging bullets. There have been so many raids lately, they're calling it concerted harassment. It's going to kick off very soon, mark my words, just like the '80s.'

Dilworth in Mallworld

We were walking the wrong way down the canal, west, towards the King's Cross development zone with its karma of ill fortune, underground fires, premeditated attacks by religious and investment-capital fundamentalists. The swirl of malevolent energies was palpable and had been for years, as faceless ghosts struggled to wrestle the truth of this place out of history and away from geological absolutes, buried rivers, disturbed burial mounds. That great collision of railway terminals – King's Cross, St Pancras, Euston – formed another geological fact, embedded in the matter of London. Having demolished and dispersed the Euston Arch, losing the inconvenient rubble in the backrivers of the future Olympic Park, there were grand project (GP) plans afoot to retrieve and reassemble the former obstacle: as a heritage quotation made serious by the huge bill for this exercise. Here was another futile attempt to rewrite the mistakes of the past: as with the return of Christopher Wren's Temple Bar to a place it had never been, Paternoster Square. To be lost among naked pastiches and jumbled statuary in a phoney Italian piazza, a project waved through on the strength of its avoidance of concrete brutality and late-modernist self-regard.

Dominant colours: dirt-rose, morbid soot, pigeon shit. The railway stations have been around so long they have become accepted natural features. Like cliffs or mountains. London grows its fossils by accretions of indifference. Vagrants return, nodding and ducking like cormorants, to the same perches and hollows.

The faces of travellers are pinched. They know about the bad thing. And all the forms it takes: viral, carnal, feral. Inevitable. They have seen the bad thing, felt its breath. And they dream it. With eyes wide open. Waiting and watching. Waiting for the bus, the lights, the mirror-flash of the speed-camera. The nudge of the petty thief at the cash machine. The spray of a fellow sufferer's germ donation wet on your neck. The thrust, into your midriff, of that free newspaper which is not free, but a minor contamination. The agreement that you are too tired to graze on anything better than television promos, football rage, war-horror blamed on someone else. Scapegoating. Flower-draped returns of the flying dead.

When Alan Moore scripted a comic-strip version of one of my fictional characters (looking alarmingly like his creator), in the 1910 cityscape of *The League of Extraordinary Gentlemen*, this balding Nazi dentist in the long green coat mutters, 'King's Cross though . . . I'd advise you to be careful. The place is a myth-sump, invites apocalyptic thinking, dangerous agendas hurrying to make their connection.'

Renchi Bicknell and Steve Dilworth barely connect. They are in discrete but parallel stories: that they are both artists, practitioners, only emphasizes the space between them. The weight of Steve's potential commissions and his cynical (or innocent) interplay with the realpolitik of GP funding are matters Renchi struggles to comprehend. The Glastonbury man walks and he waits. He solicits necessary difficulty, learning the etching process to undertake a series blending his own pilgrimages across England with a commentary on Blake's interpretation of Bunyan.

Both of the artists, the painter and the sculptor, chose to position themselves at a distance from London; one in the West Country, the other in the Hebrides. So this towpath excursion is undertaken on neutral ground. They have been sucked inwards by the gravity of the monumental schemes of land revision in the Lower Lea Valley. Renchi, playing off 2012 Mayan prophecies, fills his pockets with crushed glass from breakers' yards in Hackney Wick. He photographs wall art – crocodiles, skulls, teeth – which he sees as representing a spirit of opposition to the blue fence and its CGI-visions. Paint itself, dripping, smeared, is truth. Guerrilla artists, whatever their motives, collaborate with the architecture of ruin.

Living arms and hands intertwine with bindweed and yarrow. Pink-gummed mouths grin on concrete stumps.

Back home, Renchi made his paintings. But he returned to London, several times a year, to loop the Olympic Park and to extend the catalogue of loss. Banks of wild flowers, messages sprayed on a waste pipe. He registered disappearance and the pace of evolution, by weather, season, human intervention, from the period of his work as a Chobham Farm labourer, a gardener in Victoria Park, to the speedy present of GP invasion technology.

But the story is never so simple. Sweet Toof, one of the most prolific of the Hackney Wick muralists, achieved his transfer. I walked down Brick Lane, wondering at the pace with which territory cannibalizes itself, until there is literally nothing there, beyond the captive shadow, the eidolon. A stencilled name on the window of one of the new galleries caught my eye. On Fournier Street, Gilbert (or George), stepping out to post a letter, has to consider how much the act is a performance: how deep do they have to go to brush their naked toes against reality, whatever was here, forty years ago, before they put themselves up for sale, as prints of prints (and functioning humans also)? Tracey Emin, polite but confused, challenges a film crew in Princelet Street: why aren't they shooting *her*? Existence for a name artist is confirmed by regular infusions of publicity. He or she is a celebrity diabetic waiting for that insulin hit, the appearance of the latest diary extract, the photograph telling them just where they were last night. Accepting and sustaining a career fat with the illusion of success is a noble and self-sacrificing destiny. Wealth and fame are insufficient rewards for the pains and renunciations attendant on remaining an artist beyond art. When you are no longer visible in the magazines, the broadsheets, you are nowhere. A conical heap of mouse-dirt in an empty Whitechapel attic. Look at the fear engraved on those brave and troubled faces.

Sweet Toof had come indoors. They found him. At the precise moment when pressure hoses and industrial scouring agents were stripping paint from the concrete pillbox on the Greenway, reducing untold layers of graffiti to grey, the leading Hackney Wick bandit was a name on a window in Brick Lane. I kept going. I didn't check out the show. There's altogether too much art noise. I'm beginning to think that Gustav Metzger was right with his proposed strike: show nothing, make nothing, until the world changes. Taking a ride, back from the Wick, my companion pointed out an elderly man on Roman Road, encumbered with plastic bags, narrowly failing to persuade the bus to stop. 'It happens every day. Gustav Metzger. The driver takes a perverse pleasure in judging just how close he is going to let him get, before he pulls away.'

His art strike abandoned, Metzger's work was everywhere I travelled: Bexhill-on-Sea, Manchester, Edinburgh. Be as intransigent as you like, as much of a purist, they will search you out, the curators and promoters. Nothing is more seductive than the myth of abdication, silence. Nothing succeeds like well-managed failure. We live in an age of compulsory retrieval, exposure, downloading. With the boxed set of CDs as the final humiliation.

Steve Dilworth was in London for a reason. He had been shortlisted by Westfield to produce a suitable work of public art for the monster mall at the edge of the Olympic Park. When I met him, soon after I left Chobham Farm, in the early 1970s, Steve was the fiercest, truest to raw material, sculptor/maker I had encountered. In Cheltenham, I saw (smelt, felt) the crows he squashed, in some oily solution, between sheets of glass. I believe that, within weeks, they leaked and disintegrated. Dilworth was a scavenger and poacher, tolerated as gardener or handyman in a cottage on a private estate. He had grown up in Hull, and retained an icy, axe-carved Nordic profile, emphasized by beetling ginger brows: as he roamed and ravaged, settling anywhere but the home town from which he had escaped.

Dilworth was the kind of ecologist who kills and cooks and eats: no theory beyond action. He wove curtains of glossy, reeking eels. He stitched salted pigskin figures. He carved elaborate caskets of whalebone, to contain – take his word for it – stormwater taken at midnight from the bay.

He removed, with his family, to a house on the edge of the sea, on the Isle of Harris: to enjoy a harsh subsistence life, scouring the shore for molluscs for the evening cauldron, and dead things, birds, hares, even cats, for his shamanic practice. The whole business, as he stuck with it for so many years, was unexploitable. Some of the smaller stones, polished and crafted, were seductive: as pipes, whistles, fetish objects. But everything was conducted on his own terms. The difficulties, the hardship, the muscular energy contained within his necrophile art. There were no workshop assistants, no explainers. A rusty old deep-freeze unit stuffed with ex-seagulls, roadkill, the battered detritus of the Atlantic.

Steve's hospitality was legendary. A table for discussion, anecdote, drink and talk, through the long, dank, dripping afternoons of the Hebridean winter. The island, in its tribal allegiances and attitudes, as well as its geology, was spectacularly other. Steve told me that Stanley Kubrick, with the use of judicious red filters, discovered in the rock fields of Harris a convincing equivalent for Jupiter, for his film *2001: A Space Odyssey*. I never saw so many car wrecks alongside twisting ribbon-roads in a landscape that had no use for twentieth-century frivolity. Dilworth, restless and driven, was in the right place. However furiously he worked, he was out-sculpted by the processes of weather, a place where time was just beginning.

After a lucky find on the beach, Steve proposed an arch made from a whale's jaw. The plan was accepted by sponsors, before being blocked by local opposition, caught up in family feuds going back to the Jacobites and beyond. But his work started to appear in sculpture parks and gardens. Never tamed, aerodynamic in polished bronze, the Dilworth beast-boxes were exposed in London galleries, and described in the formal language of Arp and Brancusi. That's why we were walking down the canal in the direction of King's Cross.

Coming off the water, the revised topography around the King's Place development, at the back of the great railway terminal, was disorientating: resistant glass blocks, swirling winds wrapping debris around the legs. There is no obvious access to any of these revamped

warehouses and architectural calling-cards. No sense of the function they perform. Twenty minutes inside King's Place, Renchi
decided, was the outer limit of human endurance. There is a low-
level electronic hum, enough to keep the nerves on edge, before
stoking them with a caffeine hit at the coffee franchise where shifty
transients are trying to look as if they belong. Temperature is
cranked that notch too high: the building doesn't need you, keep
moving. Open-plan newspaper offices. Corridors that are galleries.
Galleries that are corridors. Subterranean seminar facilities for cultural pep talks, presentations, performances. And two pieces by
Steve Dilworth. One of which, a brazen bug-on-its-back out of
Kafka, has been sited right beside the down escalator. The Hebridean imperative, frozen in corporate ennui, fights to assert itself: as
a structure independent of its environment. Culture clients are
tempted to treat the smooth bowl as a receptacle for polystyrene
cups and greasy wrappings. Anything left lying about is cast in silver
and displayed in a glass cabinet.

Steve is in town for the preliminary assessments, a courtesy tour of
the Westfield building site, some triangle sandwiches curling under
strip lights. As we advanced on 2012, so the nightsweat desperation,
to find proper GP sculptural ballast, ratcheted up: the vision men
tossed out a £15-million teaser. I met a veteran of many successful
public art commissions at a memorial event for J. G. Ballard at Tate
Modern. Her first life-changing inspiration, she told me, was being
taken as a child to see Ballard's exhibition of crashed cars. Shift of
context, that's all it takes: the outside brought inside and re-labelled.
She'd already received the paperwork, now circulating among blue-
chip names, for something, *anything*, big enough and dumb enough
to be called iconic, as the Olympic Park paperweight. 'The budget's
getting close to Kapoor and Gormley,' she said. 'They need the
names, even if there's no money left in the pot to go beyond a
maquette. That giant horse for Ebbsfleet will never be built.'

   Dilworth wanted background information on Stratford, its history, topography, myths. The only useful advice I could offer was:

keep my name out of it. The Olympic borough of Newham had followed Hackney in declining to allow a book event, featuring a stellar line-up of dissenting East London authors and academics, into one of their flagship buildings. The show transferred to the Bishopsgate Institute in the City. Where the group photo, creased suits and severe spectacles lined up along a high table, made us look like the Politburo.

In many ways, the essential literature of the GP era is the proposal, the bullet-point pitch, the perversion of natural language into weasel forms of not-saying. Dilworth, whose art as I understood it, was raw, impulsive and essential, was obliged to collaborate with a graphic designer on a PR document intended to flatter the inadequacies of the commissioning brief.

SAIL: Iconic Sculpture Proposal. Landmark Sculpture for WESTFIELD, Stratfordcity.

Reading this strategic bilge, I winced at section headings undoing, boast by boast, everything Dilworth had previously achieved. 'Iconic and Identifiable'. 'A Signifier'. 'Connecting with the Image of Stratford'. 'Timeless and Multicultural'. 'Water Feature Engagement'. 'Environmental Concerns'. 'Safety Issues'.

Safety issues? After years of meat-stitching, harpooning, crowcrushing, rock-wrestling? The transformation was absolute. A horn, in the form of a sail, was computer-inflated to mall-dominating prominence. It accepted a social identity as a 'way marker' and 'meeting point' for blue-fence ghosts. And offered a nod in the direction of 'a long history of trading, with the River Lea connecting to the Thames estuary and beyond'. The 'conceptual core' would reach back to 'Viking occupation and earlier'. The weight was calculated at fifteen tonnes, but was deemed to be light enough for 'removal prior to the Olympic Games'.

I can't blame Steve for being seduced by the possibility of realizing funds for more sympathetic projects, or for wanting to present his work on an epic scale. Mallworld is where the money is, if you are not the kind of marquee name to underwrite the regeneration of a landfill site down the A13, a mining operation outside Doncaster, or a maritime City of Culture. And if, bollock naked, you are not allowed to bestride the Alps like Hannibal.

Dilworth was one of those who made the China trip. With the architects, politicians, car salesmen and poets. Renchi, when he travelled, favoured the high country: Nepal, the American Northwest, Peru. Trail-walking, camping, sketching, taking part in spiritual exercises and native ceremonies. Steve, inspecting stone-carving operations for one of his commissioned public sculptures, was a mid-air Sinologist, shuttling between past and future Olympic venues.

We listened to the stories of his adventures, the meals eaten, the craftsmen encountered in a south-eastern Chinese city given over to the production of white stone lions for restaurants in Hull and Peterborough. A few weeks later, when he had gone back to Harris, Dilworth was generous enough to present me with the handwritten journal of his trip to a tourist city in the Fujian Province.

Friday 30th March 2007. Well, here I am, my first full day in China. Still jet lagged, couldn't sleep for the electric buzzing, cotton wool stuffed in my ears.

About to be picked up to be taken to the stone yard, to inspect the work. First impressions – big city, funny start. Cathy met me at the airport, flagged down a taxi and jumped the queue. Police stopped taxi, told off driver for taking us. Taxi nearly crashed, oil in the road. Pleased my credit card is recognized by hotel, worried when phone on plane, and in airport, didn't work.

Driver came unstuck on the bridge coming back into Xiamen, cut up a car. No real damage, but the other party wanted to call the police, lots of shouting. Police took photos. The driver had a habit of noisily clearing his throat every 20 minutes and spitting out of the window. He came with me to have noodles. Every time he had a sip of beer he insisted on clinking glasses. Taught him to say 'sláinte'.

The stone yard looked impressive and the work force gathered round. Took their pictures and drank cups of tea, then off to restaurant, private room and seafood lunch. Dried fish, a kind of small whelk, two types of fish, squid, soy bean stalks, chilli sauce, rice. Prawns. Too much to finish.

On the drive out the pollution combined with fog was dispiriting, all that crap in the air. On the way back the sun was yellow-orange in the sky, doing its best to get through.

Saturday evening, 31st March. Everything seems either to be under construction or from the late Sixties – People's Revolution? Bought a couple of dried sea slugs, some dried pipe fish, dried cockles (I think). Photos of odd fish, crabs, frogs, in front of a restaurant. Tempted to step inside and ask for a live frog to go.

A museum of freak animals, two-headed sheep, a live dove with 2 extra deformed legs and a tortoise that needed space. Animal husbandry is not a big priority in China. Felt really sorry for the squirrel turning aimlessly in a cage. Cage was locked. I couldn't release it, without ending up in gaol.

Back on the mainland island of Xiamen (the ferry shuttles back and forth), then off for a foot massage. It was like getting beaten up (by a young woman, about 20 maybe). God, I felt the pressure points, but after an hour completely relaxed: when she left the room, I didn't notice. Cost 28 CNY (about £2), ridiculously cheap. I felt relaxed at last. All paid for by Cathy.

Monday 2nd April. Yesterday I went to the Buddhist temple. Beggars gather here. A young boy with seriously deformed skull. A girl playing on a stringed instrument looked blind, skin tight, ear almost gone. Others with lumps for feet. No social security. Sink or swim. Rather sink if it were me. Living in the hotel in the lap of luxury and seeing abject poverty is odd, can't do anything about it, give a few yen.

Afternoon: watching TV in hotel. Thunderstorm outside, quite cold. Off to restaurant at six for wedding celebration. First, get some flowers for the bride.

Meal made up for everything. Rice spirit is strong. Wine a bit rough. Food kept coming, this was the final bash after weeks of celebrating. Each day different.

Started with sweet soup, then every kind of sea food. Jellied sea worm, jelly fish. Clams in shells, big crayfish, fish steamed. Black chicken soup. Just kept going. Chestnuts and broccoli. Ending with sweet soup. Lots of toasts and clinking of glasses. They wanted to see if I drank. Years of living on Harris came into its own.

Wandered into a bookshop and bought a drawing pad and a book of Chinese blessings. A tea shop. A Chinese guy sat down and introduced himself - Michael - retired from running a restaurant in San Francisco. Spends half his time in Xiamen, the winter in America. Drank so much tea. Oddly enough, tea is very expensive, even by western standards. Shops specialize in one type of tea only. As it gets older, so it gets more expensive.

Wednesday 4th April. To the stone yard, to see the progress. Knocked out by the work, just polishing stage to complete.

Struck by the amount of sculpture, every 50 yards, both sides of 6-lane road into town. Something for everyone, classic Chinese humour to contemporary art.

An old lady was attempting to cross the 6-lane road with a cow in front of her. My driver used his horn, instead of slowing down. People pull straight into the road in front of on-coming traffic. Zebra crossings are killing zones.

Beggars in the market. I'm an easy and obvious target. Guy with no arms, thalidomide type, got a dollar. So did another poor soul. Don't know what to do, maybe check out the university gallery.

Friday 5th April. Checked my emails. Joan tells me that there is just £800 left on the credit card. Did the hotel help themselves when they swiped it? Or has there been some other sort of fraud? Asked Joan to give me a call, while I try to figure out what the score is. My worst nightmare. Trying not to panic. Thinking about worst case scenarios.

Back from a long walk into the old market. Caught again by beggars, three of them. I gave one a dollar to help my karma! Stopped at least twice by gaggles of girls wanting to have photographs taken with me. Bought a CD of Chinese music and a sable brush. Still stressing. I'm not sure I will sleep at all, but I'm too tired to care.

There are various possibilities

a. Get the collector to pay direct.

b. Get my dealer to pay in lieu of money from show.

c. Kill myself.

d. Get my brother to pay.

It's 2am in Britain and I will miss my flight if I'm held up in any way.

Came back to find them in the middle of cleaning the room, so went out for another walk. Thought I'd have a foot massage. Should have guessed there was something not quite right. Shown into a room with maybe sixty or seventy reclining chairs. Started to take off my boots and socks. Guy came in and said, 'No foot massage'. Another guy offered girl for sex, so I left.

Phone call from Joan at 5am. £800 has disappeared from the credit card account but there is still enough left to pay bill. Big relief. Will find out what the score is on my return. Obviously some fraud going on.

Last night playing pool with Cathy's boyfriend. Big upstairs hall, maybe eighty tables. Pint glasses of cold tea. Back at hotel about 11.30. Had a beer and listened to the cabaret, two Chinese girls singing something that sounded like it came from the Robin Hood, Prince of Thieves film.

Tried to find the new city art museum – vast, but still being built. Great sculptures of sails. I find the 'can do' quality very impressive and inspiring, when I think of the commissioning process back in the UK. You might as well not bother. Serious money is needed to do anything on a reasonable scale. All that 'community' rubbish and hand-wringing arty social workers.

Had an attack of balance disturbance, floor like a boat. A bit worried, but I won't dwell on it. Took one of the pills the doctor gave me the last time it happened.

Back to the tea shop to meet up with Michael – who didn't show. Had an entertaining time drinking green tea and learning Chinese. Going to karaoke tonight.

The sculpture yard town is by the sea, although I didn't realize this until my last visit. Six-lane road, loads of statues, some Christian things. A bit like Basingstoke or maybe Slough. Evidence of new building everywhere.

Sore throat. Down at the stone yard, dusty as hell. Work is fine. Talk about transport. They seem to know what they're doing. Everything should be fine. Home tomorrow.

I don't suppose I'm that different from most Brits who have never been to China but have fixed opinions about human rights, dog eating, military dictatorships.

I remember talking to some guys in a stone yard in Aberdeen. Most of their work being done 'out in China, for a bowl of rice a day'. I'll have to tell them now, it ain't like that.

There is something genuine in this experience, the mid-air cultural tourism. But I don't, from Steve's journal, know quite what it is. The food, the massage, the beggars, the fraud: they are all available on Bethnal Green Road. And the dust. Yellow sun behind the fug of development. Dilworth's relish for the fish and the tea and the museums. His exposure to beggars, cripples, caged animals. His apparent lack of interest in the totality of the landscape, how this city connects with the river, the port, the rest of China. It becomes overwhelming, those days waiting for your soul to catch up. The flash-memories of wife, daughters, home.

I remember a television documentary taking Jim Ballard back to Shanghai, the family house like a Surrey stockbroker's villa where another life might have unfolded. How it required extraordinary feats of self-interrogation to contrive a valid response to the accidents of biography.

A man, at Ballard's Tate Modern memorial tribute, introduced himself as the second-biggest collector in the world. He had one of about fifteen copies in existence of the pulped Doubleday edition of *The Atrocity Exhibition*. Very recently he had acquired a prize item: a single authenticated brick from the now-demolished school, adapted by war into the Lunghua camp, the cave of memory in which Ballard was interned for those formative years that made him a writer.

Westfield Wonderland

To cheat the future and find out what was coming to Stratford, I headed further west: to Shepherd's Bush. A giant Westfield mall had now opened, with the approval of Ken Livingstone, central government, style magazines, and anyone else with a weakness for the sublimely ridiculous. The madness to which we were terminally mortgaged had arrived in the disguise of a sleek, vanity-project swimming pool, looking as if it were there to demonstrate the readiness of some ambitious provincial city to welcome the Commonwealth Games (circa late 1950s, early 1960s). A chlorine-green block, brand identity in italicized script, rising out of one of those nuisance clumps of urban wilderness that occupy grunge nowheres between busy feeder roads. Doing nothing, up for grabs. The excuse for a traffic-jammed ramp. Westfield, this post-architectural storage shed, giving nothing away as to form or function, is both a beacon statement and a portal to the underexploited west of old suburbs and dormitory clusters. Vanished railway towns. Villages waiting for the canals to revive. The planning thesis being to free up congestion by taking more cars off the road: they will all be stacked (at a price) in Westfield's limitless parking bays. You can connect, from the revamped Shepherd's Bush station, with Croydon and Brighton. And if the journey ahead is fearsome enough, you'll be in no hurry to leave. Westfield is a metaphor for eternity, as a waiting room, a zone you can't escape, never having properly arrived.

When I fall into conversation with one of the dozens of photographers roaming this winter wonderland, he is astonished to learn that there will very soon be *another* Westfield, a duplicate of the duplicate: out east, in Stratford. This definitive non-space, a managed illusion, is nothing more than a rehearsal for the grandest project of them all, the zillion-pound consumer hive that is the only guaranteed legacy of the 2012 Olympics. The final solution, the great theory of everything, has achieved resolution: Westfield. Where art meets aspiration. A toy box constructed to look as if it had been put on earth to star in a disaster movie. To straddle a fault in the earth's crust. To go up in flames. To come apart in waterfalls of tumbling, slow-motion glass.

No question about it, the funny-money retail cathedral is New Labour's response to the meltdown of the financial markets. A spectator sport for those who can no longer afford to service the debt on their debt. Shops are strictly for browsing. The profit is in the car park. In coffee rewards. And fast-food pit stops for low-ranking BBC personnel taking any excuse to get out of White City: for a glimpse of sky, between studio labyrinth and this enclosed and airless city of non-penetrative consensual consumption.

Current political dogma chimes with Westfield's philosophy, as revealed in a set of lavish promotional brochures, so self-important that you expect them to appear soon in some dealer's rare-book catalogue: 'Being and Buying. Lifestyle, not just product.' Jean-Paul Sartre-lite for shopaholics. Walter Benjamin doing Saatchi-speak. A dying political regime, having presided over a shitstorm of mounting hysteria and unpoliced greed, lets us understand that it is our civic duty to shop until we drop. The twin Westfield estates, subsidized traffic islands, are the contemporary equivalent of the baroque churches Nicholas Hawksmoor thumped down in lawless riverbank regions of East London. Goodbye six-inch nails, mousetraps, brown paper, bottles of ink, sugar buns, evening newspapers. The anarchic horizontal pedestrianism of the Bush is superseded by the verticality of the secure monolith. Exclusion zones with parking for 4,500 cars. The selling point of Westfield is that it's easy to get away, to go somewhere else. New station, new connections, new roads: when you are here, you are not *here*. It is barely worth struggling out of the car. Turn straight round, after that compulsory coffee hit, and you might beat the rush hour.

What my new photographer friend doesn't get, the thing that makes him so nervous he needs help to secure his tripod, is the fact that he's been snapping away for an hour and he hasn't been arrested. There's plenty of visible security, but they behave like Photoshop clones: other-worldly, have-a-nice-day smiles, open-handed waves. Retail parks of the old school, Lakeside or Bluewater, are defined by a total prohibition on freelance imagery. Lift a camera, as I once did, in the car park of Ikea at Thurrock, and you'll get an insight into what the Berlin Wall was about. Try coming up with a coherent explanation of why it's worth recording the pattern of lines on the grid of parking bays or the colours on the trolley of the Kwik Fit squeegee operatives. When they allow you to photograph anything that takes your fancy, you know something is out of kilter. You've accessed a whole new game. When there is nothing to hide, you are in the wrong place.

'Roads surrounding the 23-acre mall were in chaos last night with up to mile-long tailbacks,' reported the *Evening Standard*. 'Motorists complained of half-hour queues to travel just a few hundred yards.' And this despite a £200-million upgrade on the traffic infrastructure (closures, eternal road works). The major jam is in reaching the jam, escaping the low-ceilinged short-term-Heathrow parking bays. It's a form of a reality TV endurance test, played out on 680 CCTV cameras. 'I'm a consumer, get me out of here.'

Journos and puffers eager to take on any excursion that gets them out of the house came to a near unanimous verdict on the Westfield experience: wow! They loved it, almost as much as they once loved the Millennium Dome. 'Never had occasion to go near such a thing before, but it's rather jolly. The food, *you can eat it*.' Tame hacks suspend reflexes conditioned by dismal expectations of motorway service stations and airport holding pens to deliver their tributes to bling enterprise, strictly-come-shopping frivolity. Blizzards of top-dollar PR – 'think try-out zones, pop-up stores' – launch the vast permafrost barn like a James Bond film premiere. Like the Turner Prize on ice. A complimentary champagne bar soliciting thank-you notes in the form of column inches.

The western suburbs are parasitical on Heathrow, not Kensington or Knightsbridge. The new Shepherd's Bush mall (twenty minutes by cab from check-in) is a duty-free zone, an improved and extended version of the downtime limbo of waiting-for-your-flight-to-be-called. More shopping, less flying. It's as if they took the former West London Terminal at Cromwell Road and filled it with discounted Harrods stock for a year-long sale. Then re-assigned upbeat hostesses in combat make-up, heels and name tags to point out the nearest exits. Heathrow is as much a period piece as J. G. Ballard's favoured emporium, the Bentall Centre in Kingston-upon-Thames. The model for his fundamentalist mall in *Kingdom Come*. Airports are so solipsistic these days, so embar-rassed about their role as bucket-shop service stations, less glamorous than the Watford Gap, that they have taken to hiring philosophers to make them sound more interesting. Like prisons, oil rigs and Championship football clubs, Heathrow made a play for our sympathies by signing a writer in residence. Hoping that, in a flush of positive media coverage, we would forget about the mountains of lost luggage somewhere in Italy and the escalators that refused to escalate. Ballard reckoned that airport roads are the same everywhere: sheds, generic hotels, car lots, pharmaceutical companies. And a vague sense of dread. Will Self, a literalist, exam-ined the thesis by walking it.

Westfield is an extension of the Westway, that vestigial road in the sky. The landing strip of a flight simulator. A Ballard theme park from the time of *Concrete Island*. A teasing figment of a Bauhaus potentiality that never happened.

Escaping London, suddenly privileged drivers note Ernö Goldfin-ger's 31-storey brutalist stack, the Trellick Tower: which was completed in 1972, two years before the publication of Ballard's novel, his recasting of Daniel Defoe. Robert Maitland, prisoner of *Concrete Island*, suffers a blow-out to the front near-side wheel of his Jaguar, before plunging down an embankment, 'six hundred yards from the junction with the newly built spur of the M4 motorway'. Taking that invented spur for the Shepherd's Bush slip road and its connection with the western motorway, six hundred yards would land the confused motorist somewhere in the future Westfield site. Maitland is an architect. Westfield is his posthumous dream.

'Rising above the crowded nineteenth-century squares and grim stucco terraces, this massive concrete motion-sculpture is an heroically isolated fragment of the modern city London might have become,' Ballard wrote in his contribution to a collection of fragments known as *London: City of Disappearances*. 'Westway, like Angkor Wat, is a stone dream that will never awake. As you hurtle along this concrete deck you briefly join the twentieth century and become a citizen of a virtual city-state borne on a rush of radial tyres.'

By describing what he saw before him, a vision of multiple realities, Ballard located Westfield before it was conceived, before it achieved its optimum state as a laptop doodle. Construction was unnecessary and ill advised. Fiction road-tests the future without obligation to buy. Novels, dreams that do not fade, hook themselves on the perimeter fence of the culture like flapping rook wings of black plastic. First the variants appear, consciously and subconsciously, in other books. Then films, television. And, finally, GP architecture: the art of original quotation. Robert Maitland's Jaguar, catastrophe in suspension, surfaces (along with the Defoe reference) in Chris Petit's 1993 novel, *Robinson*. The narrator, falling-down drunk, is taken into a multi-storey car park, given the keys to a Jag, and invited to put his foot down when he hits the Westway.

Questioned about this sequence, Petit said that, at the time of writing, Ballard was not a direct influence. He was remembering his own film, *Radio On*. Being high on a tower block, suffering from vertigo, getting the panoramic shot of a car leaving town. 'The car,' he wrote, 'seemed to drive itself, responding to the merest suggestion, whispering forward with us cocooned in leather-bound silence, protected behind the cinemascope windscreen.'

Robinson opens with twin epigrams. One is from Ballard: 'Deep assignments run through all our lives; there are no coincidences.'

The other is from the poet Weldon Kees, a man who vanished, perhaps jumping from a bridge, perhaps changing identity. Kees writes of: 'Robinson alone . . . staring at a wall.' At the unreadable blankness of Westfield? A barrier separating retail drifters on their elevated terraces from the ghosts of the hinterland, the crazed drivers flirting with suicide. And reading London's disposable ruins as recovered temples in the Cambodian jungle.

'A thin yellow light lay across the island,' Ballard wrote, 'an unpleasant haze that seemed to rise from the grass, festering over the ground as if over a wound that had never healed.'

A strip of land, trapped between stilted urban clearway and snarled feeder roads, ripe for the virus of investment capital. The block-building could be, but is not, a flagship hospital. A bug-breeding facility storing otherwise eliminated Victorian poverty plagues. A rumour factory like its neighbour, the White City BBC complex, where sweating politicians are being patted with powder, before going into a glass cubicle. Where they will be ventriloquized by sharp young men, outside the window, waving clipboards, nodding or miming throat-cut gestures.

Westfield does what airports do and does it better: the escalators work, you don't lose your luggage, there's a wide choice of near-food. And, above everything, swimming and swirling, there is: *light*. 'Very eclectic, very bold, very London.' Miniature clouds caught in the triangular panels of a celestial roof. Manufactured light. Imported light. Quotation light: waterfall-chandeliers of fizz and flash, star-fields of shimmer and glint. A ballroom of the vanities. We should be waltzing through the galleries, admiring our own reflections, not creeping like zombies in diving shoes.

I started to write a letter to Ballard, describing the Westfield set in terms of *Kingdom Come,* and all the other fictions and essays he had produced, in anticipation of this event. But it was pointless. The space had substance as somewhere imagined, not experienced. Psychopathic potentialities, tried and tested in Ballard's honed language formulae, made the *fact* of the mall seem dull and obvious. It is not that his stories prophesied a certain type of architectural folly: they made such things redundant, ridiculous. And therefore perfectly suited to the landscape into which Australian developers had brokered a loud introduction. The trick with Ballard's invented architects, Robert Maitland in *Concrete Island*, Anthony Royal in *High-Rise*, is that they don't build anything; they suffer the consequences of building. Materially successful, detached, they are the equivalents of the deracinated poets who populate the mythology of the Chilean novelist Roberto Bolaño. Poets are speakers, silenced by the world: invisibles. Architects are watchers, connoisseurs of entropy, appreciating from a high balcony the physics of smoke and sunlight across a burning city.

'I remembered my last moments in the dome,' Ballard wrote in *Kingdom Come*, 'looking back at the fires that raced along the high galleries from one store to the next . . . I watched the spectators around me, standing silently at the railing . . . In time, unless the sane woke and rallied themselves, an even fiercer republic would open the doors and spin the turnstiles of its beckoning paradise.'

I've never been much good at recognizing a division between fiction and reality, past and future, this place and that place. Does it help to know that Chris Petit, ransacking his memory-bank for *Robinson*, recalled the Jaguar he bought, second hand, on the day of his son's birth in 1984? Does the tyre that blew on Ballard's Ford Zephyr lose legitimacy by being shifted from Chiswick to the Westway? Photographs taken, after the crash, leave the vehicle, according to the author, looking fit for Athens or Havana. Petit, speaking of days riding around East Berlin in a white Jaguar, the only one in town, is smoothing the routine for a future novel. Ballard has frequently credited his friend and partner, Claire Walsh, as something more than the inspiration for the character Catherine in *Crash*: Claire *is* Catherine. 'Shall I call her Claire?' he asked. 'Better not.' But the narrator remains: James Ballard.

Now, after more than forty years in Shepperton, after numerous interviews, accounts of deckchair, Delvaux duplicates, overgrown yucca in window, Ballard was unwell. Sick enough to relocate to Claire's flat in Shepherd's Bush, in the lee of Westfield. Closer to hospital and oncologist for those unforgiving sessions of chemo, less therapy than stoically borne endurance test. A memoir, *Miracles of Life*, is an elegantly composed realignment, generous in spirit, of the accidents of autobiography, the tricks and tropes of a long career. In organizing so much material, paying tribute to so many dead colleagues and loves, reconciling hurt, dissolving feuds, he crafted the most perfect fiction of them all: the imitation of truth.

A number of Ballard's favoured restaurants, where he entertained family and friends, were hit hard by the advent of the Westfield monster. And by the strategic relocation of BBC staff to Salford, a banishment many found hard to endure. The Hilton Hotel, close to the Shepherd's Bush roundabout, was a conveniently neutral site for interviews and public debriefings. 'The biggest problem facing civilization,' Ballard observed, 'is finding somewhere to park.' There was a slot, on the other side of the road, opposite the hotel. The only occasion I can remember when he became a little tetchy and abrupt, suspending his reflex bonhomie, happened in a late-season deluge. A broadsheet portraitist, oblivious of Ballard's age and frailty, pushed him to pose on the concrete island of the roundabout. You can see the idea: road, rain, film noir mac. 'One more, just one more.' The photographer grabbed him by the elbow and thrust the distinguished author into the whip of traffic. Courtesy has its limits. In turning his back, and striding away, Ballard was signalling the final dissolution of human spirit from a topography that could be abandoned to ghosts, developers, image-jockeys and architects who never go into the office.

'But what is Westfield actually *like*?' you demand. It's like everything, as I've been struggling to tell you, and it is nothing. Like the stuff we used to call money. Forty minutes, palms sweating, teeth on edge, is my record in the Bluewater quarry. In Westfield, it's a comfortable two hours before the over-cranked heating system and the low-level electronic hum saps my energy to the point where a jolt from one of the twenty-two coffee outlets won't mend it. That's the really disturbing thing, Westfield is like everywhere.

'Boutique restaurants. Eat anywhere in the world without leaving West London.'

The floating mall is a pristine Dubai air terminal. A motorway university in Uxbridge. The headquarters of Channel 4. A private hospital on the Peterborough ring road. A canalside arts venue in King's Cross. A David Adjaye Idea Store (ex-library) in Whitechapel. A sleek logistics bunker in Beckton, low enough not to be a hazard to incoming aircraft. Westfield is copywriting made manifest. A template for faux-Ballardian prose. The hype is the truth: *the only secret*. In smoothly curated non-space, you operate below (or above) the level of ordinary human experience. You are inside the art and you are the art. Step on the elevator to retail heaven and you are making a political decision: pro-Olympic Park, blue-sky thinking. You have cast your phone-in vote for politics without alignment. You are a premature coalitionist, as rubber-smooth as Cameron-clegg. The only building in London with greater dissociation from the surrounding landscape is the new council property in Hillman Street, Hackney. Westfield has a warmer welcome: they can't wait to swipe your credit cards.

My journey from Liverpool Street on the Central Line was swift and uneventful. (Which was, in itself, an event.) I took the scatter of white stone eggs at the entrance, where you might expect benches, to be a sculptural gesture, the Brancusi head lice of an aspirational icon: before weary shopper-performers stumbled out of the hangar to straddle them. The stones are exhibits on which to perch, but not sprawl (no vagrants, no readers, no drinking schools). At Westfield, inside is outside and outside is inside. Live green hedges authenticate enclosure, while metallic trees, frosted with silver ball bearings, dress the avenue of approach. The premature gush of a water feature duplicates the wave patterns of an undulating roof.

The proper response, stepping through the mall entrance, is a happy slap of enchantment: a great tree of the world with dancing shadows. Friendly personnel at check-in stations will give you a map if you're too dumb to operate the touch-screen features. Westfield has an abundance of choice: if you are after handbags or knickers. I have a shopping list with four items. An inkjet for my printer. Contact lens sterilizing solution for my wife. A foodie book by Richard Corrigan for a relative. And one-hour development for the rolls of 35mm analogue film that I've been shooting so promiscuously. One out of four isn't bad. Travelling on to Oxford, I got the rest, in seven minutes, on the High Street. But in the Shepherd's Bush retail cornucopia? No inkjets (no Ryman). Contact lens fluid only available in bumper packs. Corrigan: not in stock. One branded photo outlet is exclusively digital and the Boots processing counter is unmanned. 'Our store colleagues are happy to help.' If you can track them down. I do, eventually, and get my rapid service (but not in the size I request). 'Do you have a Boots card?'

The Westfield hangar, in which customers do their own harvesting, is themed around an ersatz otherness. Reality is spun like sugar: PR made actual. Kiosks and 'concierge desks' soothe the flow of aimless pedestrianism. Comfort stations are plentiful, a lot of space for ablutions, but only three male troughs per unit. My soap dispenser wasn't working and had been replaced by a self-squeeze plastic bottle. The Ladies' cubicles, also in groups of three, are in dark wood, and reach to the ceiling. A claustrophobic experience, so I'm told. Theatrical, intimidating, and attended by first-night queues.

With uniformed police walking around in couples, with controlled exits, floors above floors, figures endlessly processing, there is a suggestion of the Panopticon prison. Relieved to be back outside, in the damp air, I rested for a moment on one of the steps. When I arrived home, I found lines of black lead striped across my pale trousers: a penitential metaphor. Every day the narrow trenches on these steps are refilled. You have to be spry to avoid a soaking from the cascade that can suddenly erupt from another ledge under a screen of genuine-fake greenery. Retail athleticism and Westfield are the perfect marriage. The Shepherd's Bush fortress is a memorial to a humbler event, the 1908 White City Olympics, marketed on heritage postcards as 'The Great Stadium'.

From 29 July to 14 August 1948, this part of London was the focus for the post-war Olympics, the 'Austerity Games'. A triumph of bodging and fudging, making do. We were bankrupt anyway. Competitors slept in Nissen huts, camped in RAF barracks, rode on buses. They slogged through mud and clay. The whole flickering black-and-white affair ran like an Ealing Comedy sports day. The human element was visible, unsmothered by corporate interventions. Nothing was torn down, there were no primary strategic objectives, no directions of travel. The city was already in ruins and athletes arriving here from around the world, sharing the lean times, helped to bring London back to life. Athletes were still within the compass of ordinary experience: survivors of war, schoolgirls, housewives, students, factory workers taking time off. The cult of elitism – fat-cat officials, slipstreaming politicians, reserved traffic lanes, Mayfair hotels – was not yet established and endemic. Nobody realized that the presentation of the event was bigger than the event itself: that gold medals were a measure of development potential. That the labouring competitors were tramping the ground flat for Westfield.

As 2012 approached, the GP mindset exhibited itself in a series of funded debates, seminars and 'Urban Laboratory' manifestations. I attended several of these, sometimes being invited to perform as a token dissident. The shocking aspect was quite how large the regiment of fixers, puffers, bagmen, and conceptualizers, parasitical upon the Olympics, actually was. Correspondents were appointed years before the stadium started to rise from the radioactive soil. Design for London imagineers. Legacy Masterplan magicians. Parks and Public Realm core philosophers. Leisure space enablers. Sustainable development consultants. Team leaders for integrated solutions. And, worst of all, weasel subversives, such as myself, enjoying their status as sanctioned critics corrupt enough to accept a fee for preaching disaster.

One show trial, under the appropriately resurrectionist title of 'Growing a New Piece of City: Designing an Olympic Legacy for 21st Century London', took place in an anatomy theatre. We were under instruction to talk for no more than ten minutes. All of the participants were on the payroll, deeply mortgaged to the vision of the Olympic Park. They were smooth, lean, smart. They didn't get their hands dirty. They were uncontaminated by any kind of dust. I pictured: open-plan offices, ethically sourced coffee, foldaway bicycles. These were not bad people, they had families, friends. They went out for meals. They talked about war, poverty, music, films, property prices and eco-apocalypse (especially that). But they would not, and could not, do time.

I was convinced that my earlier hunch was right: buried inside the oval of the stadium was a particle accelerator. Relativity, the old Lea Valley space–time mush, was being scrambled. Outside the circuit of the blue fence, voodoo snakes, big-mouth crocodiles and eviscerated chickens were screaming on walls: Berlin '36. Mexico City '68. Munich '72.

Every speaker, words lost as they lisp into a defective sound system, has a laptop presentation. 'Big ideas delivered in 100 pieces.' They show the message on a screen. Then read it out. Ten minutes become twenty-five. The same maps, charts, projections. Lavender beds. Water features. No mention of money, toxic waste, dust clouds. The GP bureaucrats are hypnotized by banality, the abdication of content, infinitely obliging statistics. They can't stop until the computer programme runs out. Nanoseconds expand to deny oxygen to screaming brain cells. Systems closing down. You don't drift out into a contemplative reverie, seeing the Lea Valley as it once was: the state I achieved by sitting on a chair for the artists of the Eton Mission in Hackney Wick. We die into the inevitability of this horror, looping dead images until we begin to believe them.

People came up afterwards, none of them British, exiles living in

Hackney, Tottenham, Walthamstow, with versions of the same question. 'What can we do?' 'How can we stop it?'

'Nothing,' I said. 'The fix is in and it goes all the way. Bear witness. Record and remember.'

China Watchers

The history of contradiction lies in the ground of the body image as a co-ordinate of the written sound-play, so calibrated with signifying exchange that every part offers an assembly 'in the swim'.

– J. H. Prynne

Ben Watson, who juggled identities as late-punk poet and card-carrying member of the Socialist Workers Party, the SWP, accused me of promoting no values in the contemporary world beyond a belief in poetry. And he was right. Although that ragged umbrella kept the rain out, some of the time, it was never as cunning a device as the tarpaulin hood Ben used to stop himself going blind from the leakage of a stone-crazy theology: Frank Zappa, J. H. Prynne, William Burroughs, Walter Benjamin, free-jazz improvisation, language-hallucination, orthodox and unorthodox Cambridge Marxism, and (of late), with some tenderness, family. Which is to say that whatever knots, ethically, philosophically, you tie in the tongue, it comes down to the pattern of words on the page. The grunt of performance. The shape absence leaves on the landscape. Poets were dying too fast and it hurt.

The secret of Roberto Bolaño's great literary project, beyond his physical disappearance at the optimum moment, and the spectral record of movement, Chile through Mexico City to Spain, was this: poetry is conspiracy. Poetry is a virus. Poets, sick with pride, chosen and cursed, habitués of the worst bars, the grimmest cafés, night-birds, defacers of notebooks, feed on the glamour of truth. Immortality postponed. They are owl-heads, hawkers of misremembered quotations. Solitaries jealous of their hard-won obscurity. The Chilean novelist dies in another country, thereby securing his status and, more importantly, the *visibility* of his thick and complex novels. He maps a vagrant territory previously accessed in early Wenders or lethargic single-take sequences from Antonioni's *The Passenger*. Architectural sets in which death waits, unappeased. The Bolaño template is located in the drinkers' legends that grew up around the mysterious B. Traven, sitting at the foot of John Huston's bed, when he came to shoot *The Treasure of the Sierra Madre*. And in stories of Buñuel, banished to Mexico City to reinvent a fiercer brand of surrealism, and discovering instead the baroque beauty of slums, poverty, violence and fate. White light drumming on a bloody road.

Bolaño exploits apparent flaws, the shifty, unemployed and drifting nature of poets, as a key to unlocking the corruptions of history. A woman poet, a friend of poets, hides in a lavatory stall throughout the invasion of the university, at the time of the 1968 Olympics in Mexico City. She is sainted: the sole witness. Her unreliable confessions, her visions. Her physicality: how impossible it has become to carry the burden of memory through a rapidly diminishing life. The knowledge of hurt. And the hurt of knowledge. The way Bolaño's devices and desires, his American Nazis, his decadent European academics, all those readers of forgotten books, zero in on the killing fields of Mexican border towns fouled by ugly international industries, drug wars and the never-ending rapes and mutilations of expendable women. Newsprint fodder for late-rising poets. For the poetry that comes when poetry is over.

Locally, in the dog days of the GP era, between the rabid snarl of Thatcherism and Nude Labour's yelping corruption of language, poets stood down. Good poets. Poets it was painful to do without: Douglas Oliver, Barry MacSweeney, Bill Griffiths, Andrew Crozier, Richard Caddel, David Chaloner, R. F. Langley. And now, as I come to write this, Anna Mendelssohn (who was also known as Grace Lake). Peter Riley, a poet and former bookdealer rumoured to spend much of his time in Transylvania, circulated the news. 'Addenbrooke's Hospital, Cambridge, from the effects of a brain tumour. She had been seriously ill and disabled since June.'

Mendelssohn was a Bolaño character before the event, before the epic novels were contemplated; a life of poetry as (and in) politics. Shifting identities. European connections. Abortive actions. State retribution. And just that Bolaño quality of noble, slightly absurd defeat: broken monologues of accidental grace. With nobody, beyond the cabal, really listening. Poems surfacing, from time to time, in invisible booklets. A fact which neither diminishes, nor validates, their quality. It is, in the end, such an obvious demonstration of what the condition, the non-choice, of becoming a poet means: maddened productivity, confirmation of exilic and discounted status. The growing certainty that it is all for nothing.

Whenever I met Mendelssohn, which wasn't often, and usually in Cambridge (which doesn't count), I felt challenged, wrong-footed. There was a false note in whatever I was peddling. My membership of a covert society, to which you could not be elected, had long since elapsed: I was still working the same jaunty prose routines. Failing to keep quiet, failing to let the voices through, uncensored. Failing to fail. I could hear Anna Mendelssohn, in her borrowed boy's sweater, muttering as I read.

'A dead typewriter in a city where friends are made by appointment only,' she wrote, in her Grace Lake persona. Re-remembering, and reconfiguring, the London of 1971. My urban-pastoral Chobham Farm days. Her time in the Hackney commune, in Amhurst Road, as part of the Angry Brigade. When the blue Volkswagen of the Special Branch spooks arrived, the raiders from Stoke Newington found Anna Mendelssohn still in bed. They asked for her name. 'Nancy Pye,' she replied.

'Upon returning to this country in 1970,' she later commented, 'I was attacked, my own poetry seized, and my person threatened with strangulation if I dared utter one word of public criticism. I was unable to return to university at that point and was silenced.' The poet's gift for self-dramatization is obvious. The sense of being adrift in a world of symbols. At the mercy of poetry's unforgiving truth. Which arrives early and out of synch. Like Soutine's bedbugs nesting in the inner ear.

*

The poem of the city is a memory-construct. I didn't know how much longer this place could tolerate me. My radar beacons were going down at a furious rate, the buildings by which I navigated. Rain, washing away bridges in Cumbria, gloom-glamed canalside Hackney. A pub for a doomed estate, and before that for the working canal, made a last desperate attempt to rebrand: as the Overdraught. A mirthless joke soon to be given a punchline when its windows were steel-shuttered, while property jackals hung their boards in place of the pub's overpainted sign.

The filling station on the corner passed through all the stages on the way to entropy in a few months: functioning petrol pumps with attached inconvenience store (beggars blocking the doorway), potential artwork seductive in its abandonment, caravan invasion by dispersed Hackney Wick squatters. Then: bailiffs, boiler-suit heavies. Single torched caravan with demonic edgeland slogans. Tyre dump. Weed reservation backing on deleted laundry block. Yawning, flapping roof-structure above concrete pillars. Shell occupied by rats: fetid black box. Sweating walls lurid with anathemas on developers, bankers, politicians and named enforcers.

VOODOO IS BARBAROUS CAPITALISM CLOAKED IN MAGIC.

I thought about leaving London for a few months, travelling around the country to investigate and record sites of collapsed lottery-funded millennium projects, ghost-milk architecture. Many of these GP disasters had been wiped from the files. They never happened. The New Labour era was about a remorseless push towards a horizon that must, of necessity, remain out of reach: the next big idea. And about the mistakes of the past, best handled with a blanket apology delivered by a low-ranking minister, soon to be rewarded with a joke peerage. I would also make it my business to interview surviving poets, not as unacknowledged legislators, but as witnesses. Witnesses to their own dissolution. The ones in remote Welsh cottages. In flats on the south coast. In service stations perched on windswept northern hills. It was either that, a journey from which I would never come back, or China. The six orbital motorways of Beijing.

Mid-air people come in all shapes and sizes. The Beijing Olympic movie, regiments of perfectly synchronized, colour-coordinated figures, swaying and rippling in a stadium vaster than the desert which surrounds it, was world-changing. The breathtaking ballet of individualism disciplined in the common cause had been in rehearsal for a thousand years. Access to untapped wealth, a limitless labour force, all that *geography*, was overwhelmingly attractive. Business-men, advisers, curators: they twitched to the poetry of the masses. They orgasmed appreciation. Like Steve Dilworth, they kept journals: in the form of digital snapshots, vacant blogs. Academics were drawn by the romance of Arthur Waley and Ezra Pound. Translations of classical Chinese poets at the dawn of the modernist era, a scouring of our flaccid English lyric. They honoured William Empson, who was suddenly back in fashion, for his eccentric tenure as a teacher in China and Japan. The oriental gig was much more attractive than a duty visit to some vodka binge in Moscow: tractor factory, opera, state museum.

The significant landfall, for me, was the manifestation of J. H. Prynne on the 'banks of the Imperial canal in the eastern city of Suzhou, during the summer of 1991'. A fruitful contact was established between the most accomplished and formidable poet/teacher of these islands and a collective of local experimentalists. In an Afterword to a gathering by this Chinese Language-Poetry Group, Prynne wrote: 'The exotic remoteness of that location at once bids to compose an allegory of displacement, which in turn demands a fully prepared resistance.' The liquid haze of a canalside watercolour is drafted into Prynne's analysis of the problems faced by unsponsored poets who have found a legitimate dynamic in the field of difficulty. In being where they are: with no compulsion to decamp. Both sides of this poetic collaboration are engaged but properly wary: the setting persuades them to strike out, with reckless commitment, in 'the great aquarium of language'. A conference is convened at Pearl River. In June 2005 a select band of English poets accompany Prynne on his return flight to China. Their intention? 'To make forded crossings from English into Chinese and from Chinese across into English.' There is a language of the world made from 'wit, scepticism and cantilevered invention'. And now, suddenly, everything is in flow; currents are powerful, we lose our footing and look to be swept away.

It was the influence of this fable, revived symbols in a traditional landscape, that prepared me for the discovery of an expelled Chinese poet who was about to publish a book set on my own doorstep. Bloodaxe announced: *Lee Valley Poems* by Yang Lian. I loved the idea of this new angle of approach, even before I chased down the proof sheets. And, eventually, the book itself. A slender thing with reeds in mist.

'There is no international, only different locals,' says the poet. Now I would have to find him and learn how such a project had come about. Without admitting it, I was searching for a withdrawal strategy. Somebody capable of remaking the Olympic Park without the burden of prejudice and bitter resentment. A neon moon in the yellow river.

Yang Lian among the Hasids

Matías Serra Bradford arrived from Buenos Aires to deliver a lecture on Borges and Cortázar, a state-funded and well-attended event. He told me that Borges, in his final period, welcomed visits. The eyes were gone, but he was listed in the directory. Accessible to anyone who picked up the phone. He talked in a whisper of the London that never was: of Stevenson, Arthur Machen and M. P. Shiel. Like many Anglophile Argentines, the old man read more widely and eccentrically than our local critics, who seem to prefer pastiche to the real thing. He made better use of that reading too, understanding essence but forging it into something new and strange. A genial Minotaur in a mildewed labyrinth.

If poets were the hidden arbitrators, Matías was a conduit, a cut-out man, brokering exchanges between cultures and continents. He published, in an English-language newspaper in Buenos Aires, substantial essays on figures who barely registered in their own country. He might discuss Patrick Hamilton alongside David Gascoyne and Julian Maclaren-Ross. He edited an anthology, *La Isla Tuerta: 49 poetas británicos (1946–2006)*, gathering up a secret history that ran from William Empson, W. S. Graham, Nicholas Moore, by way of Prynne, Raworth, Douglas Oliver, to Bill Griffiths, Brian Catling and Barry MacSweeney. Facing texts, English/Spanish: Matías made the translations. 511 pp. Stiff buff self-wrappers. A quiet brick to hide among the stacks of smart-academic or dust-bunker bookshops across Europe. One of those objects, I imagine, to be adapted by spies for code systems. No innocent civilians would be plucking this one from the pine shelves.

The questing catholicism of Bradford's reading was demonstrated when he alerted me to an account of the curious passion Arthur Waley developed for the Lea Valley. The distinguished

Sinologist, collector and translator, liked nothing more than taking a skiff on the murky and polluted Hackney river. Hubert, Waley's brother, described Arthur, head in clouds, ignoring the floating dogs, drowned cats, fizzing scum from factory pipes, the sewage outflow. What he admired was: 'The abrupt way London ended there.' The River Lea was more than a border, more than a link, carrying walkers or rowers out into the Thames, back into rural Hertfordshire. With its reed beds, marshes, herons, kingfishers, wooded horizons, huge skies, the Lea was a crude but haunting translation of a classical Chinese landscape. Enough perhaps to let Yang Lian find what he was tracking down, in his exile, his estrangement: a clean page for the word-shapes he wanted to inscribe. 'Water tells nothing,' he wrote. 'I hear the boats in my body.'

Stamford Hill in the rain. Mushroom-men command the pavement. See-through prophylactics over the black trilbies of Orthodox Jews. Long black coats scurrying, with purpose, ballasted by plastic-protected bags, large enough to be constantly shifted from hand to hand. Wigged women and their captive children. Never the two together, the men and the women. Young males dressed old, burdened or given status by their uniform of difference. Is there some inherited ocular weakness? They don't see outsiders, invaders; they walk right through, push us aside. Time is a value. There are no wanderers, no open agendas. I have witnessed the youths, coats off, scampering in Springfield Park on Sunday mornings, chasing footballs, but I've never seen an Orthodox man rambling up the Lea, sprawled on a bench staring at the water. 'A bench,' Yang Lian says, 'sinks deep into its own nature.'

The Chinese poet, now living on the crest of the hill, above Abney Park Cemetery, beyond the Morrisons superstore, was born in Switzerland in 1955. He spent his childhood in Beijing. In the 1970s, along with so many others of the academic and diplomatic classes, he was sent into the countryside. His family were put to work on an agricultural commune. He remembers writing his first poem, after the death of his mother, by the soft light of a paraffin lamp. When he came back, years later, to revisit the village, it had been wiped out by a new pre-Olympic motorway.

Back in the city, Lian joined the group of poets associated with the literary magazine *Jintian*. His poem 'Norlang' was criticized by government agencies operating an 'Anti-Spiritual Pollution' programme. After the Tiananmen protests and the savage state response, he chose to become a poet in exile, settling in London in 1997.

I watched Lian perform, giving interviews at conferences and literary festivals in Germany: he was intense, voluble, committed to his perceived destiny. Which he laid out in what New Labour would call a mission statement: 'Give me a single breath and I will grow roots, penetrate the soil, probe shingle and magma, and hear the sea through every artery and vein of groundwater, sharing the voyage of every navigator since the dawn of time.'

No modesty, false or otherwise, flouted here. Yang Lian was unashamed of his calling and his lineage. He saw the V of wild ducks in flight, crossing his Stamford Hill window, and took them for a welcome sign, a letter in his personal alphabet. He remained in one place long enough to number the last apples on a neighbour's tree. He spoke of a process of self-excavation, worrying at the water margin he discovered on his doorstep, the deep metaphor that was Springfield Park. He relished the silence of this tributary street, its dark-coated ghosts like confirming elders of a previous existence in another country.

I was a few minutes early and I walked down towards the railway embankment at the end of the street. Notices boasted of how random plantings, trackside weeds and wild flowers, tough black poplars, were now a protected nature reserve. I remembered Matías Bradford's grandfather, a London boy from Croydon: how, aged fourteen, he had emigrated to Argentina, to work on the railway. And never returned. His fluency in Spanish, after sixty years, was modest. But he endured, thrived.

Stoke Newington has a way of absorbing exoticism, giving shelter, without fuss, to writers such as Joseph Conrad and Yang Lian. Toleration without celebration: the Chinese poet, with his spacious flat, his scrolls and bowls, books and bleached bird skulls, passed unnoticed. With his wife, Yo Yo, he operated a literary website: the 'snow-white' skeleton of a small bird was their icon. This fetish, retrieved from the marshes, reminded me of Steve Dilworth and the hierarchies of dead things waiting for his intricate caskets. Nature-sculptures found, not made. Made to be found, then hidden. Antidotes to the inflationary tendencies of Westfield's public art, the blustering towers of Stratford. The compulsion to force the crowd to look up and ignore the ground beneath their feet. The delicate snail-shells on which they are about to trample.

Yo Yo poured the tea. Her husband, in the push of numerous projects, the fever of publication, apologized for the curb he would have to put on our conversation. Discreetly, he watched the clock. He was discomfited by the fact that he had been too preoccupied, that morning, to wash. His hair was long, his eyes hot. He was fit for purpose and pumped to expound a story made from fixed elements, around which he circled, again and again. Taking breath, punctuating the monologue with excited emphasis, he struggled to bring a sentence to resolution. It wasn't, in truth, a conversation at all: an audience with a privileged person. A poet. I placed the recorder on the table and off he went.

I have been travelling, all over the world, many times. It's not that I am everywhere, but everywhere is inside of me. This is true of Lea Valley. We base our individual discoveries on the idea that both the place and we ourselves are new, or renewed by the dialogue between place and ourselves. It is not a general Lea Valley but my Lea Valley. Lea Valley is very special and different from other places.

I myself am a valley, like my poem. Or like a river. The movement goes down. Every poet is an archaeologist of now. The layers of this time are within the moment of where we are. It's not cancelled time, but all time brought into one moment. I feel Lea Valley is a wonderful chance for me to see how deep the self, or selves, could be.

I did some research on this area. Lea Valley is part of London today, but it was once the border of Saxon and Viking kingdoms. There was a Roman camp in Springfield Park. An ice age made this landscape. All of those realities are part of myself. All those layers make a dialogue of my memories, including other layers from other places. I write about other rivers: Hutuo, Hudson, Parramatta. All those rivers I have been to before. They become part of Lea Valley, within the riverbanks. Lea Valley is me. I am the Lea Valley.

I don't try to compare the Olympic experience in Beijing directly with what is happening in Lea Valley. But it's a general problem of the world, this commercial use of landscape. I witnessed the destruction of history in Beijing. History and classical Chinese culture have been totally covered over and destroyed by so-called globalization, by ugly buildings. That is a new way to cut our memories, to root them out.

Lea Valley is being destroyed all the time. It is always being destroyed: by old industries, football grounds. They transform everything. The authorities have tried their best to convert the marshland, the original view, to a more commercial use.

As poets, we know that we have become important. Only by our deep experience, our studies, can we keep the soul of the landscape. We can remember the original creative power we gain from the land. I am now a British citizen, but, when my stranger's eyes look on Lea Valley, I recognize how rich are the links between the depths of the local and my experience of other places. I deeply hope the London Olympics are not only for commercial gain, but for the discovery of this other spirit. The invisible link between this land and mine.

The key word, not only for Lea Valley, but all other matters, is aware-ness. Poetry is the best way to show understanding and awareness. Lea Valley must be a base of spirit, not only a base of sport. The government and the commercial bodies don't know that vision or have that under-standing. They think of Lea Valley as a place of nothing. They don't have a vision of real development, the development of the mind. They only see more buildings. We, the poets, need to tell them, or at least to write down, that awareness is our poetry. I hope to suggest that Hackney does something based around the fact that there are so many writers in Lea Valley. The council should think about Lea Valley and literature. Festivals are the real Olympics, the Olympics of the spirit.

When I walk in London, I love those so-called canals. They're beautiful. London is pretty low-lying, a lot of marshland. Chelsea was originally marshland. Now of course it has the most expensive buildings. Luckily, we have a small piece of marshland that has been left, here in Hackney. When I walk through these marshes it is hard to believe I am almost in the centre of London. It is both wild and alive. It reminds me of the wild geese, crying as they cross the sky. In Chinese characters the flying shape is exactly the character for 'human'. It is the sign or symbol for 'homesickness'.

In Lea Valley context, this homesickness is not only for China, but for man. For the original life of the land. Those wild geese remind me of this, otherwise I would be cut off. If we lose awareness, we can become so poor, so boring.

Beijing has changed more in the last thirty years than in the previous thousand. It's a huge change. Remembering Communist times, the Cultural Revolution, when people were living in extremely poor conditions, I'm not totally against that. You find that the classical will almost always be destroyed. The serious culture, the intellectual culture, is very different today. All those changes, including the introduction of a measure of democracy, are important. I'm happy to see people talking about democracy and not just mouthing hollow slogans.

For the last fifty years, or even more, what happened in China was a kind of disaster. Based on unawareness. Based on huge emotion: all the way back to the Opium War, Japanese War, Civil War. The Chinese people have not undertaken a clear introspection. They have not built up a good understanding of their own cultural traditions. Therefore, they don't know what were the good things in that tradition. For quite a long time they tried to abandon everything. But no one can abandon a tradition, since the language is inside the people. Tradition controlled everyone. Secretly,

*subconsciously, we were unaware. The young men, idealists, found them-
selves joining the power game and ending up as bigger or smaller dictators.*

*That's why we have a place now called China. A place that I totally
refuse to recognize as the classical China. I always say that contemporary
China is hanging between two cliffs. The classical is one cliff, the Western
or international world is the other. We have to make, in a good way, a
bridge. A bridge which is creative and transcendent. But which, in its bad
way, is so shallow and so rude.*

*London has always been a base for exchange between the very high culture
of China and England. You tell me that Arthur Waley loved the River Lea?
Lea Valley has a link with classical Chinese landscape. The water, the
waves: it has a classical Chinese melancholy beauty. I'm totally not surprised by Waley's love for this place. The moon in the river. Huge clouds.
The skies are so dramatic.*

*So, to come back to where we start: human beings are always inspired
by nature and the discovery of nature in themselves. You have a link
between man and his discovery of nature and roots in locality. Then you
find you have a link with all great classical poets in all languages: Goethe,
Homer, Dante, Li Po, Du Fu. Everyone.* This is the key: we translate
everyone into ourselves.

*If we think of the new Olympic structures in Lea Valley as being like
Beijing, we should understand that in China the Games were run as a dictatorship toy. A part of the propaganda of Communism. The apparent
links between the two Olympics are so shameful. It would be shameful for
London to think that the Olympics would only be done for commercial reasons.*

*The only deep energy that happens inside these epochal cultural trans-
formations, in China and in Britain too, is the poetry or the eyes of poetry.
Then we could say, there is a link, and a very great link.*

*The landscape is inspiration, I think. The external landscape is an
inspiration in front of our eyes. But, finally, poetry builds up the inner
landscape, inside our hearts and minds. Inner knowledge also includes all
the spiritual understanding in the idea of forms and in discovery of landscape. This is what brought the human soul to connect with the Olympics*

in Greece. The transformation of external landscape into inner landscape, that is the power of spirit. I don't know how, but if somebody can see this point, then anything is possible.

We must do our own projects, not only for an audience but for ourselves: deep discoveries, between poets, and therefore between two languages, two cultures. *Image by image, sentence by sentence,* inside of the form. We don't understand the language of the other – but our understanding through poetry, like bolts of lightning, leads us forward. We see how language moves, and that is such a beautiful experience. Both languages are so interesting.

The deep dialogue between Chinese and English is like a dialogue between time and space. The Chinese language has been transformed from 3,000 years ago until today. And the transformation, good and bad, is proved by thousands of great masterpieces. There must be something unique inside that language.

The English language is the language which covers the biggest space in the world. Very different colours to the same language. How to judge the poetry? This was the real meeting point between China and England. Real discussions about what is the meaning of global, what is the meaning of a cultural exchange today. I come back to the idea of the international within the local. That has to be the dialogue, between the depth of the different roots. We can have a real internationalism, not just a commercial level of internationalism, causing us to fall into emptiness. Which would be a great pity and a disaster.

Lian's loved and recognized reed beds, the Walthamstow Marshes, acted as a reflective mirror between his own flat, with its accumulation of memory-objects, and the home, on the far side of the river, of one of his translators, Pascale Petit. They would meet and discuss the progress of the work in a borderland café. 'To Lian's eyes,' Petit said, 'the café walls are banded Mesozoic rock where Li Bai and Du Fu's shadows pass, each drunk on their own solitude.'

This is the loss we fear most: the contemplative solitude of the water margin, its accumulation of voices. Rivers and canals are stitched into our sides, changing and not changing, showing the rays of the rising sun and the transit of clouds. I came to Hackney by tracking the towpath out of Camden to the mysterious expanse of Victoria Park. I made my compromises with the life of the place by establishing a way out, up the Lea Valley: which was scarred, revived, inscribed along every inch of its urban-pastoral beauty. The Lea solaced Izaak Walton, Arthur Waley and, in our own time, the photographer Stephen Gill. The explanations of its power are always different. Whether it offers a willow-shaded fishing spot or edge-of-city grounds for wandering and cycling, the attraction lies in its accessible obscurity. The knowledge that nothing is explained or morally improving, overwhelmed by great publics schemes.

Water is memory. Erasure, inspiration. Without these canals, navigations, buried streams, the urban narrative clogs and chokes. If the Lea Valley were lost, I would walk away. There are other rivers, other stories. In which, like Yang Lian, to swim blind, to search for myself.

An afterthought troubled me. When the police who raided the flat in Stoke Newington wrote up their notes, how did they know how to spell Anna Mendelssohn's fictive surname, Pye? It might have been Pie. I remembered, quite fondly, a cartoon strip in a Dublin evening newspaper which we used to read as students, the adventures of a certain Professor Pi. This bumbling eccentric had a fondness for afternoon cinemas and his mythology was soon confused with that of the philosopher Ludwig Wittgenstein, who was much discussed in pubs and even sampled as text by a few show-offs. Wittgenstein was one of us, he had an Irish period.

There was also the Hitchcock connection, another enthusiasm of the Dublin years. The politics of the great-bellied Buddha director were even more dubious than my own. They were a politics of control, a benevolent dictatorship of German-inspired taste, obsessive preparation, malign fate: he recognized the bomb that went off in a bus in *Sabotage*, his reworking of Conrad's *The Secret Agent*, as a technical flaw, a sin against the laws of suspense. The boilerplated head of Hitchcock in the interior courtyard of the flats built on the site of the Gainsborough Studios gave him the look of Chairman Mao, an enigmatic master-dictator with absolute command of the laws of space and time. And an assembly line of robotic ice-maidens available to perform at his whim.

Politically, *Topaz* in 1969 was the nadir: a film that might have been produced by the CIA, an anti-Castro folly as successful as the invasion of the Bay of Pigs. *Torn Curtain*, out of its time, playing on stereotypes and prettily fraudulent backdrops, in an East Germany out of Hitchcock's pre-war espionage thriller period, was more appealing. The good Germans around Leipzig belong to an underground organization dedicated to passing scientific information, about bigger and better bombs, to American agents. They have a symbol that they sometimes scratch in the dirt: the sixteenth letter in the Greek alphabet, the symbol for the ratio of the circumference of a circle to its diameter. Pi. A symbol with the resonance of a Chinese character painted on a scroll. A shape that reminded me of the mushroom-hats of the Hasidic men in the rain.

Anna Mendelssohn's final booklet consisted of twenty-seven acrostic pieces based on the word 'poetry'. Its title was *Py*.

Privateland

Crisis

The identity-dissolving spread of water shimmers and shifts, its channels clearly demarcated, favoured by birds I fail to recognize: it covers the world. There is no solid ground left in my dreaming. Close to where the shore must once have been, oil-fed cormorants skulk on rotting wooden tripods, made from the ribs of sunken ships. Sea swallows river.

London has been, and will again be, obliterated; its vanity, its pride. Crocodile-dissidents, myself included, take pleasure in the Old Testament finality of eco-disaster: woe, woe. Disaster for who exactly? Not ecology. Ecology is indifferent. Ecology is pragmatic. The creaking and crumbling of icebergs, the melting of the polar caps, the opening of the mythical northwest passage, all of this is good news for doomsday professionals: the failed presidential candidates with their blockbuster movies, the corporate entities funding good works while despoiling the planet. And the usual reflex artists rounded up to sign petitions, mournfully accepting air-mile gigs in endangered places. Queue here to book passage on the latest ship of fools heading for Greenland to respond to the obvious with inflated metaphors.

During my brief interlude as an art historian at the Courtauld Institute, after Chobham Farm and other industrial episodes in the marginal lands, I found myself returning, obsessively, to the Museum of Mankind in Burlington Gardens. I was on borrowed time, a married man with a young daughter, no prospects, no funds. And about enough proficiency in French to follow a rugby report in a sports tabloid, or to nod over subtitles in a Godard movie. My immersion, by slide show, in Cézanne and the contentious beginnings of cubism, was racing towards banishment, tactical withdrawal. In another life, I could have spent a fruitful year with

Picasso's *Demoiselles d'Avignon*. They were excellent company, those bone-carved ladies of the south. A chorus of voices, parrot-shrill or Gitane-husky, I could never begin to translate. The African masks, the brothel setting, the fierce distortions: they were the cover story for my trips to the ethnographic museum. The galleries were cool and quiet, little-visited. The morality of storing and displaying tribal fetishes, shamanistic drums, carved tusks, grave goods, didn't trouble me, not then. They were an important element in my London mythology. They were so nakedly themselves: a goad towards the kind of poetry I wanted to write.

Walking through these dimmed rooms, I thought about how cubism affected my reading of the labyrinth of Whitechapel streets; how crimes splintered, beginning everywhere at once, unresolved, re-enacted by those who could not break their compulsion to reach the last page. To see the past as an ongoing conspiracy. Yang Lian described the Lea Valley in a present tense that included both traditional forms and future imaginings: all one, earth, water, cloud, held within the envelope of his physical being. Starting with the sound of my footsteps on the polished floor, the inspection of Peruvian pottery, jugs like the ones my great-grandfather brought back to Scotland, I projected rafts of work for the years ahead. I would try to break London down into scraps of forgotten books, postcards, accidental discoveries – and, above all these, unreadable and overwhelming, the fact of the Thames. Skin without body. Body without skin. The dark passage: out.

It hurt, coming back, to find the museum cancelled, captured: an annexe of the Royal Academy. The pharmaceutical giants, GlaxoSmithKline, were sponsoring a show entitled 'Earth: Art of a Changing World'. In keeping with the Anish Kapoor event, on the other side of the Burlington Arcade, this eco-extravaganza focused on the rude colonization of a classically proportioned public space. Kapoor's paint guns and trundling clay-block railways exorcized any lingering piety left in these solemn, high-ceilinged chambers, with their dainty cornices and established hierarchies of value. Meanwhile, in the former Museum of Mankind, glass-fronted cabinets were exposed in their nakedness, like political prisoners awaiting interrogation. The death-of-the-planet message was visible in expensive HD panels, or minimalist interventions published on an epic scale. Where there was truth, there was poetry, free of dogma and relatively unpolluted by patronage: Cornelia Parker's hanging, fire-blackened forest, conceived as a response to Joseph Conrad's *Heart of Darkness* (by way of the chemically defoliated jungles of Francis Ford Coppola's *Apocalypse Now*). Tacita Dean, a favourite of J. G. Ballard, exhibited blow-ups of Slavic disaster postcards with handwritten director's notes. Downbeat endings, she revealed, were contrived by Danish film-makers, for export to Russia; Europe and America preferred a lover's embrace, a smiling child.

The piece that hit me hardest hung like a vertical river, a thin waterfall, a scratchy torrent of pulsing light. A strip of film playing without camera or projector, self-exposed, on a loop which never returns to its starting point. Ruth Jarman and Joe Gerhardt, operating as Semiconductor, composed *Black Rain*: 'from raw visual data recorded by NASA's Solar Terrestrial Relations Observatory (STEREO), a pair of satellites that track interplanetary solar winds and coronal mass ejections heading towards Earth.' You need to be that far out to get the picture. Privileged bleating doesn't mitigate original sin. The ultimate condition of everything is *river*: light, mass, form. Torrents of cosmic dust and the post-human shrieks of all sounds since the dawn of time rushing backwards into a forgotten echo. Successive ice ages are coded blips on the surge of a crystal-particle tide.

The formal columns of the pseudo-classical building cannot support this troubled energy field. Overcoated figures, shaking off the rain, step into the darkened room, pause contemplatively, before moving on, up the stairs, to where Antony Gormley is giving an interview about his *Amazonian Field* for a British Council website. And where Heather Ackroyd and Dan Harvey are explaining why they brought home 700 acorns from Joseph Beuys's oak plantation in Kessel: only for 400 saplings to wither and die. Or be devoured by English squirrels.

Poets, long before the days of drug-company patronage, researched, debated and confronted the anguish of the planet. In the summer of 1967, at the Roundhouse in Camden Town, the Cambridge anthropologist Gregory Bateson spoke about melting polar ice caps. The listening poets fell on the metaphor. 'The end of the world?' said Allen Ginsberg, 'I'm worried about my windows in New York. Peter Orlovsky's sanity. He flipped out and they put him in Bellevue.' Twelve years earlier, in October 1955, Ginsberg launched 'Howl' at the Six Gallery, a converted auto-repair shop in San Francisco. 'Howl' is apocalypse, self-evidently; a long-breath chant intoxicated by entropy, dying cities with hard-cocked messenger angels, state madhouses and Russian endings that don't end. The ecstatic repetitions, the biblical groans and sticky clusters, carry the poet down to the black water where all human narratives dissolve. 'Shoes full of blood on the snowbank docks waiting for a door in the East River to open'.

Reading with Ginsberg at the Six Gallery were Gary Snyder and Michael McClure, both registering in quieter, steadier voices, a poetry of place, of threatened birds and beasts, poisoned wheat, lifeless seas: of being in nature. Gnosticism, they called it. Ethnopoetics. Achieved works made from direct experience: and nothing like the dim pedantry of the copywriting on the explanatory cards at the Royal Academy 'Earth' show. Which concentrated, as if up before a war crimes tribunal, on explaining precisely what they were not doing and how we should take it.

Snyder read his 'Berry Feast', an invocation of the Native American first-fruits festival in Oregon. McClure's poem, 'For the Death of 100 Whales', was inspired by an article in *Time* magazine, reporting on the activities of 'seventy-nine bored GI's', armed with rifles and machine guns, taking to the ocean from their 'lonely NATO airbase on a subarctic island', to slaughter a pack of killer whales. Wounded mammals were attacked, and torn apart, by other members of the pod, deranged by the unremitting hail of fire, the lethal corralling of the Arctic cowboys. The West Coast poets, through forms of adapted shamanism and years of ethnographic study and practice, became figures of inspiration for an emerging generation with an interest in self-sufficiency, trail-walking, Buddhist communes: the original land, its gods and spirits.

It had not been a good year, the devastation of the ecology of the Lower Lea Valley, with the loss of allotments, unofficial orchards behind abandoned lock-keepers' cottages, native shrubs, wildlife habitats, disturbed the balance of a substantial chunk of London. The corridor between the Thames and the orbital motorway. The folk memory of a broader and more vigorous tributary. But it was the betrayal of language that caused most pain: every pronouncement meant its opposite. *Improving the image of construction. Creating a place where people want to live.* Promoters spoke of the regeneration of a blasted wilderness, underscored by high-angle views of mud paddocks forested with cranes, but omitted to mention the fact that they had created the mess by demolishing everything that stood within the enclosure of the blue fence. They warned of the huge budgets and paranoid security measures required to counter the threat of terrorism: a threat they provoked by infiltrating this GP park under the smokescreen of a seventeen-day commercial frolic. And coshing the public with years of upbeat publicity. The product placement of those who are beyond criticism, wheelchair athletes (who will struggle to use the impossibly tight lifts of the Stratford International Station) and young black hopefuls funded to enthuse about training within the shadow of the emerging stadium.

Gregory Bateson, in his 1967 Roundhouse talk, 'Conscious Purpose Versus Nature', explained how Dr Goebbels believed he could control Germany, at the time of the 1936 Olympics, by creating a vast communications network, and by suppressing any unapproved alternative versions. If it is broadcast, it must be true. Here was the template for the imagineers and spinmasters of the present moment. You can buy a postcard of the Houses of Parliament, but you are no longer permitted to take a photograph. You face interrogation, forced deletion of images, under emergency powers: Section 44 of the Terrorism Act, the Public Order Act, the 'Stop-And-Account' legislation. There is a basic flaw in control-freak psychosis. As Bateson points out, the controller in his high tower, like Fritz Lang's demonic Dr Mabuse, requires a network of spies and informers to report back on the efficacy of the propaganda. The entire agenda is about *responding* to what people are saying about the grandiose schemes. To strengthen his grip, the controller adjusts his pitch to deliver what he decides the voters want. Or what they should want. What they must be *made* to want. With police cells, camps, non-person status for those who favour another narrative.

2009: Xerox history. Bodies shipped back from war zones, resource-devouring invasions. Black propaganda. Floods. Washed-away bridges. Swollen, rushing rivers. A year of rogue viruses and viruses that failed to multiply. I needed the skies of the Thames Estuary, unpeopled tracks through the reed beds and salt marshes of the Isle of Grain. A healing walk before the bad thing took its definitive form.

A river expedition, mouth to source, would carry me away, so I hoped, from confusion and information overload. The Thames was a kind of empty scroll, a way of postponing engagement with China. Gary Snyder recorded in his journals how he sat writing, or drawing, Chinese characters, but said that the activity had no particular significance. It was a way of emptying the mind through reflex physical action. Like the rhythms of a day's walk. At that period, Snyder laboured on the docks, and spoke of 'the necessity to roam at wild'. He followed the cat-tracks of San Francisco, plotting the moment when he would be free to dive, once again, into the great void. Years later, an established man, an authority, he travelled with his son to the ocean's edge and reported how the body of a river, when it approaches low ground, is 'all one place and all one land'. This was the world-river I had been dreaming about. A mantle overspreading the wide earth.

While I was making my plans to quit Hackney, I checked the transcript of the Bateson speech. There was no mention of polar ice caps. That must have happened during one of the informal and frequently heated discussions that took place, between the main events, in odd corners of the Roundhouse. I had forgotten or mis-interpreted much that Bateson said: he was focusing on the interplay of mind and its extension into the biological world. He explained how disturbing information can be processed to shine like a pre-cious stone, so that it never makes a nuisance of itself, by forcing us to *act*. He used a phrase that perfectly described the liminality of the mouth of the Thames Estuary, where nothing is resolved and pearly sky leaks into grey sea. Bateson discovered a 'semi-permeable' membrane between consciousness and the natural world. By means of my projected walk, I wanted to erase that 'semi', and to allow total mind, with all its negative capacity, to wash away into a grander self: the thick-running river, London's Thames.

River of No Return

On the rough lawn in front of the improved Haggerston flats, there is a chart, behind misted glass, in a wooden cabinet designed for community notices. The cabinet features an optimistic map of the Olympic legacy. The text is indecipherable. The blot representing a portion of the Lower Lea Valley, shrouded in folds of grey, reminds me of the Hoo Peninsula, a secretive landscape at the mouth of the Thames Estuary. I should be out there now. It is the only solution to the spiritual crisis: another walk. I have been brooding on Peter Ackroyd's notion that the Thames is a river like the Ganges or the Jordan, a place of pilgrimage. I carried Ackroyd's 2007 epic, *Thames: Sacred River*, as I plotted my expedition along the permitted path from mouth to source. My bias, which I will attempt to overcome, tends towards the more cynical view ascribed to William Burroughs by Jack Kerouac. 'When you start separating the people from their rivers what have you got? Bureaucracy!'

Having triumphantly ghosted London's autobiography, Ackroyd's obvious follow-up was the Thames: origin of the city, passage between the eternal verities of deep England and the world ocean. Drawing on the example of Hilaire Belloc's *The Historic Thames: A Portrait of England's Great River* (1914), Ackroyd discovers in this 214-mile journey, from Cotswolds to North Sea, a mirror for national identity. The river underwrites an imperialist pageant of royal escapes, murdered princelings, futile rebellion. Richard II is rowed downstream to confront Wat Tyler and his peasant army. Unable to call on anything as formidable as the Metropolitan Police's Territorial Support Group, the boy king refuses to step ashore. Ackroyd is quick to notice how time curdles in certain places, an eternal recurrence, a singularity in which dramas are fated to happen, with a different cast, time and again. Walking where there is nothing familiar, nothing to stimulate personal memory, we are not ourselves; we must begin afresh, and that is the excitement.

Much of the Thames bank was allowed to vegetate among the spectres of heritaged history, riverboat pilots peddling nursery myths, Traitors' Gate to Houses of Parliament, until the land hunger of Thatcherism recognized this absence of narrative as the primary trigger for regeneration. In Peter Ackroyd's philosophy of time as a vortex, the invention of 'Docklands' signalled a return to the old-fashioned values of piracy. Empty docks were reborn, by a process of internal colonization, as a new commercial empire: the Spanish Main on our doorstep. Planning regulations for the Isle of Dogs, that unlucky swamp, were shredded to facilitate a shelf of Hong Kong towers. Michael Heseltine, a wild-haired visionary, Klaus Kinski to Margaret Thatcher's Werner Herzog, pushed Docklands across the Thames to the East Greenwich Peninsula. The Millennium Dome concept was a remake of *Fitzcarraldo*, a film in which suborned natives (expendable extras) drag a paddle steamer over a hill in order to force a short cut to more exploitable territory. The point being to bring Enrico Caruso, one of the gods of opera, to an upstream trading post. An insane achievement mirrored in the rebranding of the Dome, after its long and expensive limbo, as the O2 Arena, a popular showcase for cryogenic rock acts: Norma Desmond divas and the resurrected Michael Jackson, whose virtual rebirth, post-mortem, gave the shabby tent the status of a riverside cathedral.

But the reimagining of the Thames was not limited to East Greenwich, conceptual settlements were also imposed on vacant brownfield sites along the floodplain in Essex and Kent. Every act of demolition required a rebooting of history: as hospital or asylum vanishes, we thirst for stories of Queen Elizabeth I at Tilbury or Pocahontas coming ashore, in her dying fever, at Gravesend. The documented records of the lives of those unfortunates shipped out to cholera hospitals on Dartford Marshes, or secure madhouses in the slipstream of the M25, can be dumped in a skip. Politicized history is a panacea, comforting the bereft, treating us, again and again, to the same consoling fables.

The tributaries of the Thames are the veins and arteries of a finely balanced ecosystem: this is another Ackroyd proposition. They are anthropomorphized, made into supplicants, handmaidens to the titular stream. The Lea quits its sylvan source to endure a penance of foul industries, travellers' camps, waste-disposal plants, 'until eventually it finds its surcease at Bow Creek'. Ackroyd responded positively to the regeneration of areas where deepwater docks lay idle and warehouses were occupied by artists and premature economic migrants.

London is unchanging. The golden-hour liveliness of Canary Wharf bankers, as they fan out through a chain of dockside bars, under the shelter of those ubiquitous patio-heater palm trees, is a revival of the riverbank life, at the time of the 1812 Ratcliffe Highway murders described by De Quincey: 'manifold ruffianism'. Where the film-making poet Derek Jarman saw Silvertown with its abandoned flour mills as a site for dervish dances and the orgiastic rituals of a punk apocalypse, Ackroyd underwrote the rhetoric of regeneration with a post-historic parade of music-hall grotesques, satanic architects and angel-conversing alchemists. He provided political opportunism with a sympathetic mythology. Ripples of psychotic breakdown, financial and ecological catastrophe, located by J. G. Ballard in the hermetic towers of *High-Rise* (1975), were limned by Ackroyd, with characteristic generosity, as the first green shoots of recovery for a poisoned wasteland. Ballard's dog-roasting balcony dwellers inhabit a premature version of the Thatcherite Docklands that *Thames: Sacred River* labours to re-enchant. By describing, in such cool forensic prose, the worst that can happen, Ballard purifies the ground, making the new estates inevitable, but devoid of spirit. Darkness has been experienced, and survived, in the act of writing. Conversely, Peter Ackroyd, with his heroic and uplifting attempt to neutralize the pains of history by suspending them in a cyclical charivari, ensures that the bad thing, the thing most feared, will return.

With his faith in London as an organic entity forever renewing itself, Ackroyd looks kindly on the official script for the 2012 Olympics. Torch-bearing processions, naked gladiators, flat-pack stadia, are right back in vogue. 'The river,' Ackroyd says, 'will once more become the highway of the nation.' Jarman is dead, leaving behind, as his testament, the film of a blank blue screen, the empty transcendence of the coming Olympic fence. A captured sky. Punks and anarchists expelled from their Hackney Wick warehouses, caravans, rubbish skips. Doctor Dee is not at home.

To get back to the Thames I had to follow one of the less celebrated streams, the Northern Sewage Outfall, now rebranded as the Olympic Park Greenway. It seemed appropriate to visit the Beckton dispersal area, in part as a walk dedicated to Ballard, to whom I would report, and in part as an investigation of an emerging topography of sheds, retail parks and landscaped gardens made from decommissioned industrial sites. A zone whose defining structure was ExCel London, a green-glazed slab on the Royal Docks, alongside the City Airport; a spacious and secure hangar in which to stage arms fairs and conferences that bewail, at shameless expense, the collapsing money metaphor. The bill for the G20 dinner for 200 VIPs, their assorted interpreters and security operatives, came to £500,000. It was calculated that each diner glugged through £140 of fine wine.

These lavish gatherings, behind closed doors, have their uses. Tony Blair, it was later revealed, had secured the Olympics for London, by jetting off to Sardinia to kiss the ring of the Italian prime minister and media magnate, at the villa where he had enjoyed so much hospitality. Signor Berlusconi, piratical bandana protecting his latest scalp rethink, took a breather from a round of hectic entertaining, to listen sympathetically to Blair's petition. It was a scene straight from *The Godfather*. 'You are my friend. I promise nothing but I see if I can help.'

Colourful block-buildings hunkered into naked escarpments. Shiny boulevards going nowhere. Virgin developments whose balconies are teased by incoming air traffic. They fan out from the sinister ExCel aquarium. The bombed gasworks in which Stanley Kubrick restaged the Vietnam War have been overlaid with off-highway shopping colonies that can be read as a pop-up catalogue of our consumer habits and addictions: an archaeological trawl from the ruins of the Woolworths barn alongside the arsenic-poisoned hump of Beckton Alp to the superstores of Gallions Reach. Some of these enterprises disappear before they can be mapped. The aisles are broader than the lanes of the adjacent A13. Breakfast substitutes are available at any hour of day or night. When you are allowed to walk freely, without challenge, along the flank of ExCel London, there is nothing happening. Nobody at home. No flame-throwers or manacles on display. A cliff of glass, like frozen rain, filtering interior palm forests. ExCel is unexplained: like a plant house teleported from Kew Gardens. No point in sending the postcard to Ballard, he did it for *New Worlds* in the 1960s.

The sacredness of the Thames beyond Beckton is not easy to quantify. It is a territory where the gravitas of the river excuses layer after layer of botched political initiatives, strategic malfunctions, half-completed or newly abandoned developments. The scheme for a bridge that would have connected the North and South Circular roads, and given London a second orbital motorway, was aborted by Boris Johnson: it was too closely associated with the former mayor, Ken Livingstone. Thames Gateway is a geographical area and a philosophy for which Johnson has no enthusiasm. Boris champions the *Eagle*-comic wheeze of an airstrip-island at the mouth of the river, out beyond Sheppey. Where wind farms compete in weirdness with sea forts, those platforms on stilts, deserted by radio pirates, hippie communes and the secret state.

I reported to Ballard on how the retail parks give way, after a strip of tolerated wilderness, to an unfinished road guarded by off-watch police cars, whose edgy occupants are hiding their faces in the jaws of jumbo burgers. Near the river, secure buildings disguise their identity and purpose, they are indistinguishable from outer-rim universities or open prisons. One of these sleek sheds confesses to dealing in Logistics and Management. The motivation behind all this clamour is Olympic overspill. 'Thames Gateway: The Shape of Things to Come.'

The cover of the brochure is a split-screen illustration. A female athlete, arms raised aloft in a triumphalist V. And on the facing page, three tower blocks ramping from a riverside marina. Here, in CGI hyperreality, is the promised legacy. 'World-class sporting facilities will be available for use by the local public. The largest new park in London since the Victorian Era – the size of Hyde Park – will provide a delightful new local facility.' Meanwhile: you can buy into Gladedale's waterside apartments, where double-glazing keeps out the roar of planes bellying in over the Thames, before skidding on to tarmac at the City Airport. 'Get the Buzz' is the unfortunate strapline. The bridge on which you stand, keeping your head down to watch jets banking steeply to avoid the pyramidal summit of the Canary Wharf tower, has been named in honour of Sir Steve Redgrave.

After hacking through brambles, detouring around Magellan Boulevard, Atlantis Avenue and a boarded-up missionary hut, I found myself outside the perimeter fence of the steel-grey monolith of Buhler Sortex Ltd. Two men wearing crisp blue shirts with identity badges were lunching beside the river, dipping lethargically into yellow cartons. 'It's all we can find,' one of them said. 'We have to go to Gallions Reach, there is nothing within five miles.' They elected to take the air, looking across at Woolwich and Thamesmead, where new estates grow like bindweed: near-neighbours to HM Prison Belmarsh, that upgrading of the Dickensian convict hulks. Buhler Sortex, so they told me, make food-processing machines. They render meat. The original factory was in Stratford, where they enjoyed pubs, cafés, some life. It was compulsorily purchased as part of the initial Olympic push. They were relocated to this empty quarter, between the sewage works and Royal Albert Dock.

After the buddleia and butterflies of the permitted riverside strip, I headed west towards Silvertown and the Thames Barrier. If you travel, thinking about a particular writer, he will provide the chart for the mental landscape through which you pass. Even the photographs I was taking came from another era, a roll of outdated black-and-white film had been sitting on my desk for years. Out of nowhere, on a stretch of defunct nautical enterprises and blind-windowed dockers' pubs, a Chinese arch appeared. Decorative and newly painted, the gateway to a secret city.

LOON FUNG NOW OPEN. EAT AT OUR NOODLE BAR.

White stone lions with Harpo Marx wigs. A warehouse displaying a profusion of richly scented produce, packets of tea with exotic designs. Fat red-gold fish, in bubbling tanks, avoiding the eye of potential diners. My meal of mushroom noodles, 'hot and tasty', washed down with gunpowder tea, cost £3. I asked Ballard what, after all his years in Shanghai, was his favourite Chinese dish. 'Roast beef and Yorkshire pudding,' he said. 'At home, we never dreamt of eating the local food.'

The purest Ballardian set, poised chronologically between *High-Rise* and *Millennium People*, was an estate on the edge of the recently created Barrier Park (architectural planting in the deep trenches of an old dock). 'The clocks seem to pause,' Ballard wrote, 'waiting for time to catch up with them . . . Money, always harder-wearing than asphalt, helped to repave the streets.'

I came back to Silvertown, to show this new park to my wife. Between the riverside gardens and the estate was a flyover on concrete stilts and a grove of palm trees, discounted and left to its own devices. Through the tropical thicket, you could make out the silver helmets of the Thames Barrier and Derek Jarman's Millennium Mills from *The Last of England*. A snake, disturbed in the undergrowth, struck at Anna's foot. When she got home, she found two neat puncture wounds. The worst of the venom, she reckoned, was absorbed by the webbing of her boot.

I told Ballard about a leaflet I picked up in the café at Barrier Park. It explained how one of the incomers to the flats had decided to operate his own neighbourhood-watch system, by forming a surveillance film club. Other members of the community could contact him by email and they would share footage, caught on mobile phones, recording the behaviour of suspect youths. An image bank would be established and the anonymity of the snoops preserved. As we penetrated the jungle, the wild garden with its cracked paths and ramps, we knew that we were on film. Somebody would have to try to explain our eccentric incursion.

I found a photocopying shop on Bethnal Green Road, to duplicate a few sheets of my snapshots, to go with the letter to Ballard. The young Asian girl who operated the machine came suddenly to life. The flats on the edge of Royal Albert Dock: *that was where she lived*. What a mistake! The isolation. The lack of community. The drive to Gallions Reach retail park for a bottle of milk. She had been all her life in the buzz of Bethnal Green, then her family fell for the idea of a riverside apartment. Now she looked forward to coming to work, coming home to London. Street markets, lovely tat. Rip-offs and banter. Bright bangles, ceremonial saris. A world that had made itself and thrived, adaptable and remorseless.

Against the Grain

Peter Ackroyd begins at source, the first trickle, Cotswold springs. He opens with a deluge of facts: length, comparison with other rivers, number of bridges, average flow, velocity of current. Then moves rapidly to 'river as metaphor'. So that the two tendencies, the empirical and the poetic, coexist: striking examples found to confirm flights of fancy. And all the time he is walking, from limestone causeway to salt marshes, but keeping the accidents and epiphanies of these private excursions out of his narrative. The only vignette he offers from the epic trudge is presented as a 'river omen', a superstition. At Erith he found a bloody blade, a stained white T-shirt and a roll of Sellotape. Hikers, less sensitive to correspondences, taking the knife for fisherman's kit, would moan, coming out on the Crayford Marshes, about the tedious detour, those extra miles alongside the snaky Darent to the A206 and back: no footbridge. Afternoons disappear, among huts, paddocks of shaggy horses, driftwood fires, scrambler bikes and wavering golden beds of reeds.

Ackroyd sees a walk towards the source of the Thames as a journey made backwards, away from human history. But that is the direction I decided to take; the legends of the Isle of Grain, from William Hogarth's drunken boat party, through Robert Hamer's film *The Long Memory* (1953), to climate camp protests at Kingsnorth, were history enough for me. Ackroyd provided my starting point: London Stone. This beacon, on the east bank of the Yantlet Creek, is said to mark the point at which the Thames merges with the North Sea. 'The song of the Thames has ended,' he wrote.

Walking west, I reached Ballard's Shepperton after days of misadventures and forced diversions: before niggling doubts sent me back, yet again, to my starting point near the village of Grain. The true pilgrimage, in the Ackroydian spirit, could only begin after touching the London Stone. I had stepped off from the wrong side of the creek, a spit from the symbolic beacon, but it wouldn't do. The Crow Stone on the Essex shore and the London Stone in Kent: an imaginary line, spanning the Thames, joins them. This is all the information Ackroyd has to offer. How he reached the London Stone on his own expedition, and how he felt after so many hard miles, is not revealed. The author, as embodiment of London, dissolves into the cold water of the North Sea.

Studying the Ordnance Survey map for the Thames Estuary, I saw no good reason why I couldn't walk along the shore from Grain, by way of Cockleshell Beach, to the London Stone. Or, failing that, down a track past Rose Court Farm to Grain Marsh. But maps are deceptive, they entice you with pure white space, little blue rivulets, a church with a tower, the promise of a shell-hunting foreshore: and then they hit you with tank traps, warning notices.

MILITARY FIRING RANGE KEEP OUT.

Rusting metal poles looped with barbed wire. A pebble shore protected by sharp-angled Vorticist obstructions, concrete blocks crusted with orange lichen. Wrecked cars turned on their backs and absorbed into nature. Footpaths doubling into aggregate dunes, dark-shadowed lakes. Refuse dumps dressed in meadow vetchling and rosebay willowherb. Cattle, on strips of land between creeks, might be part of a real farm or target practice. Across the marshes, in the soft haze, smokestacks of constantly belching power stations.

When the coastal path failed, I tried a quiet back road: running, very soon, up against ponds reserved for the angling club of Marconi Electronic Systems and the elite fishermen of BAE Systems. A huddle of police cottages monitored access to North Level Marsh and the London Stone.

PRIVATE M.O.D. ROAD. RESIDENTS AND VISITORS TO POLICE COTTAGES ONLY.

I backtracked, walked for hours – and eventually found myself on the wrong side of the Yantlet, near the colony of huts and holiday homes where any upstream Thames pilgrimage should start. The only standing stones were a blunt obelisk commemorating the 'completion of the Raising of the Thames Flood Defences between 1975–1985' and a compacted cairn, like the remains of a fireplace after a bomb blast, from which the plaque had been removed.

The tactic of culling inconvenient elements from a map went back, as did so many other aspects of the GP era, to Dr Goebbels. Baedeker guides, as Vitali Vitaliev points out in *Life as a Literary Device* (2009), were subjected to censorship, for the first time, in Hitler's Germany. 'Strategic areas, such as railways and bridges, were removed from the 1936 edition of *Baedeker's Berlin and Potsdam*, published for the Berlin Olympic Games.'

On the edge of the frame, whatever your direction of travel through the Isle of Grain, the belching stacks and trumpet-mouths of power stations remind you that this is a working landscape. Its seductive emptiness is a consequence of an invisibly enforced, but always felt, exclusion policy. Without an invitation, a hard hat and protective vest, you trespass on these salt marshes at your own risk.

Children of the middle classes were getting their first taste of counterterrorism, increased levels of state paranoia. Well-meaning, university-educated, self-elected friends of the planet were experiencing dawn raids: the trashed flat, seizure of books, papers, laptops. They were being arrested, processed, released, or brought to trial: before the contemplated action happened. They were pressured into becoming informers. They time-travelled to a 1967 mindset of tapped phones, spooks with cameras in a van across the road, infiltrators in every group, agents provocateurs heating up demonstrations.

The fiercest reaction was reserved for opponents of the energy industry. This was where the crunch would surely come and politicians were taking no chances. If your face appeared in the movie of the Kingsnorth Climate Camp, among the loose confederation of tribes opposing E.ON's coal-fired power station, you could expect a wake-up call at your home address. The Kent police who held individual protestors arriving at the camp, often for more than an hour, while they were searched and photographed, defended their actions. 'National security. War footing. Afghanistan. The 2012 Olympics.'

Helicopters hovered throughout the night. The agreed route of the protest march was altered without explanation. Ministers, responding to media criticism, made much of the seventy officers who suffered injury during the battle of Grain. When the relevant documents were acquired under the Freedom of Information Act, it was revealed that only twelve of the injuries had any direct connection with the demonstration. Other war wounds included: being 'stung on the finger by a wasp', succumbing to heatstroke, lower-back pain from sitting too long in a car, nasty headaches, loose bowels.

I continued to push west, towards Oxford, but any hope of narrative continuity was undone by involuntary flashbacks and surreal forward visions, like a character getting on a plane in a paranoid American TV fantasy. When you travel beside water, time is plural, personality dissolves. We are in the story, but we are not the story. Place dictates its own terms and conditions.

I was trudging into Reading on my reverse Ackroyd walk, when I realized that I would have to return to the Yantlet Creek. The sight of the London Stone across the narrow rivulet was an inadequate response, my walk through the salt marshes counted for nothing: hands-on touch was required. The unviolated obelisk, 54 kilometres from London Bridge, marks the downstream limit of the authority of the City of London Corporation. The fact that it lodged on forbidden ground made it more appealing; if I failed in this quest, my expedition was without substance. True to Ackroydian dogma, I pitched it pretty high: the stone had become the symbol of liberty. To reach it was to release the riverside reaches from a cloud of unknowing. The madness of Thames Gateway colonization. Military zones struck from the map. Rebranded domes. Swine flu. Floating airports. Press packs and laptop presentations.

Before parking in the village of Grain, near the unwelcoming pub named after Hogarth's rollicking peregrination of 1732, I drove to Kingsnorth through a *Red Desert* aftertaste of roads too well made to be comfortable. Private railways screened by poplars. Chimneys like disconnected prosthetics. Silos (as sinister as the word). Lagoons that looked like oil slicks. Corrugated fields where silver lakes were exposed as sheets of crop-forcing plastic. When I left the car outside a yellow-signed café in a reservation of rubber-shredding sheds, the early-morning lanes and grazing marshes were somehow bereft. E.ON UK are demonstrating all the standard strategies of exclusion: cameras, warnings, a scrambled-egg security gang manning checkpoints, high fences around a nature reserve. The energy brokers patronize wild birds, passerines, nesting avocets and rarely seen bobtailed godwits. If a bucolic cyclist weaves down this country lane, he will be wearing a large identity tag on a string around his neck. (Jimmy Savile fixed it.)

Bill Oddie turned out, in 1989, to open the purpose-built freshwater pools of the Kingsnorth Nature Centre, which is closed and shuttered today, fence draped with prohibitions.

NO PERSON SHALL DIG, TRAWL, DREDGE OR SEARCH. ENTRY TO THIS AREA IS A BREACH OF SECURITY AND WILL RENDER YOU LIABLE TO PROSECUTION UNDER THE SHIP AND PORT FACILITY (SECURITY) REGULATIONS.

Agribiz fields, shielded from the Medway by an embankment, are edged with sunken tractor tyres, making shrines of the connection points to an hydraulic irrigation system. Wind sings in pylon cradles. The power station hums. Rabbits break cover. Skylarks tread air. Two tiny creatures I later identify as yellow wagtails bounce from the path.

The death of J. G. Ballard was not unexpected, but it is still shocking, and now a quality is missing from this place, and from the microclimate of London. Acknowledging that a writer, whose work we have come to rely on, is out there, alive and active, sustains us. The non-specific headache, the dry throat, they are not caused by the sickly electromagnetic field, white dust on the road. There is a persistent black hole in the landscape, a broken connection between optic nerve and retina, a measure of loss.

Making another attempt at the track across Grain, I pass unmolested until I reach the row of police cottages. A large lady, interrupted in her domestic duties, accompanied by a scrawny youth in a vest, stands her ground. 'Excuse *me*.' I do. It's not her fault. She is a manifestation of everything laid down between Yantlet and Medway. And I'm carrying a large rucksack and have a shirt wrapped around my head to keep off the sun. Pale Taliban. 'You can't come down here. Notices.'

I notice the spike of what I assume is the London Stone, frustratingly close, but I'm not permitted to pass. This woman knows nothing of the stone. 'Go back the way you came.' It's an enviable morning. After I detour around the cottages, to sit watching swans on a back channel, I am ready to abandon the mission. Ackroyd reckons this landscape has not changed in 2,000 years. He speaks of it as an escape from the world.

When I slunk back, defeated, to the village of Grain with its single shop and pub forbidden to wearers of muddy boots, I noticed a powerful woman in a bright blue singlet, hoop earrings, cigarette in mouth, swishing a Flymo one-handed around the ornaments in her front garden. She didn't have gnomes. There were two shrunken policemen book-ending her front door: a helmeted constable with upraised truncheon and a sadistically bland commander in peaked cap, hands clasped behind his back.

But it wasn't quite over. At an art event in a squatted charity mission in Hackney Wick, I bumped into the photographer Stephen Gill. I wondered if Stephen was up for a kayak voyage across the Yantlet. A week later, at 6.30 a.m., we dragged the inflatable, paddles, life jackets, camera bags, down the track from Allhallows. The mouth of the Thames Estuary was choppy, white crests and a gusting east wind. The tide was out. Stephen noticed how the big ships, in an orderly queue, were riding at anchor in the deep channel, off

Southend. The Yantlet Creek was a fast-flowing trickle, banked with mud. 'Let's go for it,' I said. We dumped our kit and waded out, jumping from insecure foothold to foothold, to arrive on a sandy beach of Crusoe novelty. Not a footprint. Strings of seaweed, shell, plastic tidewrack. A wild-flower fringe smelling like a herbivore's tangy breakfast.

The London Stone on its slippery islet is a fossil-embossed obelisk perched on a plinth, which has been constructed from sodden masonry and calcified wood. This weathered tooth is like a monument to a drowned city. There is a memorial aspect, but nobody can remember who or what is being celebrated. The higher your name on the obelisk, the more it is obliterated. It's almost as if the sailors on a sinking raft had carved their titles on the mast. Captain William Ian Pigott. Captain B. J. Sullivan. Rear-Admiral Horatio Thomas Austin. Blind witnesses to a walk that I could now resume in good heart. Picking up a smoothed triangle of London brick, roseate, and good to hold, I had my fetish to carry along the river path to a distant Cotswold field, the source.

I treated Gill to a major fry-up at the Kingsnorth café. The rubber-stripping operation had a yellow truck parked at the gate: HOGARTH TYRE SHREDDERS. An Ackroydian coincidence? The owner admitted that the painter was his inspiration, the way he nailed the follies and foibles of a corrupt society. This man commuted to Grain, daily, from a home near the Chiswick Roundabout. It was Hogarth's Chiswick aspect that he was commemorating. The Grain part of the story had passed him by. 'You learn something every day.' The big tyres cost £1,000 each. Minor flaws are easily smoothed over and the reconditioned jobs can be knocked out at £300 a pop.

After a farewell stroll on Grain, introducing Gill to an endlessly fascinating terrain, we would return to London. Coming through the zone of dunes and solitary trees poking out of rubble islands, we paused at the perimeter fence of the military firing range. If these tidal marshes are so dangerous, why are cattle allowed to roam? Why do horses stick their inquisitive noses over gates that mark the 'demolition boundary'? A kiosk, its window-flap rattling in the wind, has been perched on stilts. An unmanned forward-observation post like a portable toilet for the rock festival that would never come. A name was stamped, grey on grey, above the steel-shuttered window: OLYMPIC.

Future History: Allhallows to the Dome

Anna came with me. Rucksacked and booted, sandwiches prepared, it felt as if we had finally made the break. We could follow the Thames to Oxford and beyond, why not? When light lifts over the rim of the marshes, there is a challenging sharpness in the air. The place is undisturbed, almost as I remember it, carrying on its furtive transactions, requiring neither acknowledgement nor attention. Allhallows-on-Sea: a landscape imagined by a blind man.

Crossing a causeway, past the pub and the hut colony, decisions have to be made, paths divide. The direct rush at the river never works: trenches, rivulets hidden in reeds. The big sky is clear, for the first time in weeks, no rain, a pinkish emphasis over Southend. Behind us, a ring of interconnected power stations leaks vertical columns of white smoke into the still air. This is one of the special places, nudging the open sea, giving access to the Medway; half-exposed with flat fields of cattle and horses, barbed-wire fences, broken sheds. Salt marshes against a beach of detritus left by surging tides. Hoo is occupied by people and buildings that have chosen to drop from sight. Those who know it only from helicopter swoops, downloads of unreliable maps, are excited by grand schemes for runways, wind farms, settlements assembled overnight from kit.

In the early 1990s, at the time when I was plotting *Radon Daughters*, less a book than a career suicide note, I haunted Grain. Frustrated by the greyness of current political initiatives, a tragic limbo between two forms of dysfunctional conservatism, I looked for the right set in which to rehearse apocalyptic oil fires and bomb outrages; before they happened, as they inevitably would. Driving over the Weald towards London, in December

2005, the Buncefield horror was a meteorological singularity from my lost novel: that membrane of pollution, the sun-masking caul over the M25, was black, thick, foul. An inspiration. And a confirmation. Writers will go to any lengths to rescue a drowning project.

This fissured corner of the Thames Estuary sucked poetry from entropy. Drawing on anecdotes overheard in a cavernous pub, in mourning for the days of smugglers and traffickers, I found my characters a farmhouse in which to hide. You could smell London on the river's sour breath, but you looked out on a broadening chan-nel. Less than an hour from Whitechapel and the pressure was off. In caravans and chalets, along the edge of the marshes, boredom is refined, by managed despair, into that emptiness of mind sought by monks and prisoners. In bunkering down on the Isle of Grain, you did your time, uncaptured, unsupervised. Stories happen without the teller.

Launching the new walk by photographing Anna outside the British Pilot pub was plunging straight back into the sea-fret of a Stephen King shocker. Into *Radon Daughters*. 'An off-limits anachron-ism proud of its non-history, its forgetfulness,' I wrote. 'The only customers are inbreeds with mercury eyes, their credit exhausted.' There is nowhere else to go, you have become a stateless ghost. 'Detached from the city, the voyagers had no life. No points of ref-erence, nothing to hate. London Stone was a mockery, a name on the map, a minor geological feature marking the entrance to the rivulet.'

I came to the British Pilot with Chris Petit, when he was researching a film inspired by the Essex Range Rover massacre, the period when club doormen became the dominant players in a culture of ecstasy-peddling, cross-channel cannabis importation. And torture by kitchen implements, DIY accessories, in imposed Barratt estates on the cliffs above Thurrock Lakeside. Gyms that looked like clubs and clubs like gyms. Steroid psychoses: coke, speed, puff and all-round red-eyed craziness. Wrenched teeth in fluffy towels. Sticky puddles on laminate floors. Patterns of blood-spray stencilled on aubergine walls. Quentin Tarantino helming *Location, Location*.

Petit had the idea that a writer, so far off the scene that his collected journalistic effusions had just been published as a posthumous tribute, could do the dialogue. This burnt-out junkie, by keeping away from daylight, hunkering down with cats and computer, acquired a Hunter-Thompson-of-the-suburbs reputation. He blogged bands nobody knew. He riffed on throwaway gestures by actors who didn't act. The man had a genius for disappearance. He hadn't print-published for years: if he did get around to you, you were mutton on the slab. The Essex Boy patter he delivered for Petit was magnificent in its madness, Jacobean arias of linguistic mayhem. Which was why the director bundled his man into the tomato-coloured Merc, where he sprawled, buttoned into his father's tweed coat, with as much enthusiasm as James Fox riding to his fate at the end of *Performance*.

Exposed to raw estuarine backchat, for a heavy session in the British Pilot, the writer was supposed to pick up a notion of how lowlife actually spoke: in grunts, obscenities, mindless repetition. Providing the dialogue track for a silent television screen wreathed in plastic roses. Debating the plots of soap operas set in other pubs.

I never saw a human creature so manifestly out of place, so exposed. Food: the writer stared at it, without lifting a fork. Cold turkey contemplated cold turkey (in solidifying gravy). Filtered sunlight, insinuating through dirty windows, burnt like an industrial laser. He flinched and hid behind a trembling newspaper. With his dark glasses and spastic attempts to get the drink to his mouth, the regulars took him for a day-release outpatient. And, being superstitious, gave him plenty of room. If they spoke at all, we were too far away to hear it. After an hour or so, knowing that he'd crossed the border between reality and nightmare, and there was no going back, the ex-writer turned to me. 'I have absolutely no idea who I am. Please take me home.'

*

To get here, we've driven through several Thames Gateway settlements, barely out of the wrappers, named and abandoned. Red roads dying in landfill dumps and overgrown quarries. Like Petit's scriptwriter, the whole Medway catchment is drying out, addicted to enterprise culture but unable to stomach it. Folk who have bought into off-road dormitories, straight from the brochure, are aggrieved at discovering 'problem' families and other inconvenient malcontents living alongside them. Property values plummeting, no escape: broken windows, wrecked motors, miles from anywhere. The social engineering reminded Petit of Poland, without the churches. The dubious morality of Germans planning sports fields and leafy walks around future barbed-wire camp sites. Garden cities out of extermination facilities.

Judith Armitt, who stood down after a year as chief executive of the £9-billion Thames Gateway regeneration project, defended her perceived failure by saying that she'd been landed with an impossible 'alphabet soup' of agencies, all bickering over conflicting plans. When the performance of this particular GP was mauled by the Public Accounts Committee, Yvette Cooper, the housing minister, unveiled her vision of an 'eco-region' showcased by a Royal Opera House 'Production Park' in Thurrock. And an International Institute for Sustainability. (Which would, I assume, be entirely self-funding. While sustaining a raft of bureaucrats in the style to which New Labour had made them accustomed.)

The chalet colony, through which I walked with Anna on that bright morning, was larger and more cheerful than the neighbouring villages. Nobody needed an expulsion order to move in. Allhallows-on-Sea was a rational grid of customized dwellings, neat, well kept, and served by a leisure centre, combining fun palace with restaurant, bar, kiddies' playground. A holiday camp taken over by the natives. Picture windows gazed on the river. Interiors gleamed with catalogue furniture, with green plants and widescreen televisions. Patriotic flags hung proudly on white poles. Here was an estate that had grown up organically, a community demonstrating its affection for a small strip of the working Thames. A trailer park with suburban aspirations. A garden city in the Garden of England.

I wanted to see more of this place, so we approached the restaurant complex, hoping for breakfast before our hike through marshlands to Gravesend. The security guard, the only black person visible in the camp, is courteous and obliging. With our rucksacks, multipocketed waistcoats, and failure to produce a dog, we don't fit. But alien status is not an absolute disqualification. He waves us inside.

Red-nose clowns are beating juveniles with sausage-balloon truncheons. Breakfast parties in smart-casual leisurewear porter groaning trays of budget scoff. Pints of lager chased by mugs of grey tea. Clean white trainers for men with silvery, swept-back hair. Gold identity bracelets, heavy watches and fading tattoos. Walnut-tanned ladies with sunglasses nestling in plump hair. Beyond the picture window, their kids are whacking tennis balls and sometimes each other. And beyond the play area, ranks of gleaming 4-wheel-drives and sabbatical taxis.

There is much competitive flashing of credit cards. An overhead screen is running Jade Goody footage, but nobody is paying much attention: a deathbed wedding for the former dental nurse from Bermondsey. It struck me that Ballard might have appreciated the way obituary tributes for the 'reality star', who went shortly before him, overlapped and intercut with his own. The death thing. 'It can happen to anyone,' Jade said. And she was right. 'Watch more television,' was the Shepperton scribe's playful advice to an interviewer. 'I'll take *Hawaii Five-O* over a book launch any day.'

The death-wedding was credited as 'a Jade Goody Production'. Ballard, as ever, was on the money. *The X Factor* is the lead item on the evening news bulletin, followed by a climate change conference and Tony Blair's chum, the Italian prime minister, being smacked in the smile by a model of Milan Cathedral.

*

The marshes: St Mary's, Halstow, Cooling, Cliffe. There is a broken concrete sign lying in the sand: PUBLIC FOOTPATH. And footprints leading away to a promise of blue sky; thorny scrub on one side, reeds on the other. After the chalet camp, it seems as if the track is open, waiting for us; the rumour of London and whatever happens after that. Oystercatchers thread, in their hundreds, across the estuary. A woman dragging, and dragged by, the unusual combination of a drooling Rottweiler and a shivering-thin greyhound, comes off the marshes and into the leisure park. She nods at us, knowing something we have yet to discover.

The promised path disappears into quicksand, floating islets, military exclusion zones. The broad Thames grumbles at our side, a working river, an accidental wildlife sanctuary. The first morning is a process of deprogramming, killing the urban twitch; not saying much, being together. Such a short distance from London, this silence. Strategic pillboxes on shingle bars. Then, for an hour or more, nothing. Moving easily, we make constant adjustments to the varied terrain. Wet-footed, stone-spiked, or lifting from springy turf, we are chasing no particular story, we drift like logs on the dark water. The walker vanishes into the walk.

When the blue pup tent appeared, on a strip where marram grass meets sand, we were ready for conversation with other hikers, coming from the west, from Gravesend. Two men, of about my own age, silver-bearded, pink-skulled, in long shorts and proper boots. For a moment, I thought I had encountered Renchi Bicknell and myself, in a parallel universe, an expedition I'd forgotten. But they are natives, men of Kent, archivists of the foreshore. They tell us that the restlessness of the oystercatchers, their migration to this side of the river, is caused by disturbances in Essex, building projects, oil refineries.

After an exchange of itineraries, we push on. One of the natural philosophers scampers after me. He has a checklist of information to impart: the church tower at Grain, wartime forts, torpedo ramps. And William Hogarth's peregrination of May 1732. A little troop, after a night's drinking in Covent Garden, took passage from Billingsgate to Gravesend. An impromptu jolly: river voyage, enough walking to work up a thirst, dung-throwing, singing, hop-scotch, larking with sailors, token antiquarianism. Gravesend to Chatham on foot. To Allhallows. By water to Sheerness. Hogarth voided his bowels on gravestones and was whipped with nettles. The hiking party – a merchant, an attorney, a painter of prospects – were well aware of earlier topographic excursions. They wanted to investigate unfamiliar territory and to make a record. They knew about the twelve years John Leyland devoted to his *Labory-ouse Journey* (1549) and the *Perambulation of Kent* (1576) undertaken by William Lambarde. Churches, tombs, castles, inscriptions: pedestrian tours were justified by the impulse to bring back useful information, relics of periods and places around which a coherent narrative could be fabricated. The journal-keepers, the makers of primitive maps, the wandering men of the sixteenth and seven-teenth centuries, manufactured the concept of England as a noble myth. They smoothed their own flaws and fears by taking them-selves into the wilds of Norfolk, Yorkshire, Wales. Spies for truth. Hobbyists serious enough to risk everything to make a contribu-tion to books published in heaven, celebrating the foreign countries of our native past.

A memorial stone near the orange-crusted seawall: THE EASTERN BOUNDARY OF THE JURISDICTION OF THE COMPANY OF WATERMEN LIGHTERMEN OF THE RIVER THAMES. Taking coffee from a Ther-mos, I notice a group of black office chairs stuck in the mud. We have seen no other walkers since we parted from the men in the tent. Sheep, yes. Patrick Wright, I remember, interviewed one of the shepherds, a Wordsworthian solitary comfortable with the seasonal mists and frets into which his flocks would vanish. The human animal is represented by slogans sprayed on concrete bunkers, blockhouses, roofless shelters. The CHATHAM BOYS have been here before us, travelling down what they call their WHITE ROAD. The dates of the camp are recorded. It's like coming across an abandoned guerrilla outpost in the badlands. A territory purged of ethnic difference, a beer-can retreat for union-flag fundamentalists.

While Anna rests, I wander off to inspect the unmapped village laid out as a target for assault, war rehearsals. Low buildings could be mistaken, at a distance, for haystacks. Up close, the uniform houses are disturbing, stranger than Tyneham, Wright's Dorset hamlet, the one that 'died for England'. Nobody has ever lived in this settlement. It was built on a grid pattern like a military camp. They kept their wild gardens inside the walls. They did without roofs. The Chatham Boys left the area well alone, it was not to be reached on a scrambling bike. Empty quarters along the Kentish shore are colonized by varieties of camp: caravan, pleasure. Holding camp. When you reach a boundary zone, it is marked with giant sheds and secure enclosures known as 'parks': retail park, business park, science park. Car park. Parks you need permission to enter. Parks with barriers like frontier posts. Parks with shivering lines of captive trees, artificial knolls shaved closer than carnival dancers in Rio.

Tony Frewin told me how the Vietnam War came to the Cliffe marshes. It was Tony who led Stanley Kubrick to Beckton as a stand-in battleground for *Full Metal Jacket*. The reclusive American director motored, at a steady 40 mph, from his country-house retreat in Hertfordshire to occupy the A13 development corridor, just ahead of the superstores. The destruction of the Beckton Gas Works, begun by squadrons of German bombers, was fulfilled by restaging the madness of Vietnam. Canny location hunters like Frewin will always be a decade ahead of the game, discovering parcels of land fresh enough, and cheap enough, to be worth invading.

The Beckton story has been told, but Kubrick's raid on the Kentish side of the river is less familiar. Frewin was responding to ground already dressed with submarine pens, pillboxes, forts and quarries. War shadows were there, overgrown with edgeland jungles.

'One of the best locations I found for *Full Metal Jacket* was the track leading from Cliffe to the Napoleonic fort on the Thames,' Tony told me. 'We returned it to Vietnam: refugees, palm trees, helicopters, US marines, tanks. A stunning shot.'

I like the way he says 'returned', as if the marshes had been Vietnam before, implicated in the conflict, waiting for the procession of ghostly marines and burning children to become visible. Making that stereophonic soundtrack, the clatter of helicopter blades, part of the fabric of a Napoleonic fort. The broken landscape of lakes and disused quarries around which we now struggled in a laborious detour.

I encouraged Anna, who was beginning to flag as we drudged over endless fields and paddocks, with reminiscences of the Clarendon Hotel in Gravesend, where I hoped to find us a bed for the night. Scramble bikes chewed tracks into half-demolished forts and batteries. We made our connection with the permitted Saxon Shore Path. The old port, where so many ships once waited on the tide, had suffered a terrible collapse – which some natives, when I asked them about it, blamed on the Bluewater retail park. The last mile into town was a classic of withheld funding, trickle-down entropy; a tracking shot through rusting chains, corrugated sheds, and nettle-alleys between storage sheds. The Clarendon, where I sat drinking with Brian Catling, after a day exploring Tilbury, had closed. Stucco was chipping away from cream walls, exposing patches of damp brown. The hotel, like everything else in Gravesend, was up for revision.

Narrow streets with nautical amnesia skidded down to the river. Under a mural of the presentation of Pocahontas at the court of James I, attended by first-people Americans with punk hairstyles, we found a Sikh minicabber who offered us accommodation above a kebab house. Which turned out to be miles away, through unforgiving suburbs: in the direction we had just walked. Exhausted, fed on the meaty fumes with which the candlewick bedspread was saturated, we slept. Next morning, unwilling to add another taxi supplement to the cost of our lodging, we tramped back through ugly ribbon development, searching without success for an open café.

Clearing Gravesend early, having no good reason to stay, we reached the rebranded O2 Arena, the former Millennium Dome, on the outskirts of Greenwich, by the second night. It was a long day's haul, about which much could be said, but most is better forgotten. Like the years of New Labour.

Going back to a tree, close to the pier, where I had buried my shard of brick overnight, I thought about how W. G. Sebald would have handled this situation. He speaks of launching a walk into emptiness: to dispel emptiness. He checks out of hospital with a nonchalant spring in the stride, as he contemplates the melancholy hours ahead, advancing, notebook and camera at the ready, through a 'thinly populated countryside'. Those friends, those memories: Kafka, Michael Hamburger, Thomas Browne.

Gravesend was made for Sebald. For the way he crafted geography, banishing the tedious bits, the inevitable frustrations that can't be turned to account. The journey becomes a monograph of significant encounters, non-spaces dignified through translation: Norfolk as a lyric poem of bereavement and alienation. Carpets of London rubble, terraces blitzed by squadrons who tracked the Thames, were removed, by convoys of lorries, to lay out East Anglian airfields for horrendous revenge raids on Germany.

But Gravesend, this Sebaldian opportunity, the starting point of Joseph Conrad's *Heart of Darkness*, the garrison commanded by 'Chinese' Gordon, martyr of Khartoum, would have to wait for another writer. I could feel the reproach in the planks of the jetty, in the hanging smoke from the power station on the Tilbury shore. A meditation on colonialism, on Lytton Strachey's debunking of Gordon, would not be achieved or attempted. Not by me. Not today.

I met, on the streets of Whitechapel, and again in a Hackney church, an undervalued poet who had been a friend, a walking companion, of Sebald. He told me, when I questioned him about it, that he used to meet the German academic at Liverpool Street Station. He wasn't quite sure, but he remembered Sebald having the use of a basement flat in Princelet Street. The Spitalfields poet conducted him on excursions to junkshops, where they scavenged for the postcards Sebald employed so deftly in his published texts. But there were solitary walks too, when the Norwich-based writer explored Jewish burial grounds and labyrinthine courts in search of another kind of emptiness; the provocation for sentences, measured paragraphs, interweavings of documentation and invention.

CHEAP WAREHOUSING AND YARDS AVAILABLE NOW. FLEXIBLE LEASES. IMMEDIATE VIEWING AND OCCUPATION.

The security guards who questioned me, on previous expeditions, had decamped, crossed the river. The Thames port had slumped into its Conradian, between-tides limbo. Much of the available energy was expended on protesting about a glass stump: GRAVESEND SAYS NO TO TOWER. Or fretting over a megamosque on which, as bloggers fumed, Ken Livingstone wanted to spend £100m of taxpayers' money. On all other topics, Gravesend yawned.

Empty camera boxes stare at brambles breaking through tarmac. Obscenities left unfinished when the aerosol ran out. Heritage prompts have been slapped on this exhausted whore of the river like nicotine patches: empty forts, stopped cannons, a dead princess (Native American). I never saw a town with so many hair salons. And so many men with heads like polished stones. They were shorn more frequently, and much closer, than sheep on the Grain marshes.

The highlight of the morning was a tour through the concrete works in Northfleet. Spokes of sunlight through grey dust, nobody challenges us. We pass under an arrangement of clattering pipes, chutes, drums. Ships park alongside a private dock in a web of shadows. At the heart of the operation is a statue of Britannia; helmeted, enthroned, magnificent in her detachment from the noise and the dirt, the men and the trucks who pay her no homage. She's built on an Egyptian scale, a queen without a kingdom. Massive limbs are draped in angular folds. She had been conceived, under Vorticist influence, just after the First War. The statue is the only white object in a microclimate of grey, air you can barely force into the lungs. You feel it solidify. Another mile and we will be statues ourselves. Britannia commemorates the workers who died in the Great War, 1914–18. Names are visible but clogged with years of industrial pollution. Occupations are listed: Labourer, Gauger, Cooper, Horse-driver, Trotter, Stower, Clerk, Machinist, Trimmer, Warehouse Boy. Being here, powdered in the soft dust churned up by lorries, has preserved her integrity: a strange hieratic beauty. She does not age. She is not for turning.

The breakfast, at the coffee stall on the edge of the Ebbsfleet retail park, was one of the best of her life, so Anna reckoned. She may have been influenced by the need to rinse the dust from her mouth and the hours spent drudging through chalk quarries and streets from which all cafés and convenience stores had been excised. They have been obliterated in the push for a Channel Tunnel link, an Olympic staging post. The black hole that was Ebbsfleet is now the very model of the GP future-zone. Giant blue sheds. Frenzied roads. Long-haul lorry drivers staring at maps. A dozen men, gathered around a tea urn, texting furiously to find out where they are.

As we drizzle brown sauce over butter-melting, bacon-egg-sausage sandwiches, washed down by mugs of steaming coffee, we are interrogated by other diners. This river walk we are undertaking to London: *where's that?* A woman, with the clear, ice-chip eyes of an Amundsen, tells us about her recent adventures in Bluewater. 'I went early. There was nobody there. It was the end of the world.' Drivers, with refrigerated cargoes, find themselves marooned at the breakfast stall when their satnavs give up the fight. You can't navigate to a place that hasn't happened yet.

NEXT STOP EUROPE.

A monster hoarding announces its abdication from the mess of downriver Kent. They want you to upgrade, at this point, to the CGI version of the road, the promo for Mark Wallinger's 164-foot white horse, his mocking tribute to figures carved *into* hillsides by our mysterious ancestors. Chalk outlines that can only be viewed by shamanic flyers and superior beings on spaceships. The Wallinger nag, an inflated cornflake-packet toy, bestrides the Ebbsfleet quarry, and dominates both road and station, glorying in its scale and emptiness. As a travelling shot sweeps you around the iconic phantom, the promo reveals a spanking-new housing development. The look-at-me horse is intended to divert attention from a process of ripping, gouging, erasing. This dumb beast, twice as big as Antony Gormley's crucified steel angel, is costed at £2 million. It doesn't matter if it is actually built or not. It looks great in the movie. If it behaves like a police horse and lets one drop, the emerging Ebbsfleet estate will be buried in steaming compost.

We can smell the marshes but we can't get at them. The warehouse zone, parasitical on the promise of Ebbsfleet's European future, has expanded like a boom city, a gold-rush camp of provision warehouses and showrooms with nothing to show. Gravel beds have been laid out with Mexican plants and the sort of geometric ponds pioneered at motorway service stations. Anna asks a young man in peaked cap and blue uniform if he can point her in the direction of the river.

'There is supposed to be a lake somewhere around here,' he says, 'but I've never seen it myself.'

'The Thames? It's a very large river.'

'Sorry.'

Negotiating a tight avenue of self-reflecting glass is like putting your trust in a corporate brochure. We find ourselves back on the river path. Around the headland of the Swanscombe Marshes is the skeletal span of the QEII Bridge, twin lines of stalled traffic, sunlight glinting on windscreens. The warehouseman's imaginary lake is busy with container ships stacked with new cars, or heading downstream towards gravel-dredging operations and concrete works.

The walk dissolves into pylon prairies, scrapyard suburbs, decommissioned fever hospitals, landfill dumps – and constant attempts, against the grain of natural resistance, to throw up riverside towers and estates. Ingress Abbey is now a gated community. Greenhithe a tolerated village. There are more retail parks. More surveyors. The Crossness Sewage Treatment Works features a splash of landmark architecture that reminds me of Terry Farrell and his dockside intervention in Hull: a fat block with a curved back, a whale jigsaw made from glass panels.

'Handling enough sewage to fill 20 Olympic-sized swimming pools every haul,' boasts the notice. And I can believe it: teal, sheldrake, oystercatcher, curlew and redshank, they are all out there. Feeding on the sludge, paddling through meaty London-waste mud. Crossness copywriting comes in Braille for sight-impaired wanderers: 'Industry and wildlife will be your companions.'

The last time we passed this way, we were held for an hour, thanks to an 'incident' in the sewage farm. Which the embarrassed copper, pressured by aggrieved hikers and cyclists, finally revealed as a visit from the Prince of Wales. We witnessed the big black car, the procession of outriders and helicopters. The suited dignitaries, frozen on the steps, breaking into excited chatter as the cavalcade swept through the gates. A tray of MBEs in the post.

But that's where we were now, ejected from new developments, clomping around token wildlife reservations, deafened by planes on a holding pattern, or swooping low towards the City Airport at Silvertown. Anna Minton in her 2009 polemic, *Ground Control*, prepares us for the coming nuisance from above. Stratford City, the Westfield supermall, are about to launch a new urban-control device, the UAV (Unmanned Aerial Vehicle). Drones operated by the American military for spying and assassination in Iraq and Afghanistan. It is expected, according to Dr Kirstie Ball, a surveillance specialist, that the flying cameras, tried and tested in the Olympic Park, will become a permanent feature of London life. By 2012 there will be no perceptible difference in techniques of control employed in war zones and in homeland development zones: making the world a safer place for shopping.

Northwest Passage

If you manage to stay upright on a balcony as springy as a ship's gangplank, in wind that rips around this eighteen-floor obstruction, the view of the Woolwich Ferry is unimpeachable: downriver London at its reeking, clanking best. Red sun, grey water. The conceit, that this new tower will make an adequate stand-in for Ballard's *High-Rise*, doesn't play. A couple of twists in the Thames, beyond the Barrier, and it's already too far. The tension in Ballard's 1975 novel comes from its severed connection with long-established reservations of money and influence. His gated community, in its vertical stack, is specifically located on the north bank, two miles from the City. The view, across the river from *High-Rise*, is dressed with concert halls, medical schools, television studios. In other words, Ballard has folded the map, conflating the South Bank culture-zone, between old and new versions of St Thomas' Hospital, with the coming Docklands development. The whole story of landscape piracy neatly packaged in a single panoramic shot. A scrupulous economy of means, as always.

And now a radio programme, responding to real-estate spin, decides that one freakish tower block, overlooking the river, is as good as any other. Walls are made from ricepaper. Furniture is minimalist, scaled down to create the illusion of space. Mirrors do what they can. The hanging silver-ghost TV is skinnier than a postcard. The show flat is like a room in an airport hotel: with the expectation that you'll stay for about the same amount of time as you'd get in compensation for missing a connecting flight.

Discussing *High-Rise* in Woolwich, we are doing what Ballard did all those years ago, nudging the narrative a few miles further out, into unwritten territory where the consequences of warped utopianism are not yet visible. Those who have been seduced by the lifestyle pitch, averting their eyes from what is actually going on, are not Ballard's alienated professionals, his architects, psychiatrists, graphic designers. Those premature New Labourites have headed in the other direction, towards Chelsea Harbour, Putney and Richmond. That's the rule. Live upstream of Westminster and invest your bonus east of Tower Bridge.

A set of 'executive apartments', Rushgrove Gate, was fabricated in Woolwich by Imagine Homes, a company run by Grant Bovey, husband of television presenter Anthea Turner. So far, so Ballardian. But the force of place, as Anna Minton revealed in *Ground Control*, undid this pipe dream. Bovey announced that all the flats had been sold 'off-plan' before they had been placed on the market. Units in the riverside tower we visited for the Ballard radio programme were selling fast, the lady with the dangerous heels told me: £350,000 a pop and they are fighting to bag them. One day soon there will be a high-speed riverboat service, a new bridge across the Thames. Woolwich has secured some Olympic gunplay, target shooting, to underwrite its pretensions. But, just at this moment, the glass stack is primped and polished and as empty as the aftermath of a fire drill. They're happy to let a radio gang mooch about for hours, while they wait for the next off-piste speculator.

Bovey pulled off a considerable coup in flogging the entire block, in a single package, to an investment company called Veritas. A company with whom he was on excellent terms: he happened to own it. The *Financial Times* revealed that, in the six-week period when the Woolwich apartments were on offer, not one sale had actually been made. The only enquiries came from companies trading in accommodation for homeless people. Investors, Minton points out, receive an excellent return from local councils paying a premium to make up for the tragic shortfall in social housing.

When I hiked through Woolwich with my wife, we recognized the furthest point at which the cultural outflow from the Millen-

nium Dome, that admix of flash-art and hucksterism, was manifest.
The Royal Arsenal, armourers to Empire, had converted their bar-
racks and parade ground into apartments, bistro-bars and nude
male figures. Rusting sub-Gormley artworks in a defensive circle.
The sculptural troop stood on the cobbles, waiting for the word of
command, ready to storm the converted storehouse where James
Wyatt was once Surveyor of Ordnance. A chipped statue of the
Duke of Wellington was relocated, with a new dedication by the
Prince of Wales, on 16 June 2005. Was his royal highness doubling
up, after a visit to the sewage treatment plant?

Shortly before the O2 Arena opened to the public, I arranged to
meet Chris Petit for a day's walk, between the shamed Dome and
the restored Wembley Stadium. In doing so, all unknowingly, we
anticipated the progress of the Olympic torch, with its shuttle
across town, avoiding Free Tibet demonstrators, jumping on and
off unscheduled buses. Petit had some interesting ideas about the
relationship between the philosophies of New Labour and the
National Socialists in the Germany of the 1930s. I wanted to test
my faith in the northwest passage, as a metaphor and a practical
solution. We would walk out of my knowledge and through districts of London where Petit had perched at earlier stages of his
fitful career.

Psychogeographers talked up the northwest passage as a residue of Tudor England, the period when Dr John Dee could be
both an imperial map-maker and an alchemist, a man primed to
receive the dictation of angels. With time, the myth of escape
moved away from records of expeditions mounted for their trade
potential by Sir Hugh Willoughby, Stephen and William Borough.
It was a high-risk enterprise, this squeezing through ice floes, over
the top of the world, between Atlantic and Pacific, searching for
the 'Arctic Grail'. Englishmen, from Sir Martin Frobisher in 1576 to
John Franklin in 1845, ventured in uncharted oceans. The Franklin
expedition, like a missing chapter from Mary Shelley's *Frankenstein*, solicited catastrophe. Rumours of cannibalism. Fatty human

traces in blackened kettles. Frozen air clamping hard on human vanity.

The cost of walking through riverside territory anchored by the flaccid Dome is disorientation: no firm horizon, history subverted at every turn. Wanting to brief Petit, and to test my pocket recorder, I suggested a pause in Greenwich for a cup of coffee.

'When did you come up with this theory about Nazi techniques of spin and control influencing Blair and his gang?'

'There was no immediate moment of realization. I noticed how New Labour developed the habit of forming a divisive bureaucracy in the way that the National Socialists did, in the Hitler period. All those mysterious quangos. I made the banal observation that New Labour was a young party in the way that the Third Reich was new and untested, most of those guys were in their thirties or forties. And as a result they saw themselves as strangely unaccountable. Jonathan Meades pointed to the fact that the Nazis were all foreign in the way that New Labour are Scottish. Hitler was Austrian. Meades listed a whole lot of them. Uncanny parallels.'

'Was Blair anything more than a game-show host with messianic pretensions?' I said.

'If you look at him now,' Chris replied, 'he's like a shape-shifter. One can't quite remember him. Thatcher, one has strong memories of: as a personality. Blair is a ghost.'

In his loden coat and brown trilby, Petit had the aspect of a character from that Geoffrey Household thriller *Rogue Male*. Public school. Regimental background. Name and rank only. It was tempting to think of him as a deerstalking assassin from the 1930s, after bigger prey: the Führer in his Alpine lodge. Petit favoured the jaded ennui of a colonial adventurer returned to a corrupt metropolis and warding off an imminent descent into melancholia and madness by some highland romp involving heretical Catholic conspiracies, golf courses and handcuffed Russian women with ladders in their sheer black stockings.

He was a terrific Household enthusiast. Household, Buchan,

Erskine Childers. All that man-against-nature, future-war stuff. The locations. The detachment. The plain prose. He told me that Peter O'Toole, who gets Hitler in his crosshairs, in Clive Donner's 1976 film of *Rogue Male*, did a bit of cricket coaching in the nets at his old school, Ampleforth.

'O'Toole turned up just across the road from where I lived in Willesden Green. His house was not much different from the one we were in. The thing that cost him was a very expensive divorce. He had been in Church Row in Hampstead, a very nice Georgian house. But, like the rest of us, he finished up in Willesden Green, where he cultivated those fast-growing trees and put Mexican gaol-bars over the front window. He was the world's worst driver. You'd occasionally see him coming straight at you.'

The Meades interpretation of New Labour politics inspired me to repeat viewings of Petit's feature films. I realized that the underlying themes had been German all along: military occupation, cultural leakage, 24-hour cities of deep assignation. *Radio On*, the 1979 road movie, London to Bristol, was wholly European: a stranger's eye on English landscape. The back-to-back German films that followed – *Flight to Berlin* and *Chinese Boxes* – were weirdly posthumous. They know, before the credits roll, the game is up. They predict what *Radio On* has already achieved. And they are interesting enough to be saved from the oblivion of an afterlife on DVD. Which gave Petit considerable satisfaction. Unseen (and unchallenged), his lost works acquired a mythical status. He appreciated, before the rest of us, that there was only one city. And its name was Zeroville. In time hip young German critics flew to London to search him out. They discovered 'a grey-bearded Godard-like' figure of luminous integrity, the walls of his modest flat covered with a collage of photographs, maps, dates, quotations. A film, without budget, that nobody had to make. The only commission worth accepting, Chris said, is the one that is self-assigned.

We had one day, crossing London, to test my fixation on the northwest passage. Petit, it was soon revealed, favoured a swerve to the east: the flat countries, polders and dikes. The Baltic, Poland. He spoke of the willed flights of writers who plunged headlong into the fire. Louis-Ferdinand Céline and Francis Stuart stumbling towards spectral after-images of Dostoevsky in the ruins of Stalingrad. I babbled about surfing the curvature of space–time. About an escape from Hackney.

The trick in this territory is to keep the O2 Arena on your blind side. At a distance, the big tent squats comfortably among yellow-grey chemical alps, rotting jetties and sliced-up cargo boats. Leave the thing alone and it might work. The surrounding area, fenced off, dressed with unexplained structures, is a precursor of the coming ecology of the collapsed grand project. Hard to decide, as CCTV cameras swivel, if it's an English Guantánamo or a car-boot sale waiting to happen. Left to its own devices – at considerable cost to our pockets and to the reputations of everybody involved – the Dome exclusion zone is a notable addition to the downriver microclimate: spears of grass breaking through tarmac, artworks degrading into their industrial origins. Toy-town estates in primary colours laid out in contradiction of everything that envelops them. The Dome reeks of compulsory celebration, yellow candles stabbed into icing sugar. The original gas-holder, with its skeletal armature, is the wrapping around a wedding cake that has turned to dust. Nowhere better to smell the rancid hormones of the next terrorist outrage than in fumes coming off stalled traffic trying to squeeze into the Blackwall Tunnel.

You can define the ground between Greenwich and the Thames Barrier very easily: every inch has been either decommissioned or recommissioned. The Trinity Almshouses are slapped down against the brutal grey mass of a defunct power station that hasn't decided what to do with itself. (The Tate Modern option is no longer available.) Chris Petit perks up. The monumental self-assurance of this blank wall inspires him to lift his mobile-phone camera, the eye in the palm of the hand. I like the way his images avoid cultural sponsorship and aspire to the point where they are unexploitable. Digital sketching. Of late, Petit speaks of a return to the era of home movies, chamber performances, films shot to be looped in empty rooms. A ghostly voice whispering over surveillance footage from misty retail parks, wet autobahns, frozen docks. The poetry of unacknowledged quotation. Of defeat without regret. When he discusses Céline's flight from Paris – a hunted man limping on bamboo canes, between collapsed hotels and renegade contacts in a Götterdämmerung Berlin – there is a light in his eyes. For Chris, all roads lead east. Poetry and autopsy work well together. Dead places sing. This Wembley expedition is a farewell letter to the commissioning process.

Our river walk is about suspended permissions. That cargo ship carved up on the foreshore might be a Third World recycling operation or a visionary sculpture by Richard Wilson. Iron hulks rust in mud. Antique skiffs and wherries are colonized by dead nettles and meadowsweet. The stink of bone-boiling vats, brewing, the manufacture of chemicals, gave the East Greenwich peninsula its special quality. The smell soaks into your clothing, the pores of your skin. Rat-grey mounds of aggregate mask the unlovely Dome: a wind-propelled spacecraft abandoned on a lifeless planet. Nothing to sustain human existence. Nothing to exploit.

Coming to terms with our trajectory across London, Petit taps childhood memories of King Vidor's 1940 epic, *Northwest Passage*: in which Spencer Tracy sets fire to a Red Indian village and fords a raging torrent by forming a human chain. Colour was the thing, back then, bright as a comic book. And the business of provisioning. That's what Chris liked most in westerns, the bit where they ticked off the shopping list: salt pork, rifles, beans, coffee. That and the optional scene when the Indian maid goes down to the river for an early-morning dip.

The only naked figure on the foreshore is hidden within Antony Gormley's *Quantum Cloud*. The artist's phantom self takes shape as you move past the blizzard of scrap that contains it. *Quantum Cloud* is a slightly forlorn memento of the cultural confusion that attended the launch of the Millennium Dome. Petit recognizes the jetty, with its barriers and steady-stare of surveillance, as a processing facility for economic migrants. The logical use for a failed grand project, hidden behind a secure fence, is as a prison camp. He shivers at the memory of shuffling through airports with dubious paperwork and too many items of hand luggage. Your soul is left behind. You don't resemble that stranger whose portrait is stuck in your passport.

Chris tells me that Céline describes this experience very well in *North*, a memoir published in England in 1972. Confronted by the authorities in a ruined Berlin, the crazed French doctor submits, along with his wife and his fellow collaborator, Robert Coquillaud, to a new set of photographs. The result is horrifying, like post-mortem Polaroids: faces have collapsed, the story of their escape engraved in flesh. Coquillaud acted in pre-war films like *Pépé le Moko* and *Le Quai des Brumes*, under the name of Le Vigan. After the Liberation, he spent several years in prison, before fleeing to Argentina, where he appeared in movies obscure enough to interest Petit. 'A man I could have used in *Chinese Boxes*,' he muttered.

I asked Chris about his own passage to Germany. What was he getting away from?

'I first went to Berlin in '76 or '77 for the film festival. It was one of the few cities that I made a point of going back to. I was given a very good trip by *Melody Maker*, to write about German music. I said I'd do it if they let me take the train. I stayed in station hotels. I finished up in Berlin.'

'How did it feel?'

'Like an historical city, there was still a wall around it. I'd been shoved off as an army brat, aged seven, to the Ruhr, so there was a point of personal interest to the exercise. I was very much at home in a garrison town, which was divided into four states. An extremely nice city in which to drive. Berlin was a honeycomb, a city I needed to understand and to which I related.'

'Comparing it to London, any major differences?'

'There were loads of things missing. There was no bureaucracy, that was all in West Germany. The people were either very young or very old. And the old ones tended to be women, because all the men had died in the war. The middle-aged professional classes weren't in Berlin. They were in the west where government was. It was always an odd city in terms of what you *didn't* see. And the big shock of going back in 2009, after so many years, was being surrounded by men of my own age, fifty-year-olds, very prosperous. What they brought with them, in terms of restaurants, certain kinds of clothing, wasn't there previously.'

'Was there much traffic, when you were making the films, across the Wall?'

'I would say that the porous society, the meeting of the film world with various kinds of criminality, drugs, and so on, goes back to a combination of military occupation and the black market. Berlin was a city of transferences. When we were shooting *Chinese Boxes* – which was made for nothing – we couldn't afford to hire a musician from the west. So we went east and used Günther Fischer, who was very high on the cultural ladder, completely webbed into the secret state system. You don't end up, as we discovered later, in that position without being approved and connected. In 1984, I was cruising around East Berlin in Günther's white Jaguar: wonderful! So all that thing of crossing borders, and that sense of it being a city of assignations, made it *more* Borgesian than Borges's "tattered labyrinth" of London.'

There is no time to cut through the defensive ring, to enter the building site of the emerging O2 Arena. The hours are slipping away. Much of the post-architectural sprawl of the new millennium is about size, wrapping; Christo drapes hung over nothing very much. The David Beckham Academy has understood the requirements perfectly: a humped tent slung across two full-sized football pitches and available, at a price, for corporate hospitality. The whole deal is part of the AEG (Anschutz Entertainment Group) package. Beckham will promote the Dome and be transferred, for a substantial fee, to LA Galaxy, a football club in which Philip Anschutz has a significant stake.

On this bleak Monday morning, the academy is deserted. Leaflets flag up soccer training for local kids and five-a-side kick-abouts for bankers from across the river. Specialist medical care is provided: MRI scans, X-rays, 'expert surgery', consultations with Gary Lewin (physiotherapist to Arsenal and England). You have more chance of getting treated in the tent than in any of the threatened hospitals on the fringes of London.

When we investigate the interior, we are directed to a side chamber, a shrine of religious fetishes. Cabinets of plastic-patinated Beckham football slippers. Disembodied voices rehearsing the triumphs of the legend from Leytonstone. Semi-divine representations of the Boy David. Fame as a religion. Commandments made significant by repetition. *Impossible is Nothing. Positive Visions Lead to Positive Realities.* A doctrine that meets with the approval of Anschutz, a conservative Christian of the Evangelical Presbyterian persuasion.

The lines of spindly trees, long avenues diminishing into closed estates, remind Petit of a recent trip to Poland.

'What was interesting about going to Auschwitz was its location. It's exactly where the retail parks would now be. The shed is the answer to everything. The whole process was industrial. It did what New Labour did: decentralization. What you've got with National Socialism and New Labour is the rise of the architect. New Labour was all about architects, chefs and stand-up comics. At Auschwitz there was a travelling show called "Attack of the Clowns". Quite chilling that.'

'You see a parallel here?'

'Himmler planned Auschwitz as an ecology park. He wanted the farm, he wanted the herb gardens. You could take the East Greenwich peninsula and put it in the middle of Poland. It would be a perfect fit.'

'The wrong kind of planting?'

'My prediction, after the collapse of the grand projects, is eco-fascism. If fascism is going to return, how will it look? How will they manage population control? My novel *The Human Pool* had quite a lot about how you deal with mass extermination. I think they'll do it next time in the form of an epidemic. An uncontrolled epidemic.'

'So we'll all be running to the East?'

'Poland is great. It's completely unsponsored. If you're going to do a remake of *Radio On*, set in 1979, you'd do it in Poland. I can understand why the Poles are so happy here. The motorway runs from Berlin to Auschwitz, straight through, no speed limit. Poland has exactly the quality that Callaghan's England used to have. And the food is just as bad. The villages and the light are the same. The only difference, making it slightly Irish, is the presence of those churches, huge great churches. The giving of directions is Irish too. We were looking for this SS recreation centre. And we were sent on a wild goose chase. The only thing about the village I can remember is a bar called "Hate". In English.'

Picking up the pace, we enjoy a proper road with charity shops and a grandiose cinema converted into a Chinese wholesaler. All the signs confirm that we are travelling in the right direction: a block of public housing on the shifty border of Greenwich and Deptford is called Ballard House. It is attended by a shrug of terminal businesses: off-licence, video hutch, Mace grocery. Deptford keeps it own company, happy to be divided from heritage Greenwich by the fouled Ravensbourne River. Everything nudges you back towards the river and the notion of a voyage out. Behind a scrapyard is an eccentric memorial to Peter the Great, who came to London to learn the art of shipbuilding; the hard way, hands-on, in the naval dockyards. Beyond Peter's monumental throne, and the court dwarf (featured to exaggerate royal size), is a pier for the ferry that services the Hilton Hotel. I take a snapshot of Petit alongside a sign that says: GREENLAND PASSAGE. Hoar-stubbled, eyes narrowed, he's ready to climb the gangplank for a doomed Arctic Grail expedition.

Unfortunately, the ferry isn't operating and the pier is pad-locked. To get at our northwest passage we have to cross the river.

Pedestrians can't broach the Blackwell Tunnel. So it's Rotherhithe, one of the grimmest experiences London can offer; a tiled bore beneath the Thames, a dirty-white drain shared with vans, motor-bikes, company cars.

Fumes. Clattering blades in ventilation shafts. The backdraught from trucks pushing you against the curved wall. The descent seems to go on for ever. I thought I had died down there and that this unknown place was my eternal destiny. But O2 was the real fantasy: an involuntary flashback as we tramped alongside the submarine traffic.

A company man, Alistair Wood, had been deputed to conduct me on a site visit to the revamped Arena. Under commission from an architectural magazine, I was kitted out in buttermilk tabard, hard hat, boots. I remember the way the tent sucks the energy out of you. The Anschutz operation was more focused than the hysteria of New Labour's Millennium Dome launch; that desperate casting about for significant content, when it was obvious that nobody had the faintest idea what to do with the paradox of a cavernous yet claustrophobic space. Now plans are hardnosed and practical: an arena for the Rolling Stones and an exhibition floor for an artefact of similar age, the mummified King Tut. The Anschutz spinners will do what they can to pump life into this dreary enclosure. Restaurants, TV sport, shopping: a combination of Bluewater and the defunct Docklands Arena. Rock shows in which the tribute bands are all originals: miming, drowning, and confronting monster blow-ups of their own ghosts. Around 1,500 workers are beavering away to make the best of what they've got, some fancy cladding and a cliff of breeze-blocks. Coloured lights are projected on to grubby canvas to disguise wounds made in construction.

A casino deal would have completed the Las Vegas makeover: before that was scuppered by mean-spirited publicity following Deputy Prime Minister John Prescott's acceptance of Mr Anschutz's hospitality, down on the ranch, in 2005. The white blob of O2, seen from across the river, is like Prescott's complimentary cowboy hat. With the brim torn off. Philip Anschutz collects Western art, paintings by George Catlin and Frederic Remington. One of his fortunes came from oil drilling (selling a disastrous fire as the set for a John Wayne movie). Bugsby's Marshes have always dripped with oil, whale blubber rendered in cauldrons to bathe the Victorian city in soft light.

Anschutz holds all the cards; if he doesn't pick up the tab for this unholy mess, nobody will. So if he wants 2,000 spaces for cars, they'll start painting the grid. Right now. (Thereby unpicking, at a stroke, the eco-boasts of New Labour's Millennium Dome.) Alistair Wood tells me that his daily journey from Southfields to Docklands takes around an hour and a half, and involves the packed, nose-to-armpit hell of the Jubilee Line. It's a rare day when he finds room to open his newspaper. Multiply this experience by a quantum factor and you see what's coming, along with flash floods of global tourism, for the Olympic Park. Mr Wood also reveals that Anschutz was eyeing up Wembley Stadium. One nocturnal excursion, one glance through the tinted windscreen at the hinterlands, hooded predators in the shadows of the Olympic Way (old Olympics, forgotten dreams), dissuaded him. East Greenwich was the consolation prize. The offer that couldn't be refused. By a government desperate to bury history. Or to save it for their self-serving, pension-fund memoirs.

There is an object I want to show Petit in King Edward Park, Shadwell. It's a ventilation shaft that drops down into the Rotherhithe Tunnel. The shaft is screened, occupied by Irish workmen. The gaffer, on the mobile in his car, gives me permission to look behind the security fence. It's still there, the stone block with its tablet in memory of Sir Martin Frobisher and the other navigators: 'Who, in the latter half of the sixteenth century, set sail from this reach of the River Thames near Ratcliffe Cross to explore the Northern Seas.'

*

On familiar ground – mine, then Petit's – we make shift across London: north-by-northwest. The walk walks us as we check off the memory-prompts: Royal London Hospital, the old Kray brother pub, the Carpenters Arms, steel-shuttered and under offer. The white Hawksmoor obelisk of St Luke's, Old Street. And Chairman Mao's peeling effigy on a wall at King's Cross, near the old *Time Out* offices where Chris worked as film editor. The development pitch, around the mainline station, with its Channel Tunnel champagne bar, is of a different order; serious money with expectation of a serious return. East Greenwich is frontier territory: circuses, pirates, unquiet spectres of labourers in dirty industries.

'In 1978,' Petit said, 'I realized that I was about to become unemployed. I wasn't going back to *Time Out*. We bought a flat in Primrose Hill because Camden was the only council who would lend money to unmarried couples. Gloucester Avenue: £12,500. I was never any good at the inner-city thing. I was a child of the suburbs. I was stuck in that northwest passage of London for about twenty years.'

After a brush with a blind pavement-cyclist and his snarling cross-breed, we know we're in Camden: torched massage parlours, drug touts, cul-de-sac estates on the edge of the railway. And that old engine-turning shed, the Roundhouse. Which has been revived, rebranded, and patronized by a list of the great and the good. Petit commends the toilets. Forty years ago I was here filming Allen Ginsberg at the Congress of the Dialectics of Liberation, that epic conference of the counterculture. A moment like the Putney Debates, with the common soldiers, anarchists and fundamentalists, after the English Civil War. Such freedoms signal the end of a cycle: a cleansing of the atmosphere before an era of oppressive legislation: Cromwell or Thatcher. The coming of the lawyers. Trimmers. Politicians. Apologists.

Confirmation that we're walking the true line, Greenwich to Wembley, comes when I notice the lobster-red figure of a naked Gormley multiple, perched on a Roundhouse ledge: a potential jumper. From this point on, we are cataloguing former Petit properties. He reckoned to get a film and a couple of books out of each new address. He was tracking his old master, Céline, to the Willesden of that supercharged 1964 novel, *London Bridge*. Céline is the genius of public transport, using bus journeys as the best method for a total derangement of the senses.

'I wanted to go somewhere nobody in their right mind would pick,' Petit said. 'Kilburn came pretty high on the list. We bought a house at an address we never learnt to pronounce properly: Streatley Road. £27,500. Five bedrooms. You arrive as an immigrant, in the way the Irish did. Kilburn was my boundary. Twenty minutes down the line from Stanmore. I'd grown up on an army estate, civilian housing for military personnel.'

'How did it work out?'

'The thing I liked about Kilburn was that it was three turnings from Marble Arch. It was that combination of the Bronx and the Irish. If you went into Irish pubs with an English accent, they told you to fuck off. I got a lot out of Kilburn in terms of production.'

Snow is falling, wet and secret, like gossip: on sullen dormitory streets, railway suburbs. There are few shops, no pubs, little to break the conformity of boredom. A zone for reforgotten BBC producers. We pass the room where Chris looked out of the window as he wrote his script for *The Hard Shoulder* and realized that the missing ingredient was Kilburn. The termite life of the main road: submerged avenues, narcoleptic tributaries.

Willesden Lane is another kind of northwest, a true frontier. Welsh chapels converted into Buddhist temples. Coloured domes. A culture-shift leading to a high street of defiantly urban energies, mostly black, with a trace of Polish melancholy. *Polskie Delikatesy*: RED PIG. Swine skulls on hooks, tongues out for inspection. Micro enterprises, worshippers at strange shrines. Kabul before the invasion. An active market. With illegitimate trade goods: fruit, cloth, opium, Stinger missiles. Grumbling rumours of the North Circular Road on our event horizon.

'I remember going to a legendary Chinese restaurant on Willesden

Lane,' Petit reminisced. 'I drove up there thinking: "This is the arse-end of nowhere." I was reminded of Ballard driving past a wretched, lime-green Ford Granada. He said, "What a horrible car." Six months later, he found himself owning one. That was exactly my experience of trying to live in Willesden Green.'

The halo of the new Wembley Stadium appears, out of the twilight, over the end of a dim street with about as much conviction as a painted backdrop from Hitchcock's *Marnie*. The architect's signature flourish mimics the missing brim of John Prescott's white Stetson. We are closing on an arthritic symbol of Empire; exhibition sites accessed through a buffer-zone of storage units, Ikea and Tesco superstores.

'The northwest passage is fucked,' Petit says.

The searchlight-bathed bowl of the stadium is protected by yellow-jacket security, crowd-control barriers. An unused stadium is a sad place, overwhelmed by the politics of absence. The potential for evil. Trains run into darkness. End of the road. End of everything. A car park filling up for a nocturnal event to which we have not been invited.

We stand on the Olympic Way as clinically white punters emerge from the Wembley Park Station and shuffle towards the arena. Like some form of reverse evolution. We try to guess who is tonight's big attraction. Elderly folk. No funny costumes. The arena holds 12,000 people. O2 expects to seat 20,000. A Moonie wedding? A celebrity spook-speaker? A convention of northwest-passage initiates? The following day's paper provides the answer: Dolly Parton. 'The sheer wonderful weirdness of it all,' said the *Evening Standard*.

There is no way back from this terminal edgeland. Our paths divide. Petit wants to investigate an off-road hotel made from container units, before he picks up the hire car and drives to the Baltic. To flesh out his film-without-film, his Museum of Loneliness. I don't have that option. I have to walk, that's part of the unspoken contract. I can't return to a place that is no longer there, my Olympic Park banishment is absolute. I think I'll aim at Morecambe. Where the former Arsenal and England defender Sol Campbell cried 'No mas, no mas' on his comeback career.

Upstream Pavilions

It was the Chinese hour. Before joggers, cyclists. Coming from a distance, along the river path, an intermittent plosive puffing; breath under pressure, arms pumping across chest. *Powww, pwah. Poww.* A low-slung concentrated woman, in Mao cap, sees us, sees through us, with no recognition or acknowledgement. None required. My groans, involuntary, are memory-provoked; painful scenes from the past replayed and re-edited as we walk. Every step highlighting an episode best forgotten.

'Don't do *that*.'

I wince, but say nothing, as Anna mutters loudly against dog people who do not scoop, litter bandits shedding packets as they gargle on morning phones. Dogs stimulate conversation. Dogs are sociable; while they sniff rears, lick bollocks, frisk and bound, leash-holders exchange canine gossip. We slalom through twisted cones of unbagged shit.

Chinese walkers pick their circuits with care, paths around stadiums, approved stretches of the river. They never pause. They do not rush: fit for purpose. Exercise undertaken before these unresolved strips of waterside London are *visibly* empty, witnessed only by cameras and security guards in kiosks.

We are headed for Oxford. The source of the Thames, beyond that, was a sort of coda, to be investigated, but of no great consequence. Oxford is the alternative capital; when London falls, royalty retreats upstream. Charles I and his louche court made free of the medieval colleges. Hitler left Oxford well alone, not a bomb fell, even on the industrial car-making suburbs. He planned to take up residence in the area, slighting Churchill by establishing his headquarters within a few miles of the old bulldog's birthplace, Blenheim Palace. Oxford is where the brown Thames meets the causeway of oolitic limestone, running from Bath to Stamford: honey-trail and honeytrap.

Within my own peculiar mythology, Oxford was the outer rim of London, the rind, the river-gate: as defined by Ford Madox Ford in his 1909 essay, 'The Future in London' – one sixty-mile sweep of the compass-pencil from a fixed point in Threadneedle Street. The arcane, the hermetic: they pushed against the flow, or went with the tide, to this other capital, the city of secret streams, privileged institutions, chained libraries. Capital of spooks and code-breakers. Established drunks and gluttons for preferment. The operators of television's *Morse* franchise got it right, time unravels at a gentler pace among inward-facing architecture, enclosed gardens protected by narrow doors.

Elias Ashmole carries off, by cart, the books and artefacts of the Lambeth gardener John Tradescant. He founds a museum in Oxford. Giordano Bruno lectures on the new cosmology and is pronounced a heretic. Oxford, I suspect, will hold some clue, now as always, about the interpretation of England as an argument between poetry (spontaneity, intensity) and politics (the rest). I come back to Ed Dorn and his six-part poem from *The North Atlantic Turbine*; how aspiration flows west, by train or by water, in the temper of sexualized attention. Riding out of Paddington, watching the soft countryside of the Thames Valley, he sits among the long-haired love-children of a dying imperialism. The eros of water-light plays on golden girls and golden stone: 'the beautiful Jurassic lias'.

I'm resigned to it, but Anna fumes with each forced exit from a route that is so busy bigging itself up: STRICTLY NO ACCESS TO RIVERSIDE WALKWAY. I see now where the O2 rebranding comes from; deliberate confusion with Oz: Philip Anschutz as the Wizard. In a few minutes, I'll be whistling 'Somewhere Over the Rainbow'. The post-architectural shells and green-glass helmets of the Thames Path are friends of Dorothy: glitzy, camp, hollow. Scarecrows in full slap dancing in a dustbowl. My experience, of taking a tour around City Hall, that blob of Xeroxed New York, was pure Oz. The more

I saw, the less there was: a knot of angry teachers with placards, outside the entrance, provided the only reality. Airport security: card-swipes, identity checks, shuffling lines. The process took longer than the climb to the viewing platform, which was the main purpose of the building, a perch for television interviews. The Tower of London and Tower Bridge as a backdrop for weather reports. Sound behaved in strange ways. From the public gallery you could hear the whispered asides of mayoral advisers, while keynote speeches were mushy and inaudible.

At London Bridge, Anna gets a call. If you carry a phone, you are electronically tagged. A family crisis: she will have to go home. I will push on, step out. I hope we can reconnect after a few days. I read an interview with Rory Stewart: diplomat, royal tutor, kilted hiker through dangerous places. Travel-writer in the tradition of Eric Newby, Patrick Leigh-Fermor, Bruce Chatwin. Stewart is sitting somewhere in Shepherd's Bush, averting his eyes from the Westfield hangar. Dusk is falling. He decides, on a whim, to stroll down to Oxford, to one of the colleges with which he has a special relationship. He probably composes a lecture as he goes. He will arrive in time for breakfast. My god, how fast does the man walk? Following the meandering river path is going to keep me busy for four or five days; Stewart yawns, stretches, knocks off the miles to sharpen his appetite.

A member of the audience challenged me after a talk I'd given at some seminar room in Oxford. 'You're not *really* a walker, are you?' He was right. Day tripper, excursionist. No Richard Long straight-line epics for a few pithy words, hundreds of miles to produce a single image. I did it the other way, modest distances for torrents of justifying verbiage.

William Shakespeare, high-domed, full-cheeked, is advertising tours on the side of the Globe Theatre. There are never-ending improvements to the image of construction. Fences around fences. It's that moment of the day, shortly after dawn, when hot yellows and reds are reflected in the glass panels of culture bunkers. Leaves uncurl on needle-thin paper-bark trees. TEMPORARY EYESORE is stencilled in black on an orange barrier. A scribbled message on a scrap of paper beneath Southwark Bridge: A CITY ON THE BRINK.

Heritage London. Funfair London of Ferris wheels and Japanese fish tanks. Secret State London: a memorial to resistance fighter Violette Szabo and the wartime SOE. *Carve Her Name with Pride*, Virginia McKenna as the martyred heroine. The period of British films restaging the Second War went on twice as long as the real thing.

Why did the Festival of Britain, in 1951, feel so much better than the launch of the Millennium Dome and the construction of the Olympic Park? I was eight years old. It was one of my first trips to London. Then there was the river, which I loved straight away, the boat carrying us between the exhibition site on the South Bank, with its *Eagle*-comic Skylon needle, and Battersea Park with its pleasure grounds and dodgem cars. The show, coming out of war, austerity, rationing, was at the heart of London, not banished miles downstream. Ealing Studios made a film about a family barricading themselves into their doomed terrace, to repel bulldozers clearing the ground for the grand project. Bureaucrats relent, allowing the house to remain as a festival exhibit: the typical English home. When the allotment holders in Waterden Road proposed the same ruse to the Olympic Development Authority, they were expelled within weeks. By 2009 the will of the alphabet-soup quangos is absolute: more consultation, swifter destruction. Direction of travel.

The Central Office of Information documentary, *Brief City* (1952), brought the Festival of Britain right back to me. The voice-over speaks of 'fierce little boys filled with their secret purposes'. School caps, ties, white shirts, grey shorts. It was summer, the men were in gabardine coats, puffing on pipes, and the women carried large white bags as they hobbled in difficult shoes. The architect Hugh Casson wanders the site with Patrick O'Donovan, who represents the sponsors, the *Observer* newspaper. They smoke, they stroll, ordinary figures in the crowd. There were 8.5 million visitors, but the project was not universally popular. Telephone operators at the box office were reported to answer with a brisk: 'Festering Britain here.'

Casson knew what he was about and his concept was not strangled at birth by spinners, politicians, land pirates. He spoke of 'leisured gaiety': kiss-me-quick hats and fairground novelties alongside solemn Henry Moore figures. Popular-science gizmos and models for New Towns tested on a compliant audience. There would be no vaunting processional ways, no grand vistas, no cardboard rhetoric. The South Bank site was plotted like a series of rooms, opening out, one from another. 'London,' Casson told us, 'is a city of secret places.' He wanted to conjure that sensation of coming across a country lane nestling among uniform suburbs, the hidden garden overshadowed by grim warehouses. Wren churches flanked by Italian coffee bars: the Fairway Café, the Dairy Bar, the '51'.

The Thames would remain an 'off-stage presence', unstressed, vital to the city's sense of itself. The view across the river to the north bank was acknowledged: as a backdrop. 'We didn't want any resounding pronouncements,' Casson insisted. He designed hanging walkways, stairs, passages, so that visitors would get unexpected glimpses of light on the river. Where fences were necessary, they maintained the integrity of the site, with its bright 'nursery colours', against the overwhelming weight of London soot and dirt outside. When darkness fell, searchlight beams swept over dancing crowds, in serious holiday mood, jitterbugging, foxtrotting, in hats and long coats, to the sounds of a full orchestra in evening dress. Premature Europeans taking pleasure as a duty. End of an era. Captured on film, lost in the archives.

Battersea Park holds a vestige of the festival period in its gracious riverside walk. From the steps of the gilded Peace Pagoda you can look across the Thames to the Chelsea Physic Garden. Taking my breakfast on Battersea Bridge Road, among soft-shirt architects and resting actors perusing the broadsheets, I contemplate the good life of this stretch of the river. I have already crossed, by Vauxhall Bridge, to the north bank, to avoid developments around Nine Elms. I return to the south side by Chelsea Bridge. Beyond the park, spindly Albert Bridge has its own prohibition: ALL TROOPS MUST BREAK STEP WHEN MARCHING OVER THIS BRIDGE.

Broad avenues, dappled light. My Thames walk is a gentle marathon, the miles drift effortlessly; the balance between riverside development and awkward ghosts like St Mary's Church, Battersea, where William Blake married Catherine Boucher, is manageable. I echo Céline: 'On foot, at a sprint, my private Olympics.' I get through it, get it done, these new clusters of superior towers, shrouded wharfs, flamingo-pink extrusions reflected in potential marinas. The smooth folk, under blue umbrellas, taking coffee at round tables, are computer-generated, but content among neat beds of yellow and red flowers. The fabulous harbour, the promised future, is pink-on-blue: no green spaces, no embankment. Electrified towers advancing to the river's edge.

Near Wandsworth Park, I encounter the first walkers of the day, a map-around-neck group of sheepy seniors hitting the Wandle Trail. 'Tony Trude,' we are informed by a notice on the bridge, 'moored his houseboat and watched river life.' The boat sunk in 2001. What happened to Tony is not revealed.

Six young women are being trained in the use of invisible skis. They reactivate the northwest-passage metaphor with a clumping synchronized dance across imaginary snowfields. A man in a tight grey suit is shouting into his phone. 'I talked with the chairman this morning. I told him what was happening with Nigel. We're screwed.'

I stop to pay my respects to another riverside St Mary, the little church of the Putney Debates of 1647. At that time, 40 per cent of locals were watermen. A ferry carried travellers across the Thames to Fulham. Many notables, officers and common soldiers from the English Civil War, were present: Ireton, Thomas Rainsborough, Edward Saxby, John Wildman, William Goffe. That story is now a matter of recordings and pamphlets. Hard chairs, nothing elaborate in the way of pews, have been arranged on three sides around a plain altar table. Children take non-denominational instruction. 'These toilets are permanently closed.'

After Putney, the river is about exercise and pleasure. Boathouses, tracks for cyclists keeping up with rowing eights, bellowing at single scullers. Richmond is an English Arcadia; the grand villas, the follies and grottoes begin. Private roads for rifle and pistol clubs. Seven miles out from London, Catholics and other heretics were permitted to take up residence. That sense of exile can still be felt. At Ham House, I can't hear my own breath for the din of leaf-hoovering devices. The river is screened. The official path, much employed by joggers and dog-walkers, becomes a tunnel through tightly planted scrub. A stone needle at Teddington marks the end of the authority of the Thames Conservancy: 'Landward Limit 1909'. And the final stretch also of whatever cultural ballast I have carried from the Isle of Grain; we dream now of tame English villages instead of the open sea.

Kingston-upon-Thames is a pivotal place. I investigate the baroque reef of Bentalls, Ballard's favoured shopping centre; he drove there from Shepperton to make his Christmas purchases. The experience informed his final novel, the messianic *Kingdom Come*. 'The suburbs dream of violence,' he wrote. 'Sheltered by benevolent shopping malls, they wait patiently for the nightmares that will wake them into a more passionate world.' Bentalls has been here for ever; its 'benevolent' domination of a busy through-route seems as long-established as All Saints Church, with its fire-blackened union flag, ironclad memorials, and crowning ceremonies for ancient English monarchs. Kings married rivers: to command them, to control bridges – and to contemplate, like Ballard, the violence of love. Battle wounds heal in the marmoreal embrace of shadowy, incense-filled interiors and in the aisles of shopping centres illuminated by racks of glittering trade goods. A hundred mute flat-screen televisions are playing the same image: black smoke over an industrial wasteland. Plane crash? Oil fire? News report or CGI fiction?

I had been invited, once before, to a rendezvous at Bentalls. They were making a *South Bank Show* profile of Ballard. He had said generous things about *London Orbital* and it was thought that I might be a suitable talking head for a soundbite on shopping malls. Television is about phone calls from researchers who want you to do the research for them. About repeat calls and last-minute cancellations. Cash-in-hand promises dissolving into paperwork.

Ballard was unwell, they said. He couldn't travel. The mall piece would be done without him: in Bluewater, in a Kentish chalk quarry he had never visited. Jokingly, at the end of another film, he gave me my instructions. He thought he was playing the voice on the tape from *Charlie's Angels*. I saw him as the ghost of Hamlet's father. Everything was turning into Denmark. 'Iain, I've just passed the baton on to you. I want you to blow up the Bentall Centre and Bluewater. Your assignment is to destroy the M25.'

It appeared, from the multiple screens in the John Lewis complex, that somebody had beaten me to it; thick black plumes over a six-lane motorway. I made a quick sweep of the Kingston charity shops and now I wanted a cup of coffee. Picture windows stare across the Thames at a new red-brick estate, with pleasure boats parked right outside.

The self-service cafeteria was deserted. A young woman in a blue overall, red-gold hair tied back, attractive patina of freckles, stood behind me, cloth in hand, waiting. The table gleamed: no smear, no telltale rings. My orange juice was untouched. A Swedish fork lay across sturdy granules of scrambled egg. She didn't budge, she wanted something.

'Why is it, do you think, the best film critics are deaf?'

She had clocked my book. I found a tattered and taped copy of *Nouvelle Vague: The First Decade* by Raymond Durgnat in one of the charity pits. For half the price of my coffee. She was quite correct. I met two of the best of the breed, Durgnat himself and Manny Farber. I sat down with them for meals in noisy restaurants. And regretted an opportunity missed as both men struggled to pick up sound. Cinema was posthumous; Farber was painting in San Diego and Durgnat was being rediscovered when it was too late. That slight deafness distances the nuisance of the world and confers an aura of withheld wisdom, a disdainful but not cynical intelligence. They read the image with such clarity, made the sharpest connections, imposing their own subtitles. They knew that film was not all there is.

The waitress was a student at a local facility known as The Centre for Suburban Studies. Nobody was required to go anywhere; to walk, roam, or drive to fungal villages growing out into the flatlands around Cambridge. 'We do it all online,' she said. 'Satellite mappings. Google Earth.'

She sat down, opposite me, there were no supervisors in sight; she reached for my book. *Des Femmes Disparaissent*. An emotive still: a thin dark man with a gun standing behind a blonde woman (not unlike Janet Leigh). She has hands (which do not look like her own) clenched over her mouth. 'All French gangster films,' Durgnat glosses, 'are unconscious parables for the political scene.' The man is North African. The woman's shoulder straps are white.

'You've taken his chair. This character I knew.'

She drained my coffee, rim of froth over a downy moustache.

'He came here, between lectures, for a coffee and a croissant. To work on his book. He said there was no appreciable difference between libraries and cafés. Students only turned up at his classes to eat. They sat in ranks munching burgers as he read from Marc Augé's meditation on non-places. While they licked their fingers and texted.'

The creased academic, with his ponytail and black leather jacket, told her that he spent most of his life at the wheel. Two days in Kingston, one in Loughborough. He lived in Brighton. The kids were with the second wife in Liverpool. It was difficult to know if he was in a service station or a new university. Campuses were the garden cities of the motorway, more bars, banks, health centres than any failing county town. Lectures were like extra features on a DVD of travel.

He no longer wrote, he stared at the river. He asked for his coffee black and thought about taking up smoking again. One day he left the folder behind: nothing but unattributed quotations. 'Death ceases to be a definite boundary.' 'Place becomes a refuge to the habitué of non-places.' 'The film made him feel like someone watching a film.' She kept the John Lewis carrier bag. The man in the leather jacket never came back.

The Lemon on the Mantelpiece

Molesey congratulates its Olympic oarsmen: Andy Triggs-Hodge, Tom Jones, Acer Nethercott, Steve Rowbotham. There is a tablet in memory of the 'world's first ever manned balloon flight' by James Sadler in 1785. Green parakeets squawk in innocent apple trees.

Light rain was misting my spectacles by the time I reached the outskirts of Shepperton. The river path was blocked by a large two-tone Jaguar saloon, white and racing green: XJ MOTOR SERVICES. The upstream settlement has evident twenty-first-century loot, as well as Edwardian weekend villas and chalets. I record a blue plaque to the literary giant they choose to commemorate: THOMAS LOVE PEACOCK LIVED HERE, 1823–1866. Modernist white cubes with picture windows animated by reflections of light on water. Natural metaphors for liquidity in a time of recession.

Before I search out somewhere to sleep, I head for the station. That's where Ballard met me when I visited him. I never saw the inside of his house. We drove to a riverside pub and sat under whirring fans. I wondered why, after his great success with *Empire of the Sun*, he didn't relocate to one of those balconied, sharp-edged properties that were so attractive to the convalescing architects and blocked advertising men who populate his books. Foolish thought. Ballard was a working writer, first and last; the *where* of it was not to be disturbed. Fixed routines served him well; so many hours, so many words. Breakfast. *Times* crossword. Desk overlooking a natural garden. Stroll to the shops to observe the erotic rhythms of consumerism. Lunch standing up with *World at One* on the radio. Back to the study. Forty-minute constitutional down to the river. TV chill-out meditation: *The Rockford Files* rather than Kenneth Clark.

The interior landscape of the suburban semi was a mirage. The more you studied it, the cannier the decision to settle the family in Shepperton, all those years ago, appeared. It was far enough out of London to limit the pests, the time-devourers. When journalists gained access they were mesmerized by the reproduction Delvaux canvases propped on the floor, the aluminium palm tree, the lounger in the front room; dutifully they repeated the standard questions about surrealism and how *The Drowned World* was saturated in Max Ernst. The house in Old Charlton Road was a premature installation; a stage-set designed to confirm the expectations of awed pilgrims. But it was also a home in which the widowed author brought up three children who are always laughing in family snapshots. A refuge and the generator of some of the most potent myths of our time: one of those myths being Ballard himself, the safe house, the good father.

Ballard may be the first serious novelist whose oeuvre is most widely represented in books of interviews. And whose future belongs as much in white-walled warehouse galleries as the diminishing shelves of public libraries. He was so generous to those who found his phone number, so direct: he rehearsed polished routines – and always agreed, with unfailing courtesy, that the world was indeed a pale Xerox made in homage to the manifold of his fiction. A late moralist, he practised undeceived reportage, not prophecy: closer to Orwell than H. G. Wells. Closer to Orson Welles than to either. Closer to Hitchcock. Take out the moving figures on staircases that go nowhere and stick with hollow architecture that co-authors subversive drama.

Spurning critical theory, Ballard joined his near-namesake Baudrillard as the hot topic for air-miles academics. Students who have lost the habit of literature recognize, in the Shepperton master's forensic prose, intimations of a hybrid form capable of processing autopsy reports and invasion politics into accidental poetry. The incantatory manifesto, 'What I Believe', deploys Ballard's favourite device, the list: as he curates a museum of affinities.

I believe in Max Ernst, Delvaux, Dali, Titian, Goya, Leonardo, Vermeer,

Chirico, Magritte, Redon, Dürer, Tanguy, the Facteur Cheval, the Watts Towers, Böcklin, Francis Bacon, and all the invisible artists within the psychiatric institutions of the planet.

It was almost dark when I got there, after a street occupied by Indian restaurants, Chinese takeaways, charity and novelty shops. Scenographic maps known as 'Road Rugs' were on special offer at £22.95. Petrol pumps and service stations on which to wipe your muddy feet. A close-cropped man, hedge-hopping Old Charlton Road, spotted me as I lined up the shot.

'A writer bloke lives in that house. We've been out here twenty-five years. I've never set eyes on him, tell the truth. But he's been on the box.'

The silver Ford Granada is tilted at a drunken angle, like a sinking cabin cruiser, in the vestigial driveway. The privet hedge has been trimmed, the napkin of lawn made tidy. The Crittall window of the front room is overwhelmed by the sinister fecundity of a yucca. There is a cheerful yellow door with an inset panel of dark glass. The rear elevation is gritty with pebbledash. Perched on the wooden fence is a cut-out Sylvester, the Loony Tunes cat, waiting to pounce.

It is easy to understand how Ballard, after he lost his driving licence in the 1970s, found everything he required within an hour's walk, in any direction, out from this house. The ford where Martian invaders from *The War of the Worlds* crossed the river. Film studios. Reservoirs. Airport perimeter roads. And the footpaths, playgrounds, woods and streams he never felt the need to describe. Territory in which his three children grew up and thrived. That is the particular magic of his final book, *Miracles of Life*: how, through minimal changes of emphasis, he revises his mythology to give readers the illusion of being guided, at last, close to the heart of the mystery. A mystery which is somehow incarnate in the hidden spaces of the bereaved Shepperton property.

Even now, when Ballard was removed to the care and comfort of his friend and partner, Claire Walsh, in Shepherd's Bush, the house seemed possessed by a form of illumination not on stream to the rest of Old Charlton Road: the afterglow of decades of scrupulous composition. The physical effects we impose, in default of sentiment, to compensate for the writer's troubling absence. Fay, Ballard's elder daughter, told me that in her childhood the house did indeed stand out from its shrouded neighbours.

'When I was young the lights used to be on the whole time, even on bright summer days. Daddy loved the idea of brightness, intensity, as if we were living in the Med.'

In too much pain to take the wheel, Ballard returned to the old house with Fay. It was strange now, this installation her father had created from the objects of his private obsessions: Ed Ruscha postcards, Paolozzi silk-screen prints, a lurid corduroy sofa. A domesticated Kurt Schwitters assemblage, in which the writer could actually live and work. Producing the books his daughters did not read.

'I hadn't visited Shepperton for many years, until the summer of 2008, when Daddy was quite ill,' Fay said. 'I remembered a dried-up orange sitting on the mantelpiece in the nursery. I walked through the door and it was still there. I said, "Oh my goodness, you still have the orange." He looked at me and he said, very quietly, but seriously, "It's a lemon." It must have been there for at least forty years. I don't see the lemon as something eccentric. It's not a relic. It's covered in dust. It hasn't been moved. It's obviously important to him. And it's very beautiful.'

The front room, guarded by the spiky fronds of the yucca, was known, in an echo of colonial times, as the nursery. Fay presented Ballard with the plant, his Triffid-like co-tenant, in 1976; a Christmas present from Marks & Spencer. It was repotted several times and addicted to regular hits of Baby Bio. Fay reckoned that, influenced by the Ballard story 'Prima Belladonna', the yucca learnt to sway and sing. The nursery was the family television room, where supper was taken. An unused exercise bike, now a junk sculpture, faced the substantial set.

Chris Petit, who did make it out here, with a film crew, told me that he felt Ballard was comfortable in this constricted space because it reminded him of the internment camp, in the way that his parents' Shanghai villa was a translation of Weybridge. Unseen horrors beyond the immaculate lawns and protective screen of trees.

When international royalties and film rights rolled in, Ballard, modest and circumspect with consumer durables, commissioned copies of two Delvaux paintings destroyed in the Second World War. Brigid Marlin, who undertook this project, wanted to paint a Ballard portrait. He agreed, visiting the artist in her studio in Hemel Hempstead, and inviting her, in return, to recreate the lost works. One of which, *The Violation*, was placed in his study. Fay remembered how her father loved feeling 'as if he could walk into the painting and be part of the landscape with these beautiful women'. The propped-up Delvaux stood like a permanently occupied mirror to the left of the author's desk; with a long window, looking over the undisturbed garden, to the right.

Ballard was fascinated by technique, craftsmanship. When Fay, herself a painter, became a student of art history, he would discuss the anonymous interior spaces of Francis Bacon compositions and enthuse over the synthetic colours of carpets in hotel lobbies and airport lounges. As a young girl, Fay perched on the corduroy sofa in the study, mesmerized by a Max Ernst poster, *The Robing of the Bride*, in which the feathered cloak of a naked birdwoman reprised the blood-orange tones of the ridged material on which she was sitting. She trawled through the shelves of reference books: Dali, Warhol, Bacon, Helmut Newton. And other less obvious interests. Reviewing a Stanley Spencer biography in 1991, Ballard proclaimed the Cookham painter as the last representative of an 'innocent world before the coming of the mass media'. In a gesture of recognition, he said: 'Small Thames-side towns have a special magic, each an island waiting for its Prospero.'

Playing along with telephone interrogators, Ballard claimed that, like William Burroughs, he would have preferred to be a painter. Meaning that he lived by the discipline of the studio, infinite variations on a menu of established themes and motifs; that his books were sometimes collaged and cut up like *The Atrocity Exhibition*, so that degraded scene-of-the-crime photographs were palpable beneath the charged surface. He could move a narrative through time and space by a cataloguing of objects, buildings, machines. Burroughs, in his final period in the red cabin in Lawrence, Kansas, did indeed become a painter and an elective surrealist, a recorder of dreams. He would tend the cats, pick up his prescription, and blast away at cans of paint. The house, through vanity portraits by visiting celebrities, remembers him.

'Daddy produced two sculptures in the garden,' Fay said. 'I was very young, four or five. Sculptures made with milk bottles, chicken wire and concrete, slightly in the style of Henry Moore, but moving towards Paolozzi.'

The sculptures have vanished. The only record of their existence is a family photograph, taken in the garden, and reproduced in cropped form on the jacket of *Miracles of Life*. The three children, school-blazered, hair-ribboned, are delighted by something out of shot. Ballard, in dark sweater, white shirt, neat tie, smiles indulgently. Behind the fat cigar dangling from his hand, a minor sculptural intervention can be located: three diminishing Dali mouths stacked one above the other. The cement used in this work was also employed to make a monument for his son's pet rabbit.

There were Ballard oil paintings too, much later, with strong primary colours. And painstaking Dali copies undertaken to find how it was done: the bread, the rocks, the clouds. These things have disappeared. But typographical collages, like ransom notes to an alien culture, have survived: the provocative advertisements Ballard made for Dr Martin Bax's *Ambit* magazine. The ads display oblique fragments of text against found images. Claire Walsh, Ballard's conduit to the information superhighway, is presented in these pieces as an early muse. One of the photographs was taken in his Ford Zephyr – he was loyal to Ford – after Claire came close to drowning, when she plunged into the sea in Margate, wearing a coat and wellington boots.

The younger Ballard had active contacts in the London subterranea of the 1960s. Michael Moorcock, collaborator in mischief, editor of *New Worlds*, joined him on a whirling carousel that led them towards Burroughs, Borges and Eduardo Paolozzi. But the two writers were never more than tourists on the skirts of the hive at Muriel Belcher's Colony Room. 'There were a couple of drunken days around Bacon,' Moorcock told me, 'but Jimmy and I tended to make our excuses and leave, because we were really family men and wanted to get home in time to fetch the kids.'

The Ballard of Brigid Marlin's portrait is a St Jerome of Shepperton: bare table, pencil and manuscript. He undertook numerous European pilgrimages with Claire Walsh, as they investigated the genius of Velázquez, Goya, Dürer, Manet. 'He loved Netherlandish art,' Claire reported, 'especially Van Eyck.' In London, on Sunday afternoons, they haunted the National Gallery in Trafalgar Square. When I followed in their footsteps, before moving around the corner to the National Portrait Gallery, to search out the Marlin portrait, it was not on display. 'We've left him in the dark,' the man at the desk said. 'Much better for preservation. We can only show writers the general public request. Like Jane Austen.'

I looked for a lemon by Francisco de Zurbarán to represent the decaying object on the nursery mantelpiece. The closest I came was a still life of oranges and walnuts by Luis Meléndez. It wouldn't do, Ballard was nothing if not precise. He said what he meant and he meant what he said. The lemon, according to Lucia Impelluso, is a potent antidote to poison and a symbol of 'amorous fidelity'.

Fools of Nature: To Oxford

Castle walls: Walter Scott-land buzzed by Heathrow's oversubscribed flight path. Faith keeps the jumbos up there, faith we no longer have. A silhouette of heritage real estate stamped on a tin tray. This riverside avenue, under ancient trees, from which random plebeians are ruthlessly excluded: Royal Windsor, nemesis of walkers.

THIS IS A PROTECTED SITE UNDER SECTION 28 OF THE SERIOUS CRIME AND POLICE ACT 2005. TRESPASS ON THIS SITE IS A CRIMINAL OFFENCE.

Much of the official Thames Path, after Shepperton, is nervous of uninvited guests. Savage dogs are name-checked, never seen. NEIGHBOURHOOD WATCH. NO ACCESS TO THE RIVER. The upstream property portfolio is a mirror of our times, shifting from customized baronial (turrets, lawns, gazebos) to Carmel (California) glass-and-pine: the lifestyle deck, the private dock. A waterside balcony occupied, in one case, by a Blues Brother mannequin sprawled on a designer chair. The epitome of cool is when you can afford to hire somebody to chill for you. When you are too lazy to be lazy.

The more pretentious mansions are being re-conceptualized by IT operations, corporate hospitality, money religions. They take the 'bank' part of riverbank very seriously. You invest in the historic Thames. You buy into the pleasure principle as a matter of business. But it's challenging to be always on show. You don't want grockles fouling the vista, lime-green anoraks gawping over the garden gate. The royals take the privacy fetish to extremes. Not content with park, castle, mausoleum, home farm, they insist on fences inside fences. They shunt ramblers across the water for an infuriating trudge down a busy road, through scrub woods and open fields: to the commuter-hamlet of Datchet.

Wouldn't I, if I had the equity, be out here too? A Mr Toad on the Thames: boat, swimming place, picture window? For sure. I have fantasized, most of my London life, about living in Narrow Street, Limehouse, on the bend of the river: with the comforting knowledge that it can never happen. My relish for this section of the path comes from voyeurism, a puritan kick at advancing through scenes from which I am barred, English arcadias that remain tantalizingly out of reach. I haven't noticed a single swimmer anywhere from Gravesend to Maidenhead. Many rippling blue pools on manicured lawns, no plungers. No medicated Burt Lancaster, in scrotum-pinching briefs, Australian crawling, length after length, down chlorinated puddles that mock the flowing river.

Ghosts are out in the morning mist, shivering among the willows, appearing and reappearing on the road ahead. I saw my late father, at a point where sodden roots dropped into a woodland pool. The fine sand looked like a beach of gold coins. The dead come back three times, so they say. Their dreams and ours share common space in the water margins. I saw Ezra Pound, black hat, long coat, going down into the Underground in Kensington, a year after I'd visited his grave in Venice; crossing the lagoon to San Michele, the isle of the dead. Slender craft, elegant mourners: the Venice of Nicolas Roeg's *Don't Look Now.* We want what ghosts can't have, heat. Warmth. Engagement. They lead us on, bone masks waiting for the right ventriloquist.

As I walked the Thames, I made lists of my own, photographs of diversion signs, private roads – and records of riverside camps, from the bivouac on the Isle of Grain to this hooped tent in the undergrowth near Bray. I was dodging around in beechwoods, trying to frame the crenellated white mansion on the other shore, where Hammer Films did their bit for the export trade by reinvigorating English Gothic with homoeopathic doses of Christopher Lee and

Peter Cushing. The pup tent was hidden by a covering of twigs, in a primitive hide, and guarded by a wolfish dog. I was sure that I had seen the tent before, several times, but the owner, if he was inside, did not show himself.

It was late in the year to be sleeping rough. My Thames excursion spanned the seasons. I kept breaking away, pushing the circuit further and further out: Liverpool, Manchester, Leeds, Sheffield, Hull, Middlesbrough, Gateshead. Taking whatever was offered by way of casual employment as itinerant culture preacher. And then returning to pick up where I left off: with that tent, the unknown camper, scouting the ground ahead of me. I had wasted so many months wondering how I could find a way out of London. Now, as a result of the Olympic Park enclosures, I had to accept the fact that there was no going back. Long hot days across the estuarine marshes dissolved into a deliriously rufous autumn in established woodlands between Maidenhead and Cookham. Detouring, yet again, I come on a picturesque cottage offering Kundalini yoga, serpent-power sex: 'with immediate results'. Massage therapy, home-made chutney. Off-shore investment advice, honey from local hives. The Stanley Spencer Gallery is closed, but the graves are always open in the little riverside burial patch, that 'holy suburb of heaven', where the eccentric painter now lies. Cookham resurrections wind back time like an old clock, deceased villagers yawning and scratching towards a second Thames baptism. Turk's boatyard, the setting for Spencer's swan-upping ceremony, and for Christ's appearance at the village regatta, has been converted into private flats. To come here, early, to row up towards Marlow, picnic, swim, was our favourite family outing. Stanley Spencer, that most grounded and domesticated of English painters, was more adventurous. He made it to China, on one of the first culture-binge exchanges, in 1954. He managed a couple of paintings of the Ming tombs on the outskirts of Beijing and a few sketches from the air. He lost a stone and a half in weight and never left England again.

Taking refreshment in an empty gastro pub, I found that

Ballard's interest in Spencer came into sharper focus: men of the river, choosing to keep London at a distance, while distilling a peculiarly English brew of perverse but undeceived sexuality. When Ballard, having lost his driving licence, took to walking around Shepperton, there was a moment of revelation: 'Through the tranquil TV suburbs moved a light as serene as any Stanley Spencer had seen at Cookham.' The dozy riparian settlements with which these men had such lengthy associations are now branded with their names. Cookham trades on Spencer, on the landscapes he turned out to pay his bills. Shepperton is yet to find a way to exploit Ballard.

The Ballard character in *The Kindness of Women* decides that it is time to take a Thames cruise and Cookham is the chosen destination. His partner, hoping to liberate the 'prisoner of Shepperton', is not enthusiastic. 'Too many angels dancing in the trees. Be honest, do you really want to see Christ preaching again at the regatta?' Ballard, his arm around his girlfriend's waist, as she grips the wheel, elects to look back at what he is leaving behind: 'the film studios and the riverside hotels, receding from me like the Bund at Shanghai'.

The impetus to complete this Thames walk came from an old wound: I was fulfilling, in actuality, an imagined journey from an earlier fiction. In *Radon Daughters*, my characters undertook a triangulation between three mounds: Oxford (with its hidden well), Cambridge (view of historic colleges), and the removed earthwork that once stood, ring of trees at the summit, beside the Royal London Hospital in Whitechapel. They walked, my creatures, keeping journals. And I felt it my duty to stay ahead of them, to base the fable on truth, a record of the hard miles. Time squeezed. I was still scrabbling about as a bookdealer, doing bits and pieces of journalism to stay afloat. Necessity overtook research: I marched, my unwilling shadows alongside me, as far as Marlow. Then I cheated, nudged the bogus journal forward to Dorchester-on-Thames. And tramped the last miles to Oxford in company with Renchi Bicknell and Chris Petit, who was using a new video camera to log projected expeditions around the 'perimeter fence' of English culture.

We acknowledged Paul Nash's Wittenham Clumps, his *Landscape of the Vernal Equinox*. Petit's interest in Nash extended about as far as those frozen seas of metal, abstracted scrapyards of wrecked fighter planes: *Totes Meer*. His attitude to landscape was German; the era of feature films was now over, but he was never comfortable without a pylon at the edge of the frame. He told me that he had endured his only English studio picture, an underlit Strindbergian version of P. D. James's *An Unsuitable Job for a Woman*, in Bray. What he remembered most about the experience was the caravan of chancers and parasites, hanging around the shoot, flogging dubious Rolex watches, designer drugs, sporting underwear. Like blackmarketeers in the rubble of a captured city.

I tried, without success, to draw out Renchi's memories of a hike from Hackney to Swansea, then the west of Ireland: all gone, visionary highlights emerging decades later as engravings. Walks overlapped walks: as films, paintings, poems, books read and books abandoned. The Thames Valley, even in clammy mist, when no excursionists were up and about, was overpopulated. Writing was selective quotation. In the novel, in *Radon Daughters*, the journalkeeper, as he stands on the bridge at Day's Lock, rejoices in the knowledge that one of his companions has destroyed the manuscript of a lifelong work from which he could not, otherwise, have extracted himself. 'He has absolved me of the complexities of the past. We hymn the emptiness of the landscape: corduroy mud, pylons, private orchards. Least known, most favoured.'

The clamp of ice, an abrupt transition into Cormac McCarthy bleakness, bit at my finger ends, splitting skin; rutted mud made field margins into a balancing act. The river was frozen in narrow channels around locks. I squeezed my shard of red brick for warmth. I passed two humans that morning, sliding through Marlow in the direction of the station: a languid Shelley-youth, trailing Isadora Duncan scarf, unbuttoned cuffs, smoking his breakfast, in company with a keen, bespectacled black girl talking very fast about electro-static attraction. 'You *want* to be a doctor?' drawls the young man. 'Why would you want to work with *sick* people?' He shrugs into his velvet jacket. He turns up the volume on his ear bud.

After Henley the hit of the wooded slopes, witnessed from a footbridge over the lock, is sublime. It's one of those moments when we see so much more than we know: the surging, ruffled water, skeletal black trees, ink strokes diminishing into the point where river meets sky.

My breakfast in the town, suitable café found after a lengthy search, was excellent: Italian. With fresh orange juice, real coffee, crispy bacon. And conversation with a friendly waitress. I noticed a Wyndham Lewis title on display in the window of an antiquarian bookseller: *The Ideal Giant*, his first separately published literary work. An item I didn't possess, and couldn't afford, even if the shop were open. Another life, move on. Let Lewis lie dormant among the glassine ranks of blind Huxleys and barking Woolfs. These bookish enterprises, embedded in commuter villages, are indistin-guishable from superior funeral directors: preserved tombstone volumes, miniature marble headstones. Your name in places you don't want to find it.

The man with the tent was drinking at a frost-slicked picnic table. He was waiting for me, a spare can punctured and hissing like a gas-canister time bomb.

'What took you so long?'

Did he know me? Was he aware of the interest I'd taken in his campsites? The dog snarled, but didn't move. The man was dressed in hooded parka, multipocketed camouflage trousers and serious boots. I'm hopeless with faces, background artists from deleted films are more familiar than my immediate neighbours, but this person, so firmly positioned over his clutch of blue cans, rang all the bells. Like a backwoodsman from *Deliverance* cutting through the screen. He took off a leather glove to carve a hunk of meat for his hound. LOVE-HATE knuckles: one broken and white, a bolt about to pierce tight skin. A compass rose tattoo. Chobham Farm, Angel Lane. The long shed. Cribbage on a packing case. Mick.

'Still living down Hackney?'

He picked up the conversation from a 1970s tea break, interrogating me, the newcomer, and giving nothing away in exchange. Where he slept. With whom. He noticed the way I fiddled nervously with the smoothed fragment of brick I'd carried from the Isle of Grain.

'Swap.'

Mick offered a closed fist. Giving up my totemic stone was abdicating from the purity of the walk. I wanted to bury it at the spring from which the Thames flowed. But the exchange, eye to eye, no looking down, had to be made. Cold: an ice cube scalded my hand.

'With all the work on the Olympic site, some bastard is going to find the platinum drum. You can only get there by water.'

I left him at the table, watching me, as I pushed on, saying that I had to be in Reading before it got dark, to find a bed for the night. Mick had the scornful expression he'd perfected in his crib. The certainty that I was playing at it, a faker, a person who wrote about walks he hadn't achieved.

By Sonning Lock, evening closing in, I heard the yelps of a female cox driving a reluctant eight to one final push: that saw them trapped in the ice. Blades scratching uselessly. Like bird claws. No purchase. The thin shell with the steaming Reading University athletes was wedged, a symbol of elegant impotence. They scraped, faster and faster, on the thin ice sheet into which they had reversed. The young woman's reflex barks of command tapered off into the silence of the coming night. A bitter cold fingered their burning lungs. The imprisoned craft, a membrane between the heat of the oarsmen and the black river, adjusted to its novel status: part of the picture. Bare trees. High wall. Lock. Voyeur with raised camera. All of it fading into the enveloping darkness.

I took Mick's chilled object from my pocket, the metallic wafer. I had seen such a thing, once before, in Stratford. A silver nugget like the one young Freddie set rocking on the table of the brown-panelled pub. A mercury messenger for a new communion. Carry it to the abbey at Dorchester-on-Thames. Leave it there, a fee against my entry to the city of spooks and spires.

It was high summer when Anna rejoined me, taking an early train to Reading. I had been drawn away, back north to Liverpool, then Ireland, Holland, Norway, Sweden, but we were reunited in time for my birthday. I planned an easy first session, a night in a river-facing pub in Streatley, before our Dorchester return and a stroll to Oxford. There was also, guided by Mick's platinum tablet, a recon-nection with the period of Chobham Farm walks, a group photograph on the bridge at Streatley, by the sign for the Swan Hotel. The Ridgeway, the Icknield Way, the Thames Path: they intersect at this point in the river. Chalk grassland to the south, but-terflies, orchids. Highway to the megaliths.

Reading claims possession of an ORACLE, but it turns out to be a sprawling retail park. A woman, extricating herself from this zone, tells us that she is heading towards Paddington, then Bloomsbury; she has no map and not the slightest notion of what sits in her way. Floaty chiffon, turban, bangles: she's as feathery and vague as a lost guest from Garsington Manor, snubbed by Lady Ottoline Morrell. Our conversation is interrupted by the din of a helicopter revving up on a riverside pad no bigger than a trampoline. The intrusive black bug is the first of many, the Thames along this reach is a runway for impatient commuters, airport hoppers who don't have the patience to urge their chauf-feurs through snarled motorway traffic.

The going is easy, but we are never more than tolerated intru-ders: private schools, fenced woods with notices in Polish warning off unlicensed fishermen. River cruisers (nautical caps, large gins) churn out a steady wash. Concrete pillboxes in tangled under-growth. A fragrant lady from the Baltic in tailored uniform checks us into the Streatley hotel.

A pre-dinner amble tells us that the Bloomsbury Morrells, patrons of weekending artists, more Huxleys and Woolfs, were the big local brewers. They took care of the laundry for their labourers and organized seaside outings in due season. We return for a celebratory meal and a few drinks, while we sit watching the lights on the river. There is a corporate function, involving numerous mobile-phone instructions and revisions, on a floating restaurant.

Heading, none too steadily, for a welcome pillow, Anna kicks the sharp corner of the big bed and breaks a toe. Dosed with painkillers and brandy, the swollen digit strapped, she tramped on, making the best of it, for another two days: Dorchester, Oxford, and out to the station.

Those academics who weren't in their pods on motorways were wandering friars on the footpaths of England. Nature-writers like Edward Thomas and Richard Jefferies were rediscovered and revalued, their downland walks invigilated by keen-eyed young men in khaki shorts. Robert Macfarlane, Cambridge lecturer, tree-climber, champion of wild places, led the way back to the era of ambulatory essays on dew ponds, standing stones, pilgrim tracks. He came off the Icknield Way and over the bridge to Streatley. Slipping awkwardly, he suffered Anna's fate: broken ribs. 'Bone for chalk,' he told me. Forfeit paid for access to the Ridgeway, a geological shift experienced in the nerves and sinews. But Streatley also trades in the more indolent literary tradition of messing about on the river: Jerome K. Jerome's trio of incompetent excursionists, unaware that they were pioneering soft-commission TV fodder for moonlighting comedians, came ashore to stock up on provisions. Local pamphlets have it that the opening scene of Kenneth Grahame's *Wind in the Willows* is set on the backwater beside the old Streatley Mill.

In 1893 Oscar Wilde was persuaded by Alfred Douglas, his Bosie, to take a house for the summer in Goring, across the bridge from Streatley. Walking with the poet Theodore Wratislaw into woods that slope down to the Thames, Wilde paused, stood for a moment, and said that he was satisfied. This view was as much as he wanted to experience. Let whatever lay around the bend remain a mystery. Wilde's biographer Richard Ellmann interprets this as a gesture of unease, intimations of coming pain and distress. In Goring, Wilde entertained his guests by sculling in a blue shirt and pink tie. Like an unelected member of Henley's famous Leander Club. He wrote the first act of *An Ideal Husband*.

In Wallingford, Anna searches for a chemist. We have a pint in the courtyard of a coaching inn. The bristling Russian waitress, slamming the glasses down, says: 'This is *not* what I do. I am scientist.' A frail old lady in Shillingford tells us that we are occupying her bench, she comes out every afternoon at this time to smoke a cigar. In Dorchester, we admire the Jesse window, genealogy taking the form of a loaded tree. An orchard of saints perched like partridges. In Abingdon we sit beside a troop of care-in-the-community folk on an outing to the pub. They are calm, taking food in measured fashion, slow and steady, where their minders leap for phones, trot backwards and forwards to the bar, kick doors, screw up newspapers, rush outside to smoke. Never failing to remind the disadvantaged ones of what a fabulous time they are having.

Through our long and uninspired Oxford approach, prohibitions mount. Anna becomes quieter and quieter, as she manages the waves of pain from her broken toe. PLEASE DO NOT LET YOUR DOG FOUL *THIS AREA*. COWS WITH BABY CALVES, KEEP WELL AWAY FROM THEM. PRIVATE FISHING NO DAY TICKETS NO LITTER CAMPING OR FIRES. BEWARE ROAD CROSSING AHEAD. *PLEASE TAKE YOUR LITTER HOME*. CLEAN UP OR PAY UP. NO NIGHT FISHING BY ORDER. PRIVATE RAFTS: PLEASE KEEP OFF. POLICE DO NOT LEAVE YOUR VALUABLES IN YOUR CAR.

We pass under bridges, through pylon plantations, into the heritage zone of boathouses, parks and distant towers; Anna dropping further and further back. When I wait, at stile or lock, she says: 'I don't want to talk.' All her concentration is required to put one foot in front of another.

Staying on the river path, we go through Folly Bridge. I made so much of Oxford in my earlier fiction – terrorist incidents, episodes in pubs – that I find the city redundant now. You can play fast and loose with descriptive prose. Poetry, I have discovered, is the orgasm that can't be faked. It happens or it doesn't. No cure. If there is poetry in this place, I'm not ready for it. We carry straight on to the station, where Anna takes the train back to London. I can't do it. I head off in search of a sleeping bag. As Don DeLillo says, 'We need time to lose interest in things.'

Northland

In the Belly of the Architect

The glory of Hull, as contemplated from the Lower Lea Valley, is the certainty that there is somewhere worse than Hackney, the crappest of crap towns in a list made by idiots. I wasn't charging off to a defunct whaling port that offered a refuge to John Prescott, New Labour's token bully, and Philip Larkin, the Eeyore of English verse. Now I know better. We've been misled by stereotypes customized for export: the crooked-mouthed, wife-beating old cricketers, those would-you-credit-it pipe-suckers. And wearied by Prescott's mangled arias of self-justification and class war. (Conducted from state-owned, rent-free apartments and striped croquet lawns in the Home Counties.) Big John has spent too long south of the M62. A ripe colour photograph complementing the inevitable sideways shuffle into reality television presents a Dorian Gray portrait finished by Francis Bacon. Inside the flaccid sporran of superfluous, hard-dining flesh is the imprint of a rugged Heathcliff workingman, a union organizer who looks like a fit and glowering Fred Truman. A good metaphor for the way the north's ruined industrial heritage has been prostituted by grand projects of regeneration (new forms of colonial patronage). Beyond Kingston-upon-Hull is the most blasted of heaths, the Holderness Plain: flat, melancholy, bone-heaped, crumbling into the sea. Will Self, in a meltdown final panel in *Walking to Hollywood*, nominated the stretch between Flamborough Head and Spurn Point as the physical manifestation of Alzheimer's disease, the slow death of English memory. Men climbing prematurely from trains to piss against vanishing barbed-wire fences.

An ASBO family, deemed too recidivist for one of Hackney's more infamous estates, faced expulsion to a place they could not begin to fix on the map: Hull. Which these unfortunates, picking up their travel passes, heard as Hell. And took their leave, with down-cast eyes and Dante-tread, as if condemned to walk barefoot up the Great North Road on a causeway of burning coals. Only to discover a thrusting new enterprise zone, lavished with architectural interventions like The Deep, a flashy Terry Farrell dockside fish-tank with as much cultural relevance as the MI6 building, that Aztec jukebox on the south bank of the Thames.

A drunken man with a smashed nose was sheltering in a deep recess of Farrell's signature regeneration project when I visited Hull's marina at night. 'I've fallen off me bike,' he explained. Bike-less, and lacking coat or jacket, he huddled beside a hot-air vent, staring across the dock and wondering what had happened to the town he left behind that afternoon.

Hull City – for a few hours – sat at the head of football's Premier League. It wouldn't last, we knew that. But at this moment, Hull was on top of the world, bragging rights underwritten by New Labour's publicity machine. Chris Petit left an important figure out of his architect, cook, stand-up comedian grouping: the claret-supping, sclerotic, millionaire football gaffer with the well-exercised jaws. The working-class champion as symbol of a managerial elite. Football is money, the Esperanto we all speak. Barber-shop babble, taxi chat. A rising city with cultural pretensions requires two things: an iconic artwork and a Premier League club. Hull hoovered up serious investment: malls, pedestrianized precincts, one of those Orwellian TV screens on a triumphalist arch, put in place to antici-pate good news from the Olympics. And, as the stamp of media approval, a visitation from the architect Will Alsop in his high-wheel, off-road vehicle (with attendant film crew), to tell them where they had gone wrong.

Alsop, in Petit's terms, was a figure of the times: architect, painter, air-miles conceptualist. Metropolitan architects, presumed to have a competence in producing new skin to cover the skull of dying industries, were parachuted into the northlands as aesthetic Gau-leiters. The political classes imagine that all an economically dysfunctional area requires is a new museum: content unimportant, style paramount. Institutes of pop music, eco-parks. They were launched with millennial seed funds and lottery loot. And they failed, withering away at the first nip of fiscal reality. What the promoters never grasped is that culture is what happens between museums, on the street, in markets and pubs. Museums are sheds in which to invade the past and make it safe, nostalgia bunkers busking for oil sponsorship. Architects, like other artists of the era, flourished as masters of the pitch. Will Alsop, a charismatic documentary presenter, was himself presented with Barnsley: to dress with haloes of light until it became a Tuscan hill town.

Alsop's reputation was made with an award-winning library (and media centre) for Peckham. The building photographs well. Very few people will inspect the original, nobody is rushing down to Peckham: the reproduction is the story. A green storage unit propped on slim black rods, topped with the word LIBRARY, so that it's not mistaken for a BMW showroom. 'A library is an old-fashioned term,' Alsop says, 'which in the age of the internet, CD-ROM, fax, electronic mail, TV, videos, talking books and performing arts, seems somehow redundant.' Privately, as a favour to a friend, he designed a more modest book depository in an Islington garden: for London's biographer Peter Ackroyd. An elegant version of the traditional book- (and bicycle-) filled shed.

The Alsop project that concerned me now was his take on the coast-to-coast motorway, Hull to Liverpool, the M62. Hungry for a larger canvas than Barnsley, the architect proposed a SuperCity folded around the entire road. He published an illustrated book of supporting essays. And he promoted the idea, vigorously, with a television film. As a presence admitted to the intimacy of our screens, Alsop looks like a man who gives (and receives) good lunch; excellent company, reflex cigarette. Easy shirt, unstructured French-blue artisan's jacket. Free-flowing monologues in a seductive deep-throat growl. Projects collapse, prizes are won. There is commissioned work in Germany and in France. And lottery-funded crumbs in the English badlands, marginal constituencies unlucky enough to be noticed by box-ticking central government. A topography of virtual masterpieces that will never be built. Noughties architecture is the art of getting some other sucker to take the blame.

Discovered, nozzling his jeep on a northern forecourt, Alsop can't wait to grab a felt-tipped pen and deface the windscreen. He lights up, before taking stock of his surroundings: 'Cheap and nasty. Horrid, revolting, evil. Complete and utter shit.' Here is a motorway utopian, an architect accepting just enough work to fund his true passion, painting. Painting on windows. Cartoons teased from agribiz edgelands. Coloured pens rattle across the dashboard. Tobacco contrails improve the visual complexity. Thick gold signet ring on paw. An actor who can drive and talk at the same time. Man of the road. Service-station philosopher.

He strikes east out of Liverpool, making for the M62, heading for Hull and memories of childhood. He schmoozes the fixed camera, architecture as infotainment. 'It's about playing.' He gestures towards a ravished horizon of cooling towers, no-purpose sheds and glinting rivers. 'This is an itinerant area that you can't define as country or city.' There is nothing quite so agreeable as pulling on to the hard shoulder, to conjure, pen on glass, soft-sculptures from innocent ground which would otherwise be polluted by Barratt estates. Chris Petit, when we motored up and down the boulevards of Alsop's imaginary city, admitted that, on the whole, he'd rather take up residence in a skip alongside a smoking landfill mountain on Rainham Marshes.

Alsop needs a bed for the night. What can the road offer? Patrick Keiller, reprising Daniel Defoe's *Tour through the Whole Island of Great Britain*, for his film *Robinson in Space*, speaks with weary affection of the Travelodge franchise. You know exactly what you are going to get: minimalism. Minimal efficiency, minimal fuss, minimal satisfaction. The budget hotel, the overnight stay on expenses, is a salient feature of the SuperCity. Alsop describes the experience in terms of Chaucerian collisions.

'People don't actually meet or talk in hotels,' he told me, when I visited him at the offices of his architectural practice, in a leafy and salubrious riverside quarter of London. 'If you go to a hotel chain, it's perfectly clean and comfortable, but the public spaces aren't there. You're not expected to sit around and mingle. They're missing a trick. All these guys, particularly travelling salesmen, have a lot of stories. Hotels are not creating the stage for things to happen.'

In SuperCity, social interaction is important; partying, yarning at leisure over good food. That classic exchange between travellers, pilgrims with experiences to share. Dimly lit bars from which consenting adults walk away unscathed. One-night stands of reps, evangelists, tribute bands, traded footballers, academics without tenure, oil-company hatchet men deciding where they can close another filling station. Neon nests where transients, coming offroad with the glamour of elsewhere, make a pitch to the girl behind the counter. The nightscape of the great American Depression as reflected in film noir dreams.

With the shudder of traffic still in the vein, the hard miles between Burnley, Bradford, Pontefract, Alsop made a big decision: *they are all the same.* A specialist cheese counter, a theatre forty miles to the south, a night on the town: parochial divisions no longer play.

'If these people live in Barnsley and they want an upmarket shop, they go to Leeds. If they want a jolly good market – they used to have one of their own, but it's gone – they drive to Doncaster. If they feel like a good thrash in the evening, they think nothing of heading off to Manchester. They use this plethora of towns, cities and villages as one SuperCity. All I had to do was stretch the concept to take in Liverpool and Hull.'

Framed in the sunset window of his vehicle, this prophet of effervescent sprawl is a true icon. The hieratic representation of a sacred personage lasered into glass. Adrift on the M62, meditating on the death of locality, Alsop is as much a representative of an historical period as Vincent van Gogh, in that molten self-portrait *Painter on the Road to Tarascon.*

'If you take roughly twenty miles on either side of the M62, there are roughly 15.4 million people. Your journey can take for ever, because of the traffic. Or it can be clear and quick. That's how I came to the conclusion that it would be a very good thing to *increase* the density. All those towns and cities are charged with building more houses. What they do, all the housing providers like Wimpey and Barratt, they look at the cheap option – which is to build on the edge of existent centres. This is not good practice. There are lots of places in the middle of those cities where you can build. There is no shortage of derelict sites. There are vast tracts of car parks just waiting.'

Liverpool remains a source of regret for the London architect, a European 'City of Culture' lacking the bottle to push through risky but potentially rewarding commissions. The offer, made to Alsop's practice and then withdrawn, was for the Fourth Grace. An embellishment for the Pierhead, the Grace would sit on equal terms alongside three 'iconic' structures: the Liver Building, the Cunard Building and the Port Authority Building. Alsop, chatting to the television writer/producer Phil Redmond, employs that degraded word. As does Redmond. It's a Tourette's-syndrome reflex, when there is a whiff of regeneration in the air.

'We're looking for an iconic statement, a beacon statement,' Redmond delivers. When Liverpool came to sell itself to the colour supplements – IT'S HAPPENING IN LIVERPOOL, EUROPEAN CITY OF CULTURE 2008 – it was with Gormley-Man from Crosby Beach, staring with blind eyes at the Mersey, at the Corinthian portico of William Brown's mid nineteenth-century museum and library, and a featureless spread of CGI towers.

'This is the western gateway,' Alsop says. He loves the fact that you can drive to Hull, by way of the M62, in less time than it takes to cross London. The obvious conclusion, as he sees it, is to make all this disconnected stuff, all the beacon destinations – Tate Liverpool, Ikea Warrington, Trafford Park, Libeskind's Imperial War Museum of the north, the Lowry Centre, Terry Farrell's The Deep – into one unified smudge. A mega-development twenty miles deep.

'We won the competition in Liverpool,' Alsop explained, 'but it wasn't just architecture. There was a financial element as well.

What happened was that there was another development, King's Dock. Their own development. It went over budget. They had to raid our £70 million.' The contract was cancelled. Leaving the regretful architect musing on betrayed visions.

'The big asset they've got is the river. Fascinating streets with boarded-up pubs and wonderful sugar warehouses. If I were chief planner of Liverpool, I would be making this area as dense as possible. When you can look south over a majestic river, why do you build mediocre stuff inland, where you wouldn't want to be? It sounds very simple, but if you wake up to a good view, you feel better.'

The M62 induces reverie, Wordsworthian recollections of childhood. Alsop grew up in Northampton. There is a moment in his television documentary when he speaks about standing on a motorway bridge with his father, gazing down on the traffic, road as river, before a family picnic in an adjacent field. His father died within a week of this epiphany.

Hull, the architect reported, was the destination for a holiday with a friend whose father was in the wet-fish trade. 'It was thriving, a real fishing port. On the other side of the river, they took all the elements of the catch, crushed at the bottom of the hold, and turned them into pet food. The whole port was full of women in pinnies gutting fish. All these people lived in terraced houses which backed on to the river.'

Alsop spoke of Mr Bogg, an employer on the docks. 'They're buggers in Hull,' this man said. 'They steal my wooden fish boxes to make furniture. I wouldn't mind, but whenever they go anywhere the sods ride in a taxi.'

We witnessed those taxis. Lines of them growling in the sleet. And the weekend-partying tribes of the Humberside diaspora. And the granite banks converted into lap-dancing clubs. I came to Hull, in Chris Petit's comfortable, diesel-devouring Mercedes, to launch a test drive down Alsop's SuperCity highway. When we strolled through the icy downpour that first evening, we were hustled by touts at the doors of hard-drinking, red-light venues loud enough not to require further advertisement. The women were dressed to please: to please themselves. A girl with bootlace-ribbons barely supporting a skimpy vest sat outside a pub, chatting on her pink mobile, watching raindrops bounce off the round metal table. 'You pregnant, love?' called a passing lad. 'Your breasts is standing right out.' She was busy, he got away with the compliment. She flicked a finger.

With its generous civic spaces, close alleys, part-developed warehouses and docks, Hull endorses the Alsop project: collision, celebration, short-term migration. A party town glorying in its Premier League status, its windfall of unaccounted dosh. Helicopters shadowed us across the Humber Bridge, as we cruised into a zone of imposing stadia, retail parks and pagoda restaurants. The clatter of blades dispersed sombre flashbacks to suicide news reports. I remembered Alison Davies, whose twelve-year-old son, Ryan, suffered from a hereditary condition called Fragile X Syndrome. Ms Davies travelled by train from Stockport, to plunge from the bridge with her son. The motorway city is also a conduit for disturbed and disadvantaged people, at the end of their tether, who have pushed themselves to the limits of a specific and unforgiving geography.

There were reasons why I didn't visit Hull often enough in the past to appreciate its now obvious virtues. The percussionist Paul Burwell got an art gig up here on the first wave of development money. He liked it, found an abandoned boathouse, and stayed: in what proved to be a tragic exile. The story of which I recovered, much later, from contradictory and highly coloured reports. Burwell fell out with a community of travellers who shared his riverside wilderness. There were incidents, assaults. Beatings with iron bars. Returned from hospital, Paul took to his bed, keeping up his spirits with infusions of supermarket whisky, supplied for a consideration by one of the traveller kids. The lad turned a profit by cutting the cheap booze with antifreeze. Being of a strong constitution, used to running up ladders with knapsacks of petrol, Burwell lasted a few months on this toxic regime, before he was discovered on the frozen riverside, stiff as a board. That was the legend, the story peddled in London.

The ultimate deterrent was Philip Larkin. While the horn-rimmed spider was in residence, I kept well away. For late modernists, Larkin was a sinister librarian with a schoolgirl bondage collection in the desk drawer. The phantom at the window in Pearson Park. Hull flattered Larkin's prejudices, even as it bought him the time to hone his morbid and singular craft. At the other extreme of the poetic spectrum, the dustwrapper of J. H. Prynne's *Kitchen Poems* set Hull at the centre of a gridded chart of North Sea oil exploration. Already, in 1968, Prynne finds currency being diverted to the north-east, while real people are 'slipping off the face of that lovely ground'.

The vulnerability of Hull's geographical position is brought home by a story in London's *Evening Standard*. They report that a Russian nuclear bomber penetrated British defence systems by flying within ninety seconds of the old fish port. The Blackjack jet was carrying out a mock attack, undetected by RAF interceptors. The breach was thought to be the most serious since the Cold War. The supersonic aircraft took off from Engels Air Base, near Saratov on Russia's Volga Delta. Hull takes the first hit: for everything from the abolition of slavery to innovative poetry. From malicious investment to nuclear holocaust.

Emerging from a traditional Humberside Tex-Mex diner, where portly middle-aged men feasted, swiftly and silently, in company with young ladies to whom they were not related, Petit was handed a card for the Purple Door Club. 'Nothing's A Secret Here. £10 per fully nude dance.' Too cold and weary to contemplate a naked scamper, we ducked under the television-screen arch – HULL UFO SOCIETY MEETING, DISCUSS STRANGE SIGHTINGS AND GHOSTLY GOINGS ON! – and skated like tumbleweed down a pedestrianized shopping precinct to our flag-bedecked hotel. Where I switched on the local news to have the identities of the trio of cultural heavyweights in the chopper that buzzed us on the Humber Bridge revealed: Bob Geldof (honorary knight of the realm), Elle Macpherson (business-woman, beauty), George Foreman (ex-pug, preacher, non-fat burger griller). They had been airlifted to a covert location to pitch ideas, to punch the promotional envelope. This was no budget seminar-breakfast at a Holiday Inn. After another helicopter hop and a private plane out of Humberside International Airport, Bob and Elle were back in the Smoke for a charity black-tie bash the same evening. The Hull excursion was like a royal tour of duty in Afghanistan, a secret accompanied by a TV crew.

The following morning, raw from a sleepless night punctuated by screams, smashed glass, slammed doors, Chris discovered that his silver Merc, secure in the hotel's basement garage, had been the venue for an unauthorized party. Night staff didn't waste the opportunity to entertain in a motor of that vintage, in such leathery comfort. After cleaning out the kebab wraps and knotted condoms, and winding down the electric windows, we headed for the M62. Pausing only to pay tribute to John Prescott's favourite trough, Mr Chu's China Palace riverside restaurant. A lion-guarded, green-and-red stockade: like the set for Nicholas Ray's epic, *55 Days at Peking*. I told Chris that I couldn't accept Will Alsop's contention, one of the articles of faith around which his SuperCity thesis was developed.

'It struck me,' Alsop said, 'that if Leeds and their football team fell out of the FA Cup, the natural thing would be for the supporters to cheer Manchester United or Manchester City. Then you have a regional identity, one city.'

About as natural, I thought, as incest. And much less popular. Leeds and Manchester United as companions-in-arms? Jack Charl-ton and 'our kid' sharing a damp Woodbine in the bath? Happy-go-lucky Billy Bremner tickling the ribs of Nobby Stiles? Trans-Pennine blood feuds are often a matter of a few hundred yards of disputed ground. If there is anything that unites the whole SuperCity, it's the quality of hatred: Liverpool–Manchester–Leeds.

Badge-kissers, coin-throwers, karate-kickers: united in the obscenity of their tribal chants.

Michael Moorcock spent several years in a rambling house at Ingleton, close to the Yorkshire/Lancashire border. 'No question that the Wars of the Roses lived on,' he told me. 'The towns around Leeds all had very strong identities and a sense of superiority one to another. My friend Dave Britton says that although everything has changed on the surface in Manchester, with new council estates replacing terraces, the basic character remains the same. Markets where markets always were, violence where violence always was. The notion of supporting Leeds had him laughing like Bernard Manning.'

The M62, Petit reckoned, along that first stretch out of Hull, was almost as good as East Germany, the run he'd made from Berlin to the Baltic. Our transit was silk-smooth, traffic-light. The cooling stacks at Selby are always worth a photo or two. We pulled off-highway at Saddleworth Moor, to take in, from this rugged tump, the hazy spread of Manchester. Once again dark history infected our perceptions. You are never free of that hideous backstory, the abused and buried children. The ones who have never been recovered. And the malignant urban picnickers with their leaking newspaper faces: bottles of cheap wine, tartan rug and spade. The satanic version of *Coronation Street* spoiling the ground even now. The thing they murdered was the moor itself.

Step outside the car and everything changes. Wind cuts. A road sign for Saddleworth has the Oldham part of it peeled away like a second-degree burn, a failed graft. Limestone overwhelmed by Millstone Grit. A rough track leading to the Pennine Way. Low cloud, saturated air. Rubbish pits and tyre dumps in which unwanted things cook and sulk. Mesh fence protecting pylons barnacled with humming disks, eavesdropping equipment. Cars that stop here are suspect, furtive; out of place until the rubber rots from the wheels and they sink into the peat.

Coming the other way, east, as part of his television tour, Will

Alsop pulled in for a comfort break. 'What Saddleworth Moor needs,' he said, 'is more access roads and a fancy service station.' He clambers from his high chariot, yawns and shakes out the creases. 'Let's make a beautiful rural service area at this point. With fantastic food and unbelievable shops.' A 24-hour destination magnet appealing to the nightbirds of SuperCity. And who would they be? Entertainers, reps. Haunted solitaries. The feral underclass populating crime encyclopaedias. Gloved wheelmen in white company vans cruising a connected network of red-light districts. Tabloid monsters with claw-hammers and faulty moral wiring. Film-makers stitching swans' wings on corpses.

We looped Manchester, looped everywhere. When it works, and you float through the cinema of landscape, nobody wants to come away from the road. We'd visited Liverpool a few months earlier, to shoot a piece for the Audi Channel, driving a £60,000 luxury model from the Antony Gormley beach at Crosby into North Wales; now Petit suggested a detour to Morecambe. A detour which involved a truckstop at Carnforth that demonstrated the qualities a pop-up city should possess: efficient but unobtrusive service based around clean and functional architecture; American windows on English lethargy. Comfortable chairs, hot soup, and a silent television screen running Euro-junk football as an analgesic, a meditative panel with no emotion, no content. Electronic impressionism: lush greens, patterns forming and reforming as colour-coordinated athletes drift and sway. You can eat here, sleep here, shop here – and, best of all, park without hassle. The lorry park *is* a park, enclosed, muffled, with great shining transcontinental rigs as works of sculpture. In the approved SuperCity fashion, this refuge has no allegiance to the local; to Carnforth with its stagnant bookshop and its heritaged railway station, the self-denying ghosts of *Brief Encounter*. The truckstop was Belgium, Italy, Idaho, Oregon. In a cartography of absence, here at last was an oasis of the possible that required no intervention from planners or overexcited architects.

Morecambe, half-resuscitated, half-choked on the karma of the drowned Chinese cockle pickers, was an unresolved argument between entropy and aspiration. With a grand sweep of bay for which the inhabitants seemed to have no particular relish. A woman, out early, dragging a blind German shepherd dog, chatted with a street cleaner in a yellow tabard. 'He's moulting, luv. It's fab. Like getting new carpet for front room.'

Nothing we found along the entire span of the road had actually been built by Alsop. He explained, when I visited him in his office, that the idea of the SuperCity emerged over a period when he was involved with a group called Yorkshire Forward. 'The man in charge gave me Barnsley. Nobody else wanted it. I was rather hoping to get Scarborough. The M62 became part of my life. If you go by train, it's hopeless.'

Post-industrial muddle extended, in the London architect's bloodshot eyes, into a single hallucinatory city. A blank canvas crying out for inspiration. The poets who clustered around Hebden Bridge, exiled figures like Jeff Nuttall and Asa Benveniste, had gone. New metropolitans, chefs, ambitious curators, took their place. Raiders of the north, reivers with laptops and digital cameras, staked out the territory. The advantage of being trapped somewhere like Huddersfield or Goole, Alsop asserted, was that you could get out, fast. Back to the road. 'Manchester feels all right, once you're in,' he said. 'But it takes a long time. Nobody is quite sure where it starts or finishes.'

I carried a coffee-table book with me, the Will Alsop tribute compiled by Kenneth Powell in 2002. There was one surviving Alsop structure to be located: the toilet block of the Earth Centre at Conisbrough, near Doncaster. It dated from the era when New Labour was an unsullied novelty, rattling out promises without having to deliver. Slush funds, siphoned from millennial lotteries, were being channelled towards northern areas deemed fit for regeneration. Brownfield anaemia doctored with booster shots of fresh green capital.

'A deal was done with the National Coal Board,' Alsop said, 'to

re-landscape the slagheaps. They already had a vineyard. And a perfectly decent hut where you could get something to eat.' A nice
little project too successful to be left alone. The terrible thing happened: they got the loot.

'I remember when they rang me up, everybody was excited. They
were going to give us fifty million. Unbelievable!'

Fifty million stretched, as these things always do, to eighty. It
started to get serious. And visible.

'Jennie Page was in charge of the Millennium Commission. You
could see why she chose the Earth Centre: it was green, it was in the
north. It was not in London.'

A headline-making disaster was snatched from the jaws of a
minor local success. 'In retrospect, it was the worst news we could
have had, the granting of lottery funds. The original group lost control. They were blamed for this failure, but it was not their fault.
They never needed that huge amount of money. Our practice
designed and built the millennium lavatory. That's my only millennium project.'

Arriving in Conisbrough with Petit, after days on the road, and finding no trace of the Earth Centre, we tried the castle. The custodians
blazed and bridled: money down the drain, they reckoned. Potential
customers arriving by car at the eco-park were surcharged a fiver a
head for wasting fossil fuel. The centre lasted two years, while it
tried to figure out its unique selling point. A consensus, after numerous meetings in motorway hotels, on the direction of travel:
downhill. They offered budget archery for kids. They peddled moral
fables like a Victorian Sunday school. The story the castle-keepers
told us was that carpet-bagging Londoners came north, were given
the best jobs and houses, milked the system, and jumped the first
train as soon as the plug was pulled. The benefit of the grand project
to the Conisbrough community was zilch. The strategy, as Alsop
explained it, had been 'to expound in a vivid, hands-on way, the
principles of sustainable development'. And, in a negative fashion,
this is exactly what the Earth Centre achieved. They proved that

nature sustains itself. It abhors the despoilers of a vacuum. Abandoned mine-workings, after a few years left to themselves, have a wild beauty which includes visible traces of a previous history: the rusted rails, coils of wire, scars and fissures. The boys on bicycles. The dog-walkers.

An Asian security guard, doomed to spend his days invigilating a surveillance monitor on which nothing is happening, and wandering, step by laboured step, around the perimeter fence of what feels like an abandoned concentration camp, was pleased to have some company. Guard towers. A grass-thatched conical yurt. Slagheaps. The Alsop turrets are like stacked containers made from an experimental medium somewhere between metal and human skin. What disaster had overwhelmed this frontier outpost? Why had the promised highway never arrived?

'Combining futuristic architecture with poignant memorabilia from a mining past.' Said the sad notice attached to a skeletal metal tree, a surplus artwork.

Here, at last, was a fitting monument to the SuperCity: a wilderness loud with ghosts from a noble industrial heritage. A desolate theme park conceived from the embryonic wraiths of a discontinued future. A conceptual landscape where reality was declared bankrupt.

Will Alsop, painter of windscreens, is our Daniel Boone: a pioneer opening up territory where nobody wants to go. A grand project obsolete before it was launched. And the wrong kind of obsolete too, the junked prototype, not the soft glow of a kerosene lamp in a cabin in northern Wisconsin, as recalled by Ed Dorn; and not, certainly not, the pure obsolete status of poetry. The obsolescence that has to be earned, that has been lived through. That continues to sing and to hurt.

Freedom Rides

One close June evening, coming away from the corrupted geometry of a generic docklands development, down a nervy arterial road, Anna lost it: *where am I?* It was like emerging from a late-afternoon siesta, not knowing day from night, Hackney from Hartlepool. Was she a boarding-school pupil or a married woman? And to whose unfamiliar body, like a coat in the wrong size, was she returning? Our walk was endless, nothing fitted against anything else. The soft pornography of regeneration was challenged by minatory ware-houses, cobbled alleys and the sullen, sour-canal whiff of the real. We had travelled on the diagonal across England to achieve this: a fugue, a lurch out of time, and the loss – for Anna – of present iden-tity. There was a sudden and unexplained reconnection with her earlier child-self, a schoolgirl of this city: Liverpool. I remembered that Liverpool was the place where the young Thomas De Quincey hid away, a sabbatical in an Everton cottage, feeding his addictions, humouring amateur authors and poetasters. And inventing, by proxy, the literary festival: the writer in residence, the culture bingo at the seaside. It was from here that he set out, 'east and west, north and south', to scavenge 'all known works or fragments' by Coleridge and Wordsworth. Cold turkey, and unrecorded dérives through slave-docks and mysterious suburbs, as he braced himself for direct confrontation with the Lakeland poets. The great port was the link with every dimension.

Our visit was the necessary second stage of the Will Alsop chal-lenge: road-test the M62, the spinal boulevard of the SuperCity. Having driven it with Chris Petit, mile after mile, I understood that we had adopted the idiot's approach. We rode through a geography that was never there. *Nor meant to be.* Any attempt to use a proposal as a working model is madness. We must respect the primacy of the imagination. Here, on the overspill of the M62, is the future we are burning up, the non-spaces we must learn to inhabit.

On Berry Street I spotted what I took to be a notebook in a shop window. Mickey and Minnie Mouse, in relief, against a scarlet-varnish background. Chinese calligraphy. Minnie, in pink pyjamas, is riding on the moon. At £1.30 this was an item requiring a metal grille, security screens, and a hatch through which I had to gesticulate and mouse mime, by making funny-ear shapes. The counter clerk was a Scouse lad of about fifteen. He treated this senior citizen with the rodent fetish with the same wary courtesy he offered to a patron whose head did not quite reach the lip of the counter; a boy of ten or so who had dropped in to pick up his vodka ration. The shop specialized in booze, the Disney stationery was a sideline, a come-on for the juvenile trade. It looked like one of those shotgun-behind-the-counter bunkers in the Bronx, but was otherwise clean and full of surprises. Bottle pocketed, the child asked for a light, then a ciggy to go with it. My notebook turned out to be a bizarre collection of Chinese New Year envelopes: Snow White, Pooh Bear and a pair of horrible furless albino cats I didn't recognize. The whole pack felt like sachets for very small bribes, birthday cake contracts.

We were close to the decorative arch of another phantom Chinatown, to restaurants and warehouses recalling trade connections, a city within the city. We drifted on towards the Anglican cathedral and the bistro-bars of Hope Street. My idea was to trade on decrepitude, turning the stiff-backed, liver-spotted wasteland of a 65-year-old self to advantage, by riding across England, Mersey to Humber, on my Hackney Freedom Pass. It had been announced that crumblies with their orange plastic wallets could travel anywhere in the country on local buses: gratis. The hope being that numbers of newly privileged geriatrics would forget to come back, or take themselves off to edgeland asylums (if they hadn't been converted into gated communities). Like inner-city drinking schools, the elderly are expected to relocate to the seaside. And disappear.

Anna joined me on this freedom ride through the back roads of

Alsop's SuperCity; she had her own agenda, memories to set against whatever we would find. As, for example, the Adelphi Hotel in Liverpool, where we spent our first night. To Anna it represented the good place, that never-forgotten exeat in a time of austerity; afternoon tea served by white-cuffed waitresses in a high-ceilinged room as big as an opera house. The Adelphi, at the hub of the seatown's civic centre, close to the railway station and the grand public buildings, was a comfortable watering hole for stopover celebs and expense-account industrialists. Or so the channelled schoolgirl, her prior self, remembered: 'A magnificent lounge with its acres of armchairs and potted palms, the elegant double-staircase curving away at the far end under the vast chandeliers and the mirrored glass.' A Palm Court orchestra. Sonar echoes of Gracie Fields, the Marx Brothers, Noël Coward, and a thousand cocktail-shakers servicing platinum blondes and local politicians returning favours.

My own experience of the Adelphi was more recent. A very different movie: digital, collision-cut, sponsored. The hip advert disguised as yesterday's underground road meditation. Chris Petit, by keeping his head down and not releasing any of his substantial archive of television essays, had achieved guru status as the man of the road. *Radio On*, newly reissued in a crisply mastered print, was well received, and accepted as a cultural landmark announcing the coming of Thatcher's children and the slow death of art cinema. Chris was welcomed in Santiago and Buenos Aires and given the occasional off-peak afternoon in Richmond.

The Audi Channel, who had squatters' rights on the outer reaches of the Sky satellite network, hired myself and Petit to sit, for one day, in a top-of-the-range motor bristling with cameras. And to drive from Crosby Beach, through Liverpool docks and the Mersey Tunnel, into the enveloping gloom of North Wales. We contemplated the threatened Gormley duplicates, admiring their stoicism, as wind whipped up a minor sandstorm and curs pissed against the slender rusted legs. Liverpool, seen through the frame of our solid, purring car, was a sequence of disconnected quotations. Our present collaboration, and all the earlier films we had made, were not much more than an excuse to talk about cinema and sometimes football. It was my contention that Petit's German trilogy – *Flight to Berlin*, *Chinese Boxes* and *Radio On* (an autobahn in disguise) – formed a significant detour for anyone interested in film history. I took the opportunity of this sponsored ride, from nowhere to nowhere, to interrogate him about those days.

As we motored on, rivers and tunnels, Liverpool became Dublin, became Rotterdam, became Hamburg. That was another of Petit's preoccupations, how cities are swallowing each other, pastiching, making copies of copies. What is the future for the redundant shopping mall? Do we follow Las Vegas and settle for cycles of perpetual reinvention? Novelty sets designed to vanish. Demolition as the money shot. Pop-up cities at the whim of fashion.

'Kit Carson, who was brought in to beef up the dialogue of *Chinese Boxes*, came up with the lines about leakage across the Berlin Wall, the gangsters from east and west getting together. The plot, with its structure of drug smuggling, political connotations, the involvement of the Americans, was impenetrable. But the shoot was quite abstemious. Whole sub-plots were junked. The money was coming from Paris. By the time they realized what they were getting, it was too late to do anything about it.'

Chris had been back to Germany, for a coda to the series, a co-production he called *Content*. 'My latest film,' he said, 'is entirely posthumous. I started to think about structure. How you look at landscape, how to get from A to B. The obvious thing is not to meet anyone, not to be linear. I wanted to go back to the wind-screen and the road. I wasn't shooting anything. I wanted to go back to Berlin and on to Poland. And then, later, Dallas. The desert. California.'

Dissolution informs this Audi project too: shapes in the dark, disguised research institutes in farmers' fields. The sun was setting over a deserted quarry; across the valley, a Land Rover churned up dust as it slalomed down the track towards us. Petit recalled the climactic sequence of *Radio On*, another quarry, another car, doors open, nowhere to go. We were never, at this stage of the game, going to travel far beyond quotation. Films were now shot in an afternoon.

The new Adelphi, Britannia Adelphi (Liverpool), is the state-of-Britain film that Lindsay Anderson never quite got around to making; after rugby league in Wakefield, *Britannia Hospital* and *The White Bus*. Our breakfast bunker is packed with Arthur Lowe and Leonard Rossiter substitutes waiting for their coaches: Lakeland tours, Blackpool Illuminations. Ranked taxis offer to run three people (£45) or five people (£65), for three hours, on a Beatles circuit with 'lots of photo opportunities along the way'. Mathew Street, Penny Lane, Newcastle Road, Menlove Avenue, Forthlin Road, Arnold Grove, Madryn Street. The idolatry of exterminated Beatles is a major industry: bad boys, slick movers, sanctified by global capitalism and the Celtic passion for wakes and displays of public mourning.

Before we get that bus, we are obliged to sample the Mersey end of the Alsop SuperCity: art, food, spectacle. The Reich Chancellery weight and neoclassical gravitas of that block of halls and museums around William Brown Street is intimidating. Anna's cataleptic episode on the dock road started with a high-speed trek, the way we insult a City of Culture by cherry-picking its highlights in a couple of hours.

I like the room of classical busts, old gods drained of blood, injected with formaldehyde, chilled into marble. Titular spirits who have seen it all. Shafts of pale afternoon light falling across city fathers, emblematic lovers. The Walker Art Gallery manages its heritage cargo of accidental plunder: trophy Pre-Raphaelite madonnas, competitive topography, and up-to-the-moment, top-dollar commissions.

The picture of the month is a Liverpool cityscape by Ben Johnson. An anamorphic spread: steely blues and aircraft greys so hyperreal that you know it's another CGI fiction, another visiting card from a future that will never arrive. Johnson, after working on a reconstruction of the Urbino panel, an ideal city attributed to

Piero della Francesca, accepted a gig from Hong Kong Telecom to paint a panorama to mark the transfer of sovereignty to China. This Liverpool cityscape, from high above the Mersey, stares unblinking at a planner's dream of a regenerated, maritime city-state: with empty docks and the human element reduced to dots on the edge of the cultural quarter. 'Some of the buildings,' the brochure admits, 'don't yet exist or are currently being built.' But the accuracy of their dimensions is unimpeachable: eleven studio assistants, consultations with historians, architects and planners, ensure it.

What need then of the old Liverpool, its crooked lanes and loud cellars, its failed speculations and faded department stores? What place is there for the golf-tee spike of the Post Office Tower growing out of a Holiday Inn? Or the shop windows filled with *OK!* magazines duplicating the approved marriage portrait of Wayne Rooney and his bronzed and airbrushed bride? A major 'coming soon' development – GRAND CENTRAL – has ambitions to make Liverpool anywhere but where it is. A destination without a hinterland.

Beside the revamped docks, necrophile sentiment underwrites the heritage makeover: a glistening black Billy Fury, legs spread, gestures at the cranes hovering over new white blocks. An immigrant group signals the pathos of their conversion into a compensatory symbol. Anna remembers, coming back to herself as we settle in an underground bar in Hope Street, being brought here by coach to take part in an anniversary service, to sing in Giles Gilbert Scott's Anglican cathedral with the school choir. The dark interior of the Gothic revival church is forgotten, sound does not fade.

The point of our bus trip was spontaneity. Anna had to restrain me from jumping on the first vehicle with free seats that was pointing in approximately the right direction: kamikaze pensioners, rucksacked and black-bagged, half-smart (top half), we voyaged in expectation of the rising sun. A day of low cloud, dishcloth skies, mercury roads. Steady movement and, once aboard, no decisions to make: where you go, we go. End of the line. End of the story.

Liverpool buses, I do appreciate them. I stayed once, a terrace in the near-suburbs, with the poet Robert Sheppard. The highlight was the ride, next morning, into town: the friendliness, the breathing space, the way people carriers arrive as soon as you raise a hand. Back home in Hackney, aggrieved clients step further and further into the traffic, scanning the horizon, willing the missing bus, any bus, *challenging it*, to make an appearance. In Liverpool, travellers nod and chat, take in the scenery, discuss the reasons for their journey, cross themselves, and generally acknowledge the privilege of being chauffeured around town, in comfort, for a few coins.

Robert Sheppard, who had experienced it, full on, as rate-payer and citizen, composed a few words around Liverpool's status as City of Culture. 'Their shit's verdure but that's OK / This isn't a nature poem.' Sheppard's near-twenty-year epic, *Complete Twentieth Century Blues*, outweighed the Ringo Starr returns, the showbiz art: he cooked slow and long, with tangy sauces and bits that break your teeth. The city averted its eyes. Alsopian relativity spurns language that stops our headlong gallop, calling it a 'difficulty'. As if it were the poet's fault that we want our meat pre-chewed.

We have a pack of timetables, but none of them make much sense. I'm impressed by the PR material put out by St Helens (previously known to me as a Rugby League team, the Saints). A triumphalist player is featured on the cover of the Visitor Guide, showing off his Pilkington Activ™ sponsorship. That's the other thing in St Helens, glass. We have to get to this Eden on the borders of Liverpool and Manchester. A very Alsop-sympathetic attractor. 'One-time cradle of the industrial revolution . . . a growing regional destination of choice . . . with status as the most car-friendly place in Northwest England.' The promotional pitch is constructed around 'a landmark new internationally significant artwork'. Which has yet to be identified. It will be unveiled later in the year (subject to planning permission). It doesn't matter what this artwork is, or does, or who made it: until you have your Angel of St Helens you are just another car park off the A580. (A road number which looks to my soft-focus gaze very much like ASBO.)

If St Helens is the event horizon of our first ride, the immediate prospect, according to Merseytravel, is Huyton. There is so much room on the bus; the bus *is* a room, a waiting room in transit. Silver-grey tarmac speckled with mica. A high street running on like an infinitely extendable ladder. This ride is a transformative experience, molecules shaken, memories invoked: the cold, greasy metal, the coarseness of tobacco-infested cloth. Generous window panels break down the division between street and interior. We're clients of a single-decker with bright green poles and red request buttons. Old ladies are the only ones heading for Huyton; old ladies and their mild-mannered grandchildren. The ones who remind me of Welsh excursions in the company of women: mother, grandmother, great-aunts. I don't think, outside London, I was ever on a bus with my father.

As we pull away from the city centre, the threat of regeneration imposes a uniformity on cancelled terraces; the same blue shutters, old trade-names painted out. The long, uphill road is as unreal as the back projections outside the coach, as it escapes East Germany, in Hitchcock's *Torn Curtain*. Passengers accept their role as actors in this fiction, they acknowledge our presence, but leave it at that. The local bus service is the last democracy. Accents shift with the miles trav-elled, allegiances are a real thing: Will Alsop's elastic uniformity doesn't play. Liverpool suburbs stretch but do not sprawl. A bus is not a coach (Freedom Pass holders have to pay for a coach ride). When Alsop was being processed through the north with the Urban Renais-sance Panel and other lottery-fund commissars, a coach was laid on, never a bus. Luxuriously appointed coaches, with reclining seats and personal monitors, carry Premier League millionaires from ground to ground: Wigan, Blackburn, Bolton. In the flat-cap, Woodbine-and-pint-at-half-time days, footballers took the bus. Coaches don't stop. They have tinted windows to ameliorate blight: to prevent the curi-ous from looking in. Nobody looks out. Multinational superstars are electronically anaesthetized. Texting. Tweeting. Enduring.

Anna grew up in Blackpool and went to school, between the ages of twelve and sixteen, slap on this bus route.

'Will you recognize Huyton?'

Would anyone recognize Huyton? Whatever ghosts it once possessed, they have been rehoused. The bus station is the best of it: a flat-pack conservatory with Jagger-tongues of wilting greenery. We have an agenda here, to locate Anna's school, to validate that skein of the past, four seamless years, in which she was happy. The fissure in her life comes when she is removed at sixteen, sent off to another place, more bracing, academically challenging: a mistake. But a fortunate one for me, as our downward drift carried us both across the Irish Sea to Dublin. There were a lot of buses in Dublin.

The estate where the school once stood, pointed cliffs of red brick, has been treated in the usual fashion: residential care homes, nurseries for 4-wheel-drive mothers, secure apartments. Voices from captured playing fields. Private roads dressed with weeds. Dogs barking at our approach.

'I should never have come,' Anna said. Swimming pool, tennis courts, corridors loud with music. Brought back. Vividly present. 'The chapel gleamed with flowers. There were groups of girls in the long cloaks we wore in the winter, hoods lined with the house colours.'

My conviction that every bus station must have a decent café somewhere in the neighbourhood is disproved: McDonald's or nothing. The expedition I mount to humour my prejudice against uniformity carries us through accidents of pay-off architecture, a suspiciously well-funded library. Huyton is favoured by the legacy of its most celebrated MP, Harold Wilson (pipe in public, cigars and whisky in private). This is not one of those Californian vanity jobs, shrines to Reagan or Nixon. The Harold Wilson Library is downbeat municipal, shelves of politics and sociology for ambitious swots. But no maps, nothing local in this locality. No copies of the booklet on Liverpool's Chinese community that I failed to pick up in the city.

St Helens has the first roadblock we encounter, a blue-tape incident. Concrete police station with windows like nicks from a cutthroat razor. The low rail around the flat roof won't deter convinced (or persuaded) jumpers. A large woman in pink T-shirt, tight mid-calf leisure slacks, pink socks and trainers, is trawling a white bag for that missing cigarette. A hunched, no-neck ovoid, she seems built for water rather than the rough boundary wall of the police car park.

We need a luggage rethink. My black bag is cumbersome. I choose a rucksack from a shop on a pedestrianized traffic island. The town slumbers undisturbed around the statue of Queen Victoria and a promised comedy festival. 'The spell of the journey is upon us,' Anna says.

The Scouse accent has flattened out, the patter. When you move through unknown territory, there is no obligation to list particulars; let it drift. Shuttered pubs and roadhouses with no road. Avenues of dwarf trees barely shading patches of worn grass. Our fellow passengers are tidy, with lightweight sports-casual clothes and considered hair. They chat, some of them, turning a blind eye towards the themed George Orwell Wigan Pier pub, alongside the sanitized canal. An insinuation of pies and gravy on a bed of golden chips makes Anna hungry. But we don't have time to stop, there's another switch to be accomplished, another bus station.

A double-decker: MANCHESTER LIMITED STOP. We climb the stairs and take the seats at the front. We're going to make it – and already there have been so many varieties of custom and behaviour; a retreat from the linguistic extravagance of Liverpool. Those Wigan pies sit heavy on the stomach, even when you have only seen them stacked like geological specimens in a shop window. The bus nurdles through miles of proud suburb. A gobby girl takes the seat to our left, chewing her mobile: '*I'm* not in a mood. It's you, right, you're in the mood. You're not listening: I'm not, not, *not*.' A daily ritual, this affectionate abuse. Virtual courtship: phone-sex on a budget. She studies her nails. Places her feet, ankles crossed, on the window ledge. She alternates spite-riffs with lingering red-tongued licks at a sugar bag that looks like a plasma sachet. 'You're trying to put me in a mood, you, so you don't have to see me tonight. You don't wanna see me, I don't fucking care. I'm not in a mood, you're in a *right* mood. You are, you fucking are. Are.'

Garden plots nudge against trim estates: Manchester's emerging blot. The whale of the north displaces a lot of murky bathwater. Down which we slide, drenching pedestrians.

'Traa. Traa. *Traa*. Fuck off.'

She dismounts, leaving us alone; the bus in its descent, into the storm, is our personal limousine. A tour of brown-sign cultural highlights: Trafford Park, Salford University, Coronation Street Experience. High-angle perspectives on terraces that are still terraces. Aspirational cul-de-sacs. Tudorbethan multiples with apron lawns. Stuttering cars from driving schools with self-important logos.

We need to find somewhere to stay that is convenient for the bus station. The nest I select, over other Travelodges, has a selling point: centre-city, in-transit sex. 'Be more rock 'n' roll next time you visit . . . Indulge in one of our suites, loaded with the latest gadgetry, dressed top to toe in the slinkiest of interiors. Enjoy power showers for sharing and tubs in front of the telly . . . A doll walks in . . . well, the place was once a doll hospital, someone fix her up.'

Very Tinto Brass *Caligula*. Straight to video. Straight to drug-shame-3-in-a-bed tabloid exposé. But a decent night's king-size slumber after the shuddering of the buses, the hungry road. Segment of canal beyond double-glazed windows. Ink-jet smear of industrial heritage.

Next morning, a uniformed doorman with a branded umbrella chases us into bar-code rain.

'Car or train, sir?'

'Bus. Direction of Hull.'

Anna notices a scrawny young woman stilting towards Piccadilly Gardens. 'Little cropped jacket,' she recalls. 'Bare white midriff. Sky-high black heels. Fishnet tights, tiny denim shorts. Wide leather belt decorated with metal studs. Thin blonde hair scraped back in a ponytail.' And pushing a baby buggy, with attitude, on her way to ram-raid Mothercare. While giving her infant a good rinsing. 'I love her style, her energy. Her attitude to the weather.'

A single-decker for the climb towards Oldham's ridge, wipers going like a North Sea trawler. Cranes loom over unfinished concrete skeletons. Chinese distribution centres. Converted Methodist chapels. Junkyards, botched scams: a townscape with which I am very comfortable.

At the front of the bus is an old fellow whose portrait I have to record. A Lancashire music-hall turn, all nose, collapsed cheeks, and mouth like a ring-pull. He mumbles, rehearsing his patter, a litany of grievances. A stoic comedian who has run out of straight men. Ratty suede jacket with fake astrakhan collar. Nose dripping steadily. A stalactite mime of melancholy and malfate who makes me feel glad to be alive.

Opposite him, and totally unaware of his presence, are two young ladies of this city, beauty reps, old hand and novice, one white, one Asian. They charm us with their vivacity and rhythm. The girls are dragging demo equipment around with them, folding tables, bulky black bags. The newcomer, the round-faced Indian girl, never stops yapping. Her companion, checking with the supervisor on the mobile, has to shout. They love their work and wear it, painted masks of small perfection. They are industrially perfumed: against the urban mould of sodden gabardine, the consumptive hacking of the submarine-bus. Hooped spines of demi-cripples transported through a catalogue of tall chimneys and dark canals to their proper Lowry setting. A rattle-bag of museum-quality relics glorying in their redundancy.

At the Oldham terminal, we pass out of one timetable, through a building that reminds me of Athens airport with its ever-shifting and reconvening queues for various island destinations, into another: the connection for Huddersfield. Nobody can convince me that the cultural shifts we are registering – weight of pies, speed of speech, attitude to surroundings – could be brought within a single system. Or that such a system would be desirable. Huddersfield passengers have an upland quality about them. Braced for the Pennine transit and delighted to be riding, not marching, heads down, into the perpetual mist.

Chip shops. Chinese restaurants. Hairdressers. A slow ascent with many stops to take on students who immerse themselves in books and iPods. Getting away from Oldham involves another blue-tape incident, blood on the stones. After Saddleworth, Yorkshire announces its difference. Anna respects the labour that has gone into rows of immaculate and competitive gardens. Over damp moors, the view from the front of the bus is romance: soft grey-green hills in the distance. Farms and scattered villages.

A change of driver and, after all these silent hours, what Anna describes as 'a party atmosphere'. Like refugee families returning home after the Blitz. A young woman, loaded with bags, climbs out of the bus, miles from anywhere, the nearest farm barely in sight.

I haven't allowed time for food, it's out of one bus and straight on to the next. I'm not convinced, although I don't admit it, that we'll make that ultimate connection, back down the M62 to Hull. In Huddersfield a woman at the information desk suggests Pontefract. But we could try Wakefield. Provisioned with pork pie (an ice-hockey puck welded out of doggy chews), flapjacks and scalding coffee, we're on the move again. Difficult to sip and suck in this trembling vehicle. Up north, buses are not cafeterias in the Hackney style. The odd schoolkid deflating a crisp packet or puncturing a can of fizz, that's it. We dine with fastidious discretion, hunkered down in our seats. I hop off at the first halt to dispose of the half-drunk carton, the crumbly evidence.

A field of scarlet poppies. 'Isn't that a beautiful sight?' a woman remarks. 'Farmer must have made a mistake.'

Wakefield is no longer the town of Lindsay Anderson's *This Sporting Life*, that homoerotic psychodrama of physical hurt and otherness. Richard Harris, fists bunched in donkey jacket, makes the social ascent from community bus to showy Jag. Grudging envy to local fame. Stay on bus, lad, that's the message. Stick with your own.

We run for the Pontefract connection. But it's not Pontefract any more, it's a retail and transport hub known as Freeport. We have arrived at an outpost of Will Alsop's SuperCity. It's off-highway, grown out of nowhere. All-purpose warehouses: restaurants, white goods, fun palaces. Anonymous hotels double-glazed against the roaring river of the motorway. A consumerist oasis built from a doodle on Alsop's windscreen. But he's not the architect, Freeport is post-architectural, self-propagating; he's just the prophet.

Bus stops in Freeport are covered stands of the sort you find in the long stay car park at Stansted. There is one connection for Hull, miss it and we are done for the night. Rain falls remorselessly. Buses for other destinations come and go. Our stand is shared with two old ladies who have heard the rumour of a possible Hull transfer, a bus coming down from Leeds, but they can't confirm it. A young couple, bored and hormonal, feast like panthers. Or fast-food addicts. The girl is hungrier than the boy. She burrows under his sweater, nipping, biting. They swap wads of gum, mouth to mouth. He drains a bottle of Vimto, before drumming with the empty, kicking it against the glass. Then opening another in a sugary spray. They grapple, pinch, slap bellies. My linen trousers, I notice, are black with the road, oily dirt from picking up bags left on the floor of the bus. All my clothes are wet. I run across to the NEXT discount hangar and re-outfit myself for £7. The old ladies are cheerful, a great day out. 'We've been to Frankie & Benny's, we've had us dinners.'

Freeport is the proof of SuperCity, everybody has an unconvincing reason to come here, nobody has much motivation to stay. You could dismantle any part of it without loss. The XSCAPE block promises cinemas, restaurants, shops, bowling alleys and an indoor ski slope. Storage, distribution and self-service have combined to form a lagoon of non-space. The surrounding canal system is an opportunity for Orwell-themed pubs, boutique hotels, city marinas. The road is the only absolute. The condition of the airport – expensive parking, terrorist alerts, celebrity visitations – is the universal model for the new England. Freeport isn't a port and it certainly isn't free. Language is the final casualty.

Forty-five minutes late, our bus arrives. The young lovers were running out of permutations of engagement: her soft-cannibal assaults and his Vimto-drumming indifference. Darkness was closing in across the flatlands. We reconnected with Alsop's superhighway, the M62 to Hull.

All the passengers, sea-facing now, are women; tawny, fluffed-owl hair. It's like being in a compartment of office cleaners, on the wrong side of dawn: solidarity, anticipated exhaustion. The sights – Selby's belching cooling towers (steam from the mouth of a megaphone), bridges, motorways on stilts – are too familiar to notice, or enjoy, rattled and stiff as we are from two days of hauling bags on and off buses.

We are booked into the same Hull hotel I visited with Petit. I look forward to a free day exploring the town, before we take the train back to London. But I know that this road, the M62, has its victims. Blue trucks like a school of dolphins accompany us to harbour. Drivers are secure in their pods, high above tarmac. The soft English landscape is a film that watches you: nothing to be done. These men are exhausted, bored, but aroused by the pulse of the engine, the steady vibration of movement. Road myths of pick-ups, casual encounters at service stations: B-movie existentialism.

A lorry driver who caused a multi car pile up on the M62 last year was sentenced to four years in jail and a six year driving ban at the Hull Court today. One of the cars involved in the incident on October 19, 2007 was being driven by 36 year old Jayne Shaw. Her nephew, 17 year old Stephen Parkhouse who had just started his second year of a four year joinery course at college, was a passenger. Both died as a result of the collision.

Old newspapers, blowing in the wind, tell the same tale.

A lorry driver whose vehicle overturned onto a car on a motorway, killing a driver, has walked free from court. Ms Taylor, 63, died after the 39-tonne lorry overturned onto her car at the end of the M62. The lorry driver was acquitted despite evidence from the Department of Transport's code of safe practice which proved that the lorry was too heavy. Mr Kynaston said that he did not know that his consignment of scrap fridges and cars was an unsafe load.

Set your rig at cruise control (this driver did), at American highway speed, mid fifties: cheese-burger, cigarette, porn stash. Trousers around ankles. Masturbating as he ploughed into the stationary vehicle. Road-reverie shattered. You can break the membrane of dream.

A man called John Davies walked it. 'I spent the whole of September and October 2007 walking the motorway corridor, Hull back to Liverpool. This blog records my daily diary and reflections on the experience. The journey over, I'm resting my feet . . . I'm hoping that the break will give me some time to start to process this experience of walking . . . Thanks to the Liverpool Diocese Department of Lifelong Learning.'

The Hull bus terminal is right alongside the railway station. 'Done!' Anna says. With justified emphasis. But our journey is only beginning, these are the first flickers of a new addiction: random excursions on local buses, the Freedom Pass to Freeport. We've achieved enough to have one morning on the town, no report to be made. Back to the Old Whyte Hart for a plate of the best fish, chips and mushy peas in England: the pub where I stood in the rain with Petit. The contrast between the town's original whaling museum and The Deep, Terry Farrell's icon on the dock, is absolute. Having ridden all those miles, we have discovered that a marina is just a marina, Liverpool or Hull: different oceans, the same artworks. That pathetic family-group sculpture from Albert Dock on the Mersey has arrived on the Humber before us. In Liverpool the cast figures are emigrants, in Hull they are immigrants. Sentimental paperweights between sea and M62, idealized pilgrims walking blind through the SuperCity, shuffling between holding pens and soup kitchens. Knut Hamsun, the Nobel-winning author of *Hunger*, saw enough of England, on the train between Hull and Liverpool, before embarkation for America, to justify a lifelong hatred.

Listening for the Corncrake

Manchester has taken possession of me for good. I cannot leave,
I do not want to leave, I must not.
   – W. G. Sebald

It starts with Thomas De Quincey, with *Confessions of an English
Opium-Eater*. The recently elected godfather of psychogeography
was born in Manchester in 1785. He attended Manchester Grammar
School, where he found himself banished to a lightless crypt. At a
whim, trunks carried to the cart, he fled; unsure if he had 'eloped'
or 'absconded', south-west, to Chester and the Welsh borders. On
foot. Putting up at roadside inns. Discovering that walking was
remembering, anticipating, debating with your demons.

   Newly settled in London, in 1967, I devoured the *Confessions*. Here
was the film I would never make and the unstable model for everything I attempted to write: mountains and rivers, city as labyrinth,
gossip about poets, fast-breeding metaphors. It was De Quincey
who, brought to the city, plotted escape; until, lodged once more in
Lake District domesticity, cells screaming, debtors beating on
the cottage door, he hurtled back to town, passing himself out on the
road. This creased and diminutive figure, man of the margins, unreliable witness, was the ultimate prisoner of scholarship, the library:
writing to know himself, cultivating digression as a necessary device
to stack up the pages, in support of a painfully loved family. Every
drip of the midnight candle was a coin earned. Those twilight ram-
bles through the most obscure parks, graveyards, riverbanks, were a
method of avoiding creditors. Multiple identities were required to
keep the words tumbling out. He supported a stable of researchers
and ghostwriters: and they were all himself, toothless Tom, the

courtly and venomous gnome of London and Edinburgh. Long coat and no linen.

In London De Quincey exists in a blur of perpetual motion: if he stops, he ceases, the words don't come, funds dry up. In Manchester he is at rest, sheltering from the rain, pedestrians are a cinema of otherness, perhaps drunk, perhaps crushed by circumstance. The only route open to him is *out*. The road. Altringham on market day. Within the amphitheatre of the hills, the spread of the Cheshire plain, market gardens push at the townscape. Manchester is an island. A human stain. Daniel Defoe's sprawling village from his *Tour through the Whole Island of Great Britain* is exploded by industry; it manages its decline by experimenting with novel identities, beneath which the old, weatherbeaten gods take shelter, pissing in doorways, and remembering to forget.

Of all British conurbations – rivers, railways, airports, development opportunities – Manchester was the grandest, the most challenging: and most avoided. It was too late, the story was too rich, I would not live long enough to fix my bearings. But there is attraction, always, in navigating a place that is completely unknown. Tapping along, fierce as Blind Pew, I was a sightless land-mariner negotiating territory where I had no good reason to prowl. As a suspect alien, I could launch wild speculations in the privilege of ignorance.

Is the rain falling now? Misting my spectacles? Good. The city-centre guide is pulp in my pocket. Out of drizzle, tasting of iron, a phantom ship appears like one of the spectres W. G. Sebald mentions in his fictive memoir *The Emigrants*. Ocean-going craft confirm Manchester's status as a port by sliding down the Ship Canal, towering over terraces. A landlocked building, Urbis, sleek and unexpected, has turned its back on the River Irwell, to face the town and its compact, self-contained centre. Nobody knows, or needs to know, what Urbis actually is. It will soon be gone. Its swaggering newness is a suicide note. It's all front and no content. Most of the energy around the development went into coming up with a name: Urbis. Like a hairspray or a mouthwash. A hump of mirrors. A ski slope launched with sackloads of loot and the vague intention of becoming a shout for the city. Urbis belongs to a fleet I am learning to recognize: ships that do not travel but which are the inspiration for travel by others. Attractors brought into existence with the death of industrial process. The final act of steel-rivet technology on Tyneside is to throw up Antony Gormley's *Angel of the North*. An icon for a new theology of regeneration. The first religion to create its idols in advance of its doctrine. Construct your strange gods and we will invent the myths to explain them.

It was a simple notion: drive from London to Manchester, lodge somewhere generic, close to the airport (always a good edgelands indicator), take a bus to the centre, find Urbis (where my report is to be delivered), walk back out to hotel. Given that spine, I should be able to hang discoveries, anecdotes, on-the-hoof research, upon a single day's excursion. I thought about recording a report, stage by stage, on park benches or steamy cafés, without mediation. I junked the notion: 'Wovon mann nicht sprechen kann, darüber muss mann schweigen.' Aware of the presence of Ludwig Wittgenstein, as an engineering student, in a house on Palatine Road (the same one that W. G. Sebald's Manchester painter, Max Ferber, occupies at a later date), I consigned my ill-informed ramblings to silence. There is a legitimacy in direct speech but it has to be earned. I was never any good with dialogue, especially my own. But I keep a notebook handy and the bedroom walls are thin. The airport hotel, in which I was booked, was on Palatine Road.

Migrants, reeling from the M6 and the M56, discover in this concrete box a soothing redoubt, sound-baffled and Cold War casual. The hotel fulfils most of the criteria for one of Will Alsop's Super-City staging posts: Chaucerian exchanges, painless conviviality, commissioned art you are free to ignore. The building services its clients with minimal human intervention. Food is in trays, newspapers are stacked: help yourself. Automatic doors open directly on to a semicircular public space, deep chairs in which to lounge, big-screen sports-channel TV, sunken bar. A large man, who is wearing a T-shirt printed with MAN U CHAMPIONS 18, spurns the cricket match in progress. His companion, or carer, is a City fan. 'They should let Mark Hughes manage.'

27 May 2009. The encouraging aspect about the Urbis address we have been given is that it doesn't exist, not in my 2001 edition of the *Manchester A–Z*. Urbis dropped from the sky, fully fashioned, around the turn of the millennium. Described as 'iridescent', this £28-million showpiece was designed by Ian Simpson Architects. The historian John J. Parkinson-Bailey describes it as 'a visual and symbolic bridge between the first industrial city and the rebuilding of the centre . . . the focal point of the Millennium Quarter'.

Without prior knowledge, it would be impossible to assign a function to this post-architectural form. The sloping glacier wall in the deserted square is a memorial to a once-vital civilization. A concept building that will never become a ruin: either it is there or it is not there. The requirement to replace it, at once, with something louder and flashier is its mission statement. Urbis has been constructed like a set of empty parentheses.

Emerging from pedestrian precincts, investment opportunities created in the wake of the IRA bomb left outside Marks & Spencer, at 11.20 a.m. on Saturday 15 June 1996, we found ourselves in a provisional zone, the sort we have previously encountered in cities with Olympic ambitions and access to serious funds. The idea being to use local particulars to achieve a universal retail conceptualism, constructed around standard items of street furniture: the Ferris wheel, uniform ditches like elegies for lost rivers, beaches of post-ironic pebbles. Referencing a deleted industrial history is not the same thing as paying it respect, by moving on.

Anna, wearying of my attempt to register this absence, goes inside the berg: *urbis reception* (lower case). It has an inside? Oh yes – and racks of leaflets. 'Urbis is an exhibition of city life.' But this city doesn't accept visitors until 10 a.m. Exhibitions we do not experience include: 'Video Nation' and 'State of the Art Light Boxes'.

Tiny figures hug the flank of Urbis, heading towards their shops and offices, in a solemn, rain-slicked procession. Penitents keeping alive the traditions of the dark cathedral, the balancing structure in this precinct. In the window of the fashionable crimper Nicky Clarke, a stone-bald man is blow-drying his own polished brown skull. Like an alchemist taking a Bunsen burner to a serpent's egg.

Anna doesn't relish the atmosphere of the church across the square. I'm drawn to the association with the old town, the river as backdrop. Like Urbis, Manchester Cathedral is an exhibition of city life, spiritual and material. 'This place is full of angels,' says the brochure. A young man in silent contemplation is the only human presence. Anna heads straight for the door.

The angel flock is palpable, rooks in the rafters: in company with memory-wraiths of Manchester's industrial underclass. The brochure tells us that Urbis was constructed on ground once occupied by 'the worst slum in the world'. An area 'described, in all its squalor', by Friedrich Engels, in *The Condition of the Working Class in England*, in 1844. Engels, directing the affairs of the family cotton mill in Salford, studied economics in Chetham's Free Library.

The complex iconography of the church would take weeks to appreciate. The depiction of a child in an eagle's nest, mysterious and sinister, is glossed as a folk legend of illegitimate heirs and village dalliance. The panelling where the scene is found was once the warden's seat: the place reserved for the Elizabethan magus and geographer Dr John Dee. Dee, that upstream man, with his troop of mischievous spirits, did not thrive in Manchester. 'I visited the Grammar School,' he wrote in a diary entry for 5 August 1600, 'and found great imperfection in all and every of the scholars, to my great grief.'

The young man who seemed to be wrestling with a spiritual crisis approached me. 'You draw them like moths,' Anna muttered, on her way out. His face is smeared down one side with bloody treacle. He has been headbutting a pillar, staving in the right eye socket. He is hooded in black, but not as a fashion statement. He wears clothes from which all colour has been sucked by use. His left ear is tagged.

'Can you list the seven deadly sins? I'm stuck on four.'

'What have you got?'

'Wrath, envy, greed, lust.'

'Gluttony. Sloth.' I improvise. There is that mnemonic, SALIGIA, but can I make the translation? *Superbia, avaritia, luxuria, invidia, gula, ira, acedia.* Cardinal sins all. We must not allow ourselves to be sucked into the granite melancholy of this city with its bombs and fires.

I am out of Victoria Street, into the long stretch of Deansgate, heading south, scanning the windows of Waterstones for my own books, when I come up with the final sin: pride.

We're on the Roman road that ran from Carlisle to Chester (the direction young De Quincey walked). There is no time to investigate the John Rylands Library or to saunter through the House of Fraser, which Anna remembers in its previous incarnation as Kendal's. She was sent over from Blackpool, as a teenager, to buy a cape. Those were the days when girls were supposed to dress like younger versions of their mothers. The only humans on Deansgate are hardhats standing in quiet clusters to admire notices they have put up apologizing for the 'hassle' of major holes in the ground.

A tributary, to the right, sparks another fugue. The dentist. With her brothers, Anna came here by train to face drill, hammer and chisel, primitive oral interventions in an intimidating Georgian property. They looked forward to tea and sticky buns in the station café, after the session was over, and then found that their mouths were too numb for crumbling Eccles cakes.

St John Street, dating from the 1770s, consists of nicely proportioned town houses, laid out on land belonging to the Byrom family. A terrace of elegant properties, brass plates polished to a mirror-like sheen, end-stopped by Byrom Street, which runs parallel to Deansgate.

While Anna tried to identify the building in which she endured English dentistry, I investigated the park where St John's Church once stood. A Celtic cross commemorates the scattered remains of 22,000 Manchester people. The church, consecrated in 1769, was demolished in 1932; leaving behind a damp flower garden. Churches from a boom period, conceived out of optimism, to give thanks for continuing prosperity, fell into disrepair as the population retreated. This small park, sweet-smelling in the morning rain, is a soothing refuge. Only the intrusive tower, looming over clumps of managed greenery, reminds us that we are in an unknown city, undertaking an urban expedition. Empty benches on carpets of wet pink rhododendron petals. Water-beads dripping from spread fingers of fatsia.

I wanted to pursue the Byrom aspect of the story. I read Joy Hancox's 1992 book, *The Byrom Collection: Renaissance Thought, the Royal Society and the Building of the Globe Theatre*. Hancox discovered a cache of 516 drawings, 'once the prized possession of an 18th-century secret society', in an 'old world' house in Salford. Her brisk narrative works like a series of trapdoors. Every drawing becomes a windowless room, a poisoned flower, a spirit path. It is all here: Dr Dee in Manchester exile, Elizabethan theatres, speculative geographers. Boyle, Fludd, Newton. The Invisible College, the Royal Society and the Kabbalah Club.

Hancox quotes from Dee's private diary. 'At my return to Deansgate to the end whereof I brought them on foote, Mr Roger Krooke offered and promised his faithful and diligent care and help, to the best of his skill and powre, in the process chymicall . . .'

The ghosts are toying with us. Double-barrelled solicitors and discreet medics. Golden quacks with burnished nameplates turn St John Street into an alchemical ditch. I can see my reflection, camera raised, smeared into a wall of names. John Byrom, inventor of shorthand, was a covert Jacobite. My great-grandfather, in an autobiographical sketch published in Colombo in 1900, wrote: 'My parents were descended from an old Jacobite stock, at this time still rather at a discount . . .' Byrom avoided exposure, declining the post of Chetham's Library Keeper – but joining the Kabbalah Club in 1725, as the urban cataloguer Ed Glinert says, 'to examine the numerical pattern of the universe'.

On the pavement lay a pair of blind man's dark glasses, with one lens missing. Now the Deansgate stack, glimpsed from the old church garden, dominated our route out. This 47-storey intruder, known as the Beetham Tower, originally appeared in 2005. We were trapped within its force field for the rest of the day. 219 luxury apartments. Sky Bar. Ian Simpson, architect of both Beetham Tower and Urbis, retained the split-level penthouse for his own use. A master of the universe, echoing Ballard's *High-Rise*, he plotted an interior 'winter garden' of olive trees and oaks.

It's too wet to consult the map. The idea is to walk, as fast as possible, away from that tower and towards the aeroplanes circling over Ringway. A hinterland of railway bridges, restored canals, insolent inner-city ring roads. Old Trafford, the footballing Mecca, has to be checked out on the day of the European Champions League final, when planeloads of supporters have already been decanted to Rome.

Our drift south towards the sprawling Trafford retail zone runs slap against the Mancunian Way, a blur of multi-lane traffic with no obvious crossing points. Until we duck down to the canal path. Wall slogans on old brick have been painted over. The Irwell, Manchester Ship Canal and Bridgewater Canal carve out an urban patchwork of locks, basins, low-level green-glazed estates: conversions in the process of selling themselves to a new demographic, based on the upwardly mobile rag trade and minimart-owning elements in *Coronation Street*. Quays-dwellers, balcony people, loft-livers. The waterways are cleaner and better kept than in London, wildlife flourishes without the thorium run-off from Olympic piracy.

There is a Crusoe isolation about this passage of our walk, reef-buildings with no visible occupants, an atoll in a sea of concrete. COMMERCIAL SPACE FOR SALE. Up the ramp we plod, neurotic about the possibility of being trapped in the waterway nexus. ST GEORGE'S ISLAND: massive, free-standing letters. The developers, Dandara, are trying to promote the notion that island-life is secure, separate from the chaotic swirl of the city. Your own Isle of Man:

without Norman Wisdom. A Turks and Caicos rum-punch paradise without the tax-haven benefits. St George's Island is surrounded by defunct industries. A postal van is parked on the corner. I rap at the window, asking after the Old Trafford Stadium. 'Take a right and carry on for about a mile,' the postie says. 'You're not really supposed to walk down there, but you should be OK.'

As we emerge on the tarmac runway of the A56, you see what he means. Pavements vanish. Smooth gradients sweep down to the wide road. Trafford Park to Old Trafford is assertively anti-pedestrian. Motor vehicles zero in on the Trafford Centre, a New Town of commerce. A suburb in which everybody shops and nobody lives. Time to hide the camera. When those dawn arrests were processed in Manchester, hurried through as a consequence of secret papers being brandished for the newsreels, as the chief cop reported to Downing Street, the evidence against the suspect men came from shopping-centre surveillance tapes. Economic migrants were observed taking photographs in the Arndale and Trafford Centre malls. The Trafford Centre, opening in 1998, had a backstory that precisely duplicated the current Lea Valley development model in East London: sewage farm nominated as Olympic site. Retail cathedral out of wilderness.

Drudges with suspect rucksacks, we follow Chester Road and the signs for Old Trafford. Grandiose civic and commercial buildings have been abandoned, smashed windows and poster-defaced plywood fences. Respectable terraces are on the slide. We're peckish. When Anna spots the sign for a café in Nuttall Road, I'm happy to detour.

First: as a salute to the poet-painter-trumpeter Jeff Nuttall, who lived beyond the northern fringes of Manchester, in Todmorden. I helped to clear Jeff's books, little magazines, sets of *My Own Mag* (with all the William Burroughs material), when he made one of his life-changing flits. A great shaggy presence, wheezing hard, too large for the terraced cottage that clung to the rim of a steep river-valley road, Jeff rolled away to the Welsh borders. And a final chapter as sidekick to Lenny Henry. Walk-on bits as asthmatic judge or bent brief: the parts Ken Campbell didn't want.

The second reason to hit the café is to pay an oblique tribute to the Manchester section of *The Emigrants*. Sebald's Max Ferber hangs out, every morning, work done, in the Wadi Halfa: 'A transport café near Trafford Park . . . located in the basement of an otherwise unoccupied building that looked as if it might fall down at any moment.' Sebald speaks of how he had to 'cross beneath urban motorways, over canal bridges and wasteland'. We followed, unknowingly, in his footsteps; in that shimmer where documentation loses its nerve and dissolves into found poetry.

The café is on the upper floor of an operation exhibiting camping equipment, garden furniture and sleeping bags. We spread ourselves, coffee and cakes, at a round table, in a warehouse of pup tents and beach parasols. Rain hammers on Stretford Road, its new red blocks, trees so basic in outline that I can't believe they're real. Somebody drives along at night and staples them to the grassy margin. A flag for CHESHIRE FARM REAL DAIRY ICE CREAM flutters from the balcony that overlooks the petrol station.

Back on the move, and closing fast on Old Trafford, I pause to photograph the blue plaque on the decommissioned Democracy House at 609 Stretford Road. We don't hear this name cited very often as a Manchester luminary. 'Dodie Smith 1896–1990. Author of *One Hundred and One Dalmatians* lived here as a child. It was so quiet and semi-rural that the corncrake could still be heard.' Old suburb, new interzone. And where are the grain fields of yesteryear?

It's evident, as the two roads meet, Chester and Stretford (a tight triangle enclosing our camping-store café), that we are entering a high-investment area organized around the flow of capital, not of rivers and railways. With Old Trafford, the Manchester United ground, as the symbol – virtual and actual – of status and future intent. In this spindly construction, like a splash of frozen water, is the future of the city: MUFC aligning itself through its global support, its multicultural playing staff, with Europe and the wideworld.

Football heaven: South Korea, Portugal, Brazil, Holland, Serbia, Bulgaria. Distant glimpses of the stadium keep us circling. A satellite state has been built from the failure, fortunate failure, of two Olympic bids. The animatronics of dud proposals are being replaced by regiments of card-brandishing, car-occupying human beings.

The crunch comes when the pavement runs into a sheep-hurdle barrier. I've had enough and decide to carry on, by the most direct route, down the central reservation. Anna prefers to play it safe, she doubles back. We will meet, if we make it, outside the club shop.

It's a damp carnival: huge red flags, a Stalinist parade marching around the stadium forecourt. Traders with plastic centurion helmets and T-shirts saluting a triumph that would never happen. Tin badges at £3 a pop: European Cup Final, Stadio Olympico, Rome, 27 May 2009. I buy one, a doomed investment. GLORY, GLORY, MAN UNITED.

A group of Koreans, come over to support their battery-driven, run-all-day hero, Ji-Sung Park, photograph each other alongside the plinth with the unlikely representation of the three amigos: Best, Charlton, Law. Brothers-in-triumph. Jealous colleagues, uncertain friends. Shackled in eternity.

Anna remembers her maternal grandfather, a strict disciplinarian. He played in goal for Preston North End. The club shop, monomaniacal in its redness, has everything we don't want. I pose for a souvenir snapshot, haunted and a little crazy, beside Ryan Giggs, the superstar who shares my birth city, Cardiff. The 'Footballer of the Year' in his well-preserved dotage. And the urban walker on his last legs.

With the gentle ascent of Great Stone Road, we are in deep suburbia. You have to hike for hours, out from central London, to achieve this. A deserted car park, slick-silver asphalt, around the featureless block of a B&Q superstore in Man U colours.

Keeping a record of Olympic connections, wherever I find them, I snap the Bei Jing (Fish and Chips + Chinese Meals to Take Away), on a traffic island known as the Quadrant. The atmosphere, damp, lush, is less paranoid than on my native turf, where such a photo-graph would be impossible. The Quadrant is well tended and planted with shady trees. This walk is proving too smooth a transit to the southern fringe of Manchester. I expected a hard day's grind. What we experienced was a drift through fields, river paths and pri-vate estates re-landscaped as public parks. And an absence of people. Where were they? The bench-drinkers? The dog-walkers? The fast-striding disciples of De Quincey, a man who wrote of growing up in the family of a rural magistrate, in a district 'close upon Manches-ter, which even at that time was belted with a growing body of turbulent aliens – Welsh and Irish'.

In Longford Park, there are no aliens, apart from us, the ruck-sacked Londoners. Anna blames the economy, who can afford to be strolling about mid-morning? Trim hedges, brushed paths. Wisteria climbing over iron fences. The estate agent, who is attempting to flog a terrace at the edge of the park, has a punning name for his properties: SHERLOCK HOMES.

Coming off Edge Lane into red-brick villas with porches, Ital-ianate mansions awaiting conversion into private flats, we follow signs for the Pennine Way. And discover a village green with a pub that wouldn't be out of place in Surrey, the Horse and Jockey. Over a pint and a platter, I study Ordnance Survey 109 for the last leg of our expedition. The cover, which I hadn't previously noticed, was a photograph of Urbis, credited to Jan Chlebik. The slope of the roof, in the section depicted against a purple sky, is the diagonal we have just accomplished. Put that in your Byrom collection.

To achieve the river path, you start by walking west through a wooded nature reserve. It's no longer raining, but the clouds are low. Windbreak poplars. Yellow fields. A cobbled track alongside a beech hedge. Cows. Everything in quotation marks, a country-park experience with the comforting hum of traffic, pylons and planes. The Mersey, when we come to it, flows fast between sheer banks. Flood meadows on which, so far, nobody has any good reason to build.

Elias Canetti wrote about the period when he lived on Palatine Road and walked with his father. 'On Sundays, he sometimes took me strolling alone. Not far from our house, the little Mersey River flowed by . . . A path wound through a luxuriant meadow full of flowers and high grass. He told me the English word "meadow", and he asked me for it during every stroll . . . Another favourite word of his was "island"; and perhaps he thought of it as an Isle of the Blest.'

After the Electricity Sub Station, it is time to cross the Mersey, and to pass under the junction of the M60 motorway. The south Manchester suburbs are bereft of tags and aerosol signatures. Rusticated estates pretend the motorway isn't happening, or that it's another river. Fairmead Road. Fairmead is the name of the Epping Forest asylum where John Clare lodged, before he began his hike up the Great North Road to Northborough and Mary Joyce, his dead muse.

Yew Tree Lane has a bridge over the traffic, from which we can identify the Britannia Airport Hotel, our base in Northenden. We're back in time for tea.

As evening entertainment, before our return to London, we sign up for the trip to the airport: £4 on the hotel coach, return. The ride brought me, full circle, to the opening of Sebald's Manchester narrative. How he flew in over 'a city of countless bricks . . . inhabited by millions of souls, dead and alive'.

We were the only passengers. Anna tried to explain the reason for our ride to the driver. Why we would *choose* to stay, for a Manchester holiday, out by the airport? Did we know about the Trafford Centre? Deciding that we must be plane-spotters, the driver let us off at the airport pub, where we drank from plastic tumblers and watched a succession of planes coming in to land. Then we walked a greenway track, under surveillance cameras and along security fences, to the terminal. Where the only disembarking passengers were a group of Chinese tourists wearing surgical masks against the threat of swine flu.

After an hour, the coach picked us up again. The driver insisted on delivering us right to the door of the Bella Roma, a Pizzeria Ristorante on Palatine Road. Where, as usual, we were solitary diners, sitting under a panorama of the Coliseum, watching smart hoodies cluster around the chippie. The large man in the Man U T-shirt, from the bar at the Britannia, the one who kept his back to the cricket, had a good reason for his behaviour. We saw him being helped into the airport coach. He was twice blind: drunk and visually impaired.

We got back to the hotel to suffer the match. After the second goal went in, I switched off and wrote up my notes.

A couple of months later, I find myself driving back to Manchester. It is still there and still wet. A report I had barely finished transcribing, on my earlier expedition, was snatched away, and turned into a script to be voiced by a German actor. There were people on the move – children – marching across town, clamped to their headphones, following my unreliable directions to invented places.

I was booked into a Premier Inn and slated to give a talk in the belly of the beast, in Urbis, that giant amputee octopus. Nothing revives a city like a terrorist outrage, a rogue car bomb clears the ground and stimulates development. Contractors put in their bids before the dust settles. Designer T-shirts in the covered malls of the post-IRA Arndale Centre proclaimed: KETAMINE JUST SAY NEIGH.

Urban Splash, the architectural imagineers, are not buying into this big-bang thesis. They reckon that nothing works, as an engine for regeneration, like a failed Olympic bid. The hard graft has been done, the nexus of connections is already in place. The schmoozers are still on salary. All that deflated rhetoric has to find an outlet. Manchester was up for change. And Urbis was part of the fallout, the collateral damage, a museum of the city dedicated to cultural amnesia. Vaughan Allen, the former style journalist appointed as chief executive, made it his first task to unpick his own mission statement. 'We banned the word "museum",' he said. 'The word "museum" means things in cabinets, and we didn't have any.' Urbis was about freeing up space, while avoiding the drag of classification. You channel-hop: fashion, music, manga, gardening. Constantly changing shows. Sampling. Snacking. Hit boredom with homoeopathic doses of the same. Vaughan's buzzword was 'zeitgeisty'. 'We realized what we had created was a Sunday supplement.'

Addressing an Urbis audience, wriggling on hard plastic chairs, I felt like Willie Walsh after the opening of Heathrow's Terminal 5: when 500 flights had been cancelled and 23,000 passengers were about to depart without luggage. There was 'insufficient familiarization', Willie said, failing to understand that the nature of these non-places is that they are all too familiar, but factored to be nothing more than that. You never achieve intimacy. Tactile exploration without penetration. Photos from our earlier Manchester walk flickered behind me, in case the audience ran out of puff. The room was like a corridor furnished to cope with the traumatized survivors of a natural disaster. I summoned a submerged cabal of luminaries: De Quincey, Canetti, Wittgenstein, Sebald. All of whom got out of town at the first opportunity.

As I negotiated my own escape, two local bad boys, cans raised in salute, waved me over. 'I'm John and so's he. That stuff you were banging on about, making it glamorous: bollocks, man. Manchester's crap. We've been stuck in this shithole thirty years, we should know.' They had the scars to prove it, prison pallor dusted with carcinogenic freckles, indelible midnight stubble. Sniffing out the complimentary booze, the low-intensity fuss of a doomed opening, a new magazine too big to steal (or sell), they were the real spirits of place; foot-soldiers of the legendary Savoy Books, a subversive operation that somehow combined the peddling of pornography with patronage of valuable lost writers like Jack Trevor Story and Maurice Richardson. And the conceptual brilliance of getting old rocker P. J. Proby to record *The Waste Land*. And Fenella Fielding to trill her way, in outraged innocence, through J. G. Ballard's *Crash*.

A younger man attached himself to our little group, a walker, newly returned from Berlin. He said that he had set out one day, on a whim, from Alexanderplatz to Poland. He followed the railway line. He took no photographs, made no notes, carried out no research. There were drawings, sketches. He would turn the journey into a graphic novel.

The cold water in the Premier Inn is off. The hot tap is scalding, volcanic. You run your morning bath before you turn in for the night. Give it time to stop steaming. The electricity, so they tell us, will be cut off at 11.30 p.m.: don't get caught in the lift. Our window doesn't shut, but the bed is big and comfortable. The breakfast bar is occupied by genial bouncers and roadies, who are exchanging tales of mayhem, life on the motorway.

Back from the Urbis gig, Anna declines to eat in the empty restaurant, which is a low-ceilinged rabbit hutch, jaunty with muzak. You are safe, she reckons, with an Indian. They tell her, at the desk, that there is a recommended place 'just around the back'. Blinded by the rain, twenty minutes in, we abandon this quest. It's one of my conceits that canalside development packages come with bars and bistros and that the inner-city marinas of Manchester are now sufficiently established to have at least one of these, which has not yet been found out, declared bankrupt, rebranded, boarded over.

Steepling warehouses, black water. Out of the gloom, a fuzzy halo of neon around an Italian restaurant. It's one of those nights when five customers is five too many. The chef is drinking at the bar, resisting overtures from a pompous greeter in a slippery suit. When my fishcake arrives, after fifty minutes, it's more like refrigerated cattle cake. You graze your tongue licking it, you can't bite. 'Everything good, signore, signora?' And for once, sodden, starving and provoked, they get a true answer. 'Awful.'

There will be no charge. Snatching up her coat, Anna lets her linen napkin fall across the decorative candle, which smoulders noxiously, then bursts into flame. I throw some iced water over the conflagration and we rush for the door, leaving a charred and smoking mess. The lowlife revellers from Urbis are pissing into one of the ornamental trenches, but the rain will wash it away by morning.

There was one more walk for the following day. Stephen Bayley, the original design commissar for the Millennium Dome, had been talking up an intervention in a revamped industrial quarter of Manchester known as New Islington. Other metropolitan commentators followed his example, enduring or enjoying the ride out of town, the cab, the lunch, a congenial interview with the Stirling Prize-winning architect: Will Alsop.

'I like sitting at tables,' Alsop said. 'They are the horizontal planes of social discourse. Most proper conversations happen across a table, particularly if wine is involved.'

The structure was called Chips (as in 'cheap as') and it looked, in magazine illustrations, like an off-cut from the container stack on the A13, downwind of the landfill mountain in Rainham. This cheery intruder on post-industrial blight consisted of a block of 142 apartments, fewer than half of which would be made available under the government's 'Rent to Homebuy' scheme. The usual consultation process had been offered to locals (i.e., an opportunity to agree with what was already in place) and they were said to regard the jazzy invader with conditional affection.

'I'd like to say the name Chips was my idea,' Alsop said, 'but in fact it was the locals who came up with it.' Fat, golden-yellow, metal chips, oven-ready and heaped on the plate, beside a dollop of brown-sauce canal. Mouth-watering colour in enhanced digital representation. The big block lettering of containers in transit from the forgotten dirt-yard of Chobham Farm, Stratford. And I thought of another set of chips too: the last throw of a desperate gambler.

New Islington didn't show up on any of our giveaway maps, which meant that we were free to ramble, to follow our instincts. We had been in this unknown city just long enough to know where to avoid, how to navigate by river, canal, culture quarter. And how to rely on postcards collected from the splendid

Manchester City Gallery. Last night's Italian restaurant, I now realized, was a recapitulation of the claustrophobic gloom of Pierre Adolphe Valette's blue-tinged painting *India House* (1912). Snaky reflections in the water, warehouses looming out of the murk. After the intense and unsettling experience of a tramp around the halls, stairs, chambers, of a new (new to me) museum, with the urge to see everything and still find time to *concentrate* on highlights, discoveries, coming away with a few postcards is a necessary ritual, a ticket of release. The correspondence I received from Ballard always came on postcards, from which you could track his movements across Europe: Rome, Madrid, Paris. His unexpected interests: Caravaggio, Raphael, Titian, Breughel, Henri Rousseau. With a reserve stock, from the Tate and the Museum of Modern Art in New York: Dali and Max Ernst. Spread Ballard's cards across one of Will Alsop's tables and you possess the catalogue of the Shepperton writer's psychopathology: Sigmund Freud, Henry Ford, and the dust cloud from 'the world's first atomic bomb'. Crucifixions, velvet nudes. Hotel lobbies, magnum cities. Cannibalism on a Spanish beach.

Off-map, beyond anywhere you are advised to shop, it gets more interesting, more Chinese. Supermarkets. Factory-size restaurants catering to out-of-town wedding parties. Bilingual signs for the HSBC bank (which is already Chinese-owned). Heading in an uncommitted north-westerly direction, we achieve an orient of the heart. Green tiles and orange, wide-skirted pagoda roofs: WING YIP, CHINESE & ORIENTAL GROCERIES. GLAMOROUS CHINESE RESTAURANT. A proper street, used and occupied, evolved into a nice mix of pushy incomers and doomed survivors. In the newspaper shop they are friendly, but they don't do much in the way of news. In the kiosk-bank, the Anglo-Chinese manager sets us right for New Islington. It is more than a rumour, he lives there. And he loves it, this separation from the street, with the screening devices of contemporary design, the electronic security systems. He is delighted that we, strangers, tourists, should want to locate his building. It confirms the decision he made, his faith in a provisional, CGI future. He flips a hand-phone, taps images on a screen, a silver wafer like a device for taking your own fingerprints. He relishes this sense of entitlement, of being a pioneer, an investor in a private island: beyond Manchester, beyond anywhere. Shanghai. Hong Kong. Canary Wharf. Dubai. New Islington.

The selling point of the enterprise zone is its refusal to connect with the street, the through-traffic heading out of town, the dignified abdication of the warehouses along the cobbled canal. Everything here aspires to Berlin's death-strip, the shadowland of the Wall as it comes back to life, as scavenging film-poets exploit it: wastelots, rubble gardens, exposed cellars, immigrant kiosks, metal-shuttered booze boxes. A headlong collision between cocky architecture, tolerated public art and brazen hucksterism: new plaques on old mills, twisted avenues of girders mimicking dead forests, towpaths with panoramic hoardings making a movie of the future: HELPING TO REGENERATE NEW ISLINGTON. You could define the area, its distance from the commercial centre, as territory in which they can't, at present, afford to build another prison. Strangeways, the ugly penal colony housing most of the cast of the *Coronation Street* soap opera, is across the river, on the west side of Bury New Road.

Stephen Bayley speaks of Will Alsop's 'tipsy bravura'. The Chips stack is a prime example of the electively unfinished look, perilously balanced blocks in fuck-you colours, suitable for students, artists, city-rim campers. Copywriting for the project makes reference to vanished industries, containers, scrapyards. The effect is throwaway but not disposable. And, although it has been extensively written up, Alsop's cluster is resolutely open-ended, a work in progress. That is its charm: it feels squatted, builders stroll through at a recreational saunter, their tools have been arranged on concrete slabs, like conceptual art waiting for a sponsor. Alsop says that what he is trying to promote is 'space', unmediated, empty as a scooped skull. 'Everyone goes through the same door. You can't tell who is relatively wealthy and who's not.' Neither can you tell who works here, who lives here, and who is trying to cobble together enough material for fifteen hundred words in the broadsheets. Everybody we see through the window is carrying furniture. Natural greenery (weeds) have been set in concrete tubs in a field of stone chippings. Curls of barbed wire dress green-mesh fencing.

ISLINGTON WHARF: BUY TO LIVE. TRY BEFORE YOU BUY. LIVE FOR I YEAR WHILE BUILDING YOUR DEPOSIT (LIMITED AVAILABILITY AND SUBJECT TO STATUS. ONLY VALID WHEN PROSPERITY IS PURCHASED.)

The rain gives Alsop's containers a glaze of authenticity. Nobody is around to make the pitch. The offices for the neighbouring development, the tower block, are shut. This is as close as we have come to SuperCity: parked units, mobile homes that do not move, a vertical trailer camp heaped in a dangerous arrangement that isn't going to crash. The building predicts a community that may or may not arrive. It exists only because funding has been achieved, at a certain level; but not quite enough, so it appears, to get the thing done.

Drenched and weary, we complete our Manchester trajectory with a return, across town, to Trafford Park. That monster mall, the Trafford Centre, conceived in 1984, is more of an antique than the Victorian mills of New Islington. The Thatcherite optimism, the glitz, the Cinecittà bravado, is suicidal, insane. Fascinated by what the posthumous history of a redundant mall might be, here was my answer: a space–time singularity. White hole. The absence of gravity. This swollen epic of consumerism was waved through, in 1989, as a job-creation scheme. There were 35,000 unemployed people within a five-mile radius. No public investment was required. The centre would provide 6,500 jobs, as well as taking on 2,000 construction workers. It didn't much matter what was being built: the same argument plays for all grand projects. Coshed by an excess of retail opportunities, fast-food outlets pastiching global cuisines, multiplexes showing eight kinds of Harry Potter and four kinds of dinosaur, we flop in a phantom New Orleans and prod at some inedible oil slick, Gulf of Mexico fish substitute. If you arrive on foot, pushing your way through a hedge into the supersize car park, you are an alien, a non-consuming wetback. Get yourself spotted on CCTV using a camera and Special Branch will kick down your door, at first light, for no extra charge.

The Trafford Centre has its own microclimate and it smells like dead television. Like the aftersweat of an Oscar ceremony: hope dashed, lust curtailed, fear tasted. That heavenly dome. The Gloria Swanson staircases. The muscle beach statuary. Our clapboard Basin Street has no bougainvillea, no heady scents: it stinks of recycled air, in-transit passengers, plastic headrests. Muzak is malfunctioning in another room, there are no street bands.

'It is unlikely,' John Parkinson-Bailey wrote, 'that another out-of-town centre of such a size will ever be built.' But the Trafford Centre isn't out of town, *it is a town*, a suburb bent on making Manchester its feeder satellite. And in this aim it anticipates the ambition of Tesco: to become a primary developer, by setting their provide-everything hangars within a secure ring of blocks and towers; thrown up, with the connivance, and approval, of local and central government.

The Trafford Centre is a quantum explosion of statistics: three miles of shopfronts, twenty-seven restaurants, a food court seating 1,600 people (eventually), nineteen escalators, forty-three hydraulic lifts, banks, financial services, eighteen 'food on the go' outlets, travel agents and estate agents, lottery points, parking space for 10,000 cars. The centre is an oil vampire, a carbon-emission hotspot. A De Quincey hallucination of superimposed cultures, pub-quiz quotations: Aztec, Chinese, *Hercules Conquers Atlantis*, *The Fall of the Roman Empire*, Fred Astaire and Ginger Rogers ocean-liner modernism. Granite and marble from the quarries at Montignosa and Querleta in Italy, at £5.8 million: lottery-winner acquisitiveness on an heroic scale. Premier League Xanadu. And all of it fixed in another era, the 1980s: retro television, *Ashes to Ashes*. In the great gold rush of Old Tory/New Labour consumerism, the Trafford Centre became the epicentre: of traffic congestion, blocked roads with anti-pedestrian earthbanks, strategic plantings. A shopping city and football stadium in the same park. An extension to the Metrolink was turned down by John Prescott, the Environment and Transport Secretary, who overruled the local planning inspector, while reasserting, with a thump on the lectern, his commitment to reducing private motoring.

It wasn't long before the news came through that Urbis was blown. The thing that was never grounded, that never managed to find a workable description for the money that leaked away into the gutters around its wind-blown square, was exposed as a metaphor of foolishness, not an engine of regeneration. The icy skin reflected the world, but it was not of the world: a solid void. Redundancy notices were delivered to two-thirds of the staff, the invisibles. Urbis came into being in 2002, on the tide of New Labour boosterism, post-millennial loose change. And like all the other vanity interventions across the north of England, it crashed: the berg melted. But a neat solution was found, relocating failure, in the expectation that, after so many lies and prevarications, nobody would notice. The collapsed National Museum of Football in Preston could be transferred to Manchester. Fail better, fail bigger. Urbis will reopen as the thing they were determined to spurn, a museum, a museum of football: in a city where there are already two major enterprises running on their club shops, their global-branding initiatives, their TV channels. Urbis, it seems, is retreating to a form I remember so well from my childhood, from Blackpool's Pleasure Beach: waxworks of Stanley Matthews and Stan Mortensen, after the monochrome Cup Final triumph of 1953.

Chinese Boxes

Staying away from Hackney, and out on the road, I took any assignments that were offered, an untenured motorway lecturer, hawker of threadbare polemics: a low-rent turn. I staggered into retail-park campuses from epic detours around overturned lorries, potatoes spread across the M11, red-cone avenues, to face ranks of urban geographers, conceptual architects, land artists – never literary folk. I was spared that. When I returned home, after a few months, it was to check on outstanding invoices (outstanding in tardiness), to placate the bank, to shuffle red postcards for undelivered packets and summonses. The more I worked the less I had. Expenses piled up, nobody rushed to reward a person operating at the outer limits of the system. Promised fees melted away in massive tax deductions. Invoices were mislaid, or returned so that the expense claims could be filed to another authority in another office. There were unfortunate epidemics of Chinese flu in the finance department. At one point, after three months of delivering talks composed in transit, finessing journalism that might be profitably recycled, slapping down introductions for over optimistic reissues, I added up the figures: I was owed more than £12,000. And I had no time to chase it. Keep moving. Another suitcase, another Travelodge.

Unless you walk everywhere, the new England is unutterably strange, a carousel of disorientating jumpcuts; coming off-road is like random digital stutter. Another plate of congealed fish and chips. An invitation to join the Automobile Association. A health check by slot machine. Another lecture to deliver: a madman talking to himself in public. Sunk in apathetic reverie, like all those other ghosts in neon cafeterias, I began to wonder if grand projects had ever been successful. And if, having once failed, they could be revived. I remembered the earlier trip with Chris Petit to

Morecambe. And the Midland Hotel. That memorial to streamlined Style Moderne. To the age of the railway poster.

The sweep of bay has more cloud than it can comfortably accommodate. The pleasure to be derived from sliding back a glass door against the force of the wind, after checking in to the revamped 1930s hotel, and remarking the narrowness of the balcony, is tempered by wondering where exactly the nuclear power station locates itself, and where the Chinese cockle pickers were trapped by the tide and drowned.

While Anna rested, I made a tour with my camera, after deciding that it would be more interesting to investigate the network of small streets behind the showpiece esplanade. The pictures, when they come back from the chemist, are never right. You can't capture it. The way Morecambe has worked so hard to reverse history, to bring back the era of lidos, pleasure gardens, well-kept municipal parks: the last resort. All Lancashire – industrialists, solicitors, showmen, Masons and Rotarians – flocked to dinner dances at the Midland. Buck Ruxton, the Lancaster GP, hanged in 1936 for the double murder of his wife and his maid, was a regular at social functions. On parallel avenues, running away from the windswept front, the town carried on its real business: failing tea rooms, Eric Morecambe heritage pubs, covered markets converted into budget malls, drinkers slumped on bus station benches, dope deals of spotty cyclists on wastelots behind abandoned petrol stations.

Oliver Hill's Midland Hotel, from 1933, is a significant part of the unsunk fleet of English modernism: low, flat-roofed, rimmed with slender balconies. And always hungry for another coat of white paint. Deco curves arguing with starker German geometry. Hotel or hospital? Fresh air, exercise, sunbathing. The lull of the 1930s, the years when the middle classes felt good about themselves, when they experimented with Europe. Hill's only experience of hotels and resorts was staying in them. He came from an established family. His connections with Sir Edward Lutyens (who designed an annexe for Manchester's Midland Hotel in 1930) helped to secure the Morecambe commission. On a continental tour, Hill visited the Stockholm Exhibition, and took a fancy to the Scandinavian version of modernism. The space, the light. Like a vision of the coming Ikea philosophy.

The Midland was born out of confusion, set down on the site of a redundant harbour to act as a crash barrier at the end of a railway line. The convex side of the hotel, mirroring the sweep of the shore, faced the sea: a vision for every bedroom. A fashionable stopover for those who were part of the newsreel of the time. Rumour dresses the empty set with Edward VIII and Mrs Simpson, Winston Churchill, Noël Coward, Oswald Mosley, Coco Chanel. The rattle of cocktail shakers. Heels clicking on terrazzo floors and ankle-straps flashing over the seahorse mosaic by Marion Dorn. Hill was a promiscuous collector who invited the artists of the moment to chip in. He signed up the few he could afford: the two Erics, Gill and Ravilious, as well as the lovely Marion Dorn with her headscarf-turban, her Egyptian eyes.

Creosote-sleek London bandleaders from the Winter Gardens squabbled over bar bills with tight-lipped Lancashire funny men. Bud Abbott, of Abbott and Costello, was expelled at 4 a.m. for ser-ious 'misbehaviour'. He crawled from his taxi, two hours later, on his hands and knees, begging for readmittance. He'd seen what the rest of the town, beyond the blessed islet of this hotel, was actually like, the penitential bed-and-breakfast regimes who wouldn't let him over their sandstoned doorsteps.

The intention of the Midland, from the first, was to keep the plebs out; working men invading the entrance hall, the show-stopping space with Gill's relief panel, were instructed to remove their cloth caps. Arthur Towle, Manager of Hotels and Catering Services for the Midland Railway, insisted that trippers coming from the promenade be separated from bona fide guests. 'We must not confuse them with the class of people who will be using the hotel.' People like Trevor Howard, who was at Carnforth Station shooting *Brief Encounter*, or tooling around the Cumbrian backroads in his MG. And Laurence Olivier flashing a rictal grin at the punters, before giving them his turn, end of Empire as dying music hall, in the film version of *The Entertainer.*

The Winter Gardens Theatre, by this time (1960), was as posthumous as the Midland. But the hotel, under various management packages, struggled on. Eric Morecambe and Ernie Wise checked in – two twin-bedded rooms – at £6 a night, in June 1969. The beached concrete liner rocked with the waves. The water table was so near the surface that at high tide, or after heavy rain, Hill's flagship building would lift and sway, tugging at anchor, floating on the tide.

Pink paths. Grey scree of man-made jetty. Massing cloud curtain. The reality of Morecambe contradicts the Midland's decorative art, Gill's map of north-west England painted on the wall of the Children's Room. His cavorting sea nymphs recall an era of luscious railway posters with rippling bathing belles, capped and toned, on diving boards above the Mediterranean glitter of a freshly installed lido.

Staying in this heritage terminal, once of the railway, now of the road, I felt like an unrequired extra in *Double Sin*, one of the Agatha Christie *Poirot* episodes they shot here. Television is our method of validating the past, through archive or costume drama. The Midland was somewhere to drive away from, the town of Morecambe was too scabby to pass the audition: they relocated the action to picturesque Kirby Lonsdale. But, weirdly, in the quest for warped authenticity, set designers recreated Eric Ravilious's erased mural. The only accessible version of this obliterated artwork was banished to a mock-up of the hotel's circular café (the space allocated for well-behaved proles) in the London Weekend studios at Twickenham. As an official war artist with the rank of Honorary Captain in the Royal Marines, and intending to sketch a rescue mission, Ravilious flew out from a base in Iceland on 2 September 1942. The plane never returned. Even before the hotel opened, Gill noticed how badly the Ravilious mural had cracked and how much it required patching. He wrote to his friend: 'It seems a frightful shame to even talk of whitewashing it out, but can you possibly leave it as it is?' Northern damp seeped through the wall, paint peeled, obscuring this prophetic vision of a deserted grand-project lido, a sky of miniature parachutes, angelic invaders floating from the clouds.

Urban Splash, the regeneration quango who backed Will Alsop's Chips development in Manchester, promoted the restored Midland Hotel like a lost Ravilious. There are photographs in the local history archive of pedestrians gazing at CGI posters exhibited on the high fence protecting the site of the future hotel. White curves, blue sky: a Hockney postcard. Morecambe as Los Angeles. Palm tree, empty highway. And, by implication, naked people sharing showers in every room.

The new Midland uses design as a screening device: are you qualified to appreciate where you are? *Are you on set?* Or passing through, a one-night investor? 'No woman had anything to do with this,' Anna said of the en suite bathroom, which allowed no space for toiletries and featured a foldaway lavatory, inches from the bed. The cupboards were artworks with complicated pull-down racks. Narrow balconies offered the immensity of the bay as a challenge. Reminding us of how unreadable this shoreline is: sandbanks and rip tides, the argument between national park and dirty industry, recreation and paranoia. A fated landscape where storms wash away bridges, splitting communities, and where one bright summer day a taxi driver with a lethal armoury would go on the rampage, killing twelve people, including his twin brother, his solicitor, fellow cabbies, before taking his own life. The authorities ordered a lockdown at the nuclear reprocessing plant at Sellafield, where Derrick Bird had worked, before being dismissed for theft. Members of the plant's private security force joined the unsuccessful pursuit of the man in the car, as he roamed the backroads, culling random pedestrians. Giving a darker stain to Eric Gill's playful chart.

Diners in the Midland, basking in the privilege of that view, are hermetically sealed, separated from the town and the semi-derelict room above a defunct pub in a backstreet, where a dozen Chinese cockle pickers were lodged, before being put in a van and taken, up the coast, to Askam-in-Furness. After the drowning of twenty-three workers, in the original Morecambe horror, minders with competing triad allegiances battled for territory. Many of the cockle pickers were brought, on a daily basis, up the motorway from Liverpool. Where they slept on mattresses laid on the floor of a boarded-up house in a condemned terrace waiting for a promised development package. The wretched illegals, invisibles who kept the supermarkets supplied, were creatures of the road. Like the underfunded academics, the highway-devouring lecturers, Chinese economic migrants shuttled around a devil's triangle: Manchester's Chinatown restaurants to Liverpool to Morecambe. Always in sealed vans or met at the bus station and taken to the latest miserable flophouse. The Taiwanese journalist Hsiao-Hung Pai, who investigated this world in *Chinese Whispers*, records the words of a Tienjin woman, a cockle picker, arriving in Morecambe. 'I've always wanted to be near the sea. So I came here. But a third of my money goes to the boss. And the sea isn't as blue as I'd imagined.'

Discovering that most of the kitchen staff, waiters and chambermaids, in the high days of the Midland, the era epitomized by a photograph of Lord and Lady Docker descending the staircase in the supreme complacency of their evening wear, came from Liverpool, I knew that a return to the City of Culture was inevitable. I had an arrangement to walk through Toxteth with John Davies, the long-distance vicar, the man who tramped down the M62 from Hull to Liverpool. The one whose blog I followed when we rode the freedom bus over the Pennines.

We had met, once before, in Cheltenham. John invited me to take part in the Greenbelt Festival, which happened over an August weekend on the racecourse, and which involved a cast of many thousands camping in tents, feeding from numerous stalls, and primed to enjoy themselves whatever the weather. Having been too long in this town, at boarding school, I tended to keep well away, as from a relatively open prison, experienced, endured, even enjoyed, but done with, finished: another self, not eliminated, but buried without regret in an unmarked grave. I'd never been part of a large-scale festival, so I took up the offer of a room in a Thistle Hotel near a major roundabout, alongside the GCHQ listening station, a secure and sinister new town of huts, bunkers, masts, and apartments for career spooks. Banal off-road architecture surrounds the doughnut of the inner circle, the hooped structure where global intelligence is gathered. The unmediated babble of the world is processed in a space where you would expect to find a retail park. GCHQ is Gloucestershire's biggest employer. National belt-tightening doesn't begin to lick the sugar from this doughnut. It is awarded, each year, the bulk of the £2.4 billion set aside for Britain's intelligence agencies. On the day when we celebrated the news that we had won the 2012 Olympics, Cheltenham received, by way of an NSA interception, a message from Afghanistan: 'Tomorrow is zero hour.' The next morning, as commuters struggled to work in London, the bombs went off in the Underground. On the day after that, GCHQ completed the translation.

The underlying theme of the festival was Christian. My problem, when confronted by an expectant audience, sitting on the grass, was being carried away by the tent-show-revivalist aspect. My pitch was too spiritual. I kept banging on about the pilgrimage, the quest, the journey of the soul. The believers were much more down to earth, socially concerned, having a good time as part of the crowd, processing between stand-up comedians, bands, films, workshops, lectures. The one venue offering beer was blasphemously signboarded as: The Jesus Arms. I went on after a talk entitled 'Bill Gates, Bono and You'.

John Davies, who appeared with me, spoke of the sense of awe he experienced, standing on a hillside above the M62, 'watching the traffic steadily flowing across the high Pennines like a metallic ribbon glittering in the sunshine'. There was, he acknowledged, a dimension of wonder in the ritualistic process of motorway driving, post-Ballardian sensory enhancement, deep reverie. He spoke of the Gospels as a kind of divinely inspired Highway Code. He found my attitude towards this liminal territory, as expressed in *London Orbital*, more critical than his own: he was undergoing, in his foot-foundered exhaustion, an epiphany. The road was a metaphor, the prompt for an unwritten sermon. 'Above Asda, only sky.'

The hiking urban vicar, a compact man, close-cropped, thin-spectacled, smiling, met me on the steps of the Anglican Cathedral. He wore a worker-priest's uniform of black shirt and dark anorak, but he had writer's hands. In his rucksack he carried a copy of *Mr Tapscott*, a self-published poem by the late Bill Griffiths. An inspiration to both of us. Griffiths, with his gift for synthesis, righteous indignation, textual archaeology, was the perfect guide to the condemned terraces of Toxteth, those wide Welsh streets and decommissioned Presbyterian chapels. Bill shaped his poem around the dubious conviction of two men, Ray Gilbert and John Kamara, for the killing of a betting-shop manager in March 1981. The spark for the Toxteth riots. 'The bulging world-of-state is a crisis.' The spaces in my dialogue with John Davies, on our tour through layers of Liverpool history, parks, houses and handsome flats once owned by Adrian Henri or Roger McGough, are filled with the growling resonance of Bill's unheard voice. Patterns of language, so generously set before those who need them, are an absolute: they cohere, they are not extinguished. To fix or interpret sections of the ring-bound poem moved us along, from named address to park, to café. 'One hemisphere of the marvellous,' Bill wrote: of the streets through which we were trudging. My own copy of the poem, I notice on returning home, has a Griffiths drawing of the Liver bird, hand-coloured, with splashes of green waves.

Walking alongside John Davies is a journey through absence, neighbourhood enterprises on Rialto Corner laid over the burnt-out traces of the original riots. 'A vast area of working-class terraces reduced from a living, active community to a tinned-up wilderness by one signature sweep of John Prescott's hand,' Davies said. In Princes Road the red-brick chapel has been made into a secure island by a fence that carries the testimonials of the expelled parishioners. I was interested to note that the ubiquitous painted crocodile of the

Olympic Park, that symbol of devouring economic imperatives, has waddled into Liverpool 8. NO MORE DEMOLITION, NO MORE BULL. DREAM ON FOR REGENERATION. Cartoon-graffiti terraces have smiling faces in the windows, where the surviving streets have chipboard. No blue plaque on the house where Ringo Starr grew up. When a Beatles tour bus pauses at the end of the road, nobody gets out. In Bethnal Green, similar properties, on tighter streets, now sell for half a million pounds.

On Lodge Lane we stop for sandwiches in a bright new café called MT BELLY'S. The mugs of tea come free. I'm intrigued by what Bill Griffiths has to say about 'the attempt to raise a new set of myths, things that were neutral but archetypal'. If we fail to follow the poet's example, and to hammer out a mythology of our own, we are lost. In Toxteth, we encountered nothing but friendliness, an active interest in our presence, as we wandered the quiet streets and deserted parks. The man in the café, launching a business, fresh paint, overloaded sandwiches, topped-up mugs, hovered over our discussion. I placed my recorder on the table to capture the story of John's hike from Hull to Liverpool. 'Bill Griffiths,' he said, 'talked about how history and literature have been colonized by certain big names. He works to reclaim it. It's good to be sitting in Lodge Lane and wondering if Bill perched here himself.'

I've always had a feeling about the M62. It's been a motorway I have travelled a lot, through visiting family and friends in different parts of the north. I've enjoyed the journey, by car. I could wonder about things I could see, landmarks, just outside the boundaries of the motorway: churches, civic-looking buildings, heavy industry. These things started to raise questions in my mind. I wanted to walk to get closer to those sites. I'd done a lot of urban walks, it was the urban thing I was interested in.

I didn't see the Will Alsop thing as being workable. I was so concerned to look at specific details of each place. I was finding the differences between places, more than the similarities. The Alsop idea doesn't reflect the cultural reality. The interesting thing is to walk through the new developments and to see how individuals or small groups, small collectives, have started to make their own archives of the places where they live – with little bits of graffiti, or structural adjustments to signage.

I'd never been to Hull before. I enjoyed Hull. It seemed to be that bit apart from all the other cities on the M62 journey. It has worked at its identity. I was interested to note that the docklands development, the waterside, was built a long time ago. The original development was carried out in the early '80s. They started in Liverpool in the late '80s. They thought it out for themselves in Hull, rather than latching on to someone else's development.

Sometimes it's good to get lost, but sometimes it isn't. I got lost in Leeds, a very dark, seedy corner of Leeds, and couldn't find my way out. I had maps with me and couldn't read them because there was no light anywhere. It was a red-light area. The only people I could find were high on drugs. It got a bit scary.

I don't know anything about flora and fauna; I'm a city person. I did enjoy walking the Pennines. I spent a day with a farmer. He farmed around the area where the motorway splits in two. I anticipated, wrongly, that he would not have liked it because it was a busy motorway ripping through his land, but in fact all the farmers welcomed the road because it made them accessible.

I didn't know Manchester at all. Another element of my walk was seeing ghosts: certainly in Ancoats, where I was with a friend who had lived there for a long time. He didn't use the word 'ghost'; he was talking about lives that had been lived in that community. He could still see those people and those places. When he looked at the closed-down pubs, he could picture the people who were once sitting in them.

I met people on the road. One guy was walking it because he wanted to connect all the Rugby League grounds, which are mainly along the M62. I did get tired. By the time I reached the outskirts of Liverpool, I just wanted to get home. My legs were gone.

I finished by walking through the arena of my childhood, Crosby Beach. I knocked at my parents' door and we went together to the beach. It was a real sense of homecoming. I hadn't planned it that way. It was quite emotional to realize how much home meant to me. I used to play on Crosby Beach as a kid. And I remember seeing the changes down there, the sandhills going up.

I like the Gormley figures. I think they're doing what I've done often in the past, which is to stand looking at the view: a wide-open sea. They have a nice, gentle presence, really. There was a lot of resistance at first, with a lot of people lobbying, particularly those who used the water, like power-boat users. The placement of the figures meant they couldn't use that stretch of water any more. But the figures have grown on people. They have attracted people to the area.

I finished my three months with a month putting all the words together. I realized that what was important to me, reflecting back, was the writing. The writing was as important as the walk. You construct the world as you go.

We returned to Morecambe to make the walk across the bay, in quest of other ghosts, the drowned cockle pickers. There were prohibitions everywhere: MORECAMBE BAY COCKLE BED CLOSURES. Notices dated from April 2006. Cockling had been suspended until further notice. You don't wait for the tide to retreat and then head off, unaccompanied, across those treacherous sands; you sign on with an official guide. I had expected half a dozen excursionists not a Cecil B. DeMille mob, packing the Arnside shoreline, waiting expectantly for their Moses to part the Red Sea. It was an awesome spectacle, that afternoon, hundreds of us, setting off under low cloud, hammered by sudden, special-effects showers. A gnarled prophet called Cedric, cleft stick in hand, trousers rolled, led us on the four-hour hike to Kents Bank. He marshalled his strung-out flock with a whistle. Sandals slung around neck, jeans sodden, I stuck close to our leader as he surged forward at a good clip. The multitude spread out, small children dragged and dawdled, before being hoisted on to the shoulders of their parents. Shaggy dogs wallowed in salt-sticky puddles. We left the land a long way behind. Caterpillar treads of orange Bay Search tractors emerged from a broad rivulet and diminished in the direction of a remote horizon. Amphibious vehicles marked RESCUE alerted us to the unpredictable nature of a place where walkers could very quickly become swimmers.

Cedric sounded a shrill blast, to line us up, on the edge of a channel where the sea had rushed in. As we waded through, we felt not only the strength of the current but also the unpleasant sensation of sand eels banging against our naked legs. I took the chance to have a quick word with this man who walked alone, retracing his own footprints, never looking back to confirm that the tribe was still at his heels.

'It was three miles over there.' He pointed with his stick. 'The cockle pickers were on a high sandbank with a fast-flowing river on either side. They had no chance.'

The money earned, £15 for three sacks of cockles, was less than the potential wages to be made sweating in the kitchens of a Manchester restaurant. Or flogging pirated DVDs around mean streets. The gang bosses took their cut and charged for accommodation and food.

Rain slashing down, we slithered through a channel of blue-grey mud, before crossing dunes held together with coarse grass, and achieving firm ground. Our fellow pilgrims, seeking release, rushed into private woodland to piss against innocent trees.

Kissing the Rod

An English train. On a glorious summer morning. I am struggling to fix the precise point at which we pass over or under the M25, London's collar: without success. The railway system lays down its metal rails, ladders for commuters, with no reference to the self-consuming serpent of the orbital motorway. Rivers and railways were always my favourite transport corridors. Time to absorb the landscape; to sit, barely registering geological shifts, dipping into a book, deprogramming a clotted backlog.

I like the way the steady-stare film-maker Patrick Keiller speaks of using train-time. He is a man, clearly, who abhors waste; a hoarder of old newspapers, careful with his finances, well aware that the next gig might be the last. Keiller used trains like an editing suite: he auditioned unregistered places. Even as he tortured himself with the knowledge that he was never going to use a single shot taken from a moving carriage, not crisp enough. The fields refused to stay still. Cattle lurched. Light values changed. The windows were greasy.

In the first phase of his career, when Patrick worked, as I did, as a part-time lecturer in Walthamstow, he explored out-of-the way locales, searching for compositions suitable for a catalogue of surrealist architecture. The unfathomable mess of London, which might, if he had to evaluate it, drive him mad, was brought to book: a sewage cathedral alongside muddy Channalsea Creek in the Lower Lea Valley, a coal hopper in Nine Elms Lane, a concrete factory in Gravesend. Somewhere in the background of all these ghosted structures was a railway.

Keiller called his chosen sites 'found' architecture. A favoured technique involved spotting possibles from a train window, then making an expedition, by bicycle, to bag the view. Like sticking a flag on the moon. Accidents of transit, undescribed, went into the captured photograph; a private archive that would, eventually, transform itself into a series of groundbreaking films. What Keiller didn't appreciate, at the start, was that he was being shadowed by future phantoms: the rasping ironies of Paul Schofield, who would become his fictional avatar, delivering scripted monologues; and the mysterious Robinson, a being brought into existence as a cultural 'beard', to take on adventures the film-maker was too fastidious to experience at first hand.

In an essay called 'Imaging', Keiller describes how he set out to look for a place he had seen a few days earlier from a train window. 'It was a north-facing hillside of allotments behind the corner of two streets of suburban houses, beyond the railway's bridge above the North Circular Road.' Mounted on his bicycle, disorientated, a little puffed, he finds something else: a metal footbridge. A bridge that dictates its own terms. 'Its long, narrow walkway resembled the linearity of a film; its parapets framed the view in a ratio similar to the 4 x 3 of the camera, and its elaborate articulation, with several flights of steps, half-landings and changes of direction, offered a structure for a moving-camera choreography which might include panoramas.' The bridge, waiting all this time for an unsuspecting interpreter, was revealed to the world as the setting for two Keiller films: the launch of a new career. The whole curious process – train, bicycle, camera – drew the architectural photographer into a situation that left him no choice but to ventriloquize a previously mute element of the city. Keiller was the thing found, not Stonebridge Park.

My ride to Berkhamsted, on this blameless May morning, pushed me to read the train window as a frame for the contemplation of an exceptional group of British film-essayists. Chris Petit, of late, had been posting, on his website, fragments from his travels. He was one of those trapped by the Icelandic dust cloud in a hotel that suddenly takes on another identity, something more than a stopover. He was attending a film festival in Buenos Aires, a city which he found rather dull, architecturally, but blessed with cheap taxis. To escape, he took a boat to Montevideo, a flight to Madrid, another flight to Rome, a train to Milan. The train windows were misted, the landscape enervated and dim: he let his new pocket Mino-HD Flip camera run, uninterrupted, like the birth of cinema, and sent the result to his friends in lieu of a Ballardian postcard. 'Lesson learnt,' he said. 'If you cut out the sightseeing, how pleasant the train can be.'

My less exotic voyage into comfortable Hertfordshire was a return to the grand-project book, and to Ballard, after a number of necessary digressions, European trips, expeditions to Sheffield, Lincoln, Bristol, Edinburgh. Only the day before, I had completed, with another itinerant and restless film-maker, the hyperkinetic Andrew Kötting, the reconnaissance for a potential swan voyage, by pedalo, from the south coast to the Olympic Park. When I discussed my notion of carrying a whalebone box, by water, using a kayak like the one with which I had penetrated the Olympic backrivers, Kötting offered himself as a companion, but suggested at once an interesting variant: that we liberate a swan pedalo from the Hastings pleasure park and put to sea, around the coast to Rye. Then meander through military canals, rivers, ponds and gravel pits, to the Thames. If we ran out of water, we would drag the beast ashore, in the spirit of Werner Herzog, and manhandle it to the next launching place. Irresistible. My only stipulation was that the journey be completed before the opening ceremony for the 2012 Games. Another sweat-drenched exorcism. Another project that, by its mission statement, disqualified itself from any hope of sponsorship, even though it fulfilled all current requirements in terms of direction of travel. Towards insanity. Pure and undiluted.

Kötting hauled a plastic swan, a lure, as we walked. We were accompanied by a pair of mature students from the art college where he taught: one of them had got himself into shape for this by completing the pilgrimage to Santiago de Compostela and the other kept a record with a pinhole camera made from a Swan Vesta matchbox. Random encounters calibrated our progress.

Coming down the Swale, from Sittingbourne to Whitstable, I was pointing across to the prison complex on the Isle of Sheppey, and reminiscing about Joe Orton's holiday stretch for defacing Islington library books, when we were joined by a bullet-headed man in a hooded Lonsdale sweatshirt carrying a tin bucket. 'Seventeen,' he said. 'Seventeen poxy crabs.' A former member of West Ham's Inner City Firm, he had personal experience of Sheppey and the house on the hill reserved for the most violent offenders. Now an amiable manifestation of place, he was prepared to overlook Kötting's provocative Millwall allegiance. And to demonstrate the sexing of crabs, by tearing off their legs. On a good morning, he could fill his pail with seventy or more, limbless but gender identified, bait for fishermen. By the time we reached the headland from which a ferry no longer runs to the pub where my novel *Downriver* concluded, Kötting was sharing his sandwiches with a pair of failed royal dogs, black retrievers who didn't retrieve. Windsor Castle passed them on, so the well-bred lady explained, through contacts in hunting circles.

The walk becomes a choir of eccentric soloists, the electively unnoticed waiting to tell their tale. Around the Olympic Park, the air was so heady that men with dusty mouths were going down like ninepins. A cheery soul on a spinster's bicycle scavenged the verges, the tangled thickets around the rat traps and mesh fences; with a mechanical hand of his own devising, he grabbed blue cans flung out of passing white vans, or dumped by migrating drinking schools. He filled sacks for charity, covering many miles a day in a forlorn circuit of the razor-wire perimeter.

Beside the A11, approaching Stratford, a man collapsed, inches from the traffic. He sprawled full-length at the roadside, prodded by an ambulance team eager to tidy him away: a premature celebrant, flag of St George, hammered into a reeking coma in expectation of World Cup triumphs indefinitely postponed in South Africa. The proprietor of the sole-surviving business, a barber called Giuseppe, twenty years in the game, was surrounded by red cones and chicken wire and overweening future developments. He gripped a Stanley knife and waited for the first council official to offer him compensation. In his window was a black-and-white photograph of a sharp-suited man with a Mexican moustache, and attitude, like a Liverpool footballer from the 1980s.

I had an appointment with the painter Brigid Marlin, the one who produced the Delvaux copies for Ballard. Brigid had written to me, after reading an account I'd published of my expedition to Old Charlton Road in Shepperton. In compensation for taking on the onerous task of reproducing works for which she had no particular affection, she compelled the reluctant novelist to pose for a portrait. 'Painting J. G. Ballard was an unusual experience,' she told me. 'He was a very obstreperous model. He wanted to take control all the time.'

So many conflicting rumours were circulating, in the months after the writer's death, that I wanted to listen to an eyewitness account of the intimate process of sitting for a portrait. It was difficult to avoid contributing to the prevailing mythology: the sanctification of the Shepperton anchorite. Ballard the good father. The spurner of metropolitan flimflam. Ballard the prophet and visionary, first man of the motorway corridor. Post-mortem sentiment congeals the legend: before the inevitable reaction, the teasing out of the flaws that make us human. The way he had, over almost half a century, manipulated autobiographical routines was exemplary: until he arrived at the purest of forms, the shifting of significant detail, for that last generous book, *Miracles of Life*, when all outstanding dues were paid.

On the Berkhamsted train, I flicked through the catalogue Brigid Marlin had sent me. I could see why Ballard thought of her as a surrealist, there was that clarity of light he admired, frozen figures traumatized against empty landscapes, hair floating upwards like smoke. The technique was about precision, egg tempera suspended between layers of oil: the hyper-unreality of certain kinds of spiritual representation, like the suffering saints and Tibetan cosmologies of Glastonbury Tarot cards and New Age posters. The intention, as

I understood it, was far removed from the extravagant and virtuoso onanism of Dali. But the big shock, coming off the Kötting experience, was the discovery of Marlin's repeated swan motifs; the rape of Leda was an obsessive aspect of the oeuvre. Arching nudes, shaven-headed or metamorphosing into slender irises, were caught up by the feathered assault, the seizure.

One painting, *The Rod*, became Ballard's touchstone. He wrote Marlin what he described as 'the only fan letter' he had ever sent to a painter, after seeing a reproduction in a magazine. His fancy fed on reproductions, postcards, portable versions of masterworks with the blight of originality filtered out. The industrial processes of mass-marketing make an image more desirable, more used, less tainted by sanctimonious and elitist notions of the unique moment, the burden of ownership. An inaccurate copy was a neutered multiple to be cut out, as required, stuck on a wall, pasted into a scrapbook collage. Taken apart and reassembled as part of a pulp-magazine fiction. Ballard was claustrophobic about art events, openings: he made an exception for Brigid Marlin.

It's easy to see the appeal of this Kuwait painting from 1973, *The Rod*. The one that looks as if it could very easily have been commissioned for the dustwrapper of Ballard's *Vermilion Sands*, a collection of interlinked tales published in the same year. Marlin's painting and the Ballard jacket designed by Brian Knight are interchangeable. Insect-eyed women with flowing hair or complicated headdresses. Sand. Ruins. The same wind-sculpted towers of rock, the Monument Valley molars. *The Rod*, in its cinemascope format, is an authentic Ballard inscape produced by an artist who had never opened any of his books. Encouraged by a friend with a taste for genre fiction, Marlin put her painting into a competition for sf-inspired work: and took first prize.

There is a fever, an erotic imperative, in Ballard's pursuit. He almost believes – he has earned the right – that he can *live* in the work, move through the screen of Marlin's meticulously constructed layers of glaze into the ground of her imagination. He claims *droit de seigneur* over these preternaturally still women who are naked, draped in transparent webs, posed in woodland, beside lakes, in front of vistas of cracked earth. They are threatened by mechanized swans, beaked ravens, burning oil wells, stalled motorways, newspaper headlines. He recognizes the figure projected into *Vermilion Sands*, his 'Prima Belladonna', in the Marlin portfolio. And he suspects that the model is Marlin herself: the artist and her mirror, a metaphor for the lost Delvaux painting he wants her to recreate. So that it can sit beside the desk where he writes, every day. A permanent back projection into which he will drift and dream.

'I assumed,' he wrote in his introduction to the Marlin catalogue, 'that the wistful and even ethereal figure who appeared in many of the paintings was a self-portrait of the artist. In fact, I was quite wrong.'

This conjunction, painter and writer coming together in a studio, beyond the outer rim of London, to conjure up a vanished Delvaux, is a potential Henry James novella, of mutual misunderstanding, oblique dialogues on the nature of art and portraiture: who will write this other into existence? And which painting, Marlin's transcription of the reluctant Ballard or her revised Delvaux, is the truer mapping of the psychopathology of the Shepperton visionary?

Berkhamsted, as you come out of the station, is a *Midsomer Murders* location, without the cast, the troubled vicars, the industrialists laying out golf clubs with which they will, before the first set of adverts, be beaten to a pulp. They say the franchise plays well in France: England as it ought to be, stereotypical, monocultural, with rigid social hierarchies. I'm a little early for my appointment. I circle around the fenced-off castle ruins and up the hill. Footpaths splay out in every direction, protected by barbed wire: PLEASE DO NOT CLIMB OVER THIS FENCE. Bushes dressed with hawthorn blossom mark the borders of close-cropped fields that drop away towards a line of low hills. Llamas munch in the company of shade-seeking donkeys.

Marlin's conservatory looks out, without interruption, on a spread of greenbelt countryside. Ballard described her as 'a tall and attractive American woman with a strong personality and a lively sense of humour'. Meaning that she did not always, or ever, agree with him. And that she was able to laugh about it. In patterned blue, shades picked up in several of her own paintings, which decorate the walls, Brigid welcomes me and lays out the lunch. She is smiling, seeing the absurdity that comes with an interrogation of the past, with summoning up the presence of Jim Ballard, who so provoked and intrigued her.

I asked about *The Rod*, the painting that brought Ballard to her studio with his photographs of the lost Delvaux paintings.

It was inspired by a trip to Kuwait, where I saw all these cars buried in the sand. It was so bizarre. And the oil wells . . . The figure of the woman represents me. I used someone else to pose, but it represents a moment when I realized that my life was leading nowhere and going towards nothing. And so these boxes in the foreground, black and white, they're like coffins. The emptiness of the boxes reflected the emptiness of my life. The woman is holding burning newspapers. It was war and anti-war: the contradictions we live in. There's no middle road. And so the thought is, that the woman, if she turns round and walks through the desert of unknowing, then there is another land, which is exemplified by a sun, which has a seascape in it. And water is a symbol of truth and it's on a higher level. So one must walk through the desert of unknowing. We can't raise ourselves to a higher level. And, at the same time, I was searching for a path myself. So it was very deep from my point of view.

The uncanny aspect, for Ballard, was finding a direct transcription, as he saw it, a proof, of the stories he was composing, a few miles down the orbital motorway, in Shepperton. 'I could well understand why Leonora Chanel had come to Vermilion Sands, to the bizarre, sand-bound resort with its lethargy, beach fatigue and shifting perspectives . . . The fused silica on the surface of the lake formed an immense rainbow mirror that reflected the deranged colours of the sand-reefs, more vivid even than the cinnabar and cyclamen wing-panels of the cloud-gliders overhead.'

Ballard critiques a painting he has never seen. Marlin reproduces the inscape of an author she has never read. She is exposed, when he arrives at her studio, not as a tailored fashion plate, nor a desert-dwelling surrealist: neither Coco Chanel, nor Leonora Carrington. But a very real woman, with a history, her own agenda, and a set of spiritual beliefs for which Ballard has no obvious sympathy or understanding.

The woman in my painting was a very feminine woman, very gentle. She represented resignation and suffering. But, in a strange way, there was something in Jim Ballard that wanted, not only to dominate women, but to suppress his own female quality, his anima. He wasn't prepared to face the anima. He was doing battle with his own inner spirit almost all of his life. And, when we met, my inner paintings didn't resemble my outer persona, because I was quite aggressive and bouncy. I don't think Jim was quite prepared for this. He expected some little fragile creature.

He's not the only one who has seen my paintings and visualized a very different person. There was this disastrous trip I took across America. I was paid by this man to go all around the country and he was going to meet me at the end. He'd fallen in love with this painting I did of a beautiful eighteen-year-old. And there I was at the bus stop . . . I was never an absolute Venus. And on top of that I was forty-five. So the blow was terrible for him. It was like High Noon. He pushed me aside and kept looking for someone else. Everyone left and we were the only two people in the terminal, facing each other. Pistols at dawn.

Ballard too! He was prepared to come and overpower this fragile creature. And the fragile creature gave as good as she got.

He was saying that although he had fame he was totally uninfluenced by it. I said, 'Oh yeah, you're totally free from any kind of vanity, aren't you?' Ha! 'And any kind of egotism?' For god's sake! It was really funny.

Brigid reads the writer's face. She likes it. She wants him to sit there, quietly, while she gets to work. She fixes Ballard as a Marlin portrait, to present in her catalogue, alongside the Dalai Lama, the travel-writer Cecil Lewis, and a beribboned Queen Mother. Ballard solicits a Delvaux, brought back from extinction, colour flooding a mono-chrome print. A physical representation of the most heartfelt psychodramas of his fiction.

I didn't like Delvaux. And I don't like copying. So he said, 'If Moby-Dick had been destroyed, I'd be perfectly prepared to rewrite it.' I question that myself. I wondered if Moby-Dick would have emerged unscathed from Ballard's pen.

I thought: 'He's got an interesting face.' I hadn't read his work. I wasn't at all interested in that kind of book. I put the proposition: 'Either you sit for me or the copying is no go.' He didn't like that. He said he hated sitting. And in fact he'd ring up and say, 'Do I have to come?' And I'd say, 'Do you want your Delvaux?' I said, 'You sound like you have to go to the dentist.' He said, 'It's much worse than that.'

He arrived. I told him to sit down and keep still. He didn't do either of those things. He would get up from the chair and he would talk a blue streak. The funny thing was he was so uncontrollable. Most sitters, when you get them to sit down, and you draw them out, you get to see their inner spirit. But I'd never seen defences like those put up by Ballard. There was no way I was going to get into his inner spirit. And, instead, he starts talking to me and I realize, suddenly, that he is writing me, while I'm trying to paint him. And we're each trying to drag the other into our worlds.

He gave me the two specific Delvaux paintings he wanted. Because they'd been destroyed. That was his idea. They meant a lot to him, espe-cially the naked girl looking at herself as a clothed figure – which I thought was badly painted, to be honest. The anatomy was bad, the folds are so childish. The concept of the wallpaper, I really disliked it.

I sneakily improved those paintings, because Delvaux is not a colourist. He mixed every colour with black. Or else he never washed his brushes and black got in. They're miserable old paintings with lots of skeletons. Del-vaux is not one of my favourites, but Ballard admired him. I improved the colouring, now those paintings are quite nice.

Jim didn't detect that. He did not realize that I had made improvements. I have seen original Delvaux paintings and they are faded with a greyish tinge. Disagreeable pictures.

Ballard would never lend out those copies. They meant everything to him. Gradually I began to understand Delvaux's symbols. There's a clothed woman looking at herself naked in the mirror. That's what it is: Ballard, with all the festoons he brought into his life, gazing at the internal mirror where his real self is hiding. Without clothes. Naked to the world.

Delvaux women have such cow-like faces. They are devoid of any real humanity. They are rubber blow-up dolls. Their faces have absolutely no expression. It's as if they are mindless bimbos. And I think that's another reason why Ballard liked them.

I had a convent education. And I was also very anxious to – how can I put it? – follow a path. We had a few arguments about this. Ballard had to accept that when he came to my studio, it was just for being painted. If I worked too much on the portrait, and not enough on the Delvaux, he got very angry. But if I had finished the Delvaux too early, he wouldn't have come back to let me complete the portrait.

I met Ballard at my spring exhibition in 1986. I started the first Delvaux in the early autumn. After Christmas, I started the other one. It went on for quite a while, maybe two years, the whole thing.

He was so fascinated by art. He wouldn't let me get on with the painting. He kept saying, 'Show me some other work you've done. I want to see what you did when you were younger.'

I had my folder from art school, so I brought it down. He said, 'But you could already draw then. Show me something from when you were much younger.' So I had done, when I was about eight, little fairy books. There were minuscule fairies in them. Ballard looked at them. They were quite good for my age. He was very impressed. He put the books down, leant back in the chair, and he said: 'You were born with it.' He was trying to trace it back and find a moment when I didn't have the ability to paint and then see the point when I learnt the skill. But there was no moment.

He said, 'Could you teach me to paint?' And I said, 'Fine.' I sat him down, put up a still life – I'm a good teacher – and I said, 'Now draw the apple.' It was really funny to watch: this bold man, this bully, got a pencil in his hand, and he made a dab at the board. He did a C for the side of the apple. And then he couldn't finish it. He was frightened. He was frightened of his failure. And I said, 'It's OK, you can do a bad apple.' I said, 'There's a glass, now draw that.' 'You do it.' So I drew it. He said, 'Doesn't look like a glass.' Then, as I painted, he saw the glass coming through. He could hardly believe it. He said, 'You must teach me art.' I said, 'You'll have to come more often.' And he said, 'Couldn't you teach me by phone?'

He wanted to draw like an old master. He wanted to paint like Dali. When he was sitting, he would say, 'You're not to put this in. You're not to paint me like that. I suppose you're going to paint me like Hitler?'

I said, 'Excuse me, Jim. Do I tell you not to write like Enid Blyton?'

I would say something thoughtless like, 'You know in the book War and Peace *by Tolstoy?' And he said, 'Oh, is there another one?'*

Such a put-down.

I told him I'd read Crash. *It was the first time I saw him really embarrassed. He didn't want me to have read it. He was ashamed of it. I was very surprised. Then he said, 'Don't read that, read* The Unlimited Dream Company. *As if that was going to be holy writ. So I got it and I read it. And I thought it was even worse than* Crash. *He eats this little girl for lunch, stuff like that. Jim couldn't see that his fear of spirituality, like eating little children, was in any way peculiar.*

He used my name in The Kindness of Women. *I really resented that. The bastard, he didn't ask me. I think it was revenge.*

I really miss his interest. He was so interested in one. And he was so intelligent. It was wonderful. People sitting for a portrait, they like the fact that you look at them with totally absorbed interest. You draw them out. That's magic. I've never experienced that before. I grew up posing for my mother. But suddenly to have a guy really interested in you and asking questions with such attention. Like you are the most interesting person in the world.

Ballard told me that women could be so cruel. That surprised me. He wasn't keen to have people visit Shepperton. They might barge in on something. He didn't want to curtail his fun.

The guy had an amazing mind, a restless, prowling, animal of a mind. Reminding me of Blake's tiger, burning bright. He actually told me that he had written Crash *because he wasn't making enough money to support his children.*

Empire of the Sun was the best book he ever wrote. I met him after that. I met him after the book and before the film. I think people are very stupid to be angry at him for not mentioning his parents. He wrote a work of art. You wouldn't have felt the same about the boy if he had got parents with him. He was absolutely right with that decision, artistically.

Ballard was about control. The one pearl that he took out of the oyster of his life was this book, Empire of the Sun. *He was born to write that book. He had to have those experiences. That book is a poem.*

I knew Stanley Kubrick through his wife, we met at the art group. Stanley reminded me of Ballard, very much so. They shared a huge amount. The difference is that Stanley was very gentle with his women. He was a generous man. He deliberately limited his knowledge. But when he did need to know something, he was obsessive. But the two men were not unalike. They were built alike. Stanley was extremely eccentric, but he wasn't damaged. A lot went into the twisting of Ballard. He was a very jealous man.

After transcribing Marlin's tape, I went straight back to *The Kindness of Women*. And found no trace of the woman I had interviewed. There were plenty of other details I'd forgotten and a strong sense of how much the landscape of the Thames Valley meant to Ballard, the woods and fields where he walked with his children. And the boat trip he makes with the woman who is clearly drawn from his partner, Claire Walsh.

'In the two years since Miriam's death,' he wrote, 'the familiar gardens and water-meadows had come to my rescue, but at something of a price . . . the quiet streets with their bricky villas, presided over by the film studios, formed the reassuring centre of my mind.'

Upstairs, in the Berkhamsted house, Marlin stood smiling for the camera, looking straight at me, while I framed the self-portrait on the wall behind her: another, younger, more troubled self; a woman with bare, powerful shoulders holding a pair of spectacles in her hand, while other discarded glasses on the edge of the shelf spurn the opportunity to reflect some surreal inner world.

The telescoping of images is vertiginous: the cross-struts of the empty easel, the fields outside the window. Brigid showed me a reproduction of the reproduction, the reconstituted Delvaux – which invokes Magritte, while belonging firmly in the Marlin catalogue. The nude in the gilded mirror is arranged at the same angle as Ballard in the formal portrait, which has now 'disappeared' from public view, to the reserve collection of the National Portrait Gallery. The woman in the mirror is Ballard's female self, his anima, the stoic writer in a golden wig: stripped, breasted, hands resting modestly over her sex. The grain of the bare boards in the Delvaux is reprised in the texture of the wall behind Ballard and in the table on which his manuscript is spread out. Using the text of an actual Ballard script, Marlin copied some sentences, showed the revisions, and invented a calligraphy of her own to duplicate the mysterious process of creation. Ballard is not rewriting *Moby-Dick*, the savage epic treated as a primer for coded messages. In preliminary drafts of the portrait, he is handless, his torso a Francis Bacon smudge of white lines over blue. The manuscript is blank. Blood arrives in his cheeks in time for the finished version. He is trapped, interrupted, on edge. Pencil gripped, he looks like a man asked to draw a perfect apple. He is St Jerome, tempted, seduced away from his cell, seeing green England as a future desert.

I spoke to Brigid about swans, the walk I.had just completed with Andrew Kötting. And the swan sculpture in the conservatory, behind the chair where she sat for her lunch. 'The journey is symbolic,' she said. 'There is a pursuit and there is the running away. Maybe our whole journey is to become ready, leaving all our baggage behind.'

When I was leaving, standing at the door, she told me that I wasn't the journalist she had expected. She saw other qualities. Ballard, in *The Kindness of Women*, put it more succinctly. He understood, all too well, the unreality of waiting on a country station for the short ride back to town. 'You've been in England for eighteen years and you still look as if you've stepped off the wrong train.'

Farland

Ghost Milk

Milk is the subtlest of insults.
  – Don DeLillo

I remember R. D. Laing, in July 1967, sitting at the back of the
Roundhouse, talking about the artist and illustrator Tomi Ungerer.
How he relished the state of siege, living close to 42nd Street in
the heart of Manhattan. 'He's dressed in military uniform. He is
conscious of the smog biting into his eyes, destroying his skin,
eroding his lungs. He's aware all the time of the enormous pollution, the noise. It's impossible to smell anything any more because
all the interior environments are air-conditioned and pumped
with the most sickly scent. You can't smell each other's sweat. You
don't know who to trust.'

Now, forty years on, I understood Ungerer's attitude: homoeopathic doses of horror to prepare ourselves for the dark day.
Circumambulations of the Olympic Park were becoming an addiction. Richard Mabey, author of *The Unofficial Countryside*, a book I
twinned with Ballard's *Crash* as the great edgeland testimonials of
the 1970s, accompanied me on another forlorn excursion. He travelled with binoculars, not a camera. He pointed out the feathery
clumps of fennel growing at the cropped margin of the canal, near
the Mare Street bridge. He told me that coots and ducks would be
unaffected by radioactive spillage into the water table. They breed
quite happily, and often, in the teeth of eco-disaster. He was
impressed by the duckweed lawns clotting the Lea, near Old Ford
Lock. The telling moment on this walk came with our arrival at the
stack of yellow containers that operate, in playfully ironic mode,
as café, viewing platform and learning centre, on the Greenway

overlooking the Olympic Stadium. We explored a thicket that ran along the side of the railway, where wild nature, profligate and without imposed narrative, thrived in blossom and berry. Hacking our way out of the tunnel, we emerged on a strip of bare, baked earth beside the yellow tin box. Mabey examined, in grim fascination, a cluster of dying saplings. At which point, a young woman emerged from the education centre to tick him off for having the temerity to intrude on the few yards of precious ground reserved for the education of the disadvantaged children of the Olympic boroughs. Richard pointed out that the pathetic plantings were choked of sustenance, uncared for, coughing their last. And if she really wanted to let the children see something grow, all she had to do was take down the rickety exclusion fence and a fruiting, thrusting wilderness would sweep across from the embankment.

Among the cargoes regularly transported down the railway line, through the heart of London's major development, the site where countless thousands will soon be arriving from across the globe for the great B&Q self-assembly Olympics, are flasks containing highly radioactive nuclear fuel-rods, shipped from Sizewell in Suffolk, and Dungeness in Kent, to Sellafield on the Cumbrian coast. When the Nuclear Trains Action Group (NTAG) contacted the Olympic Development Authority to ask if these convoys would continue to run through the period of the Games, they received no reply. Mayor Johnson knows nothing, remains silent. He has other, more pressing problems.

A protest rally, marching from Victoria Park to Stratford Station, staged a 'die-in' in front of the CGI Westfield promotional panels, well aware of the official Olympic clock clicking down the seconds like the nuclear triggers in Stanley Kubrick's *Dr Strangelove*. Such oddities are part of a conflicted topography: protest into art, political rhetoric into psychotic babble. The Angel Lane bridge over the railway, the route we walked from Chobham Farm to Joan Littlewood's Theatre Royal and the High Street, has been demolished. Mounds of scoured earth appear overnight, mountain ranges of a rigid formality thrown up by some new collision of the earth's tectonic plates.

At the junction of the Hertford Union Canal and the Lea Navigation, I came across an Olympic art manifestation which stopped me in my tracks. Here at last was a conceptual piece that took the breath away. Between Whitepost Lane and Old Ford, water gushed, cascaded, out of the enclosed site, through the fence, into the turbid and duckweed-infested canal. New barriers had been erected to deny access to potential paddlers heading for the main stadium. It was shapely, the way the water folded, curved and shimmered: a dwarf Niagara coming out of nowhere.

A jogger paused alongside me, hands on knees, taking in this unexpected water feature. 'Twenty-eight years,' he said. 'And now this.' He had come from Hong Kong and settled on an estate in Hackney Wick. Every morning he ran the same circuit, now his path was blocked. He never knew when he set out which way he would be allowed to return home, or if his home would still be standing. 'There has never been such division between rich people and poor.' He gestured towards the cliff of green-glazed windows on the spit of ground opposite us: a man-made island, the triangle between the Hertford Union Canal, the Lea Navigation, and the A102 Blackwall Tunnel Approach.

This was no artwork, in the sense of being funded, approved: punctured Victorian pipes on the Olympic site. No water in the taps for much of Hackney. The security guards brought in to protect the rapidly assembled plywood barriers were old-fashioned bouncer types, amiable and suspicious, nervous of saying the wrong thing in an unfamiliar language. The inner ring, close to the stadium complex and the construction convoys, was still guarded by regiments of Joanna Lumley's diminutive and unreadable Gurkhas.

It was only when I studied privately commissioned reports of investigations into the extensive radioactive contamination of the 2012 site that I appreciated the implication of the gushing pipes. The dispersal cell holding many tonnes of treated and untreated soil, in layers under a permeable skin, was positioned right here. As Ian Griffiths revealed in an article in the *Guardian*: 'Documents obtained under Freedom of Information (FOI) rules reveal that, contrary to government guidelines, waste from thorium and radium has been mixed with very low-level waste and buried in a so-called dispersal cell.' A cell which was placed about 500 metres to the north of the Olympic stadium. The setting for the involuntary water feature.

Bill Parry-Davies convened a meeting at which Mike Wells, who had been sifting thousands of documents and invigilating the progress of construction activity with numerous photographs, gave a lucid and alarming account of his findings. You could not nominate, in all of London, more challenging ground for a landscape blitz, a ticking-clock assault on the devastated residue of industrial history: insecticide and fertilizer works, paint factories, distillers of gin, gas-mantle manufacturers, bone grinders, importers of fish-mush, seething dunes of radiant maggots.

Waste: dumped, buried. Disturbed. Distributed.

Decay.

Putrefaction.

Tyre mounds.

The crunched metal-and-glass of innumerable breakers' yards hidden behind convolvulus-draped fences, under the flag of St George. Snarling dogs. Shirtless men smashing white goods with hammers.

And the dust.

The particulates. Hot cinders.

Blind warehouses with bundles of rags and damp paper waiting for insurance fires. Petrol reek. Black ash.

Oily smoke saturates cloth, fouls underwear.

In the dirt, they prospect: the pinstripe outsiders, compliant bureaucrats. Sanctioned buck-passers.

This was where London University carried out experiments with a now-decommissioned nuclear reactor. An area so far off the official map, so hidden within a nexus of dark waterways, that it functioned as the dumping ground of choice for what Parry-Davies refers to as 'uncontrolled deposits of radioactive thorium'. In an OPEN-Dalston blog, Bill presents a photograph by Mike Wells showing 'clouds of dust, and a skip with unsealed bags of asbestos material, during demolition of the Clays Lane Estate'.

In the Leabank Square Estate, from which the Chinese jogger had emerged for his restorative morning circuit, mediating rather than remediating the territory, residents were concerned about dust from the Olympic site. 'A recognized pathway to contamination,' Parry-Davies said, 'is by a person inhaling radioactive dust particles. Thorium is particularly hazardous.' On the estate, as the summer barbecue season opened, families found themselves 'literally eating' a relish of airborne dust, a mega-chilli bite on their steaks and sausages. When their worries were published on a website, the ODA threatened the Leabank whistle-blower with legal proceedings. And sent in a dust-sweeping vehicle to patrol the yellow-brick avenues.

Rumours were rife. I was told that the only consequence of the remediating exercise was to spread low-level radioactivity across the entire landscape of the Olympic enclosure, the divided fiefdoms of competing contractors. Toxic soil removed from the stadium was stored alongside bundles of Japanese knotweed, suggesting delirious *Quatermass* mutations, vegetal Triffid creatures slouching towards Westfield to be born. Richard Mabey pointed out that all Japanese knotweed, along the Lea, is female; the bounteous harem of a single potent male plant.

The Olympic Park was a newsreel of the fall of Berlin run backwards, from present boasts about urban renewal to the bombed and blasted killing fields, as the Russian advance decimated a pitiful remnant of boy soldiers, cripples and SS fanatics, in the Götterdämmerung endgame of Hitler's insane vision of a capital made from neoclassical facsimiles. In the Reichssportfeld, beside Berlin's 1936 Olympic Stadium, tanks, emerging from the woods, demolished trenches dug for military rehearsals. A sergeant, in command of a ragtag group of frightened children, had the only bazooka. When he stood up to fire it, his head was blown from his shoulders. What remains in these ravished topographies is a category of war-zone architecture: concrete bunkers, electrified fences, unexplained posts, burnt-out warehouses, stripped woodland, fouled water.

Grand Project development is accidental archaeology. A seance with ruins.

On Dalston Lane I met the globetrotting Sicilian photographer Mimi Mollica, a native of Hackney Wick. He swerved through the traffic to embrace me: a friendly face in a bleak environment. Many of his Wick neighbours had been expelled; the free-floating anarcho-communal days were over. There was a general drift in the direction of Berlin: more space, a vibrant culture. With the capture of Hackney, there was now a clear direction of travel: Berlin or Dagenham. Go east, young man. With his rent pitched at an impossible level, Mimi relocated to one of the generic blocks on Dalston Lane. A pristine apartment in all probability conceived by a Russian developer. If I wanted to follow the story, I would have to mug up my Fritz Lang DVDs and book a flight to Berlin.

'You have a name for your book?' Mimi said.

'*Ghost Milk*.'

'What does this mean?

'CGI smears on the blue fence. Real juice from a virtual host. Embalming fluid. A soup of photographic negatives. Soul food for the dead. The universal element in which we sink and swim.'

'Crazy, Mr Sinclair,' Mimi said. 'Crazy again.'

Berlin Alexanderplatz

Great cities take a day. This is the test of a great city.
– Don DeLillo

Descending through cloud cover over Berlin-Tegel, I feel the jolt as weary metaphors turn themselves inside out. For so many years, discussing London's edgelands, the lazy reflex has been to refer this embattled topography, and the mindset responsible for it, to the old East Germany. A dystopian myth: *Germany, Year Zero*. The circle of invaders massing around a capital that was always separate from the rest of the country; more dissidents, more anarchists, an island-state mentality.

Ghosts press, taking up the spare seats, provoking memory-films of a place I have never visited. This thin-skinned cigar tube, in which we suck up dead air, craning our necks to view cloud reefs outside the portholes, is populated with earlier Tegel pilgrims, their masks stitched from celluloid. Before Peter Falk flew into town, as a shop-soiled angel, in *Wings of Desire* by Wim Wenders, the granite lump of Eddie Constantine did the job for Chris Petit in *Flight to Berlin*. 'My film is erasure,' Petit said, 'but it pre-dates Wenders, in terms of dealing with the city. Wim was hanging around at the time. He cut the trailer.'

It was Petit who found me a copy of Godard's *Allemagne année 90 neuf zéro*. Like Berlin itself, the film was new to me, even though I was in the habit of describing it. At length. Constantine, eight years after his experience with Petit, was back in Germany, hat on head, briefcase in hand, wearing a heavy coat like a shroud draped over a statue of Beethoven. He wanders the land: one of the undead on a fated pilgrimage. Godard's meticulously edited essay reminded me of structural elements in the films of Patrick Keiller. Industrial wastelands frozen in steady-stare compositions. Pertinent texts quoted. And misquoted. Constantine was twice exiled: from America – I'd witnessed him in Reno, a bit as a casino thief in Phil Karlson's *Five Against the House* – and then again from Paris, where he growled through Lemmie Caution programmers, before achieving apotheosis as a comic-strip hero in Godard's *Alphaville*. Like Keiller's invisible Robinson (drawn from Kafka), Constantine has the ambition of becoming a spy, but he isn't sure who to approach. With marmoreal gravitas, he transfers the Daniel Defoe *Tour through the Whole Island of Great Britain* to Germany: double-agent, elegiac poet, haunter of borders. A man with the profile of a dynamited rock sculpture. A spectre drifting through ruins, railing against the non-spaces of global capital, rasping the last breath of romanticism.

Old Berlin haunted my part of London. We were the Osties, but our wall hadn't disappeared, it was newly erected in blue plywood. Urban planners and local politicians, honouring the Stalinist paradigm, returned from their sponsored excursions, the hospitality of Walter Ulbricht and Erich Honecker, with eyes shining and visions of imposing a new social order on the Lower Lea Valley. An order expressed by the destruction of historic theatres, inconvenient Georgian terraces, early-modernist factories, to make way for utilitarian blocks rapidly assembled in the cheapest possible materials. Secretly, we envied Berlin its iconic symbol: the 155-kilometre barrier that the artist Joseph Beuys plotted to destroy by adding five centimetres to its height. He understood that a minimal shift in the proportions of the wall would be enough to make the world aware of the absurd *lack of proportion* in the original intervention.

1936, 2012: build the stadium and the world will come. As Christopher Hilton pointed out in *Hitler's Olympics* (2006): 'Goebbels understood that the Germans had the first organised global press relations triumph within their grasp.' Newspapers, under orders to 'use the Olympic Games and preparations for them for extensive propaganda', were advised to avoid inflammatory or racist editorials for the duration of the athletic competition. 'No attacks against foreign customs and habits should be reported.'

Following the blueprint of the construction of Berlin's Olympic Stadium and Park, New Labour were ruthless about acquiring real estate for the two-week extravaganza. Hilton explains that if Goebbels 'wanted an amphitheatre on the site, accommodating 100,000 spectators, this is what he would get'. Hitler decreed that land operated by a popular racecourse would be taken over. The owners were compensated. Short-term sacrifices must be made for future generations and a spurious 'legacy'.

Coming out of the clouds over the flat Brandenburg plain, with its neat clusters of red roofs, managed forests, traffic flowing on white roads, I put aside the queasy rhetoric of Leni Riefenstahl and *Triumph of the Will*, the throb of the engines, the man of destiny, and shifted my role-play to the romance of the burnt-out case. The English spook, hard-drinking, short-sighted, returning to a divided city to oversee some botched escape from the East. Berlin was the borderline between cynicism and sentimentality. Coffee-and-cigar breakfasts in a bar that never closes, where men in fur-collared coats play along with the pretence that a fondly recalled black market in nylons and penicillin is still active. And red-mouthed women with high heels and raw blisters can be bought on the promise of an introduction to Fritz Lang. Hitler understood legacy very well: apocalypse, firestorm, death of the gods. An architect *manqué*, he patronized the obliging Albert Speer and his 'theory of ruin value'. Speer floated the notion that civic structures should be conceived as future monuments. Broken pillars and domes excavated from smouldering rubble. Athens, with its clear, hard light, its Acropolis, was to be spared the devastation of bombing, *the ruins were already in place*. Hitler's Greek invasion was the act of a warped aesthete, a compulsive collector. It was a perverse homage to Heinrich Schliemann and his unearthing of the treasures of Troy. Imposing museums, secular temples stacked with colonial plunder, become the cultural ballast of the benignly democratic new Germany. Contemporary Berlin, bereft of its iconic symbol, the Wall, settles for an identity as a permanent City of Culture, positioned on the European map between Paris and St Petersburg. Museums are provided with their own island, surrounded by tributaries of the Spree. This is a city of museums, accessed by wide steps, propped on Corinthian columns, weighed down with overblown statuary.

This is why my reflex metaphor, new Hackney as old East Berlin, was so inadequate. Surveillance, security barriers, grand projects carried through despite the objections of local interests, we had them all in London. Our Olympic Park, according to surveys based on wartime records, was planted with unexploded ordnance. We were obliterating communities, tearing up allotments, expelling scrap-dealers, artists and travellers, to make space for a self-assembly rip-off based on Werner March's elegant oval, the 1936 Olympic Stadium. The smart aspect of March's design is that the running track, which surrounds a central area wide enough to be used by the Hertha Berlin football team, is sunk into the ground; from the air, flying in, the stadium is impressive without feeling the need to overwhelm. London has opted for the approximate model in kit form. The stadium alongside the Northern Sewage Outfall has no predetermined height. The story changes according to the latest surveys, popularity polls, responses in the media. It might be sold off to a rugby franchise. It might, with a wink and a nudge from Newham Council, and a bunch of overlapping quangos desperate not to renege on airy promises, go to West Ham. It might be wholly or partly dismantled. The best bet is another Earth Centre eco-wilderness: before O2 step in with an offer that can't be refused for a music venue and multiscreen cinema complex.

Fortuitously, at the moment I decided to make my first visit to Berlin, I was devouring a distressed copy of Alfred Döblin's 1929 novel, *Berlin Alexanderplatz*. I found it in a seemingly abandoned conservatory in Orford, Suffolk, where customers were trusted to put a coin or two in a box by the door. How I had lived without it, up to this point in my life, was a mystery. As was my shaming inability to read the book in the original or to speak one word of Döblin's language. When W. G. Sebald arrives in Orford, in *The Rings of Saturn*, he sees the shingle spit, with its Secret Weapons Research Establishment, as 'a penal colony in the Far East'.

Francis Stuart, an Irish writer with a sublime gift for being in the wrong place at the wrong time, sat out the 1940s in Berlin, half-heartedly teaching the English classics, making propaganda broadcasts and angling for a ticket to Moscow; where he hoped to fulfil his gambler's destiny as the Dostoevsky of tragic literature and spoilt loves. A good walker but a lousy linguist, Stuart developed a phonetic system for coping with German. He broke down standard phrases into sounds he could spell out on a card, symbols which approximated to the basic requirements of his exile. When I interviewed him in his old age, another kind of exile in a bungalow beside a long, straight road, an hour out of Dublin, his grunts had diminished to a single phrase: 'That's right.' Red bulb of nose, pitted like a raspberry. Pudding-basin of shock-white hair. Watery eyes drifting away to a drowned landscape. Beads of rain sliding down a greasy window. 'That's right.' Yeats. Beckett. Iseult, his beautiful wife. He fiddles with the tie holding up custard-coloured cricket flannels. And remembers the sound of wet tyres, as he sat with an English newspaper in his favourite Kurfürstendamm restaurant. My questions grew longer, with more subordinate clauses, to compensate for silence like the silence of an ancient tree. After such a life, what was there to say? Berlin brought the best out of him: ruin and treachery, flight and displacement. The novels thrive on shame and lacerating confession: *The Pillar of Cloud*, *Redemption*. *Black List, Section H*. Lovers crawling through rubble with cardboard suitcases. Hanging around crowded offices waiting for identity papers. 'That's right.' Admit everything, reveal nothing.

When Berlin prepared itself for the Russian tanks in April 1945, the pro-Nazi Irish Nationalists at Ireland-Redaktion were one of the last satellite broadcasting stations to fall silent. They went out on the attack, accusing the Anglo-American axis of handing Europe on a salver to the ravening Slavic tribes. Francis Stuart, like P. G.

Wodehouse and Ezra Pound, was given better access to the micro-
phone, as an honoured alien, than at any other period of his doomed
career. In a city under siege, poets are free to speak, on the understanding that their next monologue will be drafted in the dock.
Metaphors ran wild. A major defensive slab, flak tower and bunker,
was sited in Berlin's Zoo. Lions died in their cages. Hippos boiled in
the tanks. Surrealism recaptured the streets. Orgies were reported
at the Grossdeutscher Rundfunk on the Masurenallee, where two-
thirds of the surviving staff were women, many of them drunk and
fearful of what was to come when the Russians stormed the building. 'There was indiscriminate copulation,' Antony Beevor reported,
'amid the stacks of the sound archive.'

The physical momentum of the prose in *Berlin Alexanderplatz*
was exhilarating, like the rush of Walter Ruttmann's film from the
same period, *Berlin – Die Sinfonie der Grosstadt*. Language and image
cut fast. Trains. Bars. Songs. Black marketeers. Whores of all sexes.
Surgeons. Detectives. Berlin in the late 1920s was the world city, city
of war-damaged grotesques out of George Grosz and Otto Dix.
How dynamic Döblin's book now seems, an outgrowth of the energies of place, and how muted, in comparison, how lightweight and
strategically charming, the Berlin snapshots of Christopher Isherwood, which were laid out between 1930 and 1933. Isherwood's
material lends itself to Hollywood schmaltz, with his English girl,
Sally Bowles, swallowed alive by a full-throttle Liza Minnelli. *Berlin
Alexanderplatz* is scrupulously, sweatily, reimagined and composed
afresh by Rainer Werner Fassbinder: a tapeworm epic for our
own times, funded by new German television money in Cologne.
Actors, taken to the edge, perform miracles of choreographed
self-exposure. They are crushed but not obliterated by the claustrophobic sets that contain them. And by the troubling memory of a
book more honoured than read in a Europe that is not quite prepared to revive it.

Döblin's protagonist, Franz Biberkopf, released from Tegel Prison,
endures the shudder of the city. He leans against walls that tremble.

He finds himself in an apocalyptic vision painted by Ludwig Meidner: cracked streets and tumbling houses skewed by shock waves running out ahead of the next war. Biberkopf's tram to Alexanderplatz belongs to that cinema of lyrical documentation, to Ruttmann or *Menschen am Sonntag* (made in 1929 by Robert Siodmak and Edgar Ulmer). He is rescued from his depressive fugue by an Orthodox Jew who brings him out of the sunlight, into a domestic interior, and tells him a story.

My Berlin quest begins with a name: Alexanderplatz. It was everywhere, in all the books I skimmed as background research. And the DVDs I rented from the shop in Broadway Market: 'Alex. Alex. Alex.' Haunting paranoid Fritz Lang thrillers as a source of power, police headquarters. And in films about the Red Army Faction. Characters in Len Deighton thrillers look east 'to where the spike of the East German TV tower rose out of Alexanderplatz'. Francis Stuart, typically, abstains. 'Whatever was going on in Alexanderplatz . . . he'd forgo until he'd deciphered the urgent messages reaching the fringe of his mind.'

Reporting from Berlin, in a couple of days, was madness. I decided to walk from Alexanderplatz to the Olympic Stadium in the west of the city, by way of that triumphal avenue, Unter den Linden. Somewhere in my scrambled geography was a memory of the final stand of the Third Reich, a strip of fifteen kilometres from Alexanderplatz to the Reichssportfeld, a last redoubt guarded by Hitler Youth detachments and the terminally sick. Like Döblin's shambling bear, Franz Biberkopf, I started by finding transport from Tegel. A system of equivalents. Prison = Airport. Tram = Taxi. That familiar disorientation, the shuttle with a temporary guide, from airport to hotel. The hoardings you find in every city, the allotments, traffic lights, and walkers in shorts and loose T-shirts pushing infants in buggies.

Angela Merkel hangs from lamp posts at busy junctions. An election is pending. Colour multiples of so many politicians, willing to serve, and willing you, with hypnotic stares and professional smiles, to approve them. The women, groomed and handsome, look very much like models chosen to advertise spectacles. The style you favour is a badge of seriousness. As a politician you are not frivolous, but you are prepared to make the best of your appearance. European football managers, taking up appointments in England, demonstrate their character – firmly progressive, modestly wealthy – by their designer spectacles: Sven-Göran Eriksson, Fabio Capello. The male politicians in their airbrushed studio portraits remind me of smoothed and well-fed versions of the English cricket captain, Andrew Strauss: fit for purpose, middle management with unexceptional opinions, hard work rather than suspect brilliance. The truth is that football is now the real politics and politics a sport for those who are not quite good enough for anything else. A chance to appear on television. In the way that all Tory candidates for Mayor of London – Steve Norris, Lord Archer, Boris Johnson – opened their campaign with a minor sex scandal, enough to get them invited on *Have I Got News for You?* And thus to achieve a populist profile. The failure of New Labour, in the end, was the lack of zip in their adulteries.

'He is back in Berlin. He breathes Berlin again,' Döblin wrote. Our smart, post-Wall hotel is in Potsdamer Strasse. As you stand at the desk, going through the formalities, a young woman in a grey uniform presents a silver tray on which repose two tightly rolled white flannels. They are damp and they remove the evidence of travel. Now we are here, we are welcome. Water features trickle alongside Matisse lithographs. A glass-fronted lift, carrying us to the ninth floor, offers a dizzying urban prospect of corporate regeneration, a merchandising spectacle underwritten by Daimler and Sony. Anna admires the sleek and regular bus service, the absence of advertising slogans, pure yellow. At home, every ride is submersion in a viral torpedo, a headache-inducing cacophony of mobile-phone chatter; dirty-weary humans surprising each other with unprovoked violence or spontaneous gestures of good will. The young Brazilian who offers up his seat to the burdened woman. The vodka-coshed Russian, sprawled on the floor of a bendy 149 at 7 a.m., who is rolled like a rag doll by a sudden stamp on the brakes, and who staggers forward to strangle the driver.

Looking down from our vertical glass coffin, I see monochrome meadows, the waist-high grass and wrecked sofas of recent history, the dead-zone wandered by characters in the Wenders film *Wings of Desire*. Now there is a multiplex cinema, Cinemax, showing the same films you'll find in London's Docklands or the Trafford Centre in Manchester: *Public Enemies*, *Harry Potter und der Halbblutprinz*, *Brüno*, *Ice Age 3 – Die Dinosaurier sind los*. Across the street, fronting the Sony Center, which resembles a collaboration between the two Walts, Disney and Benjamin, is that unnecessary thing, a museum of film: film *is* memory, even when, or especially when, we don't remember it. The pattern of tourists, citizens, Wall peddlers, when observed from the smoothly rising elevator, is a form of cinema. A restaurant-bar, parasitical on the Film Museum, is called *Billy Wilder's*. Wilder, in his early guise as a Berlin journalist and writer, was part of the team responsible for *Menschen am Sonntag*, that languorous portrait of a summer city floating between stolen documentation and affectingly cynical poetry. When he returned, after the good years selling film noir to Hollywood, it was to a divided city: Marx and Coca-Cola. *One, Two, Three*, made in 1961, is an ugly work with a furious velocity. As if Wilder couldn't wait to get back to California, never imagining, some way into the future, this branded bar with its production stills and ersatz memorabilia.

The leaflet for another film museum, the one in Potsdam, has a location photograph from *One, Two, Three* on its cover. Wilder, trademark flat cap and heavy glasses, brandishes a fat cigarette like a pen with a burning tip. Pamela Tiffin: full lips, yards of distracted hair. And a name that sounds like a cocktail. Jimmy Cagney resting a fatherly hand on the shoulder of Horst Buchholz, who must be exhausted from one of the most wearisome exhibitions of overacting since the glory days of German silent cinema. In the background, the Brandenburg Gate. ACHTUNG: YOU ARE NOW LEAVING THE WESTERN SECTOR.

Wilder's machine-gun gags, his exploitation of Cagney's gangster mythology, gives the film its defining quality. Pace, going nowhere, emphasized by a punchy score. The politics, sexual and otherwise, are crude. This epic of product placement – Coca-Cola, Pan Am and the rest – should have been produced by the CIA. It makes the coming Berlin Wall not only inevitable but also desirable, a cultural prophylactic. We need a wall to save the old Alexanderplatz from this American satellite, the steel-and-glass buildings staffed by former Nazis. True speed is only to be found in Döblin's novel. An open square swirling with trams, taxis, horses, newspaper sellers, prostitutes, businessmen, hustlers and beggars. Biberkopf is a victim of mechanized hustle, being flung from one car and run over by another. His right arm is amputated, thereby saving him, symbolically, from giving the Nazi salute. But the drumming paragraphs and repeated refrains of Döblin's novel are balanced by intervals of inertia, meditation, melancholy. Fassbinder, in his fifteen-hour television adaptation, catches these moments with well-judged sympathy. Günther Lamprecht, as Biberkopf, orders three beers and a kümmel. He croons to the bottles before swallowing their contents. The whole business is enacted in a single take. Time is time. We drink the golden light of vanished afternoons in smoky cellars.

The other couple in the glass-fronted lift at the Mandala Hotel make noises of appreciation. What a view! They are wearing smart-casual training gear and have laminated badges around their necks. Insiders, with clearance to enter the Olympic Stadium, for the World Athletic Championships due to begin at the end of the week. Berlin, as a whole, is not hyperventilating with excitement at the prospect. Most Berliners are away for one of their regular holidays. Recolonizing Greece ahead of the approaching economic shitstorm.

Bruce Chatwin reports a remark by Werner Herzog: 'Walking is virtue, tourism deadly sin.' They met when Herzog visited his brother-in-law, an Anglican vicar in Northumberland, to do a little fishing. On my first evening in Berlin, in response to Herzog's anathema, I was a pedestrian tourist. The long walk, as a cure for deep-seated neurosis, was itself neurotic: as with Herzog's famous and egotistical winter trudge from Munich to Paris, to exorcize the sickness of Lotte Eisner. The director rages at the quantity of material he has to process as he limps along. I vanish into movement, erasing the obstacle of the body like a set of faded marks on paper: new ground.

Potsdamer Platz, on the sepia-tinted tourist postcard I bought, was a non-space as formulaic as a landscape by Claude. The Wall as a barrier was no more intimidating than any obstacle in the industrial edgelands of Britain. Its function was aesthetic, to cut a diagonal across the composition. A cancelled road. Unexploited wasteground with huts and wire. As a marketing device, the Wall was unbeatable. Witness, tonight, how tourists seethe and cluster to record something that isn't there. In the rubble of the devastated city, in 1945, a diarist recorded how women with blood-soaked ration cards remained motionless in long lines. 'They stand there like walls.'

On the north side of this square, in 1932, the modernist architect Erich Mendelsohn presented his Columbus House. According to Brian Ladd, in *The Ghosts of Berlin* (1997), 'the smooth horizontal bands of its curved façade accentuated the tempo of the square'. Mendelsohn embraced dynamism and discarded static forms. Photographs of Potsdamer Platz showing Columbus House in a frenzy of traffic, a blaze of electric signs, operate as one of the blueprints for the new Berlin. Mendelsohn's building was demolished. He came to England, where, in collaboration with Serge Chermayeff, he was responsible for that unlikely marine pavilion at Bexhill-on-Sea.

But it wasn't just Jewish architects, or poets and scholars, who were threatened, moved out, eliminated. The famed Berlin department stores, cities within cities, the essence of urbanism, came under attack. Isherwood in *Goodbye to Berlin* has a telling passage in which he visits one of these retail cathedrals.

'Landauers' was an enormous steel and glass building, not far from the Potsdamer Platz. It took me nearly a quarter of an hour to find my way through departments of underwear, outfitting, electrical appliances, sport and cutlery to the private world behind the scenes.'

Palatial shops, evolving from the stalls of Alexanderplatz traders as the Hollywood dream-factories emerged from their tent-show beginnings, were operated by tight families. Their replacement, the Sony Center, is corporate. Everything about it simulates urbanism. In the shuffling tourist mob you do not experience reality, you experience a facsimile of experience. An experience that has been tried and tested, on your behalf, by computer simulations. Tomorrow the whole set, under the calculated awe of its dome, could be taken down and reassembled.

Like any good tourist, I obeyed the prompts of the brochure and struck off towards that notorious photo-opportunity Checkpoint Charlie. The former wasteland, the obliterated Potsdamer Platz, was a collage of slick architectural 'statements', monster billboards masking *trompe l'oeil* building projects (while they wait for budget approval), and low-level, grassed pyramids that seem to be hiding underground bunkers. There were chunks of the Wall with customized graffiti. And a plinth of dark bricks that stands as a memorial to the martyred socialist Karl Liebknecht. To the idea of individual responsibility and a people's revolution.

Advancing on Friedrichstrasse, my steps slowed; it was overwhelming, the gravity of the past, the way that every structure had to argue for its survival. This granite museum with its baroque trimmings and bombastic statuary might be a culture hoard or a war ministry. A section of the Wall, with no pedestrian access, marks out the Topography of Terror; a strategic solution to the problem of how to represent the former Gestapo and SS headquarters. No other city would be capable of attaching biographies of victims and torturers to the same fence, alongside a glimpse into preserved underground cells. And, beyond that, the Martin-Gropius-Bau Museum of Decorative Arts.

I am most comfortable with the wild-flower wastelots. The empty spaces disguised by fake buildings painted on canvas, with scaffolding like a provocative artwork. Otherwise, the Wall is being flogged hard: headline incidents displayed as posters on a wooden fence. Tourists, dutifully, solemnly, contemplate images of images. And take more of their own to carry away. Tony Paterson in his 'Berlin Notebook', written for the *Independent* newspaper, reports that, with so little of the original Wall left to be viewed, tour buses are now filling the gaps with computerized animations. Fragments of the Wall are preserved like the tolerated remnants of London's Roman Wall, still to be found between the Tower of London and the Barbican. Making a museum of the city is one way to control access routes into the past. The contraflows of history. With appropriate signage.

By one of those predictable coincidences of urban wandering, the fence alongside the Wall at the Topography of Terror exhibition now features dot-matrix multiple reproductions of Joseph Beuys in hat. An antidote to Angela Merkel. A missing person smeared with a blood-red line. AUS PROPORTIONALEN GRÜNDEN SOLLTE DIE MAUER UM FÜNF ZENTIMETER ERHÖHT WERDEN.

Although I didn't set foot in Berlin before August 2009, I had seen, touched and admired the Wall. They assembled it in Dublin's Smith-field in 1965, when I was a student in that city: for Martin Ritt's film version of John le Carré's *The Spy Who Came in from the Cold*. Fifty workmen spent the month of February constructing a seventeen-foot-high replica in hessian, timber, plaster and tarred felt, topped with barbed wire. Richard Burton, drinking hard to keep out the cold, and Elizabeth Taylor, huddled in her mink coat, bivouacked in the Gresham Hotel, Dublin's Adlon. O'Connell Street, with its republican scars and heritage memorials, its galleries, museums, tourist traps and beggars from the east, is a diminished provincial replica of Unter den Linden. (In Dublin they blew up the triumphalist victory column, Admiral Nelson at its summit, and replaced it with a bizarre spike, on which to stack outstanding invoices when the Celtic Tiger ran out of puff.) The Dublin Checkpoint Charlie, with its wet cobbles and sixteen faithfully reproduced curved lamp posts, couldn't disguise the fact that the low houses and tight shops were wholly Irish. Bars and grocery shops with stacks of peat briquettes. But the Wall, as a brand, was ripe for export; long after it disappeared from Berlin, duplicates were built across estates in Belfast, to separate Catholics and Protestants. When the Smithfield Wall was broken up, sections migrated all over Ireland. The guards' hut, salvaged from a municipal dump, became a makeshift school for the children of travellers at Ballyfermot. Bertrand Russell sent a cheque for £25 with which two oil stoves were purchased. The Bewley family, owners of a popular Grafton Street coffee shop, provided the young pupils with free milk and rolls.

Burton, blowing on frozen hands for the obligatory Checkpoint Charlie opener, impersonates a spook called Alec Leamas. A nice echo of the Irish politician who took part in the 1916 Easter Rising, and who was Taoiseach at the time when the film was made: Seán Lemass. Now the guards' hut on Friedrichstrasse is the fake, the set occupied by actors in uniform, a parody of all those divided-city thrillers: *The Quiller Memorandum*, *Funeral in Berlin*, *The Spy Who Came in from the Cold*.

After the death of the fleeing man at the start of Le Carré's novel, Leamas takes off, lost in a melancholy fugue, like the traumatized bus driver after the London bombings on 7 July 2005, the day after we'd been given the Olympic Games. 'They tell me you walked all night,' says Control, the London spymaster, 'just walked through the streets of Berlin.'

Nocturnal Berlin is a good place to wander. It's like being on the biggest film set in Europe. A location where history contrived its most lurid dramas. 'There was no one to be seen; not a sound,' wrote Le Carré. 'An empty stage.' The present stage is heaving with beggars carrying babies, touts, tour guides. The same riff-raff, Chris Petit told me, who used to hang around a film shoot. The crowd among whom Fassbinder chose to live and work, and whose small conspiracies and betrayals he articulated to such good effect.

Better call it a day, I thought. I retreated to Potsdamer Platz. In a recently commissioned survey into spatial awareness, it was discovered that experimental subjects invited to walk a straight line, out into the desert, invariably described a circle in the sand. That's what our interior compass does when we are denied familiar objects on which to bounce our radar: we slouch back to the nearest Travelodge (or its upmarket equivalent).

Anna fancied an ice cream at a stall in the Sony Center. It was the nearest thing she could find to the real street. Up on a giant screen I watched an account of how the Esplanade Hotel, a token representation of the magical Berlin of the 1920s, was placed on railway lines and trundled into the interior of this pleasure dome. To be preserved behind perspex. Thus fulfilling the developers' promise to retain a significant historical structure. Within the microclimate of the Sony Center there is no interior, no weather. The crowd moves, slowly, without collisions, without overt surveillance. They are cowed and respectful. They can enjoy the metropolitan pleasures of eating and drinking at a café table, without getting wet or breathing petrol fumes. They gaze at promotional film clips without really seeing them. I wonder how many of them have read their Len Deighton thrillers? In *Berlin Game* Deighton has an explanation for the crazy geometry of the Wall. It came from a wartime conference at Lancaster House in London. The city was being divided up by the invading armies. The only map to be found in Whitehall came from the era of Döblin's *Alexanderplatz*. They used the administrative borough boundaries of 1928. 'It didn't seem to matter too much where it cut through gas pipes, sewers and S-Bahn or the underground trains either. That was in 1944. Now we're still stuck with it.' Nothing changes, but the will to change. After much debate, a temporary solution. Which matures into a permanent disaster.

From the first, artists eyed up Fernsehturm, the TV tower overlooking Alexanderplatz (and the rest of the city). Back in the 1960s we were all constructing these things, paranoid snoop-stations barnacled with listening devices and equipped, as a sop to PR, with panoramic restaurants. Fernsehturm, at 365 metres, announced itself as 'Europe's second-tallest structure'. A pre-Viagra thrust worthy of East Germany's pharmaceutical laboratories, the ones who dished out steroids to athletes, shaping a generation of bearded female shot-putters and flat-chested 800-metre runners who would demonstrate, through weight of medals, the superiority of their political system. Fernsehturm was redundant science fiction, but an invaluable asset, when the time came, for conceptual art by cutting-edge westerners. Tacita Dean's 2001 film, shot in colour with an anamorphic lens, was a highlight of the genre. Sitting in Tate Britain, or some other cultural oasis, you drift for forty-four minutes through a German heaven: the installation is on a loop, stay as long as you like. Indistinct cityscape. Daylight thinning. Calling her piece *Fernsehturm* made the revolving restaurant a destination of choice for a better class of visitor. London's version, the Post Office (now British Telecom) Tower in Cleveland Street, remains closed to the public, on the grounds of security: after an unsponsored intervention by the Angry Brigade. But looking down on the spectacle of the city, from Primrose Hill or Parliament Hill, you feel the buzz of malignant radio waves.

'Which museums would you recommend?' I asked Brian Catling, one of Fernsehturm's visiting performance artists.

'Museums? I had no time for museums, Berlin has some of the best bars in the world.'

Our walk across Berlin on 12 August 2009 began at Fernsehturm. In the square alongside Marienkirche, where I inspect an angel with swan wings, discreet vagrants occupy benches and reach into bags and sacks to secure their bottles. I flip, once again, to Hackney: the early-morning canal, the drinkers on their perches, the brisk walkers, dressed in black, having intense conversations in German. As our estranged artists move out of warehouse squats in Hackney Wick for somewhere cheaper and more interesting in Kreuzberg, young German professionals return the favour: journalists, architects, photographers. They sometimes engage me in conversation as they search for the mythical Dalston bars and cafés they have heard so much about. The slender spike of the mosque, away to the south, on the road to Shoreditch, was like a faint echo of the TV tower.

Today the revolving restaurant is closed to the public, a white wedding. The queue we have experienced, the complicated ticket procedure, is a reminder of the former East Berlin. But the panorama of the city, the vision of angels tapped by Wim Wenders, allows us to align ourselves and to preview the road we intend to follow to the far west and the Olympic Stadium. Most impressive is Karl-Marx-Allee: blots of vegetation, a concrete alphabet of lovingly restored high-rise estates.

When we descend into Alexanderplatz, it's not there. We've been translated into another east: Barking, Dagenham, Romford. A soulless piazza with ill-considered post-architectural interventions, a railway station and a choice of uninviting cafés. Bemused tourists carve solid pastries, glug ersatz coffee. Anna remarks on the absence of dogs and cats. We are in the wrong part of town, I tell her. Around here you have to feed on deep memory, the dogs have been eaten. Dining that evening with the editor of a Berlin magazine, I was told that dogs are plentiful in outlying areas. This was a city of foxes, he said, living in the cellars of abandoned Nazi buildings. Of wolves emerging from the surrounding woodland. Of stoats taking up residence in motor vehicles, gnawing the wires. And an army of ghosts too, the last hold-outs. Root-chewers in rags, with skulls for faces. French SS units who are never going home.

Intimations of the World Athletic Championships were on display in the window of a department store: bloodless albino figurines, pound-stretcher versions of Leni Riefenstahl's Aryan champions, kitted out in the appropriate colours for their nations. Nederland. Australia. Korea. White as lard sculptures. Muscles toned on the exercise machines visible in the gym at the base of Fernsehturm. Reflected behind the models, in a waft of cloud, are the block-buildings of the square. A city on fire. My local informant said that the authorities were nervous in the run-up to the elections: there had been a number of troubling incidents, Muslims stabbed in parks. With serious German involvement in the high-tech aspects of the Afghan campaign, people remembered the Madrid bombings. Arrests had been made, incomers and native Germans, in a house in the country. 'It's everywhere now. There are no boundaries.'

The editor pointed out that the government of Chancellor Heinrich Brüning, at the time of catastrophic economic collapse in the early 1930s, decreed savage cuts in social programmes. Teachers' salaries and unemployment benefits were slashed. A conservative administration preached parsimony – for everything except the military. Money was found for new battleships. The alien within, the Jew, was demonized. Germany moved towards the grand project: world war. By way of a building blitz underwritten by the 1936 Olympic Games, symbol of a nation's rebirth.

Unter den Linden sweeps us along, as it is intended to do, towards the Brandenburg Gate. A refreshing shower cools us. There is so much to absorb that we scarcely appear to be walking. We're on an airport travelator, a moving pavement pulling us through sites of approved memory. Isherwood recalls an incident, shortly before he left Berlin, when 'a group of self-important S.A. men', chatting and laughing, blocked free passage down this avenue. Walkers were forced to detour through the gutter. The English writer, knowing that a pivotal period of his life is over, studies the reflections of the great civic buildings in the windows of fashionable shops. He stares 'with a mournful fixity', as if to impress these images on his mind, to carry them away. To reconstruct them as marketable fiction.

The Brandenburg Gate, living up to its reputation as the location where the Wall was finally breached, is a barrier of a different kind: street performers, spontaneous musical groups, a thrash of tourists. A person dressed as a storm trooper out of *Star Wars* stands in my way. The franchise is inescapable. A lumbering Berlin bear takes off its head, to beg a cigarette from a corpse-green vampire soldier. Who has been made up to look like an oxidized military statue. The smoking bear reminds me of a card from the film museum showing Brigitte Helm in *Metropolis*, in her pre-*Star Wars* robot outfit, being given a straw to suck a drink held by a woman in a white coat. While an assistant with a hairdryer deals with the sweat.

On the north side of the avenue, Gary Cooper, that dignified American icon, marching out of *High Noon*, advertises Solidarity. 'Yup.' The sheriff triumphs before he turns in his badge. Exiled Hollywood leftists like Carl Foreman, *High Noon*'s scriptwriter, warp Western mythology. And are warped, right here, in their own turn. Coop stands tall at a frontier that is no longer a frontier. Pedestrians, and even well-behaved cyclists, are forbidden to pass through the Gate. We have to turn left, divert into the Tiergarten. Which makes us feel very much at home. The outwash of a grand project, as experienced in London, is confirmed by the closure of paths, security barriers across public highways, locked stations.

Tour guides try to nudge us into the group headed towards the Memorial for the Murdered Jews of Europe: Peter Eisenman's 'maze of reflections', a garden of sharp grey blocks. But we are caught in a crocodile of elderly, poncho-wearing cyclists who obediently push their bicycles into the permitted entrance to the park.

The Berlin editor told me that when he cycles through the Tiergarten on Sundays he encounters 'Beckett characters', vagrants with bundles, humorous malcontents. He might, I thought, have encountered the after-image of Beckett himself; not the world-famous, lightning-struck playwright, back to oversee another austere production in the Schiller-Theater, but a young unknown wanderer, philosopher of solitude. A myopic Dubliner edging close against the paintings in the museum of loneliness. He spoke, in his German diaries, of being 'done in the eye'.

At the dawn of his career, in 1936, Beckett embarked on a voyage, hoping to visit relatives in Germany, to inspect galleries and make contact with painters. 'What will Germany be?' he wrote. 'Six months walking around.' Alone in his cabin, he read L.-F. Céline's *Death on the Instalment Plan*. The perfect choice for an unknown city: delirium and derangement to set against stasis and elective exhaustion. Trapped within a Berlin that was not yet an island, Beckett tramped for hours in the Tiergarten. You can still feel the pattern of his stride in the sandy paths. And the invocation of Céline as the ultimate outcast, pariah and poet: a man with enough shrapnel in his head to act as a devil's compass, leading him onwards into the storm. In *North* (1960), on the run from retribution in Paris, the crazed doctor delivers a cumulative itinerary of disasters, from spa town to Berlin bunker to Prussian estate; betrayed and betraying, undecided as to whether he'd rather face the Russians, the last Nazis, or justice at home.

Strasse des 17 Juni, when we are allowed to rejoin it, has aspects of the Mall, Admiralty Arch to Buckingham Palace. And aspects of Phoenix Park in Dublin. Memorials glimpsed through a curtain of well-tended greenery. Wars in stone or bronze. Victory columns. I am impressed by the park workers, the neat fashion in which they arrange their tools, the way they labour to sweep paths, trim trees and water plants. When I pause to photograph a lime-green caravan with the logo of a whetted cleaver and the word CARNIVORE, two cyclists pass close enough for me to feel their slipstream. 'Kinski. Klaus Kinski!' one of them shouts.

A bowl of soup for lunch, on the pavement at Bismarckstrasse, is a welcome change of temperature. For one thing, the English of the man preparing the soup is on a par with our German. The police sirens Anna was missing are back in force, louder than Hackney. I'm not sure of the status of the Comfort Hotel across the street, but the local demographic takes a distinct lurch towards Fassbinder. Two attractive, long-haired Thai women wait, in conversation, at the U-Bahn station. A West African lady in dramatic lace tights and vivid jewellery sways through the café, down the street, and back again. Modelling boredom. There are bookshops in this area, film stores, grocery operations on a modest scale. You can try Prana yoga or patronize LSD, an outfit retailing sex videos.

After inspecting the window of a gallery displaying watercolours of the Olympic Stadium surrounded by a pack of small bears with upraised arms, I come, unexpectedly, on the confirmation that we are still following the right route. A plaque publishes the news that Alfred Döblin, novelist, playwright, essayist, lived and practised as a psychiatrist in this house from 1930 to 1933. He left Germany for

Switzerland, 'one day ahead of a Nazi arrest warrant', before settling in Paris. It was at Döblin's house in Hollywood that Fritz Lang
met Brecht, before they worked together on *Hangmen Also Die!*
Depicted on a DDR stamp, with his monkish spectacles and promi-
nent nose, Döblin looks not unlike the founder of Fianna Fáil, Irish
prime minister and president, Eamon De Valera. Döblin: Dublin.
Doubling. The author of *Berlin Alexanderplatz* denied, at the period
when he composed his masterwork, any familiarity with that other
Homeric European wanderer, Mr James Joyce.

A late-afternoon sun casts the shadows of the five Olympic rings,
like manacles, on to the clean flags of the Osttor approach to the
stadium. The rings are strung on a wire between twin brick pillars,
topped with searchlights. Access to the stadium is strictly forbidden.
Tours are suspended for the duration of the World Games.

Our approach was oblique, through a wooded area that reminded
me of the Highgate district of London. Detached properties,
houses, villas, chalets, cohabiting in a bucolic retreat. Flat-roofed
modernist experiments, obedient to Bauhaus principles, rubbed
along, in perfect harmony, with pastiched Tyrolean mountain huts
and interesting constructions in pink tin. Statues in gardens. Art-
machines glimpsed through picture windows. An enviable zone
with none of the bristling surveillance systems, private security in
cruising cars, that would be encountered in leafy Surrey or the
Epping Forest footballer fringe. No wrought-iron gates with black
lions.

In the Cold War spy fiction by which Berlin was sold to the British, Olympiastadion had another role: it was where the spooks
hung out, a centre for covert intelligence. Spooks like parks. The
former identity of this place, imprinted through newsreels of
marches and triumphs, was the Reichssportfeld. Renaming a
perimeter road Jesse-Owens-Allee doesn't exorcize the way in
which the film of 1936 was cut, to give the impression that Hitler
refused to shake the hand of the triumphant black athlete. Agonies
of conflicted opinion were endured as Berlin's grand avenues were

named and renamed, in the effort to achieve a balance between political correctness and respect for the past. We should never forget that among the last Jews held in the Schulstrasse transit camp, a former hospital in the northern suburbs, were a group of those whose racial inheritance was 'forgiven' while they helped to organize the Olympic Games.

Fascist bureaucrats dissolve into the facilitators of the new Germany, establishing connections with property developers and city councillors. Spy fiction made much of this. 'Why don't you get in touch with Olympia Stadion?' says a character in Len Deighton's *Berlin Game*. Alec Guinness, who crafted an owl-like serenity, combined with taking off his spectacles in extreme slow motion, into an illusion of Zen omniscience, revived his career by embodying the spy's spy: George Smiley. The fat man in the tight cardigan. Bowler hat and rolled umbrella. Chelsea house and flighty wife. Appearing in tactfully filmed versions of the John le Carré novels, Guinness helped sell the notion of television as superior travelogue: Paris, Hamburg, Berne. Metaphysical doubt was expressed through infinitely extended sequences where he decanted himself from a car.

In an earlier pass at this territory, Sir Alec had a cameo in *The Quiller Memorandum*, which was scripted by Harold Pinter. He shows off the Olympic Stadium to a young American played by George Segal. 'Impressive, isn't it?' he says, before explaining that the new generation of Nazis are harder to recognize, they don't wear uniforms. 'The scene, brief and played deadpan,' wrote Christopher Hilton, 'contained something unavailable anywhere else, a sense of proximity to what had been.' Nobody does deadpan, that almost imperceptible tightening of the lips, the flutter of the eyelashes, better than Guinness.

Security is courteous. The operatives are not the desperate, edge-of-legality, non-persons who endure long hours of tedium, loudly visible in fluorescent tabards and hard hats, around the blue fences of Stratford and Hackney. They are polite but firm; linguists, diplomats of refusal. I produce a card. They are respectful of cards, even though the magazine means nothing to them. The name on the card is followed by one of those impressive German pile-ups: *Redaktionsleitung*. I'm invited to walk around to the Accreditation Centre.

The Olympic Park is one day away from the opening of the World Games and there is no hysteria. The perimeter reeks, hotly, moistly, of large animals. 'A zoo?' Anna asks. 'Horses,' I reply. Remembering the popular racecourse. The past, like it or not, is something you can still smell.

The Accreditation Centre has its own, very human, stink. The armpit of the operation. Straggling queues of men, and a few women, in search of laminated badges. The aspect that disturbs the clerks about my request is that I have no interest in attending the Games. I'm happy to blink at the miracle of Usain Bolt and his telescopic limbs on television, for 9.58 seconds, before getting on with my life. All I ask is to be allowed to witness the interior of the stadium. With a business card from an unknown, but potentially prestigious magazine, my request must be treated seriously. A higher official is summoned. It takes him a moment to adjust to the fact that an intellectual, with the title *Redaktionsleitung*, doesn't actually speak German.

'Herr . . . Doktor . . . I'm afraid it's impossible.' He bows. He shakes my hand. 'A question of security. Police and so forth. At any other time, you understand . . .'

The solution is to take a lift to the summit of the Bell Tower, Glockenturm am Olympiastadion. It's too heavy a set at the end of the day: the massive steps, the dungeon-like grilles, the shadow patterns on the cobbles. The British demolished the Bell Tower and the Langemarck Hall in 1947, one year before the austerity Olympics were staged in London. What we were entering, to take our places in the queue for the lift, was yet another tactful facsimile. Werner March, purged, de-Nazified, reconstructed the whole package, between 1960 and 1963, with the expertise of one of Fritz Lang's architects of illusion. The Bell Tower, remade, was a real fake with a psychic displacement equal to that of the fatal towers in Henry

Hathaway's *Niagara* (those maddening saccharine chimes) and Hitchcock's *Vertigo*. The Langemarck Hall with its black death-cult shields, its ritual pillars, was difficult to absorb. A difficulty further emphasized by loops of sinister newsreel footage playing in the empty crypt below.

At the summit, having climbed past the original 1936 bell, we gazed down at the stadium, and the city beyond it. The blameless swathe of the Maifeld couldn't be purged of its former purpose, the strutting uniformed figures who had ridden in their open cars along the route we walked. I pointed out the Fernsehturm, the TV tower, on the distant horizon. It is a rare achievement to find an expedition so graphically mapped. 'Only he who cannot forget has no free mind,' said the exiled architect Erich Mendelsohn.

The Olympic Park extended into hills covered with dense woodland, red roofs, white blocks, the domes of astronomical observatories. Smoke slanted from the chimneys of an energy plant on the banks of the Havel. We were back with the vision obscured by the wing of the descending aeroplane at Tegel, but now some of the shapes in the spread of the landscape have acquired meaning. After the Olympic showpiece in 1936, this park leant itself to demonstrations, to military exercises. The stadium was a convenient space for rounding up those who fell foul of the state. In these woods, boy soldiers in the final insanity of the Third Reich were executed for desertion or cowardice.

Spandau, at the north-west edge of the park, is where Hitler's architect of ruins, Albert Speer, paced the prison yard for so many years. This dark-side apologist, who managed to smuggle out 20,000 scribbled sheets of warped testimony, is another proof that the critic Lotte Eisner was right when she said, 'Lang anticipated everything.' Words pouring from a caged superman, half-lunatic, half-sage: this is an accurate transcription of *Das Testament des Dr Mabuse*, a film made by Fritz Lang in 1933. And then suppressed by the Nazis. Rudolf Klein-Rogge plays a criminal mastermind, incarcerated in an asylum, controlling the city by telepathy, hypnotism and the production of endless pages of deranged script – which the authorities and their tame experts struggle to interpret.

At a time when the Situationists were honing their provocations in Paris, Speer had already embarked on the ultimate psychogeographical exercise. As with my disorientation in the Sony Center, in attempting to describe a straight line, Hitler's confidant marched in circles, following the shape of the noose he had so narrowly avoided. Round and round and round. He was flown to Spandau Prison in July 1947 and he remained there until October 1966: walking, walking, walking. He made meticulous calculations, he measured his stride and mapped the distance achieved on his self-inflicted treadmill against real-world geography.

His first excursion carried him from Spandau to Heidelberg. Every hamlet along the way was visualized. He saw more clearly than Werner Herzog on his trudge towards the Rhine. Clenched within the confines of his skull, the Munich film-maker barely notices the details of the external world: 'The tattered fog even thicker, chasing across my path.' Herzog wonders if static figures in the frosted window of a café beside the road are corpses. Speer is omnipotent, he catalogues everything. He is the invisible spectre waiting to cross the autobahn.

Muscles honed, destination achieved, the long-distance architect took on the world. Trenching the dust of the prison yard in summer, kicking aside the fallen leaves, leaving footprints in the snow, Speer pushed on in the direction attempted by Céline and imagined by Francis Stuart, across northern Germany, into Russia and Siberia. Fording the frozen Bering Straits, he limped down the west coast of America, towards the proper destination for surrealists and psychogeographers: Mexico. By now he was one of the last two inmates in this madhouse-prison. When they let him go, turning him loose into a twilight of self-justifying interviews, he was thirty-five kilometres south of Guadalajara. Starting there, I brooded, it should be possible to reverse the trek of this mental traveller, all those miles and years, back to Berlin. The demolished prison would then rise from the dirt and Speer's small plot of ground, the wilderness corner of the yard he called his 'Garden of Eden', would flower again. Revealing this escapee from the cabinet of Dr Caligari as another premature ecologist.

On the last morning of our Berlin visit, we decided to adopt the excursionist mood of *Menschen am Sonntag*, by taking the S-Bahn to the end of the line, to Potsdam. Here was the Filmpark Babelsberg, a Disneyfied reminder of the great days of Fritz Lang and the Ufa Studios, when Leytonstone's Alfred Hitchcock served his apprenticeship and witnessed the making of *Metropolis*. In Potsdam you could take your choice of palaces, museums and memorials to the conference at which post-war Europe was carved up by the victors. Mindful of Herzog, we were not tourists. We were pilgrims searching for a final structure to complete my triangulation: Fernsehturm, Bell Tower, Einstein Tower.

We were soon among green places, botanical gardens, quiet suburbs, glimpses of white sails on water. A Chinese man stood beside me, so that his young daughter could take a seat. I remembered Christopher Isherwood's excursion to a villa at Wannsee. His host, the manager of a great Jewish department store in Berlin, describes his summer residence as an English 'country cottage'. But it is nothing of the kind: 'tame baroque, elegant and rather colourless'. The sort of villa acquired, at Am Grossen Wannsee 56–58, for the notorious conference convened by Reinhard Heydrich to fix the mundane technicalities of the 'final solution to the Jewish question'. The subject of Chris Petit's novel *The Human Pool*.

Touts come at you hard as you step from the train, offering bus trips and riverboat excursions. When I confess that my sole interest today is Erich Mendelsohn's Einsteinturm, they are happy to provide me with a map. Potsdam, from the station on, is a magical topography in which visionary architecture meets astrophysics in a forgotten crease of history. A place smelling of pine-resin and good coffee.

The railway station, for some reason, is occupied by lizard-headed extraterrestrials, crouching Neanderthals, zipped apes and dinosaurs modelled in hard plastic. SMASH FASCISM! Walls at the bottom of the hill have been painted with cartoons of pylons in an electrical storm. The red-purple skies of nuclear catastrophe. We are on the right track.

Through banks of golden sunflowers and well-kept houses, we turn into Telegrafenberg, a science park open to visitors. A woman, descending briskly, asks where we have come from. 'The station.' 'By which bus?' 'We walked.' 'You *walked*, right from the station?' She is astonished and a little alarmed. It is unmannerly, she implies, to pass up the opportunity of experiencing the efficiency of public transport available in the capital of Brandenburg.

An occasional gardener is glimpsed, at a distance: this park is a silent world. One building, fronted with picnic tables, is the Polar Institute. The Institute of Astrophysics has a sympathetic connection with *Frau im Mond*, the film Fritz Lang made for Ufa from a script (based on her own novel) by his wife, Thea von Harbou. The surface of the moon was created in Babelsberg by importing truckloads of sand from the Baltic. The warp of space–time relativity is much in evidence. Equations laid out in Lang's speculative movie form the basis for Wernher von Braun's V-1 and V-2 calculations. East London is flattened by rockets rushed into production to publicize Lang's last silent film. Professor Hermann Oberth, who advised the monocled director on *Frau im Mond*, was frequently quoted by Von Braun, at the period when he was responsible for research and development at Peenemünde. He liked Oberth's proposal for a spacecraft carrying a mirror, with a diameter of many kilometres, capable of concentrating the sun's rays to control terrestrial weather and manipulate hot spots.

The migrant dunes with which the texture of Lang's moon was constructed came from beaches near the secure site where Von Braun and his associates were adapting fantasies of interplanetary travel into a technology for turning London into a lunar desert of craters and rubble. Petit told me that when the Russians arrived in Potsdam, they occupied the Babelsberg studios, dressing themselves in costumes from a Napoleonic epic and driving their cattle through the palaces and plywood cities. Terrified Potsdam inhabitants, primed by propaganda from Goebbels, were ready to believe anything, even Cossacks with shaggy ponies and camels. They accepted the latest invaders as a regiment of Frenchmen from 1815, returned from their battlefield graves to avenge the deeds of the Prussians at Waterloo.

On sandy paths, among the woods of Telegrafenberg, we are the aliens. I'm dressed in the sort of many-pocketed waistcoat associated with Joseph Beuys. To be strolling here, so far from Hackney, is as eccentric as the solitary marches of Samuel Beckett in Tiergarten, or the nocturnal ramblings of Francis Stuart, both of whom espoused a cultural relativism: curving movements through time and space, attempting to bring into focus their point of origin. Ireland is experienced most vividly when furthest away. And Dublin, that fabled walkers' city, with its crescent bay, is grooved into the memory by pilgrimages through other countries, where equivalents are found for every bar and bench. Phoenix Park into Tiergarten, Ballsbridge into Charlottenburg.

Even the contemporary boom town, spreading up the coast like Los Angeles, a cancer of failed developments and ghost estates, had a defining image for me: young women, early in the morning, smartly presented, clicking down Baggot Street into the Georgian squares with their polished brass plates, carrying trays from which polystyrene coffee beakers depend like udders. As if, in a flash, milkmaids had become women of the city. The grand squares with their trumpeted literary associations were now active in the holy hour of old (when the pubs would shut for a post-lunch lull), with upmarket prostitutes servicing the corporate clones who could not afford to take time away from their laptops. That awkward business briskly dealt with before a late return to Sandycove, Dalkey or Beckett's Foxrock.

In a Telegrafenberg clearing, we came across a group of abandoned tin huts, so haunting that I had to photograph them. A Viking settlement of upturned boats constructed from overlapping sheets of corrugated iron. A hangar for some experiment worthy of Dr

Mabuse. An exercise in mind control. I thought of a report by Francis Stuart. After walking for many miles, struggling to make sense of Berlin, he strains for a metaphor taken from his native Ireland: the iron hut.

'He continued his walk which was not, after all, the exploration of a tourist but in the nature of a pre-pilgrimage to places, at present unhallowed, which might become as haunted for him as, say, certain corners of Dublin or the row of iron huts on the Curragh plain. How little he foresaw that nothing from the past had prepared him for what was to come!'

Erich Mendelsohn's Einsteinturm was suddenly there, of its time and ours. The realized signature of an idea: deep steps, recessed windows, an unashamedly priapic form. A sketch, swift and sure, manifested in the world, creating a force field powerful enough to keep witnesses at a respectful distance. The tower grew out of a lawn, set among the woods, like the periscope of a submarine emerging from the earth. The thrust of a shamanic observatory from an era of discontinued modernism. Concrete maturing into radiant white skin.

A note was pinned to the door: 'Dear Visitors – The Einsteinturm is no museum but a Solar Observatory of the Astrophysical Institute of Potsdam.' We had walked, therefore, beyond the city of museums, beyond towers that were open to the public, sanctioned sites where tourists are invited to wonder at the achievements of past generations of men. In progressing around the meandering paths of the hill, we had triggered a more complex narrative, which would somehow play itself out against the shape of this expressionist structure.

The visionary homage to Einstein belonged in the film studios, down below us, with the wild-eyed scientists and mesmerists of Fritz Lang and Robert Wiene. In 1923, a year of hyperinflation in Germany, when loaves of bread cost 428 billion marks, Lang's scientific adviser, Hermann Oberth, published a 92-page book called *Die Rakete zu den Planetenräumen* ('The Rocket into Interplanetary

Space'). Inspired by his childhood reading of Jules Verne, Oberth – who lived, like Hitler, in Munich – contrived a text to fascinate film-makers, as well as industrialists and ambitious students of engineering like Wernher von Braun. 'Interest in spaceflight often seemed to coincide with flight into hard-right politics,' wrote Wayne Biddle in *The Dark Side of the Moon*.

The Einsteinturm, built to test the validity of the Theory of Relativity, worked in ways far beyond its original remit. Mendelsohn described it as a 'heavenly project'. The authorities in Potsdam dragged their feet over budgets and technical specifications, delaying completion to the point where the tower became operational at the very moment when Oberth's book was published. The white stump on its solid base was a launch pad for pure research. Equations formulated here were as dangerous in their implications as the Peenemünde rocket experiments that curved towards urban devastation, astral policing and dreams of total war.

Einstein's thesis having been tested and proved elsewhere, Mendelsohn's tower became an occupied sculpture conceived by a Jewish architect to honour a Jewish scientist: as well as a demonstration of the technological heritage of the defeated Reich. In its present form, after extensive restoration in 1999, the declared aim of the tower is: 'to gather data on solar and nuclear physics'. While its covert purpose, I discovered, was to shred received notions and dissolve them into the cosmic stew, a general theory of everything: physics and poetry, Dublin and Berlin. Celtic myths and the dark gods of the forest intertwined like vegetative script from *The Book of Kells*.

The physicist Erwin Schrödinger, who generalized Einstein's relativity by using four-dimensional geometry with antisymmetric components and connections, received a personal invitation from De Valera to move to Ireland to help establish an Institute for Advanced Studies in Clontarf. Appointed as Director of the School of Theoretical Physics in 1940, Schrödinger stayed in Dublin for seventeen years, fathering two children after involvements with students, and becoming a devotee of the Vedanta philosophy of

Hinduism. Individual consciousness, he believed, was only a manifestation of a unitary consciousness pervading the universe. He
apologized to Einstein for recanting on his outspoken criticism of
the Nazis, a position he was forced to adopt in order to safeguard his
tenure at the University of Graz. It was in correspondence with Einstein that he proposed the thought experiment in which a cat is
neither alive nor dead. Or both at the same time.

Affected by the vision of the tower, I returned with Anna for a fortnight's stay in Dublin, the city in which we had met as students,
but never revisited. Space–time anomalies permitted us, like
Schrödinger's cat, to be in two places at once; blessed with a special
tenderness for the sea town in the rain, as we walked or rewalked
half-remembered routes between Howth Head and Dalkey. Anna
said that she had seen more in this brief stay than in the four years
of her student life, which was now a kind of dream. A trio of old
folk, out on the razzle, made it their business to find us the site of
the vanished hotel where we spent the first night of our married
life. In the long, light evenings, possessed by an agenda of her own,
Anna tracked down the bars that had survived and the ones that had
transformed themselves into Mexican restaurants or tourist hotels.
The priests had vanished from the streets and the beggars were now
site-specific professionals from the Balkans. One night we took ourselves off to a travelling circus pitched alongside the house where
Bram Stoker was born.

   We had been on the move for so many months that it was impossible to fix our coordinates. We slumped on a bench, in a damp park,
or a windblown square in mid-construction, and the world raced
past us. Potsdam on the S-Bahn was Shepperton out of Waterloo:
woods, reservoirs, film studios, the connection to the city stretched
to its limits. Hermann Oberth's proposal for the spacecraft with the
giant mirror could have come straight from Ballard's *Vermilion
Sands*. When Brigid Marlin sent me back to *The Kindness of Women*
in search of her fictionalized presence, I found an incident that
could only happen when time was being sucked into a black hole.

Ballard and Fritz Lang, two confirmed self-mythologizers, come face to face. And it happens in South America.

'An elderly man in an oversized tuxedo sat on a straightbacked chair turned sideways to the wall. He slumped in the chair like an abandoned ventriloquist's dummy, buffeted by the noise and music, the light show dappling his grey hair a vivid blue and green. He looked infinitely weary, and I thought that he might have died among these garish film people. When I shook his hand and briefly told him how much I admired his films, there was a flicker of response. An ironic gleam flitted through one eye, as if the director of *Metropolis* had realised that the dystopia he had visualised had come true in a way he had least expected.'

The Colossus of Maroussi

For a long time I stayed away from the Acropolis . . . It's what we have
rescued from madness . . . There are obligations attached to such a visit.

   – Don DeLillo

They were going to hunt dogs with guns, the Berliner said, to clear
the streets for the Olympics. He was in Hackney now, where the
buzz was, an architect, but he had been in Athens in 2002, when the
deals were going down and the grand project was under way. And
the inspectors, flown in from all corners, lavishly lodged and entertained, were getting nervous. I sat in an afternoon pub, beside a
street market that seemed to have migrated across town from Notting Hill, close to a stretch of the Regent's Canal that had been
peremptorily closed, fenced, drained. Instead of dogs, perhaps they
were going to kill fish, or the birds that feed on them. No work was
in progress, but the exclusion zone was briskly set up and policed by
the usual yellow tabards. The challenge, trying to discommode
stubborn pedestrians, always comes from the wrong direction:
'What are you doing on the towpath?' Good question. I've been trying to find an answer for years. But it is where I am, where I like to
be, every morning. At their first appearance, the invaders assume
absolute authority, without explanation or apology. What are *you*
doing here? And from where does the conviction, about the rightness of your piracy, emanate?

The double-banked lines of narrowboats, council-tax dodgers, have been dispersed. Cyclists are thrown into the murderous stream of Mare Street. A procession of women, all ages, being taught how to swing their arms while marching (and talking) at pace, runs slap against the plywood barrier. As a precaution, the authorities have painted a white line around the former boating lake in Victoria Park. You can't be too careful of this stuff, the alien medium: water. Comb off the algae carpet, the duckweed, and prepare to airlift in a dune or two of cheap sand, with deck-chairs and parasols, for the creation of an urban beach. A rising hysteria grips the fortunate Olympic boroughs, funny money is available, in serious quantities, for those who can come up with the right kind of fun. If you are going to hunt dogs, Victoria Park would not be a bad place to start. But that's not what the German meant, it must have been his wicked sense of humour. He was part of a nocturnal cycle patrol, middle-class professionals, archi-tects, graphic designers, financial journalists, who cruise the city searching out interesting properties to squat, hip industrial sites preferred, with visible pipes and naked brickwork, Crittall win-dows.

Pre-Olympic Hackney was an open city: Bill Parry-Davies told me that he hoped to get £200,000 from the council, to allow the long-term squatter known as 'The Owl Man of Albion Drive' to relocate with his wounded birds to the country. The budget for the transport-hub slab at Dalston Junction, serving bus routes, climbed vertiginously, and without explanation, from £26 mil-lion to something closer to £60 million. The consortium involved in this project, Balfour Beatty and Carillion, was alleged to have been engaged in bid-rigging activities over public contracts in the Midlands. After what appeared to be some American-style 'plea bargaining', a reduced fine of £10 million was paid. TfL reassure us that Best Value is integral to the planning process. And central government confirm that a 'transport interchange' is essential for the 2012 Olympics. Even though, as Lord Low of Dalston points out in a letter to the *Hackney Gazette*, none of the buses using this facility will actually go anywhere near the Olympic Park.

Those dogs stayed with me when I left for Athens. I had seen film footage shot two years after the 2004 Games: loping beasts, freelance caretakers patrolling the overgrown wilderness of the futurist sculpture park that once housed the Olympic complex, out at Maroussi. Furtive ghosts in shaggy coats demonstrating a classical trajectory of fate: how those who are condemned, without justification, become the sole occupiers of the deserted palace for which they were the intended sacrifice. Now, starting early, to get to the new Acropolis Museum before the promised crowds, I noticed cats scavenging from the lip of a brightly polished litter bin; sleek, piebald creatures leaning back, using fat tails for balance, as they sniff the refuse. Pavements are rain-washed and scrupulously clean. The graffiti, in this high-visibility tourist zone, is Arabic, framed in cracked marble panels at the base of the steps like calligraphy by Cy Twombly.

The tribal dogs, wolfish spirits of place, skulking guardians of something that has been lost, circumambulate the major tourist attractions without feeling an obligation to tout or charm. They are the unculled, collateral victims of the Olympic gaze: heavy-pelted German-shepherd types, down on their luck, war veterans with a folk memory of clover-munching sheep. And fluffed-up, pinkish creatures also, on very thin legs, like wealthy matrons from the Kolonaki district caught in the rain without their dark glasses. Feral packs roamed the old city, it's what dogs do: test architecture designed to be abandoned and recall the years before they were enslaved as household pets. They scrounged at restaurants and tavernas with Balkan insouciance. While unaffiliated cats blanketed roofs like gently stirring fur underlay; they stretch, arch, settle on the corrugated iron of Monastiraki Station or the skeleton of the wrecked café, halfway up the limestone plug of Lycabettus Hill.

At the dawn of a new golden age for Greece, with Elena Paparizou about to carry off the Eurovision Song Contest in 2005, and the football team grinding out a victory over Portugal, 1–0, in the final of Euro 2004, rough-trade canines were seen, by outsiders, as a cosmetic issue. You couldn't blow billions of euros on a reef of fabulous stadiums, an immaculate Metro system, Baghdads of synchronized fireworks, and have TV coverage fouled up with drooling, belly-on-the-floor bandits, begging for leftovers and shitting on your shoes. There was talk, the Berliner was right about that, of taking them out, not with guns and blood (and ugly press): by the traditional Socratic solution, poison. But the dogs were family, and were treated as such: cleaned-up, neutered, turned loose.

The €9 billion spent on the Olympic party was equivalent to the amount financial experts reckoned investors were siphoning out of Greek banks to bury in Cyprus or Switzerland when the collapse finally came, just as I visited Athens early in 2010. The people I talked to, students, academics, film-makers, all agreed: it had been a monumental, epoch-defining opening ceremony. The children of the middle-class suburbs, out by the mountains, down at the coast, queued up to volunteer, to play their part as marshals or programme sellers. Everybody had the DVD of the firework night, it was still selling. Nobody remembered what happened after that. One young woman, a highly qualified lawyer, now working off-the-book for around €400 a month, recalled the only Olympic event she'd actually witnessed. 'There were horses dancing. Very pretty.' The story of the drug-cheat sprinters and their staged motorcycle accident, on the eve of an appointment with the testers, has been quietly forgotten. There are different takes on this kind of behaviour. 'Better a thief than a fool.' Students help each other in exams, everybody gets the same grades. The honour of the group is salvaged. They told me how they demonstrated most afternoons, stoning the Hilton Hotel, or marching to the American Embassy: their only form of exercise. Once established as a student, the hard part has been done, you can maintain that status, failing or avoiding exams, for years, as an alternative career.

The dogs I had to step over to go down the ramp to Bernard Tschumi's statement glass-concrete box, the new Acropolis Museum, were crushed and posthumous, unwilling to lift their heads from the slick floor with its spindly reflections of cypress trees. They wore blue collars, tagged collaborators whose native territory had been captured. They moved, like tourists with one of those tickets granting them access to a number of ancient sites, between quotation ruins, refusing to trade dignity for a pat on the back. Inside the museum, rack-ribbed and stalking, was the thing they had once been: a savage marble hound, from 520 BC, 'associated with the Sanctuary of Artemis Brauronia on the Acropolis'.

I came to Athens, in the clamp of this miserable weather, because my niece by marriage, my wife's sister's daughter, was in town for a month; a fluent Greek speaker who had been a student in Crete and who was now working in the Athens office of an international publisher. Calling on this connection, for local knowledge and introductions, was a very Greek thing to do: who can you exploit if not your own family? Cousins of cousins, in-laws. That's how the system works.

Some aspects of the streets around the Acropolis were reminiscent of home, of Hackney: our Olympic makeover. There were newly pedestrianized walkways, planted and primped, in place of the buses, honking taxis and competitive guides I remembered from holidays in the 1950s. Thickets of graffiti rivalled Hoxton and Shoreditch. Athens grumbles loudly to itself, on walls and hoardings: tags, slogans, territorial claims for Mao, Panathinaikos, AEK Athens, Guns N' Roses. The most obvious differences from London were that nobody carved me up on impatient bicycles, there were no wired joggers – and dogs, unmastered, did their own thing. They were not required to gum threadbare tennis balls or crap to order. The notion that the Dionysiou Areopagitou walkway, this rock-skirting path, would inspire Athenians to splurge on Lycra and air-cushion running shoes didn't work. The only joggers, in couples, threesomes, or pumping solo, were corporate Aussies and Coca-Cola executives. My niece, who smokes as heroically as any Greek, tried this circuit, before going to the office. She was nipped on the heel by one of the dogs.

Don DeLillo, back in 1983, in his book *The Names*, depicts Athens as a pivotal place, somewhere to hide dirty money, factor covert deals between the US, Germany and the propped-up regimes of the Middle East. Future terror as a black economy. Anonymous apartment blocks, thrown up near the airport, are exploited as hideaways for adulterous liaisons between risk-assessors and the displaced wives of international bankers, hard-boozing foreign correspondents and embassy secretaries. A tribal cluster of the over-rewarded, near-writers and part-time spooks, fly off to bad hotels in hot places, and then meet once more for drunken dinners, down by the sea, on their return to Greece. 'Again I stopped drinking, this time in Istanbul,' DeLillo wrote. 'In Athens I went jogging every day.' Couples, if they swim, do so fully clothed, glass in hand, duty-free cigarette wedged in the mouth.

The small hotel my niece recommended on Rovertou Gkalli was convenient for debriefing sessions with locals prepared to indulge my blunt interrogations. The paper-thin walls and that nostalgic bouquet of drains were offset by a panoramic view from the roof terrace, demonstrating the relationship between the Acropolis and the new museum at its foot; they were lit, both of them, to stand out against a living boneyard of white and pinkish-white buildings, the terracotta tiles and narrow apartments from another era. Breakfast was a necessary penance, the same self-service troughs you find in Liverpool and Manchester. The spitting coffee-sludge dispenser. Along with coachloads of young American college kids brought here to keep the business going in pinched times. They averaged three circuits of the dead sausage/rubber-egg trays and were very cheerful about it. 'Sorry, sorry. It will be better tomorrow,' the black-clad waitress whispered.

The new Acropolis Museum had 90,000 visitors in its first week. It was a confident symbol of national revival, following on from the Olympic moment. It was also a challenge to the alleged piracy of Lord Elgin, who struck a good bargain with the Turkish authorities and hacked out the Parthenon friezes now on display in their own

Bloomsbury bunker. I visited the British Museum shortly before leaving for Athens. And heard, behind me at every step, the tobacco-enhanced growl of the late Melina Mercouri, the government minister and movie star who 'conceived and proposed' the concept of that migrating honour, the European City of Culture. 'Culture,' she pronounced, 'is Greece's heavy industry.'

Along with displays of artefacts, shards, pots found during excavations for the Metro system, the new stations with their broad platforms and clean, regular trains, featured what could only be called iconic posters of Mercouri. She is positioned in front of the Parthenon, white trench coat and roll-neck sweater, with left arm saluting, yellow flowers crushed in right hand: diva of the city, substitute for the missing Athena of Phidias. When we walked out in the evening, past a little restaurant in Thissio, we were told: 'This is where Melina liked to hold court.' There is a clip of Mercouri on YouTube, a weird superimposition of *Never on Sunday* and *Psycho* – in which she prowls up to Anthony Perkins, before perching beside him to croon. 'What's it about?' he asks. 'Like all Greek songs, about love and death,' she replies. 'I give you milk and honey and in return you give me poison.'

The museum was deserted. The entrance fee had recently been increased by 400 per cent, but it was still good value. Men in dark suits, with laminated accreditation, stood about among the marble heads on plinths, among the shock of white, confirming, if you asked, that it was not permitted to take photographs. The narrative was direct and convincing, the structure was open to an enfolding geology, the temple on the hill; it was both event and quotation. This, against the incontinent stacking of trophies in that great cabinet of curiosities, the British Museum, is such a coherent pitch. The building is not separated from the city, it's not a respite, a dream with too many chambers, collisions, compartments; it tells one story, the rock. The temple and its vanished gods. At each ascending level, a floor-to-ceiling window sets the modelled Parthenon against the structure on the hill, with the dominant colour of the Doric columns shifting through the day from the yellow-brown of smokers' teeth to burnt orange to a blueish white. Sculptural fragments, torsos, limbs, blocks of stone skewered on poles, are presented like a bead curtain, between viewer and city. Entering the museum, and looking down through the glass floor, excavations are visible, earlier layers as a part of the present structure: in the same way that, wrestling with another kind of history, they have preserved a slanted glimpse into Gestapo cellars for the Topography of Terror exhibition at the Hotel Prinz Albrecht in Berlin. Hitler, as his troops advanced on Athens in April 1941, gave the order that no bombs should fall on the city. 'If we are asked about our forefathers,' he said to Goebbels, 'we must refer to the Greeks.' The neurotic compulsion to construct museums, to combine postcard art with skull-faced warriors and nude bodybuilders roaming among the stumps of broken columns, was deep in his pathology.

We followed the blue-collar dogs to the Temple of the Olympian Zeus and the National Gardens. Inspired by what I had seen, the casts of the missing Parthenon marbles, I felt the strength of the argument for their return. The experience of the actual Acropolis, windswept, expensive, hustled by tour gangs, is grim: far better to stroll the floors of the museum, to take coffee in a room with a view. Police cars screech around the tight curves of the Acropolis ascent, and the trinket-seller Asians with cheap guidebooks and concertinas of photographs, scatter among the bushes, to regroup in time for the next coach.

On the shaded approach to the Panathenaic Stadium, an African man is throwing rubber-solution blobs at the pavement, demonstrating a novelty pedestrians greet with all the enthusiasm of being invited to sample freshly gobbed, gingivitic bubblegum. There are not many walkers to be found, it takes courage and athleticism to cross furious roads. The stadium of 1896, built on the site of the stadium of antiquity, involved some new marble cladding, some restoration, but no major devastation: the elegantly banked structure was set in parkland at the heart of the city. These were the first games of the modern era. The promoter, the Lord Coe of Athens, was a Paris-based scholar called Dimitrios Vikelas, a novelist and publisher of pamphlets. They found the ideal man, an exile with a passionate sense of national identity, and no knowledge or experience of sport. Economically, the idea was madness; the currant trade had collapsed and Charilaos Trikoupis, the prime minister, told parliament that the country was bankrupt and that there could be no financial support from the government for this Olympic revival. An obliging patron was found in the person of the Alexandrian merchant Georgios Averof and a young architect called Anastasios Metaxas was commissioned to carry through the reconstruction.

Averof gets his statue. The stadium, open to view, is still in use. Thin as a steel ruler, and too tight in the curve to be in much demand for contemporary athletic championships, the Panathenaic Stadium witnessed the close of the 2004 Olympic marathon. The rightness of the placement, against pine-thatched hills, a theatrical public space within the polis, is confirmed by sight lines, the cushion of gardens and broad avenues: a civic benefit rather than a crude intervention. Anybody can stroll to the entrance, see what is to be seen: the Olympic rings are not a threat and the sleeping dogs do not stir at the gates. Flagpoles are bare. Joggers, if any can be found, are free to make the elongated circuit or to run up steeply banked terraces. But noble as the site appears, it is not entirely benign. The poet John Lucas, in *92 Acharnon Street*, reminds us that the old Olympic stadium is where 'the colonels assembled schoolchildren for parades so that they might learn to salute the Greek flag'.

Beyond the metal stream, motorbikes cascading from tributaries, is a canine salon, a defunct beauty parlour advertised with a wolfish yellow-and-blue portrait. Many small businesses of this quarter are shuttered, signed off in a blizzard of graffiti. The single functioning enterprise offers cushions featuring doggy pin-ups, pert chows and shivering, ratty, handbag things. Red-and-white ribbons giftwrap the latest auto-shunt. Even the flashiest motors are bruised and battered like old prize-fighters. But the fug, the sulphurous fume blanket of legend, seems to have lifted, and the narrow streets as we

climb towards Lycabettus Hill are dressed with trees in winter fruit.
I pick an orange and relish its sour, enamel-stripping bite. Nobody, I
am told, devours this harvest, the urban largesse; the comfortable
folk of Kolonaki set their own trees right up to the wall, but abhor
as unclean the fruit of the town. Trucks, in poorer districts, fill sacks
to manufacture a syrup that might as well be used in soap as in
sickly cocktails.

The man on the desk of our hotel, with an effortless show of boredom, a refusal to acknowledge any of the nuisance traffic through
his lobby, must have wondered what was going on. Every evening I
perched on the sofa while a procession of young women turned up
to engage in excited conversation, before slipping back to the street
for cigarettes. The lawyer, on Sunday, was late. Even on her modest
salary, she managed a car. She drove in from Falirou, on the coast,
parked with all the rest in an unoccupied low-rise development in
Fix, and took the Metro for a couple of stops. But, really, she didn't
like it: this mingling with the poor people, the immigrants. Central
reservations and traffic lights were enterprise zones run by Africans
and Asians: cellophane-wrapped blocks of cigarettes, instant valet-
ing. Walking on those gentle hills was never an option, the tram
obligingly stops every hundred yards or so. Old folk cross themselves when they pass a church.

When she arrived, in a flurry of unnecessary apologies, my
informant explained that traffic had gridlocked. There had been
another bomb incident, she was hazy about the details. Nobody
was killed. These things happen most weekends and are unreported.
The 17N group, responsible for the assassination of Brigadier
Stephen Saunders, the British military attaché, in June 2000, had
been rounded up, so it was claimed, just in time for the Olympics.
Savvas Xiros, the alleged motorbike gunman, was arrested after a
lethal device he was carrying went off prematurely. From his hospital bed, he made a long and detailed confession, naming a list of
accomplices. Bundles of explosives, along with an assault rifle and
ammunition, were found buried on a site being cleared for the 2004

Games. The current bombs, it's thought, are intended to signal the active return of 17N, which took its name from the date, 17 November 1973, when the Junta's security forces drove a tank through the gates of the Athens Polytechnic and stormed the grounds, killing a number of students. After the United States, which was blamed for propping up the Colonels, Britain and Tony Blair were 17N's principal targets, for supporting the Nato bombing of Serbia. Curiously enough, as Michael Llewellyn-Smith, a former British ambassador, reports in *Athens: A Cultural and Literary History*, the young Blair, on a student holiday in 1974, had witnessed the triumphant return of the exiled Constantine Karamanlis, after the fall of the Colonels. Blair, as we know, is not immune to the theatrical potential of flag-waving processions, the glad-handing of mesmerized supporters: the rhetoric of regime change, messianic populism. Eyes flashing, teeth barred with threatening good will. The Man. The Chosen One. The Infallible Leader.

I enthused to Anna about one benefit of the Olympic extravaganza, the Metro system: trains appeared within minutes, tickets were modestly priced and uncomplicated, stations were smart and well lit. Too many nightmares underground, stalled in overheated viral torpedoes, kept my wife well away from the London system, but here, deep below Athens, it was a pleasure ride, an outing, as we sailed towards Maroussi and the major, multi-stadium Olympic complex, built to showcase both the top-dollar panache of the Spanish architect Santiago Calatrava and the visible pride of the Greek nation. The Olympic Park, as I tried to explain, had been sited on a significant patch of ground: the memory-field of Henry Miller's undervalued travel journal *The Colossus of Maroussi*. It was written in the shadow of war – time out for Miller, the last of old Europe – and published in 1941. This was the first Miller title that Penguin felt brave enough to place on their list. Apart from some nude sunbathing with the Durrells, whose marriage was going through a stormy patch, and many life-affirming meals and marathon drinking sessions, the tone is melancholy and estranged: bad roads in worse weather, radiant ruins guarded by forgotten eccentrics. A dollar goes a long way: Miller takes a room in one of the grand hotels on Constitution Square, from whose balconies it would now be possible to look down on the massed tents of protesting unionists alarmed by threats of cuts and redundancies. Through Lawrence Durrell, Miller meets – and loathes – members of the British expat community, effete classicists and cultural carpetbaggers whose practised ironies he fails to appreciate. He also encounters, and embraces, Greek poets of the Plaka, talkers, drinkers: George Seferis and George Katsimbalis. It is the Falstaffian Katsimbalis whom Miller christens 'the Colossus of Maroussi': war-wounded, ever thirsty, a large, limping man whose life is the excuse for a cycle of epic performance pieces. So successful was Miller in mythologizing his friend from the quiet suburbs that the poet was set up with lectures for life. Durrell records Katsimbalis, his 'blood roaring with cognac', crowing like the king of the city from the Acropolis rock until, from the 'silvery' darkness, all the scattered roosters of Attica answer him.

What is fascinating, as we ride so effortlessly through the underworld towards Maroussi and the Olympic Park, is a passage in the Penguin Miller, with its red-and-white cover, in which Katsimbalis indulges, through absurdist flights of fancy, the madness of a grand-project promoter. Miller recognizes that his friend is succumbing to a peculiarly Greek condition, the striving after ancient glory in a time of war: temples in place of bunkers. Olives shrivelled on the tree. Dust on the plate. Slaves quarrying marble for the latest folly.

'He had gotten a mania for Haussmannising the big cities of the world. He would take the map of London, say, or Constantinople, and after the most painstaking study would draw up a new plan of the city, to suit himself . . . Naturally a great many monuments had to be torn down and new statues, by unheard-of men, erected in their place. While working on Constantinople, for example, he would be seized by a desire to alter Shanghai . . . It was confusing, to say the least. Having reconstructed one city he would go on to another and then another. There was no let up to it. The walls were papered with the plans for new cities . . . It was a kind of megalo-mania, he thought, a sort of glorified constructivism which was a pathologic hangover from his Peloponnesian heritage.' It's a pity that nobody reads Miller, because it's all there: the damaged, wine-fired poet playing with utopian blueprints, constructing fabulous cities on scribbled sheets of paper. De Quincey nightmares that fade in the cold Athenian dawn. Dreams that know they are dreams. All too soon the German tanks would arrive and the craziest (and most frustrated) architect of them all, Adolf Hitler, would salute the proud ruins, the inspiration for his visions of apocalypse.

Changing trains at Attiki, the mad thesis is confirmed, there is only one city and it doesn't work: blue-and-white ribbons block the stairs. Disgruntled travellers. Tunnels. Expulsion into the street. Students handing out leaflets urging immediate strike action. A bendy bus. Standing-room only. Sunday pilgrims heading out to the suburbs, to the green oasis of Kifissia, are pressed like grapes, breathless, for a lurching, swaying ride, uphill, past a seemingly end-less accumulation of small grocers, hawkers of hubcaps, warehouse sex clubs, graffiti. And a billboard with a monster, finger-jabbing Quentin Tarantino pimping whisky: I WRITE MY OWN SCRIPT.

After the cemeteries, the allotments, the euro-funded superhigh-way, we have that familiar sense of being out on the edge of things, confronted by overloud architecture. It's Irini and the Olympic Sports Complex: difficult to reach, half-forgotten, but serviced by handsome, flower-bedecked stations. The site looks like a brave attempt to comply with some CGI prophecy conjured up in Hong Kong. The parkland clients, such as they are, come from another story: suitcase survivalists offering tin trains to bored commuters. A wilderness dressed with elaborate and ruinously expensive struc-tures for which nobody has any use. A buffer of generic flats assembled as an athletes' village, a future development, then left to rot, along with random kiosks, garages, slogan-sprayed toilet blocks. An English architect with a Greek wife, who had been visit-ing Athens at regular intervals for twenty-five years, told me that the official total of thirteen deaths for construction workers on the

Olympic project was a tactful underestimate. It was closer to seventy. The pressure to deliver the scheme on time led to a nexus of subcontracting, the employment of cheap and unskilled Balkan labour. And a plethora of brown envelopes. 'They call it "coffee" money,' he said. 'Ten grand to smooth a path to the right officials.'

It is eloquent: the setting, the backdrop. Curved steel ribcages. Grandiose water features. Puffy clouds over mountains scarred with a sort of reverse glaciation: white tongues of speculative housing pushing heroically against the gradient. Sad trees withering in concrete tubs. A security person waves us through: this is a novel experience, to be granted access to a posthumous project, the symbol of a nation's bankruptcy. OPEN STADIUMS. PLACES OF CELEBRATION. A WAY OF LIFE.

We are free to wander, to burn up film on the surreal conjunctions of this mesmerizing set. Patterns of herringbone traceries, wet shadows. Girdered tunnels mimicking cypress avenues leading nowhere. The structures in the park are monumental but anorexic: a futurist city that was never completed, Kensington's Natural History Museum taken over by Disney. A museum without walls on a bulldozed meadow of mud. An island, between motorway and railway, surrounded by glass boxes, failed corporate entities, unpopular estates, scrap-metal dumps, breakers' yards, mosaic walls with laurel-wreath symbols. The death of the grand project is the history painting of our time: W. P. Frith's *Derby Day*, without the people, the excursionists, gypsies, toffs, gulled punters. All that human noise is missing, only the set itself is worthy of commemoration. Great fireworks, great razzmatazz. And then? Crippling debts. White-elephant stadiums that cost a fortune to keep empty. New roads choked with tractor protests. Airport closed. Angry, stone-throwing mobs demonstrating the consequences of fiscal mismanagement, chicanery by international bankers, a culture of tax avoidance and brown bagism. National pride suborned by a word the Greeks patented: hubris.

The site has its own microclimate: melancholy. Unnatured winds gusting around the struts and piers, the slippery walkways and mounds of unused chairs and broken barriers. Two or three swimmers completed lethargic lengths under the instruction of dark figures with hands in their tracksuit pockets. Other pools, a vast gymnasium, an indoor tennis centre, a steepling stadium overlooking a puddled garden with limp palm trees, were all deserted. The highlight of our dazed perambulation was an encounter with a small troop of men with bulging rucksacks, who emerged like phantoms out of the desert, and vanished again behind an improvised fence of corrugated iron. There was no obtrusive CCTV monitoring and no visible security presence. This was a dreamscape out of Giorgio de Chirico, who lived in Athens as a young man, attending the polytechnic, and who understood all too well that great cities achieve their essence as ruins. The Agora, Acropolis, Temple of Zeus, and all the Olympic parks and fields have museum ambitions; to be spectres of themselves in perpetuity. Labyrinths of memory made from broken columns. De Chirico was present during the first Olympic Games of the modern era. He witnessed the arrival of Louis, the Greek man who won the marathon. The crown prince embraced his champion. 'The public was delirious.' But the attempt to invoke the ancient tradition of a parallel cultural Olympiad was a fiasco. 'Dreary, tedious and above all artificial,' De Chirico wrote in his *Memoirs*. 'A destructive atmosphere of intellectualism lay over the public and the actors. It looked as though everyone was stifling huge yawns . . . But the organisers of open-air spectacles do not want to understand and continue, more through stupidity than through obstinacy or conviction, to give these clumsy performances in all countries.'

The security man in the office of the main stadium, now taken over, despite the running track, by the football team AEK Athens, gave us permission to inspect the empty, rain-slicked bowl. The recycling appeared to be successful, another example of a commercial enterprise surfing public funds. The Markopoulo Equestrian Centre, I was pleased to discover, had also found a use: corporate Australians staged inter-firm cricket matches there.

*

Our arrest came at the site of the former Athens airport, on the coast, near Faliro Bay. The whole curve of shoreline, despoiled by the perverse aesthetics of grand-project architecture, was a natural wonder. The new tramline dropped weekenders at their pine-sheltered seaside clubs. Nobody cycled or jogged on the official city-centre paths, they were out here: slow men playing football in a communal dance. A shuffle, a feint, a cigarette, and a long rest in the shade. There were hardy swimmers in the clear water. Men with comfortable bellies in tight polo shirts paddled balls with considerable force, but no venom, across high nets. Gentle exercise was a privilege, enjoyed without nannying endorsement and vainglorious expenditure.

It was suicidal to cross the road between coastal strip and airport. A bridge led directly from the abandoned zone to the runways with their grey-blue blocks given over to obscure trade fairs and expositions. The bridge was padlocked. Walls and concrete ramps were dense with graffiti: HEZBOLLAH GAME THE FUTUER. FUCK YOU HERE. MY LIFIE.

Reaching the far side, I discovered that the airfield was open to inquisitive walkers, the fence was down and there were no obvious prohibitions. Following traces of runways where we once landed, en route to the islands, I snapped tyre marks, avenues of light poles and shelters made for the 2004 Olympics. The derelict airfield was a retail park waiting for finance. I was lining up a shot of a grid of cracked tiles, in front of some glorified container sheds, when the car screeched up. The driver didn't speak much English, just two words: 'Get in.' As we bounced across the field, I remembered the fate of the twelve British plane-spotters arrested on spy charges for taking photographs at an air show on a military base near Kalamata in southern Greece; perhaps it had not been such a great idea to make a survey of this public wilderness. Anna, I thought, was looking rather tight-lipped. Images are always contentious. The idea of a lengthy interrogation, and whatever followed, was not appealing. In the Lower Lea Valley, as I heard from so many locals, film was seized and digital captures deleted: not here, photography was not the issue. The driver had no idea what we were after, unlanguaged aliens doing crazy stuff in the middle of nowhere. He dumped us back on the main road.

Out towards Piraeus, near the Karaiskaki Stadium of the Olympiakos Football Club, the derangement is absolute. The argument between vanity architecture and post-architectural infill, self-designed termite colonies wedged into every nook and cranny, is presented in all its naked absurdity. The great white monsters, with their choked plants withering in stone beds, are a beached fleet. The Peace and Friendship Stadium (which hosted the volleyball in 2004) has docked from some totalitarian regime that got lucky with oil and gas. Peering inside its cavernous depths, the acres of waxed board, I find a solitary depressive shooting hoops like a Category C prisoner enduring his hour of sanctioned exercise. Families, enjoying their Sunday at the seaside, manoeuvre around these useless mastodons, to cluster in a beachfront bar with a panoramic window on the yachts of the oligarchs, the marine-insurance brokers.

What is beautiful, in this urban steppe, is the way the official narrative is subverted. The overpasses and underpasses, the stilted highways and giant hoardings, the irrigation ditches and empty canals, the mesh fences and graffiti-splashed junction boxes, form an edgy parkland where anything could happen. Permitted paths vanish into dunes of landfill, into neurotic traffic, into functioning rail tracks and tramways. But the old road, the ghost road, the one that was here before all this madness, has become a favoured route for joggers and cyclists. The Olympic Park, that corrupted legacy, is like mid-period Fellini: kite flyers, moody urbanists in long coats, white cars parked in unlikely places, a glitter of sea you can never quite reach.

Across the coastal highway, over the tracks, is an area of balconied flats, steel-blue offices and sex clubs with screaming scarlet promises: STRIP SHOW LIVE. Multiples of Tarantino with his bottle of booze and his accusing finger. The final doodle on a white board marking the end of the Olympic zone confirms Neo Faliro as a

theme park without content: THAT HEAVEN WOULD WANT SPECTA-
TORS. A film-maker called Aristotelis, a former student of
architecture, explained it to me. 'The Games are just empty buildings, we have no use for them. But they have become monuments,
so we can handle them and live with them. We are used to living
among ruins. They are just ruins, they were never anything else.'

We learnt to time our breakfast raids between coaches. It was the
last morning and I wanted to go to the Museum of Cycladic Art. I
was intrigued to see a businessman in an ostentatiously well-cut
pinstripe suit lurking in the doorway of our fast-food bunker. The
clientele were otherwise slogan-T-shirt Americans or crinklies like
ourselves, dressed down for the culture tramp and wearing trainers.
Was this an economic indicator? Were there still deals to be done,
power breakfasts to be made, even in such a do-it-yourself cafeteria?
The man, tanned, trim of hair, swept impatiently through the tables,
giving off an aura of barely controlled annoyance, that his contact
had failed to arrive on time. Turning from the coffee dispenser, on
the far side of the room, I was surprised to see Mr Pinstripe choosing to sit back to back with my wife in an otherwise quiet corner of
the restaurant. I saw him dip under the table, get up and move rapidly away. 'Did you have something on the floor?'

And of course Anna did: her new bag. Credit cards, euros, spectacles. I had witnessed the whole slick operation and failed to put it
together in time to prevent the theft.

The man on the desk didn't want to know. 'Such things do not
happen here. Evidently, the bag remains in your room.' They had a
CCTV camera, he admitted, but such people are clever, the critical
moment would be masked by the sweep of his jacket.

'I saw it all, I could recognize him again,' I said.

'You want to become involved in a court case?'

We were permitted to use the hotel phone to cancel the credit
cards, but we must pay for the calls. The manager couldn't be sure
where the nearest police station was to be found and he wouldn't
recommend making a report: the time, the formalities.

'Insurance,' I said. 'We have to do it.'

'Greek people do not have insurance.'

On the streets the mood was threatening. The National Gardens were closed, the entrances guarded by black-beret soldiers with Plexiglas shields. Union protestors, with placards, were gathering on the other side of the road. But there was no difficulty about wandering through the opposing lines, we were unchallenged. Because the park through which we wanted to walk was secured against intrusion by those whose jobs were threatened, we found ourselves opposite the presidential palace on Irodou Attikou as the prime minister's gleaming limo swept in. For another crisis meeting. The Museum of Cycladic Art was selling itself on an exhibition of erotic sculptures and images. There were posters for the new show in town: Gilbert and George. Pride of Spitalfields.

Returned to Hackney, I found that access to the canal was still blocked. Barriers had been put up in time to use this year's cash reserves, but not one brick had been touched and no workmen were to be seen on the entire fenced-off strip. Parking in my street, for which the council charges a hefty fee, was suspended – without consultation – so that a film crew could lodge their catering vans. 'Be advised,' said the document shoved through the door, 'using these suspended bays at any point during the day will accrue a parking ticket.'

My native borough never fails to surprise: a number of the anarchists who were giving a cutting edge to events in Greece were living right here, in a communal building near the canal known as the Greek House. They flew out, at regular intervals, to take part in the action in Athens, and then regrouped in what they described as 'Occupied London'. I watched clips of protestors swarming through the narrow streets of Kolonaki, under the orange trees, marshalled by young men with megaphones. I read about the police opening fire on students at Palaio Faliro. And I saw, as if I needed to be told, how London becomes everywhere: the anarchists were making films transposing the conditions of the West Bank, restrictions endured by Palestinians, on Hackney.

That dog-culling, pre-Olympic moment had finally arrived. A local freesheet headlined a story about the growth in ownership of 'status' dogs, attack animals bred in tower blocks. The call is out: it's them or us. Urban hunts were forming to slaughter a plague of foxes, Hackney babies had been attacked in their cots. Lord Low, blind from birth, told me that he found himself trapped in his bedroom, one afternoon, with a panicked beast: which turned out to be a fox. They couldn't get rid of that hot reek. Animal rights campaigners responded by agitating about the traps set to counter the vulpine invasion. It was good to be back in a place where every edition of the *Hackney Gazette* read like a poem by Bill Griffiths.

American Smoke

> We had some very strong tea – they said it had volcanic ash in it and it
> was the strongest they'd ever had.
>
> – Jack Kerouac, *The Subterraneans*

When product arrives at the Harry Ransom Humanities Research
Center it goes into quarantine. They are humane in this well-
endowed enclave of Austin, Texas; respectful of the Masonic leyline
that flows uninterrupted from the sniper's University Tower to the
extruded nipple on the dome of the State Capitol, which has to be
the tallest of its kind in the USA, topping Washington, DC, by the
height of Lyndon Baines Johnson's Stetson. LBJ's presidential library
is on campus, near a football stadium that holds more fans than Old
Trafford.

Looking at volumes laid out in the cold room, I felt like a shamed
witness trying not to turn away from the porthole of an execution
chamber. I listened for the hiss of lethal gas. They brought the temperature right down, my guide explained, it was a kindly euthanasia,
alien bugs died in their sleep, dreaming of sweaty human hosts, hir-
sute tropics, raised veins, moist deltas of delight. And I thought of
my own status, a wasp in a bottle, flown in over the great meat-
packing hangars of the Chicago railhead. That epic confluence of
steel, horizontal ladders along which herds are transported for hundreds of miles. Unwitting bovine hitchhikers in refrigerated cars
living down to the myth of John Wayne's pathological cattle drive
out of *Red River*.

And then, coming south across the plains, small farms beside
huge baked fields and long, empty roads. Humans struggle to make
their mark on land which has been fenced, branded, but which

remains a *tabula rasa*, bereft of ghosts. Kit-settlements, off-highway clusters, are temporary installations. The natural condition is to be precisely where we are, in flight, economy-plus with extra legroom: America still a movie, a pre-composed text. Writing in London is about archaeology: trawling, classifying, presenting. Here it is the blank page of an elephant folio; hot, red-gold dirt through which clips of my favourite westerns constantly appear and disappear. Howard Hawks to Monte Hellman. Geography as morality. A quorum of my particles might catch up in a month or two, letting me know just who I am; until then, with a week's recovery time required for every hour in the air, Texas could dream me into existence, a floating presence lacking gravity shoes.

The Harry Ransom Center threw out a lifeline by purchasing what they term 'archive', otherwise known as skip-fillers. Manuscripts. Typescripts. Notebooks. Thin blue bundles tied with yellow twine. Correspondence. Forty years of scribble and grunt in eighty sacks and boxes: a still life writhing with invisible termites, microbugs, blisters on onion-skin paper. This material, stacked solid in a tin box in Whitechapel, was an insect ghetto, an unvisited Eden: until I became my own grand project and sold the memory-vault for the dollars to keep me afloat for another season. Away went a mess of uncatalogued scraps, the vanished Dublin novel, the Chobham Farm journals. Spiked scripts and yards of indecipherable poems. Letters, postcards. Telegrams (they loved those): RIP NEAL CASSADY FEBRUARY EXPOSURE ALCOHOL DRUGS MEXICO. A pension prematurely cashed in.

Ballard, when they asked him about his archive, about the drafts of *Crash* and *The Atrocity Exhibition*, the photo-collages, the lively exchanges with his peers, said that he kept nothing. Burnt: all of it. Trashed. And good riddance. He abhorred the fetishization of first editions in the original dustwrappers, the sacred relics of a writer's hidden life. Nothing. Nothing *intimate* survived. A catalogue of wound illustrations. Some black-box flight recordings. Helmut Newton nudes. Histories of surrealist art. A paperback *Moby-Dick* (because Ray Bradbury wrote the screenplay for the John Huston movie). That was the legend and we believed it. Michael Moorcock, who now lived in Bastrop, a short drive from Austin, told me that he remembered Ballard making a bonfire of review copies in a pit in the Shepperton garden.

Coming into Fay Ballard's Hampstead house, nine months after her father's death, I was astonished to find a neat stack of material we understood to have been destroyed. The collectors, the vulture dealers, the archivists: they bought the story and kept clear, giving Ballard the breathing space his strategy deserved. The man who commissioned the reconstitution of Delvaux paintings left behind an immaculately organized record of the typescripts and artworks he was supposed to have barbecued. I couldn't convince myself that I was holding a version of *Crash* with numerous revisions, strikings out, improvements. The Ballard interviews, so courteously delivered, on the phone, and in person, were fictions crafted like the rest of his work. He told us what he wanted to tell us. Not a syllable more.

'Shepperton lives on,' Fay said. 'I go and water the yucca and collect the post on a regular basis. Nothing is touched. Everything is sacred. Fifty years of life. It is very peaceful and beautiful in a timeless way – as if it never belonged to our world. I make sure the front lawn is trimmed every fortnight but there is little I can do about the car, which is beginning to look tired. I have no plans. I'm still trying to metabolize it all.'

The word hoard for future scholars remained in England at the British Library. MYSTERIOUS TO THE END: JG BALLARD'S SECRET ARCHIVE IS REVEALED. Headline writers loved the story. Sex, lies and *Hawaii Five-O* videotapes, in lieu of £350,000 in death duties. The house in Old Charlton Road was exposed as a biography of its occupier in a thousand objects: term reports from the Leys School in Cambridge, documentation from the Lunghua internment camp, the holograph manuscript of *Empire of the Sun*. James Andrews, head of modern literary manuscripts at the British Library, described the individual pages of Ballard texts as 'works of art'. Blue pen, red pen. Tippex, fading ribbon. Living alone, insulated by the residue of his past life, confirmed the author's magus-like status, another upstream Dr Dee. (I was surprised to learn that Ballard, who turned down decorations that came with the word 'Empire' attached, drove up to Leicester to receive in person an honorary doctorate in literature. Thus acquiring the title he forswore when he gave up his medical studies.) Ephemera in the Shepperton archive helped to dictate successive raids on the past, as he assembled his elegant fictions. He did not need to consult old papers. I'm sure that Ballard never took a second look at a manuscript, after the book was published. He rarely discussed a work in progress, but enjoyed a celebratory drink when the job was done. Arm around the shoulder of the Thai waitress, ordering for all the company. Another bottle, dear.

My guide to the Harry Ransom holdings, a charming young woman married to a golf pro (Austin is ringed by manicured, sprinkler-nurtured courses), produced three items to give me a taste of the treasures hidden away in grey archival boxes, in avenues that slide open at the touch of a sensor; narrow streets of high steel frames dedicated to Norman Mailer, Julian Barnes or Robert De Niro. Scripts, costumes, stills arrive on completion of every De Niro movie: more CIA research files for *Meet the Fockers* than the Kennedy assassination. But despite the madness, the W. R. Hearst-like, Xanadu-acquisitiveness of this storage facility, like a selective catalogue of human culture preserved against the coming nuclear winter, the atmosphere is calm, temperate, *clean*. It may be her smile, but the guide's easy, sure-footed passage through intimidating chasms of matter, has a humorous, even ironic touch, reflecting the tone of the whole enterprise. The Harry Ransom Center, its entrance doors incised with the clustered signatures of Joseph Conrad, L.-F. Céline, Wyndham Lewis, John Cowper Powys, Allen Ginsberg, Alfred Jarry, its grid of window panels fired by the unblinking eyes of Pablo Picasso, is the ultimate lock-up. Del Boy's Peckham garage with billionaire budget. A perfect-taste condominium of high modernist culture: Vivien Leigh's hold-your-breath

Tara ball gown cased alongside a map of Joyce's Dublin. A first edition of Conrad's *Youth* (which includes *Heart of Darkness*), inscribed to Henry James, and marked as coming from the library at Lamb House, shares space with Harry Houdini's chains and padlocks. The chaotic accumulations of writers' lives are smoothed out, labelled, rationalized, entombed in grey boxes and prophylactic glassine sleeves. Tom Staley, the southern gentleman who was in charge of this place, occupied an office that was a fantasy for every collector, for dabblers and amateurs of rarity. Walls of gallery-quality black-and-white photographs, lithographs by the masters of the modern movement, author portraits of the giants of our time. And pristine books shelved and stacked – it hurt to look at them – without there being any sense of claustrophobic entrapment, the anal-compulsive derangement of the obsessive who vanishes into his library.

And from all this, the tonnage of culture cargo held in a chilled Austin bunker, my guide put her three chosen items on a ledge for my inspection. The tiny doll-script of Emily Brontë's warring empires in a childhood notebook, like those intricate burrow-worlds made by outsider artists. Then a wedding gift, an album of Templar knights, rams' horns, topographical engravings of country estates, smeared with the drip of martyred hearts, presented to Evelyn Waugh. And, finally, the one that stopped my blood, as my guide had calculated, Jack Kerouac's ring-bound *On the Road* work-book. His word counts, his comments, as he laboured at a first draft; no free-flowing, barbiturate-fuelled, hammer-typed spontaneous composition on teletype scroll. The daily reports of agonized progress in a school exercise pad: the 1949 *JOURNALS*. Of a man whose liver would burst in a Florida retirement colony before he reached the age of fifty.

Silent avenues were like burial vaults. In a forensic lab, deep under the Texas heat, white coats stored bottles of parasites, the collateral damage of archival preservation. Murdered insects were carded for inspection. They were part of the unvisited museum. 'Domesticated Beetle found on a manuscript, lived in the bug jar, without food, air, or water, for 4 months.' They were already replete with the glue of Scott Fitzgerald's nightmares, fear-saliva from Ford Madox Ford's moustache, wax from Soutine's inner ear, dust of Man Ray's silver gelatin. Sharers in secret sorrows. Collaborative intelligences. One consciousness splintered into sentences.

We progress through this silent, air-conditioned facility, nodding to researchers in their private kingdoms, to scholars making sense of otherwise forgotten aspects of the past. There were entire libraries, removed, post-mortem, from city apartment or rural shack, and shelved in alphabetical order in secular solitude. Chris Petit speaks about curating, across Europe, a museum of loneliness. This was *that* place, serviced by kindly and intelligent agents. The Harry Ransom Center was a repost to America's paranoia, to the occult geometries of the information-acquisitive architecture of the secret state: target structures for the disaffected. I was touring an island of submarine wonders, the undestroyed evidence of vanished civilizations: available to all, a provocation for theses (which would themselves be acquired, catalogued, filed away, pre-forgotten). We came to rooms that were windowless theatrical sets, dimly lit reconstructions accurate in every detail and rarely visited. My guide took meetings, afternoon assignations, in the study of John Foster Dulles. Curators and academic bureaucrats sitting on authentic furniture, lolling on chairs where America played out her games of realpolitik. Dozing on couches polished with the leaked DNA of global decision makers.

A newly appointed young woman, who came out to lunch with us at a Tex-Mex diner, was moving effortlessly around her open-plan workstation trying to make sense of a box of Mailer's reel-to-reel recordings, a bunch of disembowelled *Mad Max* computers. One of the antique hard drives was mine: the submerged but unerased history of everything I'd written between the point when my children badgered me into wiring up, around 1997, and the day when the whole contraption was dumped in a skip in 2007. Coming back from a morning walk, it struck me that the hard-drive element might be worth rescuing, since it represented more information than hundreds of sacks of defaced paper. Now here it was, waiting for surgery. Everything else, my false starts, abandoned projects, drafts, proofs, corrected typescripts, had been sorted, listed, entombed.

Tex-Mex is generally the best option. The food was good, but in quantities that challenged the slender figures of my companions. They told me, proudly, that this was the place where Laura Bush had been socializing before she was done for drink-driving. Under a ceiling of silver hubcaps, portraits of lifestyle cars, an Elvis shrine, I learnt that I would be required, that afternoon, to identify a few of the more mysterious items in my rescued-landfill deposit.

Returned to the Harry Ransom Center, I picked up a notebook and flicked the pages. Dirt – processed, made safe – fell on the antiseptic surface of the desk. Clinker. Coal dust. A residue of the Lower Lea Valley. Of the Stratford railway sheds. English dirt preserved between pages of English paper: the work-diary jottings that became my vanished Chobham journals. I had resurrected material for *Ghost Milk* from a few photographs, reels of 8mm film, and an interview with Tom Baker. I had no use for the original, now that it had been processed through immigration. But the grit, the flakes of a place soon to be buried under the monolithic Westfield mall, that was another matter. I longed to rub the grains into my skin, to snort the essence of Chobham. The incident was such a neat conclusion, it framed a narrative. Writers are ruthless with their own lives, as well as the lives of those who surround them. Anna found these holdings disturbing, as if the story was now over. Many of the grey boxes had closing dates as well as dates of birth. When you are neatly sorted into chapters, you are sorted. Period. It seems rude to add another paragraph to the structure. Illegible notes, first draft, final version: an obituary in three slim files.

The next afternoon the Moorcocks took us to Bastrop. Linda was keen to point out the profusion of Texas blue bonnets, motorway-fringe plantings in spring abundance. The fields looked green and well kept, but you couldn't walk in them. There were no paths across this terrain. Bastrop had expanded. The sole off-highway

motel from my previous visit was downgraded by a rash of optimistic real-estate projections, with the old western-style main
street maintained as a tolerated quotation, Bath or Cheltenham
with hitching posts and livery stables. We ate, outdoors, in a
shaded courtyard. Around the corner from the Gin-U-Wine Oyster Bar, with its time-shift balcony and chicken-fried steak, I found
a shop offering Philip Roth first editions. I wouldn't have bought
one at home, but travel had prepared me for an account of 'the
enduring of old age'. *Exit Ghost*: 'Walking the streets like a rev-
enant, he makes connections that explode his carefully protected
solitude.'

Michael Moorcock, more than anything in the Harry Ransom,
was a *live* cultural resource, the London writer who, more than any
other, kept the conduit open to the submerged literatures of
Edwardian and Victorian England. He was a voracious reader and
enthusiast, ploughing back his resources from the good days into
supporting magazines for the best of his peers, British or American.
Confessing his flaws, as he saw them, the misplaced wives (running
amok on rogue credit cards), the bankruptcies, flights, breakdowns,
vanities and illusions, he never stopped the books coming, never
sold out the integrity of his vision. Libraries, built up and lost,
flowed through this man. He lodged, steady and resolute, in the
detritus of it. When I stayed in Bastrop, creeping up early to make a
cup of coffee, before trying for a breath of air, Mike was waiting at
the kitchen table, mid-sentence. To finish, or reignite, that never-
ending tale: the gossip of ghosts, the testament of the last witness
on the raft.

Texas, on the edge of the hill country, was where the word stuck
to the fence, where names that meant nothing in the realms of
cyberspace lay at peace in their graves. Among racks of sheathed
ball gowns. Mounds of boots. Watches, toys. Discontinued gods.
Like the aftermath of a benevolent holocaust. An epicentre for the
next hurricane.

Mike spoke about how the fittest of men, the ones who skipped
around town doing good works, putting up barns, were soon

reduced by Bastrop's microclimate, the wind from the prison, the Apache whistle of through-trains, to the state of cripples. He'd blistered a foot breaking in new boots at a dance, years ago, and had barely walked a step since: necrotized tissue cut back, toes amputated, long hours of treatment in an oxygen box, watching old westerns of his own choosing, singing cowboys or revenge sagas by Anthony Mann and Budd Boetticher. Having completed an all-embracing European epic, the Pyat quartet, navigating our darkest histories with an astonishing deftness of touch, Moorcock was labouring, as in his earliest days, on a *Dr Who* novel, conceived in the spirit of P. G. Wodehouse.

The Moorcock mansion was in southern colonial style, a veranda facing a wide lawn that ambled down to a quiet road. Customized properties in white and pink, self-consciously charming, were set apart in shady avenues. This section of town was exploited by numerous film crews looking for untainted iced-tea Americana. Austin, with its music, its design studios and geek entrepreneurs, attracted its share of movie stars. But no other Bastrop dwelling, I'm sure, opened directly on to the varnished melancholy of an Arts and Crafts interior: William Morris wallpaper, good pieces of furniture bought in Portobello Road at the right time, rows of George Meredith and Robert Louis Stevenson first editions. Every chamber, moving back through the Moorcock house, could have been transported to the Harry Ransom Center. Mike kept unsold stock, prodigious quantities of the back titles, in a structure he called 'The Shed of Shame'. Cats scarfed his neck, purring and self-cleansing, as he wallowed in a deep chair, his fingers racing across the keyboard of a laptop, taking, as it appeared, the oracular dictation of his Egyptian pets. Bad news or old movies played, as low interference, on a giant plasma screen. Step outside, he said, and something will bite you.

If the approach to the mansion was straight from the directory of historic Bastrop residences, Mike's study at the rear was 1960s Notting Hill, Colville Terrace, a commune of one. When I was last here, ten years ago, you could still get in. Mike worked at his computer, keeping in touch with a diverse set of friends and disciples. Now the lumber was dense enough to bar him from the memory-prompts and sacred relics that informed and mapped his multiverse. The toys had a practical purpose. Mike demonstrated how he worked out potential narratives by manipulating plastic figurines. Betty Boop voodoo dolls, *commedia dell'arte* Pierrots and Pierettes, carnival masks and Elric swords were heaped over every surface. The walls were paper histories, *Tarzan* comics, family photographs, friable magazines, newspapers: the salvage of centuries. A group shot with Moorcock and Ballard as middle-aged men, companions-at-arms, took my eye. Mike in his Russian phase, bearded, capped, piratical. And Ballard, eyes shut against the sudden flash, in dark, open-necked shirt and white jacket. They were refereed by a diminutive bookshop manager, who stood between them, ready to open twin piles of books for signatures.

Ballard was a raw topic for Mike. Much that was now credited entirely to the Shepperton man emanated from Moorcock's promiscuous curiosity, his civic conscience and his ability to put himself around: conduit to Paolozzi, Burroughs, Borges. I'm not sure, at this stage, if the details of who and when, and what exactly happened that night, actually matter. But Moorcock, the mythologist's mythologist, was drawn, despite himself, into the debate over the way Ballard was perceived by the media, the new generations of fans and readers of website interviews. When, in 1999, I wrote about Cronenberg's film of *Crash*, I plotted my path by the stories Mike told me, psychotic episodes from the motorway years, Hampstead orgies, reluctant trips to a wreckers' yard. As I came to know Ballard, a little, and to value his company, I saw how much the two men meant to each other at the period of *New Worlds*, when they met, on a regular basis, to plot their assault on a stagnant culture. Ballard would always say: 'Mike *must* come back. London is his city. He belongs here.' He gave no evidence of having read any of the books after *Letters from Hollywood*.

Moorcock never failed to acknowledge Ballard's peculiar genius, even as he wrote effortless parodies of his style. He was a midwife to the fragmented tales of the high period, the mad period, that led to *The Atrocity Exhibition*. He steered a wide berth around *Crash*, while recognizing the achievement, the apotheosis, of *Empire of the Sun*. But differences festered. The core story was not being told. One man was self-exiled, walled in by books, cats, guitars, still sweeping between half-welcome commissions and major work that editors and critics were slow to accept. The other, Jimmy Ballard, at his death, was a global phenomenon, subject of glowing tributes, a news story. He left his daughters, his grandchildren, substantial fortunes. Spielberg and Martin Amis – on screen – paid their tributes at Ballard's Tate Modern memorial. The archive, which he swore did not exist, was now lodged in the British Library. And being picked over by those who wanted to keep old arguments alive.

Meeting the biographer John Baxter in Paris, Mike found himself mounting a strenuous defence of his old friend, against tides of malignant rumour. The confirmation of anecdotes, privately delivered, gave him no satisfaction. Better to relish being away from the unforgiving Texas summer, playing Cajun tunes with the legendary Paris book-dealer Martin Stone. A huge doorstep volume of Moorcock's non-fiction – 717 pp., no indexes – had just been published by Savoy Books, a magnum opus in a small edition. The prolixity, the breadth of interest, the scatter of photographs running back to childhood, made this an invaluable source. Mike was curated in a way that was available to all: if you were lucky enough to hear about it.

Then the bugs took over.

'When I was writing here in Texas,' Mike said, 'I noticed an increase in the ant population on my desk. We won't poison the surrounding ground, so we have to deal with insects on a daily basis.' He tracked the scurrying soldiers back to a boxed set of *The Newgate Calendar*. Taking out one volume, he discovered an entire colony, eggs and all, sustaining themselves on eighteenth-century ink, the bloody records of extinct London lowlife. Literate cockroaches crept from fat Ackroyd biographies, sated on essence of Blake, Dickens and Eliot. 'I'm on first-name terms with half a dozen of them and they no longer try to carry off the cat. Domestic life in Bastrop is like being on the Discovery Channel twenty-four hours a day.'

The cave-like shops of Chinatown, with their masks and lanterns, cinnabar pillboxes, novelty crucifixions, retro-Mao posters, were as close as I was going to come to Beijing. We are on the wrong side of the Pacific Ocean. The last time I was in San Francisco, I brought home, as a present, one of those round red boxes. I loved to handle it, the cool surface responsive to touch. The diagram incised into the lid was the map of a city I had been chasing for years, a labyrinth within a series of protective walls. And inside the empty box, the colour of sea and sky: a deep turquoise.

San Francisco was a walking city. We treated ourselves to a week at the Holiday Inn on the corner of Van Ness Avenue and California as a way of deprogramming the strangeness of Texas, where I had been a kind of exhibit, struggling to live up to my papers. I climbed the University Tower and was shown the spot where Charles Whit-man, the rifleman who killed fourteen people and wounded thirty-two others, was himself gunned down by the police. The walkway on the twenty-ninth floor had been closed for years, then caged in, after students used it as a suicide platform. The clarity of the light, the tiny figures with their neat shadows, made trigger fingers itch, even among the liberal-minded humanists who took the excuse of my guided tour as a once-in-a-lifetime opportunity to inspect the site. Knowing nothing, except how to get lost in an interesting way, I led my disparate group on a circumnavigation of the university-city; its population at 50,000 students was twice the size of the small town where I grew up. Out on the highway we passed a humped structure, bigger and whiter than the Millennium Dome on Bugsby's Marshes. The membrane of the tent enclosed a pitch for football practice: funded, used, and fitting unobtrusively into the university parkland.

Around Polk nothing much had changed. We started the day in Bob's diner, with fresh orange juice and too much weak coffee.

The independent cinema which, back in 1995, had been showing Abel Ferrara's *The Addiction*, was now featuring the French gaol saga *A Prophet*. The same audience, ponytails and herb-saturated leather waistcoats, were occupying the same tired seats. Street folk, with their discretion and subtlety of movement, colonized doorways around our part of town, away from North Beach, where they had been so visible and assertive on my last visit. After the film version of Cormac McCarthy's *The Road*, a distressed shopping trolley had become the must-have accessory, heaped with salvaged microwaves, TV sets, duvets, outdated cans and cereal packets.

It was too easy to romance this town, with its contours of poverty, the locked restrooms for which café owners would dole out a key attached to some great wooden ball, to prevent street people and addicts from taking possession of their generally filthy sties. My ideal San Francisco was in place long before I came across Hitchcock's *Vertigo*. The absurdity of his necrophile voyeurism forgiven for those dreamlike drifts, Jimmy Stewart tracking Kim Novak's green Jaguar Mark VIII around the steep hills of a revised topography. Auto-courtship. All of it within a short drive of the director's favoured hotel, the Fairmont on Nob Hill. And his chosen restaurant, Ernie's on Montgomery Street. The Gotti brothers, who owned this establishment, were awarded cameos, in the 1958 film, as maître d' and bartender. The crew gorged themselves, during a morning's shoot, on salad with Roquefort dressing, New York steaks and baked potatoes, banana fritters. Hitch sent down a truckload of wine from his vineyard in Scotts Valley. In the director's vision of San Francisco, the bridges, parks and phallic towers are subservient to more significant architectural constructions: the behatted elongation of James Stewart, who walks like a man with a chronically bad back, and the baroque entablature of the Edith Head-tailored mass of Kim Novak. Who walks like an avalanche with the breaks on.

The confusion I felt, in this new place, was not simply a question of orientation: *where was the Pacific?* And why, setting off to find the poet Michael McClure's house, above Berkeley, on my first visit to California, did I drive into Oakland with Kathy Acker's stories of being flung from a car, after turning down a threesome with Gregory Corso and his pick-up, putting an edge on my attempts to ask for directions? Now, years later, we were caught in the same loop. As a tribute to *Vertigo*, we took the lift up the bell tower at the university, before hiking a long hot way, down a featureless avenue, to the antiquarian bookshop of a dealer who used to trawl the stock in our Hackney bedroom. He was ill, terminally ill, and the shop, stacked and dusty, promised hours of serious investigation. While I made a desultory pass at this, Anna took a chair, the only one in the place, and chatted to the man who was helping out. She asked for directions to the ferry; we wanted to cross the bay, before returning that evening for a reading McClure was giving with David Meltzer. I liked the sound of Jack London Square. But after misreading the first road sign, we plodded for hours in the wrong direction, deep into the projects, over railways, under elevated roads. A sheriff's car cruised alongside us for a block or two. We jumped a bus, reached the point of embarkation, another stalled marine makeover: to find white-shirted Asians, with polished black shoes, playing cricket under the palm trees.

The managed schizophrenia of my approach to the Bay Area went back a long way, to a schoolboy, roomed in the unearned splendour of an Oxford college for a hockey festival, devouring Kerouac's *The Subterraneans*. Nothing, superficially, could have been less subterranean than my surroundings, outfit or appearance. The slender Grove Press paperback, with its Golden Gate Bridge by Roy Kulman, supplied the outline of a city I had no intention of visiting. There was enough morbid ripeness, in those intense, free-flowing pages, to seduce a British adolescent operating within strictly proscribed limits. There was hot language, first and last, ahead of narrative. Kerouac's prose was confessional, stalling or lifting away with unrepressed surges of memory, before plunging into melancholia and blockage. The tang of a forbidden thing, the sex act and all its sticky mysteries. Urgent conversations, ugly solitude. Bars, cheap hotels. The ocean.

And then I discovered that San Francisco was a fraud, the true story of *The Subterraneans* took place in New York. Kerouac's junkie angel, Mardou Fox (travestied in the film version as the very white Leslie Caron), was a black woman called Alene Lee. The shift, coast to coast, allowed Kerouac to distance himself from a one-night stand with Gore Vidal. Despite these tricks, San Francisco gains a double identity, in the exorcism of past shame and the anticipation of future *Dharma Bums* visits. Kerouac's Pacific-rim town defines itself as somewhere sympathetic to poets. *The Subterraneans* is poet-truth, uncensored; street details are noted at speed, or on speed, with intoxicated excitement. The synopsis, sold to his editors, is the excuse for a frenzied monologue: the poem Kerouac was too modest or too shy to deliver at the Six Gallery reading on Union and Fillmore; where, in 1955, Ginsberg launched *Howl*, in the company of Gary Snyder, Michael McClure, Philip Whalen and Philip Lamantia. Kerouac's city of vagrants, giant sunflowers on docks by the railroad tracks, is animated by pill-fired New York psychodramas. Like Hitchcock, he takes what he needs. He makes a contribution. He invents a territory in which we are invited to lose ourselves.

When I met John Baxter, who was hard on the trail of Ballard's junkyard, the stories behind the stories from which a mythology had been expertly manufactured, he put me right about Brigid Marlin's unwelcome cameo in *The Kindness of Women*. I had misinterpreted that interview as thoroughly as I was now misinterpreting San Francisco. Scanning the 1991 novel for a feisty female painter, I missed that characteristic Ballard sidestep, the episode with a prostitute called Brigid in a Canadian hotel room: a 'strong-shouldered blonde, naked except for the silk stockings rolled down to the ankles'. And the revealing way that this cloned Ballard, in anticipation of his beloved Delvaux, finds himself 'looking at Brigid's reflection in the full-length mirror'.

Baxter told me that Ballard, unlike this celebrator of the kindness of women, never flew solo. He did his basic training and dropped out, having taken what he required from the experience, as from the dissection of corpses in Cambridge: a stock of potent metaphors. The lost painting that Marlin had resurrected – and improved, as John confirmed – had not been destroyed in the war. It had been recovered in Belgium. Thereby altering, at a stroke, the mystique of the duplicate. And the complex equation of Ballard's infinitely revised forms of subverted autobiography. Much of the writing, Baxter told me, in those early days when a morning's work was kick-started with a tumbler of whisky, was dictated into a tape recorder. The Shepperton author was not the anchorite with the pencil, depicted by Marlin in her portrait, but a suburban William Burroughs, doing the voices, testing the rhythms, over and over, to achieve flow. Rinsing hard, Ballard spat out pure gristle: CUT THE WORD LINES. TALK TO MY MEDIUM.

Prepared now for a return to Hackney, and eager to patch in Baxter's information, I shut out a snippet of conversation overheard in the lobby of the Holiday Inn, as we waited for the minibus shuttle to the airport. 'Flights cancelled.' A German, collected from another hotel, confirmed the worst: a volcano in Iceland had erupted, throwing up a dust cloud and leaving the travel industry in a state of confusion and panic. They didn't know how to spin this one and they reacted by doing nothing, closing down airports, falling back on the reflex stratagem of a clapped-out Nude Labour regime: no comment. The upbeat mode, responding to the latest disaster from the Olympic Park, was to rattle off statistics like a concrete poem. The statistics for Icelandic volcanoes were not encouraging. 'Three months,' said one of the check-in uniforms. 'Three years,' said another. 'The last time this happened, volcanic activity went on for three years.'

In a few days, a week at the most, financial imperatives would begin to bite and the fuel-guzzling, dirt-farting tubes would be back in the air, come dust cloud, firestorm, terrorist outrage. The final word is always profit. The airline on which we were booked for our return to Heathrow had nothing to offer: no news, no compensation, no beds. A weary shrug. A booking can be made for next week, but it won't be honoured. Acting promptly, we get a smaller room, right next to the lift, back in the Holiday Inn: at a higher price. There are five rooms left. Take it or leave it. Next move, the street. Eyes peeled for a Cormac McCarthy trolley.

The lobby was heaving and smelt strange, a sickly sweet blend of coconut oil, patchouli and burnt popcorn. My way to the hotel basement, where they kept the internet connection, was barred by a bearded woman with flawless skin. She was wearing a cut-off black T-shirt and her powerful arms and shoulders evidenced a strenuous iron-pumping regime. 'I'm sorry, sir. No access without accreditation.' She pointed to the board on which the day's events were outlined: plenary session on cross-gender migration, demonstrations of knots useful in bondage, whips you can trust, one-on-one massage seminars, and a keynote costume orgy.

There had been a shift in delegates since we took the morning bus. The Christian fundamentalists with the lapel badges and threatening smiles had moved out and a regiment of amiable hardcore lesbians had captured the castle. Making every trip in the lift, every weaving passage through the lobby, a theatrical performance. Anna expressed her admiration for a pair of the more flamboyant boots on display and the seven-foot jarhead responded with a flush of pride, a conspiratorial wink. Paramilitary kit, stripped from some whimpering Bruce Willis, was much in evidence. Leather cowgirls. Cyber slaves. Barbarellas in see-through plastic sheaths. The lobby, before the evening festivities blossomed into the surrounding streets, was a wedding scene from a Genet brothel: kidney-crushing corsets, eye-popping cleavages, stilt heels. Hell's Angel studs in impossible places. Streams of travestied and actual aircrew intermingled. Grounded pilots and tight-skirted hostesses dragged wheeled luggage alongside gash-mouthed Idaho librarians in fleecy Ballardian flight jackets. As the days rolled on, the hormonal reek of peanut-butter bodies and their pleasure seminars cooked up a microclimate that oozed into the cafés and bars on Polk Street, dives where traders were grateful to accept the custom of well-behaved tourists. Every ascent to our room was an adventure: we made polite conversation with one of the course leaders, a ponytailed black academic in *Midnight Cowboy* gear, carrying a supersized ebony dildo with the delicacy of a connoisseur coming home from an auction house with a bargain Giacometti.

'You can't write about this,' Anna threatened. 'They'll never believe it. I'm not sure that I do. It's not happening.'

I gave up my morning swims in the rooftop pool when the towels disappeared and the surface of the water was covered with an oily film in which you could make out the footprints of the previous night's party. Rags of costumes, the shed skins of moonlighting superheroes, were draped over white plastic loungers. I scanned rooftops for the sniper from *Dirty Harry*. The washing machines in the laundry room had a horrible death rattle. Once started, you couldn't turn them off. The only solution was to keep walking. Every day a different direction. Every night the hotel shuddered.

America, I decided before coming, would be about staying out of cars. We could hike or use public transport. After Texas, where a black limo, chauffeur in dark suit and dark glasses, met us at the airport with 'When I'm done with you folks, I'm gonna come back for Elton John', we stuck with the programme. There was a cab home, on our first night, when Anna, worn out by grandiose avenues, weird lighting schemes, unfamiliarity, felt ready to collapse. Our boutique Mansion Hotel, the driver revealed, used to be a drying-out clinic for junkies. He had done time there himself and recommended it. 'They're cool.'

I lined up with a row of dealers and conspiracy freaks nodding over their laptops in an internet café on Polk. Heathrow was shut down. Those who had taken, in panic, any flight out of the West Coast, found themselves camped on a terminal floor in Chicago or Boston. There was an invitation for me from the *Guardian*. Would I like to do a Hackney piece on how calm and quiet London was, basking in sunshine, without aircraft overhead? The city as it ought to be.

I remember Moorcock, in his *Letters from Hollywood*, telling Ballard how uneasy he was in San Francisco, where everybody he met thrust drugs at him, in the belief that he was the manifestation of his fictional mask: Jerry Cornelius, the dandy assassin. The city was so pleased with itself, he said, that it seemed to consist of nothing but societies for the preservation of defunct societies. He's not wrong about that: the spray-painted surfaces of Haight Ashbury, the Xerox bohemia of North Beach, where tragic writers have become street names. In the Beat Museum (relic supermarket), they have a large sign: FREE TO BROWSE. They don't object if you take a photo of the Neal Cassady automobile that is now definitively off-road and in the shop window.

The aspect that meant nothing to Mike, but which sustained me, was the sense of a town sympathetic to poets. They could perch for a time and make a contribution. Polk was where that astringent Objectivist George Oppen lived, a man who knew when to step back, to vanish into Mexico. He published nothing between 1934 and 1962. John Wieners wrote his first book, *The Hotel Wentley Poems*, in an area he described as 'Polk Gulch'. He had a room above Foster's Cafeteria. Poets picked up on traces and they were the traces, spoors of the real. The figures camped on rugs in doorways understood it perfectly. 'The story is not done,' Wieners protested. 'There is one wall left to walk.'

Moorcock, in a conference hotel on Sutter Street, just up from Union Square, felt trapped by too much recycling, he couldn't wait to get out. 'An old friend of Linda's has promised to show us who actually wears the peacock-feather suede cowboy hats sold in Carmel.' He had only to drop around to check out the delegates at the Holiday Inn. 'San Francisco makes me homesick,' he said.

Back at the airport, after a week walking the territory, through Golden Gate Park to the Pacific, where Anna rushed forward to paddle, and round the headland through Lincoln Park to Golden

Gate Bridge, where Kim Novak posed for the suicide jump she never made, nothing had changed: beyond the length and aggression of the queues. Information was a commodity. Nobody was flying anywhere. A state of limbo was confirmed.

I took Anna, who was beginning to feel the physical pain of her enforced separation from children and grandchildren, to the Ferry Building on Embarcadero. We sipped green tea and listened to tinkling wind chimes. My instinct was to find a boat. A ride across the bay to Sausalito would soothe our spirits. Hackney had never appeared so attractive. I thirsted for the canal path, London Fields, the lovely chaos of Ridley Road Market. Even the devastation of Dalston Lane would be welcome: as a symbol of honourable opposition by Bill Parry-Davies and his associates. But it was too late, we were banished. We had sold out to Texas. I think I knew there was no going back when two men in suits approached me after an event in the Round Chapel on Lower Clapton Road. They asked if I would stand for mayor against Jules Pipe. A hopeless business, as they admitted, in the face of a supremely efficient political machine. The Lib Dems didn't care what my politics were, I would generate publicity and bring together a number of disaffected splinter groups. The sole pitch was public accountability. They spoke of numerous scandals they were unable to make known, because of the rules of council confidentiality: manipulated budgets, million-pound payoffs hidden from ratepayers, everything you'd expect in a rotten borough. Clint Eastwood took over Carmel, I recalled, but I didn't have a restaurant to promote.

We would have to wait forty minutes for the Sausalito ferry, but we could embark, right away, for Larkspur. I had no information on this place, but it sounded bucolic and the ride took us across San Pablo Bay. It wasn't until we were snaking around the headland that I knew we were in the wrong movie. Guard towers, grey walls. The only colour in the scene was a splash of orange from the exercise yard. Sunlight wilted into Depression-era monochrome. To the Lloyd Bacon film made for Warner Brothers in 1937, with Pat O'Brien and Humphrey Bogart: *San Quentin*. The soothing voyage I contrived, as a treat for Anna, was a hop, engines at full throttle, to one of America's grimmest prisons. Forget Alcatraz. That was a tourist excursion from Fisherman's Wharf. And forget Eastwood masquerading as the only man to crawl ashore on the mainland, after conquering fierce tides. The Alcatraz rock had, over the years, been occupied by hippies and Native American tribes. Swimming clubs used that stretch as a harmless weekend exercise. A nine-year-old boy had cruised the distance several times.

San Quentin was something else: Quentin, Q. The original cyanide gas chamber. I blazed away with my camera, using up my last roll of film. All my American fantasies congealed within the malign geometry of this massively secure penitentiary, an ugly barracks built to contain ugliness. As the ferry slid towards the dock I was haunted by memories of prison-yard dialogue, the snap and spit of warring factions: Latino, white supremacist, black. Quentin was the Holiday Inn for recidivists, unAmerican hardcases, beyond parole. Time was manacled, it didn't move.

They were all here. Sirhan Sirhan, the Robert Kennedy assassin, passed through Quentin before transferring to Corcoran State Prison. Charles Manson, Dune Buggy Korps Commander, checked out in 1989. Barbara Graham, impersonated by Susan Hayward in *I Want to Live!*, died in the gas chamber in 1955. Merle Haggard, the country singer, sentenced to fifteen years for grand theft auto, served three within these walls. Caryl Chessman, convicted rapist, delayed the death sentence pronounced in 1948 until 1960. He became the first man in America to be executed for a sexual offence that did not result in murder. Neal Cassady, mythologized by Jack Kerouac and Tom Wolfe, endured a prison term in San Quentin, after being set up by an agent provocateur with a low-level dope deal. He saw his imprisonment in this fortress as a religious ordeal, during which he would correspond with female friends, by way of imitations of 'Proust's endless sentences'. Let loose in what he called 'The Big Yard', Cassady experienced a sense of 'hazelike concentration', objects and memories sharply sculpted out of fog.

A number of actors, who went on to perform as Hollywood

criminals, graduated from Quentin. There was Eddie Bunker, one of Tarantino's reservoir dogs. And the fearsome Leo Gordon: who played a major part in Don Siegel's *Riot in Cell Block 11*. A San Quentin theatre workshop made contact with Samuel Beckett before staging a production of *Waiting for Godot*. Rick Clutchey, who appeared in a trilogy of Beckett plays, was invited to attend rehearsals supervised by the playwright in Berlin. A city in which, according to the biographer James Knowlson, 'they made an oddly assorted couple in bars and restaurants: Beckett, tall, almost skeletally thin, with his spectacles pushed back onto his spiky hair, as he listened to Clutchey recounting tales of life in the notorious penitentiary'.

Built in 1852, San Quentin was the most authentic of my grand projects. And the most enduring. Baseball and other sports were offered, as a way of appeasing the insanity of an ever-expanding institution. Physical torture as an approved instrument for the interrogation of prisoners was officially suspended in 1944. This was a bad place. No sooner had we realized there was nothing to be seen except a vast car park, for commuters and prison visitors, than we re-embarked. I finished my film as we sailed alongside the red-roofed monolith with its guard towers and searchlights.

Coming ashore at the ferry terminal, we bought tickets for Sausalito, and sailed straight back out again. English spring flowers dressed the gardens of freshly painted houses in unEnglish profusion. Vertiginous steps took us to a position above the town, on the edge of the woods, where a man hosing his lawn expressed amazement at finding people wandering about with no fixed purpose. By the time we sat down in a waterfront restaurant, I accepted the fact that there was no going back. I had left my camera, the battered old instrument with which I had catalogued so many expeditions, on the Larkspur ferry. Without evidence, no story. Ghost milk. American smoke.

The food was Italian and very good. Crisp white linen, red wine. The only other diner looked like a man with a yacht, someone who comes in every day, until he is ready to voyage again. He was weatherbeaten and expensively downbeat, in the style of that hard-charging actor, namer of names, occasional author, Sterling Hayden. He was reading a thick book without moving his lips. Or taking more than a single glance per page. He had the wounded air of a weekend sailor trying to forget the lady from Shanghai. He nodded, acknowledging our right to share his space. Before he went out, he strolled over to our table.

'Good to meet another person who's been to the atoll,' he said. 'Or even the Cook Islands.'

But this was unearned glory, as I had to admit: no boat, no exit strategy. The branded T-shirt was a gift from my son, who had been marooned in the Pacific with a crew shooting some get-me-out-of-here television series. True decadence is achieved, I realized, when you pay somebody to take your holidays for you. Tomorrow we would head south for that Mexico of the mind. I wanted to know just what happened when you walked thirty-five kilometres out of Guadalajara. And then one more.

Acknowledgements

My thanks to Will Alsop, Tom Baker, Fay Ballard, John Davies, Yang Lian, Robin Maddock, Brigid Marlin: for finding time to give the interviews I have included, in edited versions, in this book. And to Chris Petit, who, beyond deep-memory interrogation, provided transport and conversation, radio off, on lost English roads. Steve Dilworth's generosity in offering the journal of a trip to China is much appreciated.

For information, hospitality, humour, wisdom, commissions, and a proper measure of cynicism when required, I am indebted to: Tim Abrahams, Angelina Ayers, Bea Ballard, Fay Ballard, John Baxter, Frank Berberich, Renchi Bicknell, Matías Serra Bradford, Michael Butterworth, Brian Catling, Judith Earnshaw, Laurie Elks, Charlotte Ellis, Gareth Evans, The Film Shop (Broadway Market), Anthony Frewin, Jürgen Ghebrezgiabiher, Gianni Giannuzzi, Stephen Gill, Benedetto Lo Giudice, Oona Grimes, Joanna Kavenna, Patrick Keiller, Fergus Kelly, Anja Kirschner, Andrew Kötting, Rachel Lichtenstein, Richard Mabey, Chris McCabe, Robert Macfarlane, Rob Mackinlay, Jean McNichol, Keith Magnum, Linda Moorcock, Michael Moorcock, Alan Moore, Leigh Niland, John Richard Parker, Bill Parry-Davies, Olivier Pascal-Moussellard, Hilary Powell, J. H. Prynne, Dave Raval, Emily Richardson, Kevin Ring, Les Roberts, John Schad, Robert Sheppard, Danielle Sigler, Paul Smith, Tom Staley, Susan Stenger, Ian Teh, Vitali Vitaliev, Claire Walsh, Stephen Watts, Patrick Wright.

Quotations from the works of J. G. Ballard are used with the permission of the Ballard Estate and the Wylie Agency. My thanks to them.

Acknowledgements

Sections of *Ghost Milk*, in earlier, unrevised versions, have appeared in: *The Architects' Journal*, *Beat Scene Press*, *Blueprint*, *Corridor* (Manchester), *Dodgem Logic*, the *Guardian*, *London Review of Books*, *Matter 10*, *Our Kids Are Going To Hell*, *Towards Re-Enchantment*. The photo of Iain and Anna Sinclair is by Grace Lau.

This book is dedicated to Mayor Jules Pipe, a constant inspiration, as he remakes the borough of Hackney as a model surrealist wonderland.

IAIN SINCLAIR

WHITE CHAPPELL, SCARLET TRACINGS

Following the fading fortunes of a predatory clutch of ragged book dealers scavenging for wealth and meaning amongst the city's hidden tomes, *White Chappell, Scarlet Tracings* reveals a present-day London rooted in a dark and resonant past. The chance discovery of a dust-torn classic is hailed as a triumph, but within its battered covers lie uneasy clues to the century-old riddle of the Whitechapel murders.

Part biography, part mystery, part exorcism, *White Chappell, Scarlet Tracings* explores the occult relationship between fiction and history and examines how their bloody collision has given birth to the London of today.

'A sane, darkly brilliant report from the back streets of knowledge and power'
New Statesman

'Extraordinary . . . ruined and ruthless dandies appear and disappear through a phantasmagoria interspersed with occult conjurings and reflections on the nature of fiction and history' *Guardian*

'A Gothickly entitled guidebook to the abyss . . . burns with radioactive energy'
London Review of Books

IAIN SINCLAIR

LONDON ORBITAL

Encircling London like a noose, the M25 is a road to nowhere, but when Iain Sinclair sets out to walk this asphalt loop – keeping within the 'acoustic footprints' – he is determined to find out where the journey will lead him. Stumbling upon converted asylums, industrial and retail parks, ring-fenced government institutions and lost villages, Sinclair discovers a Britain of the fringes, a landscape consumed by developers. *London Orbital* charts this extraordinary trek and round trip of the soul, revealing the country as you've never seen it before.

'Erudite, ingenious, exhilarating, involving, unpredictable, enchanting … as a Hobson-Jobson to the quirks of a hidden England you feared had vanished it's unbeatable' *Spectator*

'Lucid, accessible, inventive, witty' *Independent*

'A journey into the heart of darkness and a fascinating snapshot of who we are, lit by Sinclair's vivid prose. I'm sure it will be read fifty years from now' *Observer*

IAIN SINCLAIR

DINING ON STONES

Andrew Norton, poet, visionary and hack, is handed a mysterious package that sees him quit London and head out along the A13 on an as yet undefined quest. Holing up in a roadside hotel, unable to make sense of his search, he is haunted by ghosts: of the dead and the not-so dead; demanding wives and ex-wives; East End gangsters; even competing versions of himself. Shifting from Hackney to Hastings and all places in-between, while dissecting a man's fractured psyche piece by piece, *Dining on Stones* is a puzzle and a quest – for both writer and reader.

'Spectacular: the work of a man with the power to see things as they are, and magnify that vision with a clarity that is at once hallucinatory and forensic' *Independent on Sunday*

'Brilliant, startlingly insightful. A fiercely original and distinctive writer' *Financial Times*

'Sinclair breathes wondrous life into monstrous, man-made landscapes. He has now excelled his previous efforts to tread where other writers fear to ... *Dining on Stones* [is the] bastard son of *London Orbital*' *The Times Literary Supplement*

IAIN SINCLAIR

EDGE OF THE ORISON

In 1841 the poet John Clare fled an asylum in Epping Forest and walked eighty miles to his home in Northborough. He was searching for his lost love, Mary Joyce – a woman three years dead . . .

In 2000, Iain Sinclair set out to recreate Clare's walk away from madness. He wanted to understand his bond with the poet and escape the gravity of his London obsessions. Accompanied on this journey by his wife Anna (who shares a connection with Clare), the artist Brian Catling, and magus Alan Moore – as well as a host of literary ghosts, both visionary and romantic – Sinclair's quest for Clare becomes an investigation into madness, sanity and the nature of the poet's muse.

'Brilliant ... amusing, alarming and poignant. An elegy for an already lost English landscape. Magnificent and urgent'
Robert Macfarlane, *The Times Literary Supplement*

'A sensitive, beautifully rendered portrait ... a feast, a riddle, a slowly unravelling conundrum ... a love-letter to British Romanticism' *Independent*

'Hilarious and gothic, always compelling. Sinclair is alive to the rhymes and half-rhymes, echoes and coincidences in lives, literature and landscape'
New Statesman

IAIN SINCLAIR

HACKNEY, THAT ROSE-RED EMPIRE

Once an Arcadian suburb of grand houses, orchards and conservatories, Hackney declined into a zone of asylums, hospitals and dirty industry. Persistently revived, reinvented, betrayed, it has become a symbol of inner-city chaos, crime and poverty. Now, the Olympics, a final attempt to clamp down on a renegade spirit, seeks to complete the process: erasure disguised as 'progress'.

In this 'documentary fiction', Sinclair meets a cast of the dispossessed, including writers, photographers, bomb-makers and market traders. Legends of tunnels, Hollow Earth theories and the notorious Mole Man are unearthed. He uncovers traces of those who passed through Hackney: Lenin and Stalin, novelists Joseph Conrad and Samuel Richardson, film-makers Orson Welles and Jean-Luc Godard, Tony Blair beginning his political career, even a Baader-Meinhof urban guerrilla on the run. And he tells his own story: of forty years in one house in Hackney, of marriage, children, strange encounters and deaths.

Praise for Iain Sinclair:

'Sentence for sentence, there is no more interesting writer at work in English'
Daily Telegraph

'He is incapable of writing a dull paragraph' *Scotland on Sunday*

'Sinclair is a genius' *GQ*